Sport and Social Capital

Sport and Social Capital

Matthew Nicholson
and
Russell Hoye

AMSTERDAM • BOSTON • HEIDELBERG • LONDON • NEW YORK • OXFORD
PARIS • SAN DIEGO • SAN FRANCISCO • SYDNEY • TOKYO
Butterworth-Heinemann is an imprint of Elsevier

Butterworth-Heinemann is an imprint of Elsevier
Linacre House, Jordan Hill, Oxford OX2 8DP, UK
30 Corporate Drive, Suite 400, Burlington, MA 01803, USA

First edition 2008

British Library Cataloguing in Publication Data
A catalogue record for this book is available from the British Library

Library of Congress Cataloging-in-Publication Data
A catalog record for this book is available from the Library of Congress

ISBN: 978-0-7506-8586-3

For information on all **Butterworth-Heinemann** publications
visit our web site at books.elsevier.com

Typeset by Charon Tec Ltd (A Macmillan Company), Chennai, India
www.charontec.com

Printed and bound in Hungary

08 09 10 11   10 9 8 7 6 5 4 3 2 1

Contents

Contents

List of Tables

List of Figures

Contributors

Chris Auld

Chris Auld is a Professor in the Griffith Business School. Chris has been involved in sport and recreation management education since 1987 at Griffith University (including two years as Head of the School of Leisure Studies), the University of Hong Kong and the Pennsylvania State University. His research interests include the management of sport volunteers, governance in the non-profit sector and the impacts of major events. Chris has published in a wide variety of journals including *Journal of Leisure Research, Journal of Sport Management, European Journal of Sport Management, Event Management, Urban Policy and Research, Social Indicators Research, Annals of Leisure Research, Sport Management Review* and *Society and Leisure*, and is an editorial board member for the *Annals of Leisure Research*. His most recent publications include *Working with Volunteers in Sport: Theory and Practice* (2006) with Graham Cuskelly and Russell Hoye, published by Routledge.

Steven Bradbury

Dr Steven Bradbury is a Research Associate at the Institute of Youth Sport, Loughborough University. His research interests are around sport and social inclusion, with particular emphasis on young people, race and ethnicity. His work includes studies of sports volunteering as a facilitator for citizenship and social capital; racism and processes of inclusion and exclusion in amateur football; and the effectiveness of anti-racist strategies in English professional football. Recent outputs include an examination of young people and sports volunteering entitled *Youth Sports Volunteering: Developing Social Capital?* (Leisure Studies Association, 2007), a critique of the work of the English Football Task Force entitled New Labour, racism and 'new' football in England (*Patterns of Prejudice*, 40(1), 2006), and a socio-historical account of ethnic minority football clubs in England entitled *Racism, Resistance and Identity in Local Football in Leicestershire* (International Sociology of Sport Association, 2007).

Kevin Brown

Dr Kevin Brown is a Senior Lecturer in Sociology at Deakin University where he is also Deputy Director of the Centre for Citizenship and Human Rights. He has researched and published in the areas of community association, the third sector and social capital including the jointly authored book *Rhetorics of Welfare* (Macmillan, 2000) which was the first national study of Australian non-profit welfare organizations. Much of his work in this field has had a comparative international focus and he has given keynote addresses to conferences and research groups in Australia, Malaysia, Spain, Sweden, the Netherlands, Russia and the UK. He has held Visiting Fellowships at the Universities of California (Berkeley), Hull, Stockholm and the Russian Academy of Sciences (Moscow). Since 2005 he has been President of the Australian and New Zealand Third Sector Research Association. In 2006 he was appointed on secondment as the Foundation Director of Research at the Epilepsy Foundation of Victoria.

Fred Coalter

Fred Coalter is a Professor of Sports Policy in the Department of Sport Studies at Stirling University, Scotland. In 2002 Fred was awarded an Honorary Fellowship by the Institute of Leisure and Amenity Management and in 2004 he was elected a Fellow of the Academy of Leisure Sciences (USA). In addition he has been a member of the Council of Europe Working Group on Sport and Social Exclusion; a member of Sport England's Working Group on Performance Measurement for the Development of Sport; a member of Audit Commission's Working Group on Best Value in Sport and Recreation; an expert advisor to the Scottish Physical Activity and Health Council; and a member of the Office of the Deputy Prime Minister's Neighbourhood Renewal Unit's Advisory Group. He is also a member of the editorial board of *Managing Leisure: An International Journal*. He has recently published *Sport-in-Development: A Monitoring and Evaluation Manual* (UK Sport and UNICEF) in 2006 and *A Wider Social Role for Sport: Who's Keeping the Score?* (Routledge) in 2007. He is currently working with 10 sport in development projects in Africa and India.

Tim Crabbe

Tim Crabbe is a Professor of the Sociology of Sport and Popular Culture at Sheffield Hallam University and a founding member and Chair of the co-operative social research company substance (http://www.substance.coop). He has a specialist interest in the social dimensions of sport, leisure and popular culture, and a long track record of conducting both 'pure' academic and applied research in these fields as well as tailored monitoring and evaluation exercises relating to specific programmes of activity. He also has a long history of research and writing around the issues of 'race', crime, 'deviance' and substance misuse, particularly in relation to young people and contemporary cultures of consumption. His books include *The Changing Face of Football: Racism, Identity and Multiculture in the English Game* with Les Back and John Solomos (2001); *New Perspectives on Sport and 'Deviance': Consumption, Performativity and Social Control* with Tony Blackshaw (2004); and *Football and Community in the Global Context: Studies in Theory and Practice* with Adam Brown and Gavin Mellor (2008).

Graham Cuskelly

Graham Cuskelly is a Professor and Dean (Research) in the Griffith University Business School. He holds a Master of Science in Recreation Administration from the University of North Carolina at Chapel Hill and a PhD from Griffith University where he studied organizational commitment amongst sport volunteers. Professor Cuskelly has been awarded Australian Research Council funding for two separate projects examining volunteer and referee retention with the Australian Rugby Union and is Editor of the *Sport Management Review*.

Simon Darcy

Simon Darcy is an Associate Professor and Research Director of the School of Leisure, Sport and Tourism at the University of Technology, Sydney. Simon's research and teaching expertise is in public policy, environmental planning and diversity management. Simon's research interests in sport include the Paralympics, volunteerism, event impact and inclusive organizational practices for marginalized groups. Simon has published in a wide variety of journals including *Sport Management Review, European Journal of Sport Management, Event Management, Annals of Tourism Research, Disability & Society, Annals of Leisure Research* and *Sport in Society*, and is an editorial board member for the *Annals of Leisure Research*. He is actively involved in community advocacy projects and passionately believes in the rights of all people to fully participate in community life.

Alison Doherty

Dr Alison Doherty is an Associate Professor in the School of Kinesiology, Faculty of Health Sciences at The University of

Western Ontario, London, Ontario, Canada. Her research efforts focus broadly on community sport volunteerism and community sport development, and particularly event volunteerism, volunteer management, group dynamics and organizational capacity. She teaches undergraduate and graduate sport management courses in human resource management, organizational behaviour, organizational theory, international sport management, and sport management field experience. Dr Doherty served as Guest Editor of a 2006 special issue of *Sport Management Review* on Sport Volunteerism, and co-authored the text *Managing People in Sport Organizations: A Strategic Human Resource Management Perspective* (2007) with Tracy Taylor and Peter McGraw. She was awarded the 2006 SIRC Research Award for her paper entitled *The Nature and Context of Civic Engagement in Sport*. She is a Former President of the North American Society for Sport Management (NASSM).

Russell Hoye

Russell Hoye is an Associate Professor in the School of Sport, Tourism and Hospitality Management, La Trobe University, Australia. Russell has been involved in sport management education since 1993, working in Australia at La Trobe University, Griffith University, and Victoria University and in China with The University of Hong Kong and Tsinghua University. His research interests focus on the governance of sport organizations, the impacts of public policy on sport and the engagement of volunteers in sport. He is a board member of the Sport Management Association of Australia and New Zealand (SMAANZ), and editorial board member for *Sport Management Review* and the *Australian Journal on Volunteering*. He is the Series Editor for the Sport Management Series published by Elsevier: Butterworth Heinemann and his most recent books include *Sport Governance* (2007) with Graham Cuskelly and *Working with Volunteers in Sport: Theory and Practice* (2006) with Graham Cuskelly and Chris Auld.

Kevin Hylton

Dr Kevin Hylton is a Senior Lecturer in Sport and Recreation Development in the Carnegie Faculty of Sport and Education, Leeds Metropolitan University. Kevin is Course Leader for the MA Sport, Leisure and Equity and has recently returned from a promising researcher fellowship at the University of Leeds. Kevin has been heavily involved in community sports development, working with marginalized groups in different settings. Kevin's research has focused on diversity, equity and inclusion, and in particular racism in sport and leisure. Kevin co-edited *Sports Development: Policy, Process and Practice* the first substantive text on sports development in 2001 for Routledge which is now in its second edition (Hylton & Bramham, 2007). His most recent publications include Hylton, K. (2005). *'Race', Sport and Leisure: Lessons from Critical Race Theory*, Leisure Studies; Hylton, K., Long, J. & Flintoff, A. (2005). *Evaluating Sport and Active Leisure for Young People*, Eastbourne Leisure Studies Association; and Hylton, K. (forthcoming, 2008). *Critical Race Theory and Sport*. London: Routledge.

Akram M. Ijla

Akram M. Ijla is a PhD student in the Maxine Goodman Levin College of Urban Affairs at Cleveland State University. A native of Gaza, Palestine, he has served as the Director General of Ministry of Tourism and Antiquities for Palestine. Mr Ijla's doctoral research focuses on issues of social capital, cultural tourism, historic preservation and urban revitalization.

Grant Jarvie

Grant Jarvie is currently Deputy Principal (Learning, Teaching and Student Issues) and Professor of Sports Studies (since 1997) at the University of Stirling. As a serving panel member for the 2008 Research Assessment Exercise, he is involved with the benchmarking of current research in UK Universities, having also served as a panel member to the 1996 exercise. He has held established Chairs and led departments and research centres in different UK Universities including Stirling, Warwick and Heriot-Watt University. He is an Honorary Professor of the University of Warsaw and a Past President of the British Society of Sports History. His research has covered aspects of sport, health and education in other countries including Denmark, South Africa, China, Kenya and France. His most recent books include *Sport, Culture and Society: Can Sport Change the World?* (Routledge); *Sport, Scotland and the Scots* (with John Burnett); and *Sport, Revolution and the Beijing Olympics* (Berg). Grant comes from an international sporting family, acts as a panel member for the Scottish Sports Hall of Fame, and enjoys running and the odd game of squash.

Tess Kay

Dr Tess Kay is a Senior Research Fellow in the Institute of Youth Sport, Loughborough University, where she directs research into the relationship between sport/leisure and inclusion, diversity and development. Much of her work involves the evaluation of initiatives to promote sports participation and sports volunteering among young people, many of which also aim to contribute to the development of social capital. Tess also undertakes research into sport and international development, working with local agencies in Africa to develop the use of sport to engage young people, encourage educational attainment and promote healthy lifestyles. She has served on a number of social policy research networks, is a Managing Editor of the *Leisure Studies* journal and an Editorial Advisory Board member for the *World Leisure Journal*. She is Editor of *The Fathering Game*, a collection of international research contributions on the relationship between fatherhood, sport and leisure, to be published by Routledge in 2009.

Daniel Lock

Daniel Lock is a PhD candidate, Research Assistant and Lecturer in the School of Leisure, Sport and Tourism at the University of Technology, Sydney. Daniel's research interests include social identity, sports fandom and the business development of soccer in Australia. After completing his masters in Sports Development in the UK, Daniel moved to Australia to pursue his playing career in football, whilst studying in a warmer climate.

Jonathan Long

Jonathan Long is Director of the Carnegie Research Institute at Leeds Metropolitan University, and was previously Research Director at the Tourism and Recreation Research Unit and the Centre for Leisure Research in Edinburgh. Conducting research for external organizations like the Department for Culture Media and Sport, Sport England and the Central Council of Physical Recreation, he is known for his research on issues related to leisure and social justice, particularly involving social inclusion and issues of equity in sport. His book on *Researching Leisure, Sport and Tourism* was published recently (2007) by Sage. Jonathan was a founding editor and on the editorial board of *Leisure Studies* for 15 years, and is currently reviews editor for *Managing Leisure*. He is an Academician of the Academy of Social Sciences.

Katie Misener

Katie Misener is a PhD Candidate in the School of Kinesiology, Faculty of Health Sciences at The University of Western Ontario, Canada. She holds a Doctoral Fellowship from the Social Sciences and Humanities Research Council of Canada (SSHRC) and a Sport Canada Sport Participation Research Award. Ms Misener earned an undergraduate degree in Kinesiology from McMaster University and a masters of

Human Kinetics from the University of Windsor. The focus of her doctoral research is organizational capacity in community (non-profit) sport organizations. Her other research interests include fundraising, older adult volunteerism, partnerships and linkages, and qualitative methodologies. She is the current Student President of the North American Society for Sport Management (NASSM).

Matthew Nicholson

Dr Matthew Nicholson is a Senior Lecturer in Sport Management in the School of Sport, Tourism and Hospitality Management at La Trobe University, where he is also the Director of Learning and Teaching. Prior to his appointment at La Trobe University, Matthew was the coordinator of the Sport Administration programme at Victoria University, where he was awarded the Vice Chancellor's Award for Teaching Excellence. Matthew's research and teaching interests focus on policy development and practice, the relationship between sport and the media, and the contribution of sport to social capital. His most recent publications include *Sport and the Media: Managing the Nexus* (2007) and *Sport Management: Principles and Applications* (2006) with Elsevier, and *Australian Sport: Better by Design? The Evolution of Australian Sport Policy* (2004) with Routledge.

Mark S. Rosentraub

Mark S. Rosentraub, PhD, is Professor at the Maxine Goodman Levin College of Urban Affairs, Cleveland State University. Dr Rosentraub's *Major League Losers: The Real Costs of Sports and Who's Paying for It* was published by Basic Books in January 1997 and a revised edition was released in 1999. He is a co-author of *The Economics of Sports*, published in 2004. Dr Rosentraub's research has been reviewed and discussed in *The Wall Street Journal*, *The New York Times*, *Business Week*, and on ESPN's *Sports Center* and HBO's *Real Sports*. Dr Rosentraub has worked for Los Angeles, Philadelphia, Brooklyn, Indianapolis and San Diego in their efforts to build facilities. Dr Rosentraub has published more than 90 papers in journals and collections including the *Journal of Urban Affairs*, *Urban Affairs Review*, the *Journal of the American Planning Association*, *Public Administration Review*, *Public Finance Revenue* and *Economic Development Quarterly*.

Ørnulf Seippel

Ørnulf Seippel (PhD from the University of Oslo) is a Professor of Sociology/Political Science at the Norwegian University of Science and Technology (NTNU) and senior researcher at the Institute for Social Research (Oslo). Seippel's research interests are first and foremost civil society, voluntary organizations and political sociology in general. Within this field, the focus has been mostly been on sport and environmental issues. Besides Norwegian books and journals, Seippel has published (on sport) in *Voluntas, International Review for the Sociology of Sport, Sport in Society, Journal of Civil Society, Acta Sociologica* and *European Sociological Review*. At present he is editing a special issue of *Sport in Society* focusing on Scandinavian sport.

Tracy Taylor
Tracy Taylor is a Professor of Sport Management and Associate Dean (teaching and learning) in the Faculty of Business at the University of Technology, Sydney. Tracy teaches in the post-graduate sport management programme and the Executive MBA and is Course Director of the Master of Sport Management programme run by UTS and Tsinghua University (Beijing). Tracy's research interest is in people management in sport organizations. Tracy is immediate past-President of the Sport Management Association of Australia and New Zealand (SMAANZ), and Associate Editor of *Sport Management Review*. Her most recent book is *Managing People in Sport Organizations: A Strategic Human Resource Management Perspective* (2008) with Alison Doherty and Peter McGraw.

Acknowledgements

This book would not be possible without the contributions from the academics and researchers who have an interest in sport and social capital. We thank them for their enthusiasm, support and professionalism in working with us to deliver their chapters. We would also like to single out Professor Fred Coalter, one of the leading authors in the area, for his support of our ambition to produce this book. Once again we are indebted to Francesca Ford, Acquisitions Editor at Elsevier Butterworth Heinemann, for her encouragement and dedication to this project. Finally, we would like to acknowledge the wonderful support and understanding provided by our respective families for the time they gave us to complete this project.

Matthew Nicholson
Russell Hoye

Sport and social capital: An introduction

Matthew Nicholson and Russell Hoye

To build bridging social capital requires that we transcend our social and political and professional identities to connect with people unlike ourselves. This is why team sports provide good venues for social-capital creation.

(Putnam, 2000: 411)

Sport and social capital is a result of this proposition and others like it that suggestively position sport as an institution capable of creating substantial social capital. Even a cursory examination of public discourses that relate to sport and leisure reveals that politicians, academics, sport administrators, policymakers, journalists, athletes and commentators are convinced the idea that sport is a vehicle for the creation, development and maintenance of social capital is, at the very least, intuitively correct. We have deliberately used the word 'intuitively' here, as a way of signalling that these propositions and related policy declarations are often not supported by a significant body of research. While there has been a large volume of literature produced on the idea of social capital, the relationship between sport and social capital has not been thoroughly examined. The collection of work in this book seeks to critically examine the theoretical connections between sport and social capital and in doing so, highlights the central role sport plays in facilitating social integration and civic participation. We also hope the research presented in this book that focuses on the connections between sport and social capital progresses discussions of these connections beyond intuition, suggestion and political opportunism. More broadly, we expect *sport and social capital* to stimulate and provide an accessible and useful framework for public debate about the social significance and benefits of sport and how sport and other areas of public policy might be reframed to more directly facilitate social capital development.

In 2000 the Saguaro Seminar argued that social capital was an important influence on the wellbeing of individuals, organizations and nations, citing research in economics, psychology, epidemiology, sociology and political science. The Seminar, an initiative of social capital researcher and author Robert Putnam, was in part a response to what was perceived to be a crisis in American civic engagement. Claims of social capital's importance and fears for its demise have been the foci of much of the intellectual and political energy dedicated to the discussion of social capital and its benefits. As yet, the role of sport in generating social benefits, contributing to the demise of social capital or providing a vehicle for generation or regeneration of social capital is unclear. National sport policies of countries such as Australia, Canada, New Zealand and the UK refer to the role sport plays in generating social capital. However, these social capital outcomes tend to be assumed to result from more instrumental policy aims such as supporting elite sport systems and fostering greater numbers of participants in sport rather than any direct policy elements aimed at enhancing social integration or civic participation. Further, social capital as an idea seems far removed from the everyday operations of sport clubs and groups whose focus is to get a team on the field and enjoy playing sport. This chapter addresses several fundamental questions about sport and social capital before briefly introducing each of the contributions to this book.

What is social capital?

A key principle guiding the work contained within this book is that definitional similarities rather than differences are of greater importance in establishing whether social capital is a useful conceptual lens for examination of the social significance or benefit of sport. We acknowledge the argument that 'beneath the general agreement about social capital as a metaphor lie a variety of network mechanisms that make contradictory predictions about social capital' (Burt, 2000: 2). Despite these contradictions we are more inclined at this point in the investigation of the relationship between sport and social capital to embrace a key point of agreement, metaphoric or otherwise, that 'the people who do better are somehow better connected' (Burt, 2000: 3) or even more colloquially that 'it's not what you know, it's who you know' (Woolcock & Narayan, 2000: 225). In other words, there is an inherent logic in the idea that the more connections individuals make within their communities the better off they will be emotionally, socially, physically and economically. Perhaps more importantly, while it might result in a charge of naivety, we are advocates for Putnam's (1995b: 665) contention that the question of who benefits from social capital should be determined empirically rather than definitionally. We did not wish to suggest that the contributors to this book limit themselves to empirical research, for some make valuable conceptual advances, but rather that the book should attempt to establish a foundation of empirical research that contributes to the general discussion of social capital by providing some contemporary empirical evidence.

Like many before us we are drawn to Bourdieu's (1986: 248) definition of social capital as 'the aggregate of the actual or potential resources which are linked to possession of a durable network of more or less institutionalised relationships of mutual acquaintance and recognition'. As subsequent researchers have identified, the definition highlights social relationships and the resources that are made available through these relationships. Contemporaneously, Coleman (1988: S98) also identified that social capital constituted 'a particular kind of resource' and 'inheres in the structure of relations'. Similarly, Portes (1998: 6) noted that there was a growing consensus that social capital is 'the ability of actors to secure benefits by virtue of membership in social networks or other social structures', and in a later version substituted the word 'benefits' for 'resources' (Portes & Landolt, 2000). Lin (2001: 3) defined capital as the 'investment of resources with expected returns in the marketplace' and thus, social capital as the 'investment in social relations with expected returns in the marketplace' (Lin, 2001: 19).

A series of important interrelated issues arise from these definitions and their focus on resources and social relations (variously referred to as relationships, networks or structures). First, if social capital is a resource that is made available and able to be mobilized through social relations, then the corollary is that an individual's access to the resource or resources comes at the expense of others. Bourdieu (1986) noted that the volume of social capital available depends on the size of the network of connections that an individual can mobilize and the volume of capital possessed by the membership of the network. If there are finite resources within a set of social relations then one individual gains access to resources to the disadvantage of another. Thus, within the sport context it might be useful to think of a producer–consumer dichotomy, or at least consider that not all people within a social network will be better off because of the stock of social capital made available. Furthermore, if there are finite resources within a community, then those who are not members of social networks are disadvantaged by not having access to the privilege that comes with membership. In other words, a lack of social relations denies access to the resources of the network(s).

Second, as Portes and Landolt (1996, 2000) have argued, it is important to distinguish between the sources and benefits of social capital, for to confuse or conflate them might ultimately lead to the banal conclusion that the successful succeed. The unequal distribution of wealth and resources in society and across nations means that the social capital and therefore the ability to access resources does not guarantee a positive outcome (Portes & Landolt, 2000). In other words, an economically disadvantaged community might have very strong social networks, but the volume of capital possessed by the members of the network might be relatively low. In this respect social capital, or the ability to access resources, might mean that the resources of a network are optimized, yet minimal (Woolcock, 1998). Given that people participating in sport with regularity are likely to have a higher socio-economic status than those who do not, it is important not to draw the conclusion that the resources these people are able to access are as a result of their sport participation. In this context their sport participation may simply have extended the size of the network and the amount of capital available, which was considerable prior to participation.

Third, if social capital is relative to the size of the network of social relations and the volume of other forms of capital available through the network, then it is likely that people will build their social network over time and through a variety of activities. It will be rare for an individual to build their social network exclusively through involvement in one activity. Thus, social networks are the result of entangled activities, including those conducted with family, friends, workmates, fellow volunteers, etc. Clearly, the challenge for researchers generally and within this book specifically is to disentangle these activities and determine which are more or less effective in building social networks and providing access to resources (Coalter, 2005).

Putnam (2000: 19) defined social capital as 'social networks and the norms of reciprocity and trustworthiness that arise from them'. Unlike Bourdieu and others, however, Putnam did not make a direct link to resources that are available to individuals as a result of their involvement in a social network. According to Putnam (1995a: 67), 'life is easier in a community blessed with a substantial stock of social capital', because social networks foster reciprocity and trust, facilitate communication, amplify reputations and 'allow dilemmas of collective action to be resolved'. The social network is a conduit for a range of other outcomes (such as increased trust), which in turn might lead to further outcomes (such as emotional physical or financial support during a time of need). Adler and Kwon (2002: 18) explained this phenomenon by arguing that if goodwill (sympathy, trust and forgiveness) is the substance of social capital, then 'its effects flow from the information, influence and solidarity such goodwill makes available'.

It is clear that a common ground for social capital theorists is the concept of social networks – 'the core idea of social capital theory is that social networks have value' (Putnam, 2000: 18–19). We acknowledge, however, that social capital definitions vary according to ideas about what these social networks facilitate. For some, resources, access to resources and investment of resources within an expected return are central (see Bourdieu,

1986; Bourdieu & Wacquant, 1992; Portes, 1998; Lin, 2001). For others, the outcome is the ability of people to work together; communication, cooperation and positive collective action are at the core of this understanding of social capital (see Woolcock, 1998; Putnam, 2000). These two understandings of social capital are not mutually exclusive, for the outcomes of increased trust, reciprocity and communication can result in greater access to the resources of the collective. While we agree that the emphasis on resources enables a more effective understanding of power, we cannot escape the conclusion that using a more inclusive definition of outcomes might lead to an understanding of how social interactions, in which there is no exchange of resources of any economic value, make people happier and healthier.

So, the notion that social capital is the resources available to and accessed by an individual or community through social networks is a reasonable starting point, although we would advocate a broader and more inclusive definition of resources that does not reduce social capital to an economic mechanism, as well as an understanding that aspects such as trust, sympathy and reciprocity are features of the network that indicate its strength and the ability of members to produce or access resources. For example, Nahapiet and Ghoshal (1998) provide a useful way of investigating the structure of social relations by dividing social capital into three clusters, although they acknowledged that the clusters are highly interrelated despite their analytical separation: the structural, relational and cognitive dimensions of social capital. The structural dimension of social capital refers to 'the overall pattern of connections between actors – that is, who you reach and how you reach them' (Nahapiet & Ghoshal, 1998: 244). These connections, or networks, facilitate the flow of information as well as the building of relationships (King, 2004). Nahapiet and Ghoshal (1998) argue that the presence or absence of network ties is an important aspect of the structural dimension, as are network configurations. Included in the structural dimension is Coleman's (1988) notion of appropriable social organizations, in which the network might operate for purposes other than the one it was created for. The relational dimension of social capital refers to the 'personal relationships that people have developed with each other through a history of interactions' (Nahapiet & Ghoshal, 1998: 244). In this dimension trust and trustworthiness, norms and sanctions, obligations and expectations, and identity and identification are considered key factors. Finally, the cognitive dimension of social capital refers to 'shared meaning and common values', as well as collective goals and a shared vision among community or network members (King, 2004: 473).

Importantly, we wish to acknowledge from the outset that social capital is not exclusively positive, although clearly its overwhelmingly positive overtones are of interest to policymakers in particular. Rather, it has the potential to sustain communities in which the members of the community are socially, financially, culturally, mentally and physically prosperous, but also has the potential to exclude and create or sustain significant disadvantage. In this respect, Putnam's distinction between bonding and bridging social capital has merit for an examination of the role of sport. Bridging social capital refers to processes by which the development of social norms, networks and trust through social interaction links various segments of the community and contributes to the connection of disparate elements of the community, rather than reinforcing notions of division and difference (Putnam, 1995b). By contrast, bonding social capital involves the norms, networks and trust contributing to the cooperation of members within a group. Whereas bridging social capital is regarded as having a positive influence in society, organizations or communities that experience high levels of bonding social capital can have a negative impact on wider society, such as extremist religious groups or neo-Nazi gangs. In these cases the level of bonding social capital results in the community or organization being exclusive rather than inclusive. Coalter (2007) noted that the concept of linking social capital should not be ignored in the context of the operations of sport organizations, and drew on the definition provided by Woolcock (2001) that linking social capital refers to vertical connections between different social strata that enable individuals to gain access to other resources.

Why social capital?

Social capital is a theoretical paradigm that has gained increasing currency in recent years as academics and politicians alike have searched for ways to conceptualize social, economic, demographic and political changes and their impact on communities. Since Putnam's *Bowling Alone* (2000) the entrance of social capital into the public arena has been magnified, although even prior to this publication the term social capital was described as one of the 'most popular exports from sociological theory into everyday language' (Portes, 1998: 2). Like Blackshaw and Long (2005) we are fascinated by social capital's meteoric rise, particularly in the policymaking discourse, where it is variously used to provide structure or legitimacy. We acknowledge that we are disturbed by the way in which social capital appears to have been uncritically adopted within sport policy and management discourses, but are at the same time enamoured by its potential to provide a conceptual framework for investigating the social impacts of sport.

It makes little sense to ignore the social capital concept, particularly given that its political, as well as its academic currency appears to be growing rather than diminishing. The approach adopted within *sport and social capital* is to examine whether the concept has any conceptual or practical use by investigating its relationship with a specific social institution, in this case sport. The prevalence of the social capital concept within public policy generally and sport policy more specifically makes it imperative to critically assess this relationship. Furthermore, the popularity and influence of Putnam's *Bowling Alone* (2000) has meant that there is an implicit, if not explicit link between sport and social capital in the political and public imagination. Thus far the academic research on the relationship between sport and social capital has not been of sufficient critical mass to determine the nature or extent of this link, let alone determine its legitimacy. At a base level, it is hoped that *sport and social capital* provides a forum to investigate the relationship more thoroughly.

Are participation trends useful for measuring social capital and the impact of sport on social capital?

This question is prompted by the work of Putnam in particular, and specifically his use of participation trends in organized sport to illustrate the decline in American social capital in *Bowling Alone* (2000). In lamenting the decline in league bowling in favour of more individual and more informal participation, Putnam (2000) quotes figures indicating that although the total number of bowlers increased by 10 per cent between 1980 and 1993, league bowling decreased by 40 per cent during the same period. He claims that the significance of this trend 'lies in the social interaction and even occasionally civic conversations over beer and pizza that solo bowlers forgo' (Putnam, 2000: 113). Furthermore, Putnam (2000: 113) argues that the decline in the numbers of people participating in teams rather than as individuals or informal groups illustrates 'yet another vanishing form of social capital'. One of the inherent problems with this analysis, despite Putnam's concept of participation with 'a diverse set of acquaintances', is the notion that the simple act of people talking or meeting on a regular basis constitutes social capital. As one of a series of general social indicators, the trend away from league bowling has merit as part of a broader argument about the decline in social capital. As an isolated and specific indicator, however, the notion that participation is a valid proxy for social capital does not account for the way in which the social capital produced through these interactions is used.

Participation trends can be useful proxies within analyses where one of the primary goals is to generalize at the macro-level, particularly if multiple sources and a diverse range of evidence are utilized (Putnam, 2000; Van Deth, 2003). However, these same trends are less useful when isolated correlations are made to demonstrate social capital, social benefit or the strength of communities. For example, using sport participation as a measure of community strength assumes not only that there is a single type of participation that can be used to strengthen or bind a community, but that it is exclusively positive. In reality, there are different types of participation and it is likely to be positive, or negative or even neutral given different contexts and circumstances. Both these issues will be discussed in greater detail later in this chapter. Perhaps most importantly, participation trends are inadequate for analysing the substance of social capital, or in other words, the ways in which it is used by individuals, groups and communities. Membership of a club, group or association is unlikely to be an accurate reflection of engagement within an organization or within broader community activities (Putnam, 2000). Membership of voluntary organizations in particular is often devoid of specific responsibilities or performance expectations, a situation which is exacerbated if the membership is simply a sense of belonging which is not formalized through the payment of fees or dues. Therefore, the assumption that increasing the number of participants or members of an organization will have a direct relationship to the level or quality of social capital is tenuous. Indeed, Putnam (2000: 58) noted that 'what really matters from the point of view of social capital and civic engagement is not merely nominal membership, but active and involved membership'. A re-examination of the selection of prominent social capital definitions listed above reveals they do not focus on participation, but rather the benefits or infrastructure of social interactions. Social capital, therefore, is not present or reflected in the membership (or participation), but the ways in which the membership is used to secure benefit for the individual or the group. Perhaps the key to answering the question about participation and determining its importance for establishing the connections between sport and social capital lies in the deceptively simple acknowledgement by Coleman (1988: S98) that 'social capital is defined by its function'. In other words, how does participating in sport enable individuals to develop social connections and thus contribute to the creation of social capital while at the same time the very existence of social capital facilitates such involvement in sport.

While some of the authors within this book have used participation trends to illustrate the relationship between sport and social capital (which is probably necessary given that Putnam is aware that his bowling example might be considered 'whimsical' by those more likely to view political participation as a more legitimate measure), we have encouraged what Blackshaw and Long (2005), in their discussion of the differences between Bourdieu and Putnam, identified as methodological polytheism. As they acknowledged, compiling multiple statistical indicators has the attraction of being able to command the attention of policymakers and bureaucrats, but qualitative (messier) approaches are likely to tell us not only more about the ways in which sport engagement facilitates trust or reciprocity, but the ways in which this trust or reciprocity is mobilized. They are also likely to reveal more about inclusion and exclusion, within and outside sporting teams, groups, organizations and communities. Qualitative approaches are also likely to contribute to disentangling the role of sport from other social activities in the production of social capital.

What is sport participation and how does it relate to social capital?

The concept of participation is problematic when one form or type is privileged over another in terms of its ability to generate or sustain social capital. Putnam's (2000: 114) notion that 'watching a team play is not the same thing as playing on a team', and the inherent privileging of participatory (team) sport as a vehicle for the development of social capital creation, may have more to do with his classification of sport as a type of informal social connection and the position of sport in American society than the specific social virtues of engaging in competitive physical activity. In order to examine the relationship between sport and social capital a more inclusive definition of participation is required, what we would term sport engagement. We have used the word 'engagement' deliberately, rather than 'participation', to steer away from the emphasis on playing sport and include a wide variety of means by which people might engage with sport or sport organizations.

Playing sport is but one of three general forms of sport engagement, along with facilitating and watching. Sport engagement is also multi-faceted and complex. People who play, facilitate or watch sport do not do so in the same way. Rather, sport engagement is dependent on a range of variables and the status of the individual who is engaged. For example, a paid basketball referee (facilitator) officiating three games per week will engage with their sport in vastly different ways to the volunteer president (facilitator) of a rowing club who is responsible for a membership of in excess of 200 people. These differences are likely to have an impact on the type and utility of the social capital that is created, developed and maintained by these individuals. We have used the example of sport facilitator to highlight the possibility that the interplay between sport and social capital can be culturally dependent. For example, the bowling leagues to which Putnam referred are typically conducted in privately owned and operated facilities (fee for service). In fact, Putnam noted that the decline in bowling league participation is important to bowling lane proprietors because league bowlers consume three times as much beer and pizza as individual bowlers. Leaving aside the issue of the health cost of social capital development in this example, it is clear that the ownership and management of the sport activity will impact the type of engagement available to members of the community. In club based sporting systems in countries such as the UK or Australia, a significant majority of sport is delivered through the non-profit sector dependent on volunteers. In this context it becomes important not to reduce sport engagement to 'participation', particularly given the relationship between volunteering, reciprocity and social capital. The recent work by Harvey et al. (2007) that explored the link between social capital and volunteering in sport highlighted this point. They found that long-term volunteering fostered the creation of social capital through the 'investments and exchanges made by social actors' (i.e. volunteers in sport organizations) (Harvey et al., 2007: 220).

Is social capital all good, or does it have a 'dark side', and if so, is sport likely to be a positive or negative influence?

Much criticism has been levelled at social capital proponents because the positive aspects of social capital have either been emphasized or represented exclusively. The contributors to this book will actively acknowledge in their conceptual thinking, if not in their writing, that the relationship between sport and social capital has an equal chance of being either positive or negative. In this respect, we are aware that variables such as location (Onyx & Bullen, 2000) or diversity (Portes & Landolt, 2000) can be important in the way social capital is manifest and are likely to influence the creation and deployment of social capital within and through sport. Organizations that are dominated by an ethic, religious, racial or gender group are likely to have different levels of bonding and bridging social capital than organizations that are more diverse (Putnam & Goss, 2002), while some of the key negative consequences of the development of social capital include the exclusion of outsiders, excess claims on group members, restrictions on individual freedoms, and downward levelling norms (Portes & Landolt, 2000; Jarvie, 2003). We are prepared from the outset to acknowledge that sport organizations and sport teams are just as (if not more) likely than other community organizations to facilitate insular behaviour, values and norms that might engender strong bonding social capital, but limit bridging social capital (see Jarvie, 2003). Rather than operating as a site for the creation of overwhelmingly positive social capital and inclusive social networks, the inherent nature of sport and its contemporary organization might facilitate the exact opposite. The gender segregation of many sport clubs in particular makes them unique relative to other non-profit organizations.

Interestingly, Putnam (2000: 112) claimed that in America bowling is the most popular competitive sport, but unlike those sports that are highly concentrated either among young men or the upper middle class or both, 'bowling is solidly middle-American – common among both men and women, couples and singles, working class and middle class, young and old'. It appears, albeit implicitly, that Putnam was arguing that sporting activities that claim a broad and diverse membership are less likely to facilitate negative social capital and more likely to contribute to the formation of useful social networks for communities rather than individuals. However, the contribution of sport within different geographic and demographic contexts remains relatively untested and given the characteristics of sport organizations and their membership, it is reasonable to suggest that they have the capacity to engender the 'dark side of social capital'. As such, we are explicitly interested in the way in which social capital operates within sport and sport organizations 'to impose conformity and social division at the expense of tolerance' (Blackshaw & Long, 2005: 242).

Contributions to the book

This book seeks to explore the association between sport and social capital with an emphasis on the role of sport in facilitating social integration and civic participation. In seeking to undertake this exploration we have invited a number of leading authors and researchers to provide their views on the links between sport and social capital and some examples of more recent research into these links. We have grouped their contributions into three broad themes: concepts and contexts associated with the relationship between sport and social capital; analyses of the relationship between sport and social capital at the grassroots or club level of community sport; and explorations of sport and social capital in action around the world, specifically Australia, Norway, the UK and the USA.

The first of these themes, concepts and contexts associated with the relationship between sport and social capital, includes contributions focusing on social theory, sport development, sport policy and education. Chapter 2, from Tim Crabbe, provides a critical analysis of the contemporary fascination with sport's role in fostering the development of community and social capital. Tim considers the limitations of considering the role of social capital associated with the work of Robert Putnam and its quantitative evidence base before arguing for Pierre Bourdieu's more convincing approach that incorporates qualitative evidence to allow the voices of the oppressed to be heard. Tim concludes by considering the potential usefulness of a selection of new perspectives which embrace the implications of the material, social and symbolic realms of capital as they relate to the seductive appeal of sport and the role of the sports practitioner as a cultural intermediary. The third chapter of the book comes from Fred Coalter who considers the contribution of sport-in-development to the formation of social capital through an extensive analysis of a sport development programme in Kenya. Fred explores the assumptions about social capital formation that are made by policy-makers and the limits of sport-in-development's contributions to broader development strategies. The case study within Fred's chapter illustrates the dangers of conceptualizing the link between sport and social capital in simple terms (i.e. that participation in sport automatically generates social capital outcomes) as well as highlighting to us that it is sport organizations that produce and sustain social capital and that they do so on the basis of the social networks within these organizations. Chapter 4 is a contribution from Russell Hoye and Matthew Nicholson that explores how social capital has been conceptualized by policymakers in sport, the reasons national governments have focused on social capital within their sport policies, and discusses some challenges for how policymakers determine the outcomes of social capital related sport policies. The final chapter in this section, Chapter 5, is provided by Grant Jarvie who examines some of the arguments and some evidence which supports the fact that sport and education or education through sport provides a potential resource of hope which can make a difference to people's lives. Grant notes that historically sport and education have been key avenues of social mobility and, in some cases, an escape from poverty. He argues that rather than capital the emphasis should be on the 'social' in social capital and that it is therefore necessary to think of ways in which the 'social' in social science, social change and social empowerment may contribute to alternative practices and ways of thinking about sport and education.

The second theme, analyses of the relationship between sport and social capital at the grassroots or club level of community sport, comprises chapters on community sport networks, the contributions of sport clubs to social capital creation, a comparison of social capital data from sport participants in Australia and Sweden, and an analysis of sport volunteer participation rates in Australia, Canada and the UK, and the implications for social capital. The first of these contributions, Chapter 6 from Alison Doherty and Katie Misener, argues that community sport is characterized by networks of individuals who come together to volunteer their time for community sport organizations, as well as external stakeholders who have an interest in the performance of these organizations. Alison and Katie examine the nature of community sport organizations, in particular reviewing evidence of the potential for, existence of, and barriers to social capital in and through the networks of volunteers and stakeholders involved in these organizations. The chapter also provides a detailed discussion of possible directions for future research and implications for practice. Chapter 7 is provided by Chris Auld, who explores the nature of social capital development focusing on different types of social capital and their relevance to the sport club context. Chris argues that while sport clubs need to identify the means by which they can be more inclusive and contribute to the building of bridging social capital, such a strategy is not without problems nor does it guarantee that social capital will be produced.

The next chapter is from Kevin Brown who provides a detailed analysis of some selected data from an international study of social capital. In Chapter 8, Kevin shows that a mix of indicators measuring aspects of trust, connectedness, civic activity and tolerance comprise a potentially useful instrument for measuring broad aspects of comparative social capital. Importantly, Kevin illustrates that members of sport/recreation organizations from Sweden and Australia, compared to all other types of community organization members, scored significantly higher on some social capital measures, indicating that involvement in sport may indeed be a useful vehicle for the creation of social capital. The final chapter in this section, Chapter 9 from Graham Cuskelly, explores questions such as who volunteers in sport, how and why they become involved, the nature and extent of sport volunteering and how these statistics compare to other sectors in order to consider possible implications for the development and maintenance of social capital. In focusing on volunteer involvement statistics, Graham explores the possible consequences of volunteer involvement for social capital.

The third and final section of the book explores sport and social capital in action around the world, specifically Australia, Norway, the UK and the USA. Chapter 10, from Jonathan Long, examines how national level sporting institutions (in this case national governing bodies of sport (NGBs) and other national sports organizations (NSOs) in the UK) might deliver various elements of social capital. Through a detailed case study of member organizations of the Central Council of Physical Recreation, Jonathan highlights issues associated with using the social capital concept to explore what sporting institutions could do to deliver positive social benefits. The next contribution, Chapter 11, is from Ørnulf Seippel, who examines the outcome of Norwegian sport policy processes associated with facility development with a special focus upon the role of social capital within these processes. Ørnulf explores how the sport facility development policy process is institutionalized, and how the various actors involved operate within this institution. The chapter concludes with a discussion of how policy networks actually work at the intersection of public and voluntary politics. Chapter 12, from Kevin Hylton, is based on a study of the Black and Ethnic Minority Sports pressure group (BEMSport) in the UK. Kevin explores how institutional structures have systematically and summarily excluded black people from the policymaking and implementation processes in sport in the UK and then makes the connection to the ways in which social capital was used within and through BEMSport, as well as the interplay between organizations such as BEMSport and public policy.

In Chapter 13, Steven Bradbury and Tess Kay focus on the capacity of youth sport volunteering to develop social capital. They argue that youth sport volunteering is appealing in the context of a number of topical UK policy agendas, as it provides a form of social participation that potentially engages young people in community-oriented activities, empowers them as resourceful individuals and contributes to the development of citizenship and social capital. Steven and Tess analyse the extent to which young people's experiences of volunteering in sport meet these policy expectations. Chapter 14 moves our attention to Australia, where Daniel Lock, Tracy Taylor and Simon Darcy examine the role that soccer (football) played in Australian society in relation to social capital development in the last century. Their chapter analyses the recent changes in governance and strategic positioning experienced in football and the impact these initiatives have had on the sport's social capital and its constituent communities. The final contribution to the book is from Mark Rosentraub and Akram Ijla who, in Chapter 15, consider the role of sport facilities as elements of the social capital of a society. Mark and Akram examine the different ways in which a sport facility is used to advance, change or interact with a culture and society in order to develop a typology of elements that define the social capital components of sport facilities.

In conclusion we trust that the contributions from these 20 authors will extend the debate about the theoretical connections between sport and social capital and the central role sport plays in facilitating social integration and civic participation. We do not seek or expect that readers will agree with all the contributors, rather our hope is that this book will stimulate further efforts to explore the social significance and benefits of sport and how public policy might be enhanced to support the individuals and organizations involved in sport to deliver those benefits.

References

Adler, P.S. & Kwon, S. (2002). Review of the literature on social capital. *Academy of Management Review, 27*, 17–41.

Blackshaw, T. & Long, J. (2005). What's the big idea? A critical exploration of the concept of social capital and its incorporation into leisure policy discourse. *Leisure Studies, 24*, 239–258.

Bourdieu, P. & Wacquant, L.J.D. (1992). *An Invitation to Reflexive Sociology*. Chicago, IL: University of Chicago Press.

Bourdieu, P. (1986). The Forms of Capital. In: J. Richardson (Ed.), *Handbook of Theory and Research for the Sociology of Education* (pp. 241–258). New York: Greenwood.

Burt, R. (2000). The Network Structure of Social Capital. In: R. Sutton & B. Staw (Eds.), *Research in Organizational Behaviour*. vol. 22. Greenwich: JAI Press.

Coalter, F. (2005). *The Social Benefits of Sport: An Overview to Inform the Community Planning Process*. Sportscotland Research Report No. 98. Edinburgh: Sportscotland.

Coalter, F. (2007). Sports clubs, social capital and social regeneration: 'Ill-defined interventions with hard to follow outcomes'? *Sport in Society, 10*(4), 537–559.

Coleman, J. (1988). Social capital in the creation of human capital. *American Journal of Sociology, 94*, 95–120.

Harvey, J., Levesque, M. & Donnelly, P. (2007). Sport volunteerism and social capital. *Sociology of Sport Journal, 24*, 206–223.

Jarvie, G. (2003). Communitarism, sport and social capital. *International Review for the Sociology of Sport, 38*, 139–153.

King, N. (2004). Social capital and nonprofit leaders. *Nonprofit Management and Leadership, 14*(4), 471–486.

Lin, N. (2001). *Social Capital: A Theory of Social Structure and Action*. New York: Cambridge University Press.

Nahapiet, J. & Ghoshal, S. (1998). Social capital, intellectual capital, and the organizational advantage. *Academy of Management Review, 23*, 242–266.

Onyx, J. & Bullen, P. (2000). Measuring social capital in five communities. *Journal of Applied Behavioral Science, 36*, 23–42.

Portes, A. (1998). Social capital: Its origins and applications in modern sociology. *Annual Review of Sociology, 24*, 1–24.

Portes, A. & Landolt, P. (1996). The downside of social capital. *American Prospect, 26*(94), 18–21.

Portes, A. & Landolt, P. (2000). Social capital: Promise and pitfalls of its role in development. *Journal of Latin American Studies, 32*, 529–547.

Putnam, R. & Goss, K. (2002). Introduction. In: R. Putnam (Ed.), *Democracies in Flux: The Evolution of Social Capital in Contemporary Society* (pp. 3–21). London: Oxford University Press.

Putnam, R.D. (1995a). Bowling alone: America's declining social capital. *Journal of Democracy, 6*, 65–78.

Putnam, R.D. (1995b). Tuning in, tuning out: The strange disappearance of social capital in America. *Political Science and Politics, 28*, 664–683.

Putnam, R.D. (2000). *Bowling Alone: The Collapse and Revival of American Community*. New York: Simon & Schuster.

Van Deth, J.W. (2003). Measuring social capital: Orthodoxies and continuing controversies. *International Journal of Social Research Methodology, 6*, 79–92.

Woolcock, M. (1998). Social capital and economic development: Toward a theoretical synthesis and policy framework.
Theory and Society, 27, 151–208.

Woolcock, M. & Narayan, D. (2000). Social capital: Implications
for development of theory, research and policy. *World Bank
Research Observer, 15*, 225–250.

Woolcock, M. (2001). The place of social capital in understanding social and economic outcomes. *ISUMA Canadian Journal of
Policy Research, 2*(1), 11–17.

Part One

Concepts and Contexts

Avoiding the numbers game: Social theory, policy and sport's role in the art of relationship building

Tim Crabbe

Introduction

In the context of a commitment to the use of research to effect social transformation and material change this chapter is concerned to identify a more purposeful theoretical toolkit for those involved in the development of sports-based social initiatives. In recent times the notion of the 'power of sport' to do social good has increasingly come to prominence on both social policy agendas and sports management and marketing strategies. Whether it be the regenerative potential associated with the staging of 'mega events' such as the Olympic, or indeed Commonwealth, Games or the need to engage young people in purposeful activity in local neighbourhoods, belief in the wider benefits of sport has rarely been so strongly advocated.

There remains a widespread tendency within sporting, political and popular discourses to regard sport as an entirely wholesome activity for young people to be involved in, an activity which is conferred with a whole series of positive attributes to the exclusion of the social ills facing wider 'society'. There is of course nothing new about this approach. Arguably, organized modern sport owes its very existence to attempts to influence and shape attitudes within British public schools and to service the needs of the Empire through the concept of 'Muscular Christianity'. More pertinently, during the nineteenth century 'sports were to play a major part … in the creation of a healthy, moral and orderly workforce' and in shaping the values and behaviour of working class youth (Holt, 1989: 136).

Without necessarily seeking to do so, social considerations of sport have tended to be framed by such 'functionalist' perspectives which emphasize what sport does *to* people and *for* 'society' (see Blackshaw & Crabbe, 2004). In keeping with this position a number of North American studies have over the years provided some theoretical and empirical support for the notion that participation in sport serves as a deterrence to delinquency and 'deviance' (Schafer, 1969; Buhrmann, 1977; Purdy & Richard, 1983; Hastad et al., 1984). Nevertheless, whilst sports-based social interventions have long sought to demonstrate their worth through claims that they can impact upon wider social problems, there remains little definitive evidence of a direct causal relationship between involvement in sport, moral outlook and criminal or deviant behaviour (Coalter, 1989; Robins, 1990; Snydor, 1994; Long & Sanderson, 2001; Collins, 2002; Morris et al., 2003; Smith & Waddington, 2004).

Whilst Long & Sanderson (2001: 201) 'are persuaded that there is sufficient cause to believe that community benefits can be obtained from sport and leisure initiatives', they recognize that these may be small scale, exclusionary and isolated. Indeed in terms of the specific relationship between sport and crime, whilst there are reasons why sport and leisure activity might influence levels of criminality, the objectives and rationales have rarely been made clear, leaving the measurement of outcomes an uncertain exercise. Paradoxically, while it could be argued that formal images of sport may be policed through societal expectations which stress its wholesome and socially cohesive nature, at the level of experience it is precisely sport's legitimation of 'deviance' which is often most compelling (Blackshaw & Crabbe, 2004). For sport provides environments in which acts of violence, confrontation and drug use are licensed in ritualized fashion and given meaning through their association with the hegemonic masculine ideals of toughness, heroism and sacrifice.

As such, sporting activity itself does not necessarily seem to offer the most appropriate means for challenging socially disruptive behaviour. As Lasch argued, '[g]ames quickly lose their charm when forced into the service of education, character development, or social improvement' (1978: 100). Rather, the achievement of these goals is now increasingly recognized as being related to the ongoing personal and social development of participants rather than the measurable outcome of any one specific activity (Crabbe, 2005).

In offering a critical analysis of the contemporary fascination with sport's role in fostering the development of 'community' and 'social capital' then, this chapter will seek to establish a fresh interpretative framework which demystifies and enlivens the imagination to sport's role in the achievement of social progress. After revealing the limitations of more popular contemporary analytical concepts the chapter will consider the potential usefulness of a selection of new perspectives including notions of:

- 'cool', 'performativity' and the seductive appeal of sport;
- the mobilization of 'respect' and new forms of 'social control' through sport;
- the sport practitioner as 'cultural intermediary'.

In presenting these concepts a focus will be retained on their pertinence to the practical development of sport-based social policy.

Sport, social capital and communitarianism

In recent years it is the concept of *social capital* espoused by Putnam in *Bowling Alone* that has come to dominate theoretical thinking about the social potential of sport and leisure programmes. Few other ideas so closely related to people's leisure lives have had such an impact as social capital is beginning to have today. However, Blackshaw & Long (2005) have recently argued that the greater part of what Putnam offers is more an imaginary construction than a solution to social problems. This position accords with the emergence of community sport as a rhetorical device tied to conceptualizations of the 'problem' of 'deviant' youth in the context of romantic imaginings of 'community' as having been 'lost' and something to be regained.

In their critique they demonstrate the communitarian ideals which underpin Putnam's work and its relation to notions of 'civic virtue' (Putnam, 2000: 19). Since, as Delanty argues, civic communitarianism is by and large a 'Toquevillian discourse of the loss of community' (2003: 81) which, as Welch emphasizes, harks 'back self-consciously to a few key chapters in *Democracy and America*' (2001: 238–239). They also highlight the point that Putnam understands social capital in a functionalist fashion as sets of actions, outcomes or social networks which allow people and associations to operate more effectively when they act together.

Focusing on the sport of bowling, Putnam observes that the leagues of his youth with their legions of teams are no longer the dominant form of participation and that people now increasingly 'bowl alone'. In support of his thesis he uses evidence to chart fluctuations in the stock of social capital and attempts to assess the impact on social processes and benefits. The data he uses are however drawn from organizational records, databases and social surveys rather than bespoke surveys. What they seem to indicate is a very marked decline in social connectedness since the 1950s and 1960s.

... the last several decades have witnessed a striking diminution of regular contacts with friends and neighbours. We spend less time in conversation over meals, we exchange visits less often, we engage less often in leisure activities that encourage casual social interaction, we spend more time watching (admittedly some of it in the presence of others) and less time doing. We know our neighbours less well, and we see old friends less often. In short it is not merely 'do good' civic activities that engage us less, but also informal connecting.

(Putnam, 2000: 115)

Putnam seeks to assess the relative contribution that different factors have made to this decline and on the basis of his analysis suggests that:

(a) Pressures of time and money account for 10 per cent of the decline.
(b) Sub-urbanization, urban sprawl and the associated commuting contribute a further 10 per cent.
(c) Electronic entertainment accounts for 25 per cent.
(d) Generational change accounts for around 50 per cent.
(e) The overlap between (c) and (d), represents a TV generation, leaving about 15 per cent to be accounted for by other factors.

Blackshaw and Long suggest that it might be the weight of data and the associated 'certainty' of these findings that has appealed to senior civil servants, lending the appearance of a more 'scientific' approach to the argument than other writers have provided. Within our own discipline the rare emphasis which Putnam places on sport and leisure may have provided an added attraction. From this perspective sport and leisure could now be valued not only if they can create employment, generate income, improve health or cut crime, but because they 'bring people together'.

In terms of the practical use of these findings Putnam draws a crucial distinction between bonding (ties and interaction between like people) and bridging (the inter-group links) forms of social capital. However the intuitive appeal of this distinction is not reflected in his exploration of social data. Furthermore it also implies a somewhat simplistic understanding of individuals since as Blackshaw & Long (2005: 245) suggest:

the like us/unlike us presumption that lies at the heart of the distinction between bonding and bridging is hard to appreciate given the multi-dimensionality of any individual (sex, age, class, occupation, ethnicity, sexual orientation, political belief, abilities, interests ...).

As such Putnam's theoretical position is undermined by its lack of qualitative insights and positivistic orientation to research. As Blackshaw and Long go on to reveal:

essentially, Putnam develops a theory of 'community', which is based on quantitative findings from individuals and their interpretations of their individual circumstances, but which he uses in a cumulative way to theorise social networks at various idealised levels, such as 'network', 'community' and 'association' (p. 246).

Given the extent of the critique of notions of community in contemporary sociological debate (Bauman, 2001; Delanty, 2003), Bourdieu might be seen to offer a more convincing approach towards considerations of social capital. This is primarily because of his location of the concept within a proper sociological framework which accounts not only for individual agency and structural determinants but also dissolves the opposition between the two whilst considering the implications of the material and the symbolic realms of capital. Although both Putnam and Bourdieu recognize that the social world cannot be reduced to individual indicators, their ways of dealing with this are very different. Whilst Putnam relies upon statistical indicators, Bourdieu incorporates qualitative approaches to allow the voices of the oppressed to be heard.

Crucially what Putnam overlooks is Bourdieu's important point that what he calls 'the profits of membership' of civic associations and social networks are not available to everybody. For Bourdieu, then, social capital cannot be understood in isolation but is indelibly linked with field and habitus such that it has two decisive features: on the one hand it is a tangible resource made by advantage of family, friendship or other kinds of social networks whilst on the other, it has a symbolic dimension, which contrives to hide networks of power woven into the fibres of familiarity. Indeed Bourdieu (1984) suggests that power relations are a result of the constructed interests of dominant groups – what he calls the 'cultural arbitrary'. As Blackshaw & Long (2005: 251–252) put it:

That these groups have the power to classify cultural practices under conditions that put their own tastes to the fore *and* in terms of their own distaste of the tastes of others, means that they ultimately subject less powerful social actors to a kind of symbolic violence, which not only legitimises the systems of meaning constructed in their own interests, but also maintains extant structures of social inequality ... put directly in terms of sport and leisure policy, [this] symbolic violence has the effect of normalising the marginality of the poor who are treated as inferior and denied the kind of trust that they could manage public resources for themselves. This in turn not only limits their opportunities for social mobility, but also naturalises their feelings of inadequacy, because their own kind of truth about 'how to go on' does not fit into the existing order.

In many respects this accords with Bauman's (1987) acknowledgement of the new celebration of diversity and relativism which comes with 'liquid modernity' whereby the market takes over from the state in producing willing consumers rather than obedient citizens, accomplishing its ideal the minute it 'succeeds in making consumers dependent on itself' (Bauman, 1992: 98). Yet if, as Bauman has argued, consumption has emerged as the new 'inclusionary reality' or normalizing constraint, with consumers bound into the social by seduction – driven by the images of 'perfect', sexy bodies emerging from commercial gyms, the dreams of football superstardom peddled to youngsters at soccer skills summer camps, the celebrity sport stars adorning the covers of lifestyle magazines and the safely consumed images of sporting 'deviance' – the excluded non-consumers remain subject to repression.

Ultimately, it is this repression, manifest in the form of the welfare services, which reinforces the seductive authority of consumerism. Rather than emancipation from want, disease, squalor, ignorance and idleness that underpinned the creation of the British Welfare State, the welfare services now reveal the horrors of non-participation in the consumerism of the free market, by reforging 'the unattractiveness of non-consumer existence into the unattractiveness of alternatives to market dependency' (Bauman, 1992). For Bauman (1995: 100), within this repressive arrangement, 'distance' is of the utmost importance since it is not merely used to differentiate 'us' from 'them', it also allows 'us' to construct 'them' as 'the objective of aesthetic, not moral evaluation; as a matter of taste, not responsibility'. The estate dwellers are dismissed as 'vermin', 'scum', 'asylum seekers', 'immigrants', 'white trash', an underclass to be avoided, to escape from. This process is what Bauman describes as idiaphorization, which essentially marks the comfortable but anxious majority's disengagement with a commitment and responsibility for the poor.

Re-conceptualizing the social benefits of sport: Respect, cool and the cultural intermediary

If it is our intention to use sport as a means of achieving social benefit and taking responsibility for empowering the disadvantaged, it would seem appropriate to acknowledge these divisive features of consumer society and to find a set of concepts which better understand the task at hand. As such it is vital to identify a theoretical framework which escapes the predominant focus of the plethora of social interventions associated with the 'social inclusion agenda'. For these have placed an emphasis on social capital and communitarian ideals which encourage 'us' (policymakers, university lecturers, community development initiatives) to determine what is appropriate for 'them' (the poor), despite the rhetoric of community led initiatives.

In this sense we can borrow from Sennett's (2003) critique of the lack of mutual *respect* which otherwise tends to pervade the provision of services to those who are forced to abide by or are dependent upon bureaucratic welfare organizations and their representatives. Sennett presents what is essentially an argument for the performativity of 'respect' in a world that is not only saturated with contingent social relationships – or the absence of community – but also pervaded by inequality, where gaining respect becomes a matter of composing the appropriate kind of 'performance'.

Success here is measured not by mere acts or gestures but by the extent to which the performance embodies what it takes to generate respect between two communities of people who do not know and do not really want to know the full extent of each other's subjectivity. Here then, in maintaining a 'cool' distance, 'respect' and authority are based upon an understanding of the futility of efforts to impose them in a 'legislative' manner. In liquid modern times, gaining respect has become a matter of being accepted by the *other* as 'cool'.

Pountain & Robins (2001: 28) identify three key arguments around what constitute *cool* personality traits. For them cool can be recognized as:

- 'a syndrome that is transmissible via culture and has a traceable history';
- losing its 'rebellious status' and becoming the dominant ethic of late consumer capitalism;
- a 'mechanism for coping with consumer capitalism'.

Whilst the notions of *respect* and *cool* share many characteristics, *cool* is perhaps more ephemeral, with those precedents which exist to maintain it being more consistently open for change and negotiation. Connor (2003: 1) suggests that:

Cool, at its most basic, is a way of living and surviving in an inhospitable environment, a rational reaction to an irrational situation, a way of fitting in while standing out, of gaining respect while instilling fear.

This reveals a central paradox, on the one hand cool is about detachment whilst on the other it is about the performance of 'playing the game' as a mode of engagement. Cool, both enables and prevents relationships developing such that Sennett debates the notion of 'dealing coolly with others' in terms of an engagement strategy of reserve or emotional detachment. However he also uses cool in the 'warm' sense, making the point that in current times being accepted by others as cool or 'easy' is a vital part of how we *gain* respect. This use of the term cool can operate as a way of 'bridging the gap' according to a set of rules which respects the other, such that cool:

> assumes a sense of propriety, which involves knowing just how close one needs to get in order to both respect and gain respect of the other. The ideal 'cool distance' cannot be guaranteed in advance, but it needs to be neither too far, nor too close, so as not to worry the other and also not to lose the potential benefits of what a good relationship with the other can offer.
>
> (Blackshaw & Long 2005: 253)

It is in this sense that effective community sport workers are often seen in different ways to many of the other agents associated with the social inclusion agenda such as teachers, probation officers and youth workers. Part of the reason for this is that, when considering what are often regarded as 'alien' social groups, conventional policy 'speak' merely seeks to 'translate' their ways of living and thinking into its 'own' language. What effective projects are concerned to do is to operate as *'cultural intermediaries'* which seek to *understand* people on their own terms through reference to more personal experience rather than policy led language games.

The concept of the cultural intermediary has most readily been applied following the late French sociologist Bourdieu (1984) and Featherstone's (1991) use of the term as a way of understanding the emergence of a 'new middle class' which has helped to collapse some of the old distinctions between 'popular' and 'high' culture. Opening the possibility for a broadening of access to an intellectual and artistic way of life and freeing 'information channels between formerly sealed off areas of culture' (Featherstone, 1991: 10). The term is used here in relation to a different cultural axis and focus on the potential for community sport projects to help generate a class of professionals able to collapse the barriers between the socially 'excluded' and the 'included'. The cultural intermediary becomes more than just a communicator with the wherewithal to open 'information channels between formerly sealed off areas of culture' (Featherstone, 1991: 10). Rather, they act as both an interpreter and a go-between.

In this sense they are regarded as opening up possibilities, providing guidance and demystifying mainstream society rather than asserting some kind of repressive authority. The credibility of a sport background coupled with empathy amongst staff for the individual condition of those they work with can encourage young people to engage with projects, opening up potential personal and collective development pathways. Indeed for the political and social theorist Antonio Gramsci the role of the cultural intermediary, or what he referred to as the 'new intellectual', is necessarily broader than the search for conformity and control which has formerly characterized both the community sport (Clarke & Critcher, 1985) and social inclusion agendas. Rather it is about their capacity for effecting change:

> The mode of being of the [cultural intermediary] can no longer consist of eloquence, which is an exterior and momentary mover of feelings and passions, but in active participation in practical life as constructor, organizer, 'permanent persuader' and not just simple orator.
> (Gramsci, quoted in Joll, 1977: 93)

At the time of writing, whilst imprisoned by Mussolini's Fascist dictatorship, Gramsci was centrally concerned with the issue of realizing the revolutionary potential of subordinated workers and was in essence talking of trade union 'shop stewards'. In a context where work has now become far less central to the processes of contemporary identity formation, social organization and progressive politics–appropriate community sport programmes offer the potential for an alternative means of organizing and realizing the potential of socially marginalized young people by engaging in a similar orientation towards agitation and action within the context of consumer society.

What maybe significant about the new generation of sport-based interventions then is their efforts to engage disadvantaged young people through a *respect* for the cultural contexts in which they live, whilst also striving to open new avenues of opportunity and transition gateways. Through operating as 'cultural intermediaries' which *understand* and respect young people on their own terms whilst also providing access to the 'mainstream', they have the potential to open up possibilities, provide guidance and, demystify mainstream society rather than merely provide a fleeting cache of 'social capital' (Crabbe, 2007).

More than a number: Positive Futures, engagement and the measurement of success

One of the things that has marked the Home Office funded Positive Futures programme in the UK out from other sport-based social inclusion initiatives is its commitment to the development of a comprehensive programme of research, monitoring and evaluation that combines both quantitative and qualitative assessments. This was borne of the early recognition of the failure of a succession of similar programmes to demonstrate their achievements or provide definitive evidence of a direct causal relationship between involvement in sport and specific social outcomes. For in the context of Putnam's distinction between bonding and bridging forms of social capital, evidence of a programme's capacity to open social gateways must be provided by participants' willing engagement rather than the search for causal relationships.

At best, the search for specified outcomes can produce a numeric record of, for example, how many participants have not been arrested over a given period of time. However, the incomplete nature of this 'data' renders its usefulness limited. Such statistics are notoriously unreliable as, in the case of arrest figures, they ignore unreported crimes whilst the 'fact' that somebody has not been *arrested* gives no indication as to whether they have actually been involved in crime or not. Furthermore, any evidence of non-involvement in crime could never be directly attributed to the impact of a specific programme such as Positive Futures.

In this sense, successive attempts to establish a relationship between sport and singular 'outcomes' can be seen as a rather crass effort to bang square pegs into round holes. Whilst politically expedient, this approach ultimately represents a staged attempt to validate the benefits of sporting programmes rather than providing a more valid and complete account of what is actually involved in the process. As such, instead of focusing on sport itself, or any particular key outcomes indicator, Positive Futures has been concerned to gain a more complete picture of the ways in which *projects* (rather than sport or other activities) influence participants' attitudes, engagement, interests, education, employment, peer groups and relationships. Furthermore, the programme's commitment to a research process is informed not only by a determination to generate evidence of projects' achievements but also by its desire to identify ways of learning from the diverse range of agencies, staff and contexts in which the work is delivered.

This represents an important step change. It breaks with the more common reliance upon the simple reporting of monitoring statistics, but also goes beyond more sophisticated attempts to *quantify* social interactions associated with social capital perspectives. What these quantitative approaches represent is a search for a certainty and finality which is absent from the lives of the young people associated with Positive

Futures. Whilst most policy makers, politicians and media agencies may feel they benefit from clear, uncomplicated and quantifiable assessments of programme achievements, such approaches do not provide a full picture.

If Positive Futures is a 'relationship' strategy, then the success of the relationships it creates, just like our own private personal relations, cannot be 'measured' in a finite, quantifiable sense. Situations change rapidly due to myriad factors which extend beyond any pre-determined lists of 'variables'. In this context, Positive Futures were prepared to recognize the wastefulness of applying resources to measuring the point-in-time correspondence between programme activities and fixed 'outcomes'. Instead the programme chose to adopt a longitudinal approach which would seek to capture a sense of participant and project 'development' over time. Alongside individual case studies this is now assessed on a programme wide basis through the use of an engagement matrix, based on a range of illustrative indicators, which identifies five 'levels of engagement' for young people attending the projects (illustrated in Table 2.1 – this matrix is based on learning from youth work progression models and the engagement matrix developed by Darts (Hirst & Robertshaw, 2003) and is integrated into the SPRS monitoring framework utilized by the programme).

As participants move across different levels of engagement from the resistant, disconnected and self-constraining disengagement of Level 1 to the self-directed and empowered autonomy of Level 5, they connect more strongly with wider and wider circles of contacts whilst retaining their cultural antecedents. In this way and as illustrated in Table 2.2, for those who remain engaged, Positive Futures can help to build both *breadth* and *depth* into project related friendships, networks and opportunities rather than just access to 'more' or 'different' people.

Such approaches can be juxtaposed with a more populist stance through which sporting interventions are *believed* to work because they are seen to provide *relief* from a criminogenic environment. With the 'scallies', 'chavs' and 'hoodies' residing on Britain's housing estates dismissed as 'the objective of aesthetic, not moral evaluation' (Bauman, 1995: 100), a romantic fiction associated with the functionalist interpretation of sport as inculcating a sense of self-discipline, routine and personal responsibility continues to be reproduced (Crabbe, 2000). Now enhanced by the seductive glamour and performativity of the celebrity version, sport represents a metaphor for the positively imbued social values that the 'healthy' *majority*

Table 2.1   Positive futures engagement matrix

Level 1: Disengage- ment	Level 2: Curiosity	Level 3: Involvement	Level 4: Achievement	Level 5: Autonomy
Sit out and ignore activity	Watch activity	Join in with others	Complete tasks	Gain relevant qualifications
Encourage disputes	Dip in and out	Respond to instruction	Communicate with staff outside of activity	Initiate ideas
Distract others	Ask questions	Talk about experiences	Make positive statements about work	Help plan and run activities
Walk out	Listen to staff and peers	Enjoy good relations with others	Celebrate work publicly	Advise and educate peers
Make negative comments	Comment on activity	Share facilities	Make connections beyond the project	Praise work of others
Destroy/ damage facilities	Talk to others about activity	Handle conflict and confrontation with maturity	Receive accreditation	Manage conflict between others
	Try activity on own	Attend regularly		Volunteer
				Gain employment

Table 2.2   Engagement and social capital

Engagement	Breadth of contact	Depth of contact
Disengagement	Participants	Fleeting, hostile
Curiosity	Participants, delivery staff	Transitory, interested
Involvement	Participants, delivery staff, volunteers and office staff	Ongoing, engaged
Achievement	Participants, delivery staff, volunteers, office staff, partners and funders	Celebrated, committed
Autonomy	Other projects, colleges and employers	Mutually rewarding, respectful

claim as their own and which are wheeled out to the zones of exclusion in an effort to alter the behaviour and consciousness of 'risky' populations.

The danger then is that community sport might more easily be recognized as a product or vision from the mainstream rather than a celebration of the cultural achievements of the disadvantaged – a means of educating the 'flawed' or 'illegitimate' consumers in 'our way of doing things'. In this context sport might be seen to emphasize the legitimate rules of consumer society which have often proven beyond the community youth worker, probation officer and educational welfare officer who lack the cache of social and cultural capital that goes with contemporary sport. Misconstrued, what this kind of social intervention can represent for the mainstream then is an extension of the seductive appeal of its own consumer society. In this sense, part of the attraction of community sport work to the mainstream is its *lack* of any ideological critique of the consumerism which contributes to young people's ghettoization. Indeed the offer of a 'passport' or gateway 'out' is often premised upon the mediated appeal of one of the most rabidly commercialized industries on the planet.

Conclusions: Moving from theory to action

From this discussion the shortcomings of more popular approaches towards the theorization of sport's social benefits – namely functionalist and communitarian perspectives with their associated espousal of sport's capacity for generating social capital – should be clear. It is in this context that some of the possibilities associated with a series of other concepts which are more centrally concerned with the intimate dynamics of human relations are advocated. Nevertheless, as they stand, these concepts might themselves be regarded as somewhat abstract or descriptive rather than purposeful or explanatory. In this sense there is an imperative to mobilize these concepts in a fashion which actively seeks to influence and contribute to the design of the community sport project. This will involve a tripartite approach which brings together rather than divorcing theory, method and practice.

The preference would be for a set of more fluid and interpretive theoretical concepts which are made to the measure of our times rather than theories which encourage the measurement of impact in a positivistic sense. Rather than identifying indicators for the assessment of causal relationships between sport and pre-defined social outcomes we should use concepts which help to shape and re-define the purpose of community sport initiatives. It is in this sense that we might consider the extent to which programmes pay *respect* to the 'otherness' and embodied *cultural capital* of others and their capacity to take on the role of the *cultural intermediary* in engaging *with* participants.

The ability to mobilize these concepts relies upon a methodology which is driven by more intimate, participatory action research approaches in order to evaluate complex relationships and often 'life changing' outcomes. Such an embedded approach can provide a deeper understanding of the social context in which projects operate, the complexity of participants' interactions and the often contradictory and fluid impact of initiatives which would otherwise go unaccounted for through more quantitative enquiries.

Ultimately this more engaged application of theory and method places an emphasis on how community sport initiatives might be mobilized as a force for generating progressive social change rather than control and conformity. As such the imperative is to identify theoretical orientations which can challenge and reveal the weaknesses of extant perspectives; celebrate the cultural achievements and resistance of disadvantaged groups; and advocate sport's role in wider community development strategies that are concerned with transformative agendas.

References

Bauman, Z. (1987). *Legislators and Interpreters: On Modernity, Postmodernity and Intellectuals*. Cambridge: Polity Press.

Bauman, Z. (1992). *Intimations of Postmodernity*. London: Routledge.

Bauman, Z. (1995). *Life in Fragments: Essays in Postmodern Morality*. Oxford: Blackwell.

Bauman, Z. (2001). *Community: Seeking Safety in an Insecure World*. Cambridge: Polity Press.

Blackshaw, T. & Crabbe, T. (2004). *New Perspectives on Sport and 'Deviance': Consumption, Performativity and Social Control*. London: Routledge.

Blackshaw, T. & Long, J. (2005). What's the big Idea? A critical exploration of the concept of social capital and its incorporation into leisure policy discourse. *Leisure Studies*, 24(3), 239–258.

Bourdieu, P. (1984). *Distinction: A Social Critique of the Judgement of Taste*. London: RKP.

Buhrmann, H. (1977). Athletics and deviance: An examination of the relationship between athletic participation and deviant behaviour of high school girls. *Review of Sport and Leisure, 2,* 17–35.

Clarke, J. & Critcher, C. (1985). *The Devil Makes Work: Leisure in Capitalist Britain.* Basingstoke: Macmillan.

Coalter, F. (1989). *Sport and Anti-social Behaviour: A Literature Review.* Edinburgh: Scottish Sports Council.

Collins, M. (2002). *Sport and Social Exclusion.* London: Routledge.

Crabbe, T. (2000). A sporting chance?: Using sport to tackle drug use and crime. *Drugs: Education, Prevention and Policy, 7*(4), 381–391.

Crabbe, T. (2005). Getting to know you: Engagement and relationship building, *First Interim National Positive Futures Case Study Research Report.* Retrieved July 30, 2007 from http://www.positivefuturesresearch.org.uk/index.php/Section15.html

Crabbe, T. (2007). Reaching the 'hard to reach': engagement, relationship building and social control in sport based social inclusion work. *International Journal of Sport Management and Marketing, 2*(1/2), 27–40.

Connor, M.K. (2003). *What is Cool?: Understanding Black Manhood in America.* New York: Crown Publishers.

Delanty, G. (2003). *Community.* London: Routledge.

Featherstone, M. (1991). *Consumer Culture and Postmodernism.* London: Sage.

Hastad, D., Segrave, J., Pangrazi, R. & Peterson, G. (1984). Youth sport participation and deviant behaviour. *Sociology of Sport Journal, 1,* 366–373.

Hirst, E. & Robertshaw, D. (2003). *Breaking the Cycle of Failure – Examining the Impact of Arts Activity on Attending Pupil Referral Units in Doncaster.* Doncaster: Darts.

Holt, R. (1989). *Sport and the British.* Oxford: Oxford University Press.

Joll, J. (1977). *Gramsci.* Glasgow: Fontana.

Lasch, C. (1978). *The Culture of Narcissism: American Life in an Age of Diminishing Expectations.* New York: Norton.

Long, J. & Sanderson, I. (2001). The social benefits of sport: where's the proof?. In C. Gratton & I. Henry (Eds.), *Sport in the City: The Role of Sport in Economic and Social Regeneration* (pp. 187–203). London: Routledge.

Morris, L., Sallybanks, J. & Willis, K. (2003). *Sport, Physical Activity and Antisocial Behaviour in Youth, Australian Institute of Criminology Research and Public Policy Series No. 49.* Canberra: Australian Institute of Criminology.

Pountain, D. & Robins, D. (2001). *Cool Rules: Anatomy of an Attitude*. Reaktion Books: London.

Purdy, D.A. & Richard, S.F. (1983). Sport and juvenile delinquency: An examination and assessment of four major themes. *Pacific Sociological Review, 14*, 328–338.

Putnam, R.D. (2000). *Bowling Alone: The Collapse and Revival of American Community*. New York: Simon & Schuster (Touchstone).

Robins, D. (1990). *Sport as Prevention, the Role of Sport in Crime Prevention Programmes Aimed at Young People*. Oxford: Centre for Criminological Research, Oxford University.

Schafer, W. (1969). Some Sources and Consequences of Interscholastic Athletics: The Case of Participation and Delinquency. *International Review of Sport Sociology, 4*, 63–79.

Sennett, R. (2003). *Respect: The Formation of Character in an Age of Inequality*. London: Allen Lane.

Smith, A. & Waddington, I. (2004). Using 'sport in the community schemes' to tackle crime and drug use among young people: some policy issues and problems. *European Physical Education Review, 10*(3), 279–298.

Snydor, E. (1994). Interpretations and explanations of deviance among college athletes: A case study. *Sociology of Sport Journal, 11*, 231–248.

Welch, C. (2001). *De Toqueville*. Oxford: Oxford University Press.

Sport-in-development: Development for and through sport?

Fred Coalter

The United Nations, sport and civil society

In November 2003 the General Assembly of the United Nations adopted a resolution affirming its commitment to sport as a means to promote education, health, development and peace and to include sport and physical education as a tool to contribute towards achieving the internationally agreed development goals. Following this, the United Nations declared 2005 to be the Year of Sport and Physical Education via which, 'the United Nations is turning to the world of sport for help in the work for peace and the effort to achieve the Millennium Development Goals' (United Nations, 2005a: v). These goals include universal primary education, promoting gender equality and empowering women, combating HIV/AIDS and addressing issues of environmental sustainability. The wide-ranging contribution expected of sport is stated clearly (United Nations, 2005b: v):

The world of sport presents a natural partnership for the United Nations' system. By its very nature sport is about participation. It is about inclusion and citizenship. Sport brings individuals and communities together, highlighting commonalties and bridging cultural or ethnic divides. Sport provides a forum to learn skills such as discipline, confidence and leadership and it teaches core principles such as tolerance, cooperation and respect. Sport teaches the value of effort and how to manage victory, as well as defeat. When these positive aspects of sport are emphasized, sport becomes a powerful vehicle through which the United Nations can work towards achieving its goals.

Many of these statements of desired outcomes are derived from traditional and widespread ideologies of 'sport' – the development of discipline, confidence, tolerance and respect. However, robust evidence for such outcomes is limited (Coalter, 2007), both in terms of individual impacts and the associated desired behavioural outcomes. In addition to a relatively weak generic evidence base, in the emerging policy area of sport-for-development we are also faced with a widespread lack of evidence for the effectiveness of some of the core claims made for sport (in part reflecting the recent establishment of many of the programmes). For example, a UNICEF (2006: 4) publication on monitoring and evaluation of such programmes states that 'there is a need to assemble proof, to go beyond what is mostly anecdotal evidence to monitor and evaluate the impact of sport in development programmes'. For example, Kruse (2006: 8), as part of an evaluation of the sport-based Kicking Aids Out! network, stated that:

We have not come across any systematic analysis of how to understand the relationships between sport and development or an assessment of to what extent such a relationship exists – or in other words a discussion of the causal links between an increased emphasis on sport and a positive impact on HIV/AIDS. What is it with sport that could lead to such an impact – what and where are the linkages and can they be documented? … The strong beliefs seem to be based on an intuitive certainty and experience that there is a positive link between sport and development.

Kruse (2006: 8) speculates that one of the reasons for the almost uncritical belief in the positive benefits of sport-in-development is that 'it is intriguingly vague and open for several interpretations'. Although organizations had overall objectives which provided vision and direction, Kruse (2006: 27) found that 'intermediate objectives are missing providing targets for how much and when results were expected' and 'indicators are used in the application for funds, but not for actual monitoring and reporting', with the absence of clear targets 'making it difficult to assess performance'.

However, the vague and 'mythopoeic' nature of sport (Coalter, 2007) is more evident when we examine the even more ambitious claims for sport's *institutional* contribution to the development of aspects of civil society. For example, *Sport for Development and Peace* (United Nations, 2005b: 2) states that although the United Nations had previously collaborated with a range of organizations in the commercial, public and voluntary sectors, 'what was missing, however, was a systematic approach to an important sector in civil society: sport'. This is followed by the assertion of the need to 'ensure that this powerful and diverse element of civil society becomes an active and committed force in the global partnership for development' (United Nations, 2005b: 7).

In an earlier document the United Nations (2003: 14) stressed the centrality of volunteering in sport and argued that it contributes to 'social welfare, community participation, generation of trust and reciprocity, and the broadening of social interaction through new networks. Consequently, volunteerism creates social capital, helping to build and consolidate social cohesion and stability'. Further, while the concept of *social capital* is not explicitly stated, it is clearly implied by the statement that:

Local development through sport particularly benefits from an integrated partnership approach to sport-in-development involving a full spectrum of actors in field-based community development including all levels of and various sectors of government, sports organisations, NGOs and the private sector. Strategic sport-based partnerships can be created within a common framework providing a structured environment allowing for coordination, knowledge and expertise sharing and cost-effectiveness.

(United Nations, 2005c: 7)

Consequently there is a need to promote partnerships which enable resource mobilization 'both for and through sport' as 'effectively designed sports programmes ... are a valuable tool to initiate social development and improve social cohesion' (United Nations, 2003: 20, 12).

From economic aid to social capital

The concepts of civil society, social capital, 'sport' and sport's contribution remain largely untheorized in most of these documents. In this regard van Rooy (2004) suggests that within development policy the concept of *civil society* has become an 'analytical hatstand' on which donors can opportunistically hang a range of ideas around politics, organization and citizenship. Further, Renard (2006: 18) suggests, critically, that the broader vision of civil society in this paradigm is largely 'non-conflictive and not overtly political' – based on a rather romanticized communitarianism (Woolcock & Narayan, 2000). Yet, the precise nature of civil society in non-industrialized countries has been a subject of much debate (Pollard & Court, 2005), with some commentators raising questions about the widespread utility of such terminology. Others (Comaroff & Comaroff, 1999) suggest that the notion of a 'vacuum' to be filled by non-governmental organizations (NGOs) – or sport-in-development organizations – is misplaced and that the concept of civil society needs to be broader and includes involuntary membership and kinship relations. For example, a NORAD report (2002) on civil society and Mozambique concluded:

An estimated 60 per cent of the population lives according to traditional norms and structures with little notion of the state, formal laws and their rights. Governance is in the hands of indigenous/'non-state'/ 'non-system' leaders and structures that exist in many if not most areas, the leaders have legitimacy in that their position and their powers are accepted by the local communities and there is a degree of formality, structure and division of responsibilities. They have important functions in the distribution of resources (especially land), the resolution of conflicts, and in some cases even impose 'taxes'.

Many sport-in-development organizations are confronted with such complexity, with their ability to operate frequently depending on complex negotiations and relationships with existing community power structures (which will also set certain limits on the extent and nature of their contribution).

Despite such misgivings and complexities, the emphasis on the potential role of sport in civil society (partnerships, social development, social cohesion, coordination, sharing of knowledge and expertise) clearly reflects a broader shift in the 'aid paradigm'. For example, Hognestad (2005) locates the new emphasis on sport and civil society within a broad policy shift, from a reliance on economic aid to a more diffuse focus on the role of culture in development processes. He quotes the report from the World Commission on Culture and Development (1995) – *Our Creative Diversity* – which defined development as an expansion of people's possibilities of choosing, while stressing the significance of bringing issues of culture to the mainstream of development thinking and practice – 'not to substitute more traditional priorities that will remain our bread and butter – but to complement and strengthen them' (quoted in Hognestad, 2005: 3). Hognestad (2005) illustrates that the Norwegian Government's *Action Plan for the Eradication of Poverty in the South 2015* emphasizes the connections between poverty and cultural conditions and the significance of securing cultural rights as an important part of the fight against poverty. It is perhaps not insignificant that several Norwegian organizations (e.g. Norwegian Olympic Committee and Confederation of Sport (NIF); NORAD; Strome Foundation) are major investors in sport and sporting organizations in Africa.

Woolcock and Narayan (2000) argue that the new emphasis on civil society and social capital reflects a recognition that the concentration of development policy on the economic dimension was too narrow, often simply dismissing various aspects of traditional social relations and networks as being obstacles to development, rather than potential resources. In fact, Portes and Landolt (2000: 530) suggest that the new emphasis represents an attempt to repair the damage done by previous policies in which,

the removal of state protection giving way to unrestrained market forces has produced growing income disparities and an atomised social fabric marked by the erosion of normative controls. ... the trend is visible enough for policy-makers to seek ways to sensitise or create anew community bonds and social institutions.

In such circumstances the notion of social capital holds 'the promise of a ground-up alternative to the top-down policies promoted by international financial organisations in the recent past' (Portes & Landolt, 2000: 530).

The hope is that, where national and local states are weak, or not interested, organizations in civil society and the degrees of trust and reciprocity they are presumed to engender, can provide informal social insurance, can increase community participation and strengthen democracy, can facilitate various types of social development and economic growth (World Bank, n.d.). For example, the World Bank has engaged in extensive conceptual, empirical and policy-related work on social capital. This work has explored 'the various survival and mobility strategies of the poor, while also exploring the nature and extent of social relations between the households, associations and communities of poor people, on the one hand, and markets, states, and non-governmental organizations, on the other' (Grootaert et al., 2004: v).

Consequently the relatively new emphasis on sport-in-development, and the rather vague and ambitious claims for its potential contribution to development, can be understood within the context of a new aid paradigm (Renard, 2006). Just as in the UK, where new Labour's emphasis on social inclusion and active citizenship has increased the social policy role of sport (Coalter, 2007), a new emphasis on social relationships and networks within development programmes has lead to an increased concern with social capital and sport's potential contribution to its development.

Social capital and development

The concept of social capital is not new and has its roots in the classic concerns of sociology and political science with aspects of social cohesion and associational life (Portes, 1998; Field, 2003; Johnston & Percy-Smith, 2003; Farr, 2004). Although its precise meaning and relevance to development are disputed, a useful general definition of social capital is that it refers to social networks based on social and group norms, which enable people to trust and cooperate with each other and via which individuals or groups can obtain certain types of advantage.

There are three main sources of theories of social capital – two sociologists – Bourdieu (1997) Coleman (1988, 1990, 1994) and one political scientist – Putnam (2000). Although all three would broadly accept the above definition, there are significant differences in their use of the term (related to their assumptions about the nature of society, human motivation and social relationships). In terms of our concerns with sport-in-development, Coleman and Putnam are the most relevant.

Although Coleman is rarely quoted in discussions relating to social capital and sport-in-development, his concerns are clearly of relevance – the relationship between social capital and the development of human capital (education, employment skills and expertise). Because of his commitment to individualistic rational choice theory, the attraction of social capital for Coleman (1988) is that it appears to be capable of bridging the gap between the 'over-socialized' views of human action and economists' 'under-socialized' models of self-interested actors maximizing their utilities. Coleman views social capital as mostly neutral aspects of social structure and social relationships which facilitate actions and he stresses the conscious actions of individuals in the development and use of social capital. In this context social capital is:

> the set of resources that inhere in family relations and in community social organisation and that are useful for the cognitive or social development of a child or young person. These resources differ for different persons and constitute an important advantage for children and adolescents in the development of their human capital.
>
> (Coleman, 1994: 300)

Johnston and Percy-Smith (2003) illustrate that Coleman identified three aspects of relations of social capital: (i) obligations, expectations and trustworthiness of structures; (ii) information channels and (iii) norms and effective sanctions, which facilitate 'closure' of such networks and ensure that obligations are met and 'free-loaders' are expelled. The importance of such sanctions and norms lies in the expectation of reciprocity and the fact that an individual's 'investment' (e.g. time, effort, helping others) is made not for altruistic purposes, but in the strong expectation that it will pay future dividends. Portes (1998: 10) notes that Coleman laments the decline of the 'close or dense ties' associated with 'primordial' institutions based on the family and emphasizes the need to replace these with 'rationally devised material and status incentives'. As Coleman (1988: S117) puts it:

> Because the social structural conditions that overcome the supplying of these public goods – that is, strong families and strong communities – are much less often present now than in the past, and promise to be even less present in the future ... the obvious solution appears to be to attempt to find ways of overcoming the problem of supply of these public goods, that is, social capital employed for the benefit of children and young. This very likely means the substitution of some kind of formal organisation for the voluntary and spontaneous social organisation that has in the past been the major source of social capital available to the young.

We will return to Coleman below, but here it is important to note that many sport-in-development organizations place a strong emphasis on the need for young people to remain in education and some provide both social and financial support for them to do so. Further, there is a widespread emphasis on the development of various aspects of human capital (e.g. transferable social and organizational skills), trust and collective responsibility, accompanied in many cases by rationally devised material and status incentives. However, we now turn to Putnam (2000), whose version of social capital tends to dominate debates and disputes within development policy.

Putnam differs from Coleman in placing little emphasis on instrumentalism and individual choice. From his perspective social capital can be regarded as a public good, which serves to bind communities together. Social capital is viewed as an essentially neutral resource which is a property of collectives – communities, cities, regions. For Putnam (2000: 18–19) 'the core idea of social capital is that social networks have value ... [it refers to] connections between individuals – social networks and the norms of reciprocity and trustworthiness that arise from them.'

Communities with high levels of social capital are viewed as being characterized by three main components – strong social networks and civic infrastructure which are characterized by strong social norms (i.e. informal and formal rules about personal and social behaviour and associated sanctions), which both support and reinforce mutual trust and reciprocity among members of a community. Putnam's appeal to policymakers is that he is more clearly interested in the role of organized voluntary associations and *collective outcomes* (unlike Coleman's more individualistic focus). Putnam (2000) views the civic engagement, associational life and volunteering associated with social capital as important because they improve the efficiency of communities and societies by facilitating coordinated actions, reducing transaction costs (e.g. high levels of trust facilitate commerce via less dependency on formal contractual agreements) and enabling communities to be more effective in pursuit of their collective interests. In other words, social capital is not just a public good, but is *for* the public good (Szreter, 1998). Its potential value for development is indicated by Woolcock and Narayan (2000: 240) who, summarizing Fukuyama (1995), state that 'social capital includes norms and values that facilitate exchanges, lower transaction costs, reduce the cost of information, permit trade in the absence of contracts and encourage responsible citizenship and the collective management of resources'.

Putnam (2000) distinguishes between two types of social capital – bonding and bridging. The former refers to networks based on strong social ties between similar people – people 'like us' – with relations, reciprocity and trust based on ties of familiarity and closeness. Putnam (2000: 23) refers to this as a type of 'sociological superglue', whose function is to enable people to 'get by' and which works to maintain a strong in-group loyalty and reinforce specific identities. Woolcock and Narayan (2000), social scientists who work for the World Bank, identify this as a rather romanticized *communitarian perspective* within the development literature. From this perspective social capital is equated with local clubs, associations and civic groups and is viewed as 'inherently good, the more the better, and its presence always has a positive effect on a community's welfare' (Woolcock and Narayan, 2000: 229). Nevertheless, many writing within the development literature acknowledge that for many people living in deprived communities, such networks are a key resource and an important means of cooperation and survival.

It is clear that this communitarian vision is the one which underpins many of the assertions about sport-in-development. Certainly, aspects of bonding social capital could be regarded as part of the historic role of sports clubs – like-minded people (often from similar economic circumstances, age ranges, educational backgrounds, sex, social class, race and religion) coming together to produce and consume a common interest – a particular sport. If we move beyond the simple use of the term 'sport' and 'participation', and begin to conceptualize the issues around more formal clubs and organizations, it is clear that to varying degrees they are capable of developing forms of bonding social capital that provide a basis for resource mobilization *for* sport, and to a certain extent *through* sport (United Nations, 2003).

Sport, sport plus or plus sport?

Before we illustrate these issues via a case study, it is useful to note the distinction between *sport plus* and *plus sport*. The major aim of sport plus organizations is to develop sustainable sporting organizations in order to remove barriers to sports participation, train and support leaders and coaches, develop basic sporting skills and provide opportunities to develop and progress (for many young men such organizations are viewed as a potential route into professional soccer). However, such aims are rarely the sole rationale and very rarely the basis for investment by aid agencies. Almost without exception, the role of sport in contributing to broader social goals is emphasized, with sport (or sporting organizations) being used to address a number of broader social issues (e.g. gender equity;

HIV/AIDS education; citizenship education). Plus sport pro-grammes place much more emphasis on sport as a means to an end – using sport's 'fly paper' ability to attract large numbers of young people to programmes concerned with wider social and health objectives. Non-sporting outcomes (e.g. HIV/AIDS education and behaviour change) are more important than the longer-term sustainable development of sport.

Of course, there is a continuum of such programmes and differences are not always clear-cut, making generalizations about such programmes very difficult. However, this con-tinuum illustrates a key fact – that *sport* in any simple sense rarely achieves the variety of desired outcomes attributed to it and that issues of process and context – either sport plus or plus sport – are key to understanding its developmental poten-tial. As Papacharisis et al. (2005: 247) suggest, 'there is nothing about … sport itself that is magical … It is the experience of sport that may facilitate the result' – they might also add the context and organisation of sport.

To illustrate and explore some of these issues we turn to a case study of the Mathare Youth Sport Association (MYSA).

The Mathare Youth Sport Association

Mathare, in north-east Nairobi, is one of the largest and poor-est slums in Africa, with a population of about 500 000 living in an area of 2 kilometres by 300 metres (1.2 miles by 0.2 miles). It is a maze of low, rusted iron-sheeting roofs with mud walls. Housing is wholly inadequate, with most houses measuring about 8 feet by 6 feet and holding up to 10 people. Few houses have running water, open gutters of sewage run throughout, the road infrastructure is extremely poor, refuse and litter dominate the area and the local authority provides few serv-ices (http://www.mysakenya.org; Willis, 2000; Brady & Kahn, 2002).

MYSA was established by Bob Munro (a Canadian UN environmental development officer) in 1987 as a small self-help project to organize soccer. The concentration on soccer is explained by the extremely high levels of local interest, low skill entry levels and basic facility and equipment costs. It is now the largest youth sports organization in Africa, with more than 1000 teams and 17 000 members. MYSA's teams range from under 10 to 18 years of age, organized in 16 zones – the biggest league in Africa. MYSA also has two male semi-professional teams, Mathare United (Atkins, n.d.). These teams were established for two reasons. Firstly, to provide the top of the development pyramid and provide motivation and role models for the junior players – in 2004 MYSA supplied eight players for Kenya's African Nation's Cup squad. Secondly, it was hoped to develop players and benefit from transfer fees which could be used to provide economic security for the broader MYSA programme (of which more later).

Producing citizens

MYSA initially attracted young males who played on waste ground in the slums with footballs made of recycled plastic bags and twine. The attraction of MYSA was three-fold. Firstly, access to real footballs (not to be underestimated in conditions of such poverty). Secondly, organized and structured games, which simulated the professional game. Thirdly, an ordered and protective environment, which was especially important for the many street children attracted to MYSA. However, it soon developed into a much more complex and ambitious *sport plus* project, whose ultimate ambition is to produce citizens – 'the leaders needed for building the new Kenya' (Munro, 2005: 5).

A major goal is to give both young men and women a chance to take part in sport in conditions of equality and mutual respect. Sport is used to reduce young women's social isolation by providing them with a wider range of legitimate public spaces and opportunities to develop (Brady & Kahn, 2002). Although the subordinate economic and social position of young women (reinforced via often strong parental and community opposition to their participation) presents ongoing recruitment and retention difficulties, flexible programming and other measures are adopted to enable participation as players and, even more importantly, as peer leaders and coaches within the organization (Saavedra, 2005). The concentration on soccer can be regarded both as pragmatic and as an attempt to use a presumed male preserve to challenge gender stereotypes (a vital aspect of addressing issues of HIV/AIDS). With boys expressing scepticism about girls' ability to play the game, the provision of 'girls' sports' would risk simply re-enforcing deep-rooted stereotypes. In this regard Brady and Kahn (2002: 1–2) state:

We posit that participation in non-elite sports programs appropriate for girls of average physical ability and skills can meet the simultaneous needs of offering girls new venues in which to gather and breaking down restrictive gender norms … Girls' participation can begin to change community norms about their roles and capacities. In this way, sports may be a catalyst for the transformation of social norms.

Consequently, soccer is an entry point to a comprehensive, interdependent programme, in which all elements are mutually reinforcing in order to produce a form of social capital. These elements are outlined by Munro (2005) as follows:

(i) To link sport to community service.
(ii) Youth are owners and decision-makers (with the average age of elected leaders and volunteer coaches being 15–16 years). They are elected from zonal league committees to Sports Council/Community Service Council and then to the MYSA Executive Council.
(iii) Learning by doing, with assistance but limited interference.
(iv) To help youth to help themselves by helping others. Reflecting a key component of bonding social capital, Munro (2005: 3) argues that 'when you are poor cooperation and sharing are crucial for survival'.
(v) Help young leaders to stay in school. This is achieved via a points-based educational scholarship system, with points being awarded for volunteer activities (coaching, refereeing, community service).
(vi) Plan for organizational sustainability. MYSA has many decision-makers and clear lines of accountability and there is a 'retirement' policy to ensure that it remains a youth organization.

These various philosophies and practices clearly reflect components of the definitions of social capital – social networks based on social and group norms which enable people to trust and cooperate with each other and via which individuals or groups can obtain certain types of advantage. Further, this is clearly a form of *bonding social capital* as it is based on strong social ties of familiarity and closeness between people who share very similar social, cultural and economic circumstances – many members refer to MYSA as a 'family'. This is reinforced by the fact that the 60 full- and part-time employees are recruited from MYSA members (who appear to possess a deep sense of responsibility to act as positive role models). These basic elements are part of an over-arching philosophy of mutual self-help and a number of specific practices and activities which serve formally to reinforce certain values and attitudes.

The sense of involvement, responsibility and values of active citizenship are reinforced by member-involvement in decision-making at all levels, with a strong emphasis on mutual self-help – stated succinctly by Munro (2005: 2) as 'you do something, MYSA does something. You do nothing, MYSA does nothing'.

This ethic of reciprocity, which serves as a form of closure thereby reducing the problem of free-loaders, is especially important in a society where there is widespread corruption, including sport (to which we will return).

Sport plus

However, from the perspective of sport-in-development, it is essential to understand that MYSA do not depend on any simple view of 'sports participation' to maximize the possibility of achieving the desired outcomes. For example, the rules of soccer have been amended to maximize the potential to achieve such outcomes. During soccer games anyone other than the captain who speaks to an official can be sent off (a substitute player is permitted). The player then has to referee six junior matches to put him- or herself in the place of a referee before being permitted to play again. In addition, a green card is awarded to the most sporting player and is a highly valued award, as it is accompanied by educational scholarship points. This illustrates an aspect of social capital emphasized by most theorists – that the social relations/networks provide access to certain resources and advantages. As part of its commitment to helping young leaders to stay in school, MYSA has about 400 annual Leadership Awards (it also provides small libraries and study rooms to compensate for the lack of study space in over-crowded dwellings). Although schooling is free up to the age of 14 years, many schools require pupils to wear uniforms (prohibitive for many living in poverty) and in the post-14 schools, fees are required. The awards are paid to the school of the winners' choice and are used to pay for tuition, books and uniforms. Points towards these awards are also linked to volunteer, peer-leadership and coaching work.

A more general commitment to community service is compulsory for all members of MYSA, including the semi-professionals in Mathare United. The aim of the work is to increase environmental awareness and entails a 'cleanup', in which teams from the various zones clear drains, cut grass and remove litter. Although this work makes little overall impact on the overwhelming environmental problems of Mathare, the core value being emphasized here is that of collective responsibility and reciprocity – 'if you get something from the community you must put something back into the community' (Munro, 2005: 2). The extent of programme integration and re-enforcement of values are emphasized by the fact that each completed cleanup project earns a soccer team three points

51

towards its league standings – success is a combination of sporting talent and social responsibility.

Rather than reflecting Putnam's somewhat 'organic' view of social capital, the MYSA approach seems to be closer to Coleman's 'rationally devised material and status incentives' (Portes, 1998: 10), needed to compensate for the weakening of family, community and local government structures. It can also be viewed as illustrating aspects of Coleman's perspective about the relationship between social capital and the development of human capital and his greater emphasis on the more conscious and self-interested aspects of social capital. For example, initial parental resistance to girls' participation in such sports projects is frequently overcome once parents realize the educational and other benefits to be obtained via membership. Further, issues of reciprocity and trust are clearly and regularly articulated and reinforced within the organization, rather than simply assumed (or illustrated via sanctions for transgression).

Consequently, MYSA's importance goes well beyond sport or the traditional functions of most sporting organizations. In effect, it operates in a number of areas in civil society, seeking to compensate for major failures of the local and national states' welfare provision – facilitated and given coherence by soccer and soccer-related programmes. Although MYSA is a particularly sophisticated example of a sport plus organization, it is based on an approach which is widespread among all such projects – the development and use of volunteer *youth peer leaders, educators* and *coaches.*

Volunteering plus

In many traditional sports development programmes leaders and coaches are regarded simply as *inputs* – qualified sports development officers who use their professional expertise to develop programmes for local communities. However, by adopting a youth peer leader approach, many sport-in-development organizations involve young men and women at various levels of planning, implementation and decision-making, providing important experience of control, empowerment and a sense of collective responsibility (via the much emphasized status of 'role models'). In other words, *people* (or 'responsible citizens') are a major outcome of many such organizations, one that is central to their sustainability and precedes the programmes whose impacts are often the subject of evaluation.

Consequently, volunteer peer leaders, teachers and coaches are at the centre of such organizations and programmes. In addition to being a vital resource for the sustainability of the organizations, their use is also based firmly on educational and learning theory. For example, it is argued that because young people's attitudes are highly influenced by their peers' values and attitudes, peer educators are less likely to be viewed as 'preaching' authority figures and more likely to be regarded as people who know the experiences and concerns of young people (Kerrigan, 1999; YouthNet, 2005). Further, Payne et al. (2003) illustrate that, to be effective, role models must be embedded, based on the development of supportive, longer-term trusting relationships. In line with social learning and self-efficacy theory (Bandura, 1962), evidence suggests that major factors underpinning the effectiveness of role models are the characteristics of the model and their *perceived similarity to the learner*. Learning is more likely to occur when the learners perceive that they are capable of carrying out the behaviour (self-efficacy expectancy), think that there is a high probability that the behaviour will result in a particular outcome (outcome expectancy) and if the outcome is desirable – all of which can be reinforced via peer education. In this regard, Kerrigan (1999), in discussing the role of peer educators in HIV/AIDS programmes, argues that the key to successful peer education lies in the fact that it makes possible a dialogue between equals and collective planning to adopt practices which are contextually and culturally relevant – a clear form of bonding social capital. In addition, Saavedra (2005) emphasizes the special importance of female role models in sport-in-development organizations which seek to confront traditional, exploitative and often abusive social relations. Munro (2005: 4) illustrates the importance placed on role models by asking rhetorically: 'role models for youth: is anything more important in development?' He argues that in most African countries the poor are the majority and youth constitute the majority of that poor majority and that 'among the many debilitating aspects of poverty is that the poor, and especially the youth, lack confidence and belief in themselves'. Consequently, 'after food, water, shelter, health and education, nothing is more important for future development than providing good role models for our youth' (Munro, 2005: 4).

However, although accepting the theoretical legitimacy of the peer educator approach, Kruse (2006) points to the lack of research on the nature and quality of such processes, arguing that there is a lack of information about the quality of the exchanges in particular contexts (a key issue for social capital), the extent to which peer leaders and coaches are given sufficient training, the extent of supervision and support provided after initial training and their effectiveness. In this regard Nicholls (2007: 1) argues that 'the necessary support for peer educators is not always available in the resource poor and donor-driven world of development through sport'. Consequently, although there is a strong theoretical underpinning for such an approach, there is an urgent need for empirical research relating to both educational and social capital outcomes.

Motivations and meanings

In this regard, a better understanding of how such organizations actually work might be to adopt a less romanticised, communitarian, view of the *organization* and explore the potential range of motivations – from those motivated by civic/democratic/moral values (akin to Putnam), to more Coleman-like instrumentalism (Gaskin & Smith, 1997; Portes & Landolt, 2000). Clearly there is a substantial ethos of altruism, sense of belonging and collective responsibility among most youth peer leaders – values and attitudes presumed to underpin volunteerism and central to Putnam's civic virtues. However, in many cases this is accompanied and reinforced by rationally devised material and status incentives – access to educational scholarships, foreign travel to competitions (a major incentive), status within the organizations and community – which appear to be closer to Coleman's more instrumental and self-interested approach, whose attraction and power are wholly understandable in conditions of extreme poverty. The nature of motivations and incentives has clear implications for the design and use of sport-in-development programmes and for our understanding of the nature of the social capital which they produce.

The issues of motivation and meaning also raise another important issue when discussing social capital and sport-in-development – the possible differential distribution of benefits – referred to by Fukuyama (1999: 2) as the 'radius of trust'. For example, where an organization's social capital produces positive externalities (e.g. via MYSA's cleanup activities and educational scholarships) then the radius of trust can be larger than the group – an outcome clearly implied by much policy rhetoric in sport-in-development. However, while it is clear that there are collective benefits as a result of the ability of the organization to mobilize and maximize the use of sporting resources (e.g. access to limited playing space), there is also likely to be a differential distribution of social capital and its benefits *within* the organization – perhaps the collective strengths of social capital inevitably benefit some more than others. Fukuyama (1999) suggests that it is also possible that trust-based and cooperative norms are strongest among the leadership and permanent staff. For example, those most actively involved in the organization and the provision of opportunities will be those most likely to benefit via the development of their human capital and increased employability (Seippel, 2006; Skidmore et al., 2006). An example is provided by a small qualitative study of the Edusport organization in Zambia in which Mwaanga (2003) illustrates that the level and intensity of participation were key moderators of programme effectiveness – not surprisingly the youth peer leaders were more likely to benefit than simple participants. They are the most committed, have gone through the various training programmes, have experience of decision-making and perceptions of control and status, and are highly conscious of their positions (and responsibilities) as role models.

Such comments should not be taken as criticisms – to produce a cadre of highly committed and responsible youth peer leaders (especially female) in such difficult economic and cultural circumstances is clearly a major achievement. Rather, the comment relates solely to seeking to understand better how such organizations work and to the widespread concern about the limits of bonding capital in processes of development.

Is bonding enough?

MYSA clearly indicates the potential of sport-in-development organizations to compensate for certain aspects of the wider failures of national and local states, weak civic structures and disintegrating families (although it is essential to recognize that it is much longer established, more sophisticated and better funded than many sport-in-development organizations). They have the potential to develop forms of social capital by providing young men and women rare opportunities to participate in decision-making, confront exploitative gender relations, encourage ambition, recognize the value of education, develop relationships based on trust and reciprocity and provide opportunities for the development of aspects of human capital. Further, in MYSA's case at least it is clear that they have achieved both mobilization *for* and 'through sport' (e.g. the educational scholarship programme) (United Nations, 2003).

However, many writing within the development literature express concerns about the limitations of *bonding social capital* – especially for contributing to wider policies of social and economic regeneration. Clearly it can play a significant role in local social regeneration – for example, as an essential first step towards building collective confidence, cohesion and cooperation. However, concerns have been expressed about certain socio-cultural aspects of bonding social capital, what Putnam (2000) has referred to as its 'dark side' – acting to impose conformity and downward levelling, excluding outsiders and maybe even providing the basis for anti-social activities (e.g. the Mafia, urban street gangs). It is possible that while such capital can assist in community bonding, it may lead to 'defensive communities' (or organizations) (Forrest & Kearns, 1999: 1) – linking disadvantaged individuals together, but effectively excluding them from the wider society (and its resources and opportunities) and restricting routes out of poverty and exclusion. Consequently, Woolcock and Narayan (2000: 231) refer to bonding social capital as a 'double-edged sword' with strong group loyalties and collectively enforced obligations potentially serving to 'isolate members from information about employment opportunities, foster a climate of ridicule towards efforts to study and work hard, or siphon off hard-won assets' (e.g. via the enforcement of collective obligations on small entrepreneurs to make charitable gifts or fund festivals or celebrations). However, it is possible to argue that many sport-in-development organizations, with their emphasis on gender equity, education, personal development and social responsibility, are seeking to confront and replace potentially negative bonding social capital with much more positive forms – a task which sometimes leads to confrontation with wider community interests.

However, while many sport-in-development organizations manage to promote the positive aspects of bonding social capital, there is a broader danger that 'equating social capital with the resources acquired through it can easily lead to tautological statements' (Portes, 1998: 19) – in other words such networks can be 'resource poor', both internally and externally. For example, Narayan and Nyamwaya (1996) point out that, 'in Kenya a participatory poverty assessment recorded more than 200 000 community groups active in rural areas, but most were unconnected to outside resources and were unable to improve the lot of the poor' (quoted in Woolcock & Narayan, 2000: 220). Portes and Landolt (2000: 542) note that 'it must be recognised that local-level cooperation alone cannot overcome macro-structural obstacles to economic stability, autonomous growth, and accumulation'. Therefore, Portes and Landolt (2000: 546) conclude that the development of forms of social capital is a very attractive proposition for aid agencies because they can increase the yield of aid and investment (e.g. via volunteer labour and greater openness and accountability):

One must not be over-optimistic about what enforceable trust and bounded solidarity can accomplish at the collective level, especially in the absence of material resources. Social capital can be a powerful force promoting group projects but, … it consists of the ability to marshal resources through social networks, not the resources themselves. When the latter are poor and scarce, the goal achievement capacity of a collectivity is restricted, no matter how strong the internal bonds … social capital are not a substitute for the provision of credit, material infrastructure and education.

For example, Woolcock and Narayan (2006: 235) point to the limitations of civil society organizations where there is 'rampant corruption, frustrating bureaucratic delays, suppressed civil liberties, vast inequality'. Although the example is not directly analogous, it is worth noting the case of MYSA. The establishment of the semi-professional Mathare United was part of a strategy to achieve some degree of financial sustainability. It was hoped that by developing players their transfer fees could be used to provide economic security for the broader MYSA programme. However, reflecting wider aspects of corruption in Kenyan sport, football agents, in association with the Kenyan Football Federation undermined this strategy, by depriving MYSA of its legitimate share of two transfer fees. This was in addition to clear examples of match fixing, systematic siphoning-off of match fees and a failure to distribute FIFA youth development funds (for a full detailed analysis, see Munro, 2006). Although certain resolutions have been found to some of these issues, they serve to illustrate what Woolcock and Narayan (2006) term the *Institutional View* of the role of social capital in development – that civil society organizations are not simple substitutes for the state and can only really thrive to the extent that the state actively encourages them. In other words, in the absence of what they refer to as 'civic and government social capital' such well-intentioned efforts will have limited general impact. Here it is worth noting Renard's (2006: 21) suggestion that the encouragement of civil society organizations might be 'a covert ploy that is intended to have long-term effects on power relations within the country' – certainly MYSA's confrontations with the KFF raise this possibility within the area of soccer (Munro, 2006) as does more general discourse about citizenship, values and female empowerment.

Going beyond the boundary

The limitations of (even positive) bonding social capital can be partially moderated by the development of other forms of social capital – *bridging social capital* and *linking social capital*. The former refers to weaker social ties between different types of people – more colleagues than family and friends. This is less of a glue than 'a sociological WD40' (Putnam, 2000: 23) and facilitates 'getting ahead' via, for example, the diffusion of information and employment opportunities. The notion of linking social capital is proposed by Woolcock (2001), a social scientist concerned with development. Whereas bonding and bridging social capital are concerned with types of horizontal relationships, linking social capital refers to vertical connections between different social strata, including those entirely outside the community (thereby offering access to wider networks and the potential to leverage a broader range of resources). In fact, Skidmore et al. (2006: viii) suggest that broader policies to promote community participation in governance are frequently concerned with linking capital, the theory being 'that being involved in the governance of services, participants build relationships with public institutions or officials which give their community access to valuable external resources like money, support or political leverage'.

In this regard it is worth noting Seippel's (2006) distinction between *connected* sports organizations (i.e. members have ties to members of other associations) and *isolated* organizations, which focus solely on their sport and local community. The latter are a vehicle for the mobilization of resources *for* sport and may achieve certain intermediate impacts supposedly associated with participation in sport (self-efficacy, confidence) and develop certain forms of bonding social capital (with varying 'radii of trust'). For example, Driscoll and Wood (1999) explore the role of Australian rural sport and recreation clubs in periods of social and economic change and their contribution to development of social capital. They conclude that in rural areas sports clubs have the potential to perform wide-ranging sociocultural functions, including leadership, participation, skill development, providing a community hub, health promotion, social networks and community identity. However, the definition of the term 'social capital' – 'a collective term for the ties that bind us' – is rather vague, with limited analytical utility.

However, the United Nations' (2005c: 14) aspiration for an integrated approach to sport-in-development 'involving a full spectrum of actors in field-based community development including all levels of and various sectors of government, sports organizations, NGOs and the private sector' clearly relates to *connected clubs*. The extent to which clubs can develop both bridging and linking capital will vary by their type, size and location (e.g. isolated or connected; single or multi-sport; urban or rural; competitive or recreational). However, in many cases they are part of a wider 'sports community', in which participation in leagues, competitions, governing bodies, ground sharing and so on provide theoretical opportunities for the development of forms of bridging and (maybe) linking social capital, although the extent to which this is restricted to 'sporting social capital' (i.e. mobilization of resources *for* sport, within the sports community) is an important empirical question in relation to their precise contribution to broader processes of development.

Woolcock and Narayan (2000: 231) refer to the combination of bridging and linking social capital as the *networks view*, arguing that 'strong intra-community ties and weak extra-community networks are needed to avoid making tautological claims regarding the efficacy of social capital'. However, the networks view seems to be closer to Coleman's rather individualistic perspective than to Putnam's more collective views and returns us to the questions relating to the beneficiaries of forms of social capital – with substantial implications for development. For example, Woolcock and Narayan (2000: 234) suggest that 'this view minimizes the "public good" nature of social groups, regarding any benefits of group activity as primarily the property of the particular individuals involved'. Leonard (2004) offers a very similar analysis about the potential conflict between very strong bonding social capital in Catholic communities in Belfast and the need for small businesses and individual entrepreneurs to develop bridging and linking capital in order to develop and expand their businesses. Whereas bonding social capital may provide an essential collective support and insurance network for the poor, for development to occur it needs to be weak enough to permit the (individual) poor to gain access to wider and more formal institutions and a more diverse stock of bridging (and maybe even linking) social capital – MYSA's citizens must leave eventually.

It is clear that many sport-in-development organizations have the potential to gain access to forms of both bridging and linking social capital, although their relationships with national governing bodies and government sports organizations vary widely (in some cases they are antagonistic). In particular, the burgeoning international sport-in-development networks provide access to such networks and the funding and resources which accompany them. However, Renard (2006) suggests that there may be a conflict at the heart of these relationships in the new aid paradigm – between largely locally determined poverty reduction strategies (or in our case, sports development strategies) and externally imposed Millennium Development Goals, which may skew programmes and not reflect local issues and needs. In such circumstances Renard posits two contrasting sets of relationships (which can be regarded as forms of linking social capital).

One set of relationships is based on donors and recipients pursuing similar policy objectives, based on consensus and trust. It might be hypothesized that this refers to aid given to existing sporting organizations by sporting organizations in a spirit of relative altruism, in order to promote and develop sport and international sporting solidarity. In current circumstances such aid is nearly always for a *sports plus* approach, but will nevertheless be concerned with sports development and the strengthening of the sporting infrastructure (accompanied by an implicit belief in the positive outcomes associated with sport). Renard's second set of relations is based on the possibility that donors and recipients may have differing agendas. This is more likely to be closer to a plus sport perspective, in which sport's 'fly paper' properties are emphasized and sports organizations are funded, or even 'constructed', with the purpose of achieving defined non-sporting developmental goals.

With regard to the latter approach, concern has been expressed about the possible consequences of external aid to such civil society organizations. As the debt-ridden crises of many African societies have lead to a weakening of the state and institutions of civil society there has been a proliferation of external NGOs, giving them effective control of areas such as health, education and welfare provision (reinforced by the HIV/AIDS pandemic) (Armstrong & Giulianotti, 2004). Some have argued that the rapid growth in influence of locally non-accountable NGOs represents new forces of neo-colonialism, with their main leadership and strategies being formulated in the West they are viewed as promoting new forms of dependency. With regard to sport, Giulianotti (2004) has raised questions about the exporting of overly 'functionalist' views of sport by new 'sports evangelists' and questions the nature and extent of the dialogue between donors and recipients, the extent to which 'empowerment' is a clear goal. It is certainly the case that donors' frequently unrealistically high (but extremely vague) aspirations for the contribution of sport to development encourage such organizations (wholly dependent on external aid) to include objectives and programme elements in their funding applications which they might not otherwise have contemplated, which may skew their sports development and which present considerable difficulties for any attempts at monitoring and evaluation (Coalter, 2006, 2007; Kruse, 2006).

The nature of such donor/client relationships is important because of a desire to 'promote' forms of social capital, and the more general concerns that 'the essence of social capital is that it consists of activities and relationships freely engaged in by individuals' (Field, 2003: 118). For example, Fukuyama (2001: 18) warns that excessive (state) intervention 'can have a serious negative impact on social capital' and Field (2003) refers to Coleman's doubts about the ability of constructed forms of organization to provide the required normative cohesion and network closure central to the effective working of social capital – although this is clearly a matter for empirical investigation. In this regard Sport England (2003: 14) accepts that requiring sports clubs to adopt different agendas contains substantial risks and argues that 'any external assistance offered needs to emphasize that it is designed to help them achieve their aims'. As Renard (2006) stresses, such a position has major implications for the functional use of sport-in-development organizations to seek to achieve donor's wider objectives. It is perhaps worth leaving the last word on this to Munro (the founder of MYSA) (personal communication) who stated that 'the best thing that happened to MYSA was that nobody was interested for the first five years'. The implication of this is that the lack of interest and aid permitted the establishment of locally based aims, objectives, principles and processes – whether these are viewed via the lens of Coleman or Putnam.

Conclusions

In considering the contribution of sport-in-development to the formation of social capital, the key issues concern the types of social capital being assumed, the precise meaning of resource mobilization 'both for and *through* sport' (United Nations, 2003: 20) and the limits of sport-in-development's contributions to broader development strategies (e.g. we have noted Renard's (2006) suggestion that the encouragement of participation in organizations in civil society is a covert political ploy to change certain power relations).

The case study of MYSA illustrates a number of issues about the danger of de-contextualized, rather romanticized, communitarian generalizations about the 'power' of sport-in-development. Firstly, it is clear that it is not simple sports participation which can hope to achieve such outcomes, but *sports plus*; it is not sport which achieves many of these outcomes, but *sporting organizations*; it is not sport which produces and sustains social capital, enters into partnerships and mobilizes resources, but certain types of social organization. Further, evidence would suggest that some of these organizations are consciously and systematically organized to maximize the possibility of achieving such outcomes – developing forms of Coleman's rationally devised material and status incentives, rather than depending on Putnam's rather more organic perspective.

It is clear that some types of sport-in-development organizations provide inclusive sports development programmes, enabling many young people to have access to sporting opportunities and some non-sporting resources (e.g. education; foreign travel) that they would not otherwise have had. In some circumstances they offer some compensation for certain aspects of weak civic structures, disintegrating families and inadequate education systems. They can develop forms of social capital by providing some young people with opportunities to participate in decision-making, confront exploitative gender relations, encourage ambition and recognize the value of education, develop relationships based on trust and reciprocity, provide opportunities for the development of aspects of human capital – especially via the volunteer based youth peer coaches and educators. These possibilities make such organizations an attractive investment for aid agencies, as they increase the yield of aid and investment – you get a lot for your money. However, there is a wide variety of such organizations and in terms of understanding the contribution of sports organizations to development it is essential to distinguish between the social relations characteristic of forms of social capital and the (frequently limited) resources associated with them (Portes & Landolt, 2000; Kruse, 2006; Nicholls, 2007).

The type and strength of social capital (and associated resources) developed will depend on the size and type of organization (e.g. isolated or connected; single or multi-sport; urban or rural; competitive or recreational; single or mixed sex) and their relationships with the 'community' (both local and sporting) – the 'radius of trust' (Fukuyama, 1999). Further, although there is a tendency to talk about social capital in organizational, collective terms, many commentators – reflecting the perspective of Coleman (and Bourdieu, 1997) – raise the issue of the differential distribution of social capital (most especially bridging and linking) within organizations. For example, an analysis and evaluation of the developmental effectiveness of such organizations might concentrate on the roles of youth peer leaders and subsequent destinations (Mwaanga, 2003; Nicholls, 2007).

A further key issue relates to the nature of the processes involved in the formation and sustaining of different types of social capital. There is broad agreement that policy-led attempts to construct social capital may fail, as social capital is based on activities, relationships and norms freely engaged in by individuals – an analysis which raises significant issues for organizations which are almost wholly aid-dependent and are effectively encouraged to offer an economy of solutions to a wide range of social, political and economic problems. However, it is also worth noting Coleman's (1988: S108) suggestion that 'organizations once brought into existence for one set of purposes can also aid others, thus constituting social capital available for use which are set up for one purpose'.

Consequently we are left with questions about how to understand the relationships between forms of sport, forms of organization, types of social capital and forms of development, *or the extent to which such relationships can exist* (Kruse, 2006). Certainly, in the area of sport-in-development we can clearly see the truth of Pawson's (2006: 5) assertion that 'social interventions are always complex systems thrust amidst complex systems' – something frequently ignored in policy rhetoric.

References

Armstrong, G. & Giulianotti, R. (Eds.), (2004). *Football in Africa: Conflict Conciliation and Community*. Basingstoke: Palgrave Macmillan.

Atkins, H. (n.d.). *Mathare United: A Model CECAFA Club*. Available from http://www.toolkitsportdevelopment.org.

Bandura, A. (1962). *Social Learning through Imitation*. Lincoln, NE: University of Nebraska Press.

Bourdieu, P. (1997). The forms of capital. In A.H. Halsey, H. Launder, P. Brown & A. Stuart Wells (Eds.), *Education, Culture, Economy and Society* (pp. 46–58). Oxford: Oxford University Press.

Brady, M. & Kahn, A.B. (2002). *Letting Girls Play: The Mathare Youth Sports Association's Football Program for Girls*. New York: Population Council.

Coalter, F. (2006). *Sport-in-Development: A Monitoring and Evaluation Manual*. London: UK Sport.

Coalter, F. (2007). *Sport a Wider Social Role: Whose Keeping the Score?*. London: Routledge.

Coleman, J. (1988). Social capital in the creation of human capital. *American Journal of Sociology, 94*, 95–120.

Coleman, J. (1990). *Equality and Achievement in Education*. Boulder, CO: Westview Press.

Coleman, J.S. (1994). *Foundations of Social Theory*. Cambridge, MA: Belknap Press.

Comaroff, J. & Comaroff, J. (Eds.), (1999). *Civil Society and the Political Imagination in Africa: Critical Perspectives*. Chicago, IL: University of Chicago Press.

Driscoll, K. & Wood, L. (1999). *Sporting Capital: Changes and Challenges for Rural Communities in Victoria*. Melbourne: Victoria Centre for Applied Social Research, RMIT.

Farr, J. (2004). Social capital: A conceptual history. *Political Theory, 32*(1), 6–33.

Field, J. (2003). *Social Capital*. London: Routledge.

Forrest, R. & Kearns, A. (1999). *Joined-Up Places? Social Cohesion and Neighbourhood Regeneration*. York: YPS for the Joseph Rowntree Foundation.

Fukuyama, F. (1995). *Trust: The Social Virtues and the Creation of Prosperity*. London: Hamish Hamilton.

Fukuyama, F. (1999). *Social Capital and Civil Society*. George Mason University. The institute of Public policy.

Fukuyama, F. (2001). Social capital, civil society and development. *Third World Quarterly, 22*(1), 7–20.

Gaskin, K. & Smith, D. (1997). *A New Civic Europe? A Study of the Extent and Role of Volunteering*. London: Volunteer Centre UK.

Giulianotti, R. (2004). Human rights, globalization and sentimental education: The case of sport. *Sport in Society, 7*(3), 355–369.

Grootaert, C., Narayan, D., Jones, V.N. & Woolcock, M. (2004). *Measuring Social Capital: An Integrated Questionnaire, World Bank Working Paper No. 18*. Washington, DC: World Bank.

Hognestad, H. (2005). *Norwegian Strategies on Culture – and Sports Development with Southern Countries*, a presentation to the Sports Research Forum, Australian Sports Commission, Canberra, 13–15 April.

Johnston, G. & Percy-Smith, J. (2003). In search of social capital. *Policy and Politics, 31*(3), 321–334.

Kerrigan, D. (1999). *Peer Education and HIV/AIDS: Concepts, Uses and Challenges*. Washington, DC: Horizons/Population Council.

Kruse, S.E. (2006). *Review of Kicking AIDS Out: Is Sport an Effective Tool in the Fight against HIV/AIDS?*, draft report to NORAD, unpublished.

Leonard, M. (2004). Bonding and bridging social capital: Reflections from Belfast. *Sociology, 38*(5), 927–944.

Munro, B. (2005). *Role Models: Is Anything More Important for Future Development?* Role Models Retreat, Laureus Sport for Good Foundation, 23–24 November, Pretoria, South Africa.

Munro, B. (2006). *Greed* vs *Good Governance: The Fight for Corruption-Free Football in Kenya*, a paper presented at Play the Game 2005 – Governance in Sport: The Good, The Bad and The Ugly, Copenhagen. Available at http://www.playthegame.org.

Mwaanga, O. (2003). *HIV/AIDS At-Risk Adolescent Girls' Empowerment through Participation in Top Level Football and Edusport in Zambia*, MSc thesis submitted to the Institute of Social Science, the Norwegian University of Sport and PE, Oslo.

Narayan, D. & Nyamwaya, D. (1996). *Learning from the Poor: A Participatory Poverty Assessment in Kenya*, Environment Department Papers, Participation series 34, World Bank Social Policy and Resettlement Division, Washington, DC.

Nicholls, S. (2007). *On the Backs of Peer Educators*, a paper presented to the International Studies Association Congress, Chicago, IL, February.

NORAD (2002). *Study of Future Norwegian Support to Civil Society in Mozambique*, NORAD. Available at http://www.norad.no/default.asp?V_ITEM_ID=1137.

Papacharisis, V., Goudas, M., Danish, S.J. & Theodorakis, Y. (2005). The effectiveness of teaching a life skills program in a sport context. *Journal of Applied Sport Psychology, 17*, 247–254.

Pawson, R. (2006). *Evidence-Based Policy: A Realist Perspective.* London: Sage.

Payne, W., Reynolds, M., Brown, S. & Fleming, A. (2003). *Sports Role Models and Their Impact on Participation in Physical Activity: A Literature Review.* Victoria: VicHealth.

Pollard, A. & Court, J. (2005). *How Civil Society Organisations Use Evidence to Influence Policy Processes: A Literature Review, Working Paper No. 249.* London: Overseas Development Institute.

Portes, A. (1998). Social capital: Its origins and applications in modern sociology. *Annual Review of Sociology, 24*, 1–24.

Portes, A. & Landolt, P. (2000). Social capital: Promise and pitfalls of its role in development. *Journal of Latin American Studies, 32*, 529–547.

Putnam, R. (2000). *Bowling Alone: The Collapse and Revival of the American Community*. New York: Simon & Schuster.

Renard, R. (2006). *The Cracks in the New Aid Paradigm*, Discussion Paper. Antwerpen, Belgium: Institute of Development Policy and Management.

Saavedra, M. (2005). *Women, Sport and Development*, Sport and Development International Platform. Available at http://www.sportanddev.org/data/document/document/148.pdf.

Seippel, O. (2006). Sport and social capital. *Acta Sociologica*, *49*(2), 169–183.

Skidmore, P., Bound, K. & Lownsborough, H. (2006). *Community Participation: Who Benefits?*. York: Joseph Rowntree Foundation.

Sport England (2003). *Sports Volunteers in England in 2002*. London: Sport England.

Szreter, S. (1998). *A New Political Economy for New Labour: The Importance of Social Capital*, Policy Paper No. 15. Sheffield: Political Economy Research Centre.

UNICEF (2006). Monitoring and Evaluation for Sport-Based Programming for Development: Sport Recreation and Play, Workshop Report. New York: UNICEF.

United Nations (2003). *Sport for Development and Peace: Towards Achieving the Millennium Development Goals*, Report from the United Nations Inter-Agency Task Force on Sport for Development and Peace. Geneva: United Nations.

United Nations (2005a). Business Plan International Year of Sport and Physical Education. New York: United Nations.

United Nations (2005b). Sport for Development and Peace: Towards Achieving the Millennium Development Goals. New York: United Nations.

United Nations (2005c). Concept: Education Health Development Peace: International Year of Sport and Physical Education. Geneva: United Nations.

Van Rooy, A. (2004). *Global Legitimacy Game: Civil Society, Globalisation and Protest*. London: Palgrave Macmillan.

Willis, O. (2000). Sport and development: The significance of Mathare Youth Sports Association. *Canadian Journal of Development Studies*, *21*(3), 825–849.

Woolcock, M. (2001). The place of social capital in understanding social and economic outcomes. *ISUMA Canadian Journal of Policy Research*, *2*(1), 11–17.

Woolcock, M. & Narayan, D. (2000). Social capital: Implications for development theory, research, and policy. *The World Bank Research Observer*, *15*(2), 225–249.

World Bank (n.d.). *Social Capital and Civil Society*. Available at http://web.worldbank.org/wbsite/external/topics/extsocial devlopment.

World Commission on Culture and Development (1995). *Our Creative Diversity: A Report of the World Commission for Culture and Development*, UNESCO. Available at http://www. unesco.org/culture/policies/ocd/index.shtml.

YouthNet (2005). *From Theory to Practice in Peer Education*. New York: United Nations Population Fund and Youth Peer Education Network.

Locating social capital in sport policy

Russell Hoye and
Matthew Nicholson

In the introductory chapter to this book we made the point that our interest in social capital and its relationship with sport was (in part) motivated by the frequency with which social capital is referred to within contemporary national sport policies. In this chapter we identify how social capital has been conceptualized by policymakers in sport, explore why national governments have focussed on social capital within their sport policies, discuss some challenges for how policymakers determine the outcomes of social capital related sport policies, and highlight the policy convergence that has occurred in this area amongst selected Commonwealth countries.

In general terms it could be argued that the sport policies of countries such as Australia, Canada, England and New Zealand are focussed on the twin objectives of: (1) enhancing elite sport performance and (2) increasing the proportion of people involved in formalized competitive sport or physical activity (Stewart et al., 2004; Green & Houlihan, 2005; Bergsgard et al., 2007). These policies have also focussed on improving the capacity of non-profit governing bodies of sport so that they are more likely to deliver these twin objectives on behalf of their respective national governments. The overwhelming majority of funding allocated by these policies is targeted, however, toward elite interests (Green & Houlihan, 2005). Despite this focus on the instrumental goal of achieving international success in the Olympic arena and other high profile international sport events, social capital and related terms appear throughout these sport policies. The following sections identify the context in which social capital and related terms appear within the current sport policies of these four countries and interpret how social capital has been conceptualized.

Australia

In the wake of the Sydney Olympic Games, the Australian federal government released *Backing Australia's Sporting Ability (BASA)*, a policy that provides direction for the development of Australian sport throughout the first decade of the twenty-first century. In the foreword to the policy, Australian Prime Minister John Howard and the then Minister for Sport Jackie Kelly noted that the policy had two objectives: to assist elite athletes to continue achieving success and to increase the talent pool from which these champions will emerge, an objective intimately related to the concept of social capital. Importantly, they noted:

The centrepiece of our policy is a new strategy to increase community participation in sport. It is true that more players mean more winners but there are also other benefits of being involved in sport. In addition to the obvious benefits of health and fitness, the Government appreciates that sport provides valuable opportunities for people of all ages to improve themselves, display teamwork and become more engaged in community activities. Our aim is to see more sport played at the grass roots level, particularly amongst school aged children and in rural areas, where sporting groups are often a vital factor in the cohesion of local communities. To this end the Government has increased funding to encourage participation and has introduced new programmes directed at young Australians.

(Commonwealth of Australia, 2001: 2)

In the context of the BASA policy goal of delivering greater grass roots participation in sport it emphasised the need for sport organisations to be involved in partnerships between government of all levels, the business community and schools; to build links with schools, business and community groups; and to strengthen the links between sporting clubs, schools and the community (Commonwealth of Australia, 2001). Government interest in social cohesion and community building through sport is not isolated to this policy document. Almost all significant Australian sport policies have been preceded by a review of the sport system and a set of policy recommendations. The BASA policy was no different and was preceded by *Shaping Up*, a review of government involvement in sport and recreation that provided a set of recommendations for the Australian sport system following the Sydney 2000 Olympic Games. In the section that examined the contribution of sport and recreation to Australia, the report noted that 'the Commonwealth Government funds sport because it is an investment in the community' (Commonwealth of Australia, 1999: 53). Furthermore, the report noted that:

Sport fosters the social cohesiveness and unity that reinforces our sense of being an Australian. The contribution that sport makes to the Australian national image cannot be quantified, but it can be felt. The same is true for other benefits that accrue to individuals and the community through broader participation in sport.

(Commonwealth of Australia, 1999: 55)

Shaping Up argued that elite sport contributed to social cohesion, self-esteem and well-being through the development of national pride as a result of Australians watching elite Australian athletes and teams enjoy international sporting success. In other words, as Australian men and women perform well on the international sporting stage, all Australians receive a benefit through feeling better about themselves and their country. This notion of the creation of national pride through sporting achievements has been used by many countries to justify government funding of elite sport. The report also identified that social cohesion was produced at the community level, while sport was able to address social inequalities and contribute to personal development, which in turn would lead to positive social outcomes, such as crime reduction. The report made the claim that:

Sport is an inclusive social phenomenon and provides opportunities for specific groups to feel a part of the community. In a multicultural society such as Australia, sport is an important mechanism for bringing diverse groups closer together.

(Commonwealth of Australia, 1999: 55)

Shaping Up concluded that 'social and community benefits can be gained from progressive policies that utilise sport and physical activity and that this justifies Commonwealth Government involvement in providing opportunities for people to engage in physical activity' (Commonwealth of Australia, 1999: 56).

The central tenets of the BASA policy were reinforced by the Howard Government's 2004 election policy statement on sport *Building Australian Communities Through Sport* (BACTS), that, as its title suggests, made an explicit connection between sport and community. The BACTS policy continued the claim that 'sport plays a vital role in building and sustaining local communities, particularly in rural and remote areas' (Liberal Party of Australia, 2004: 4). It also repeated the claims that by supporting elite athlete success Australian sport policy helps to 'unite Australian communities' (Liberal Party of Australia, 2004: 8).

More recently, in announcing a funding boost for Australian sport for the four-year period beginning in 2006, the Minister for the Arts and Sport, Senator Rod Kemp, claimed that the increase was important because 'sport is an integral part of Australian life, and the Australian Government provides funding for sport as an investment in the community in terms of national pride, improved health, economic activity and stronger communities' (Kemp, 2006a). Furthermore, in a 2006 speech to a sport policy summit in the Netherlands, Senator Kemp reconfirmed the government view that sport acts as a 'social glue' within Australian urban and rural communities. Specifically, he noted that:

Sport is not simply about being the best or beating other countries or gaining the most medals. From events like the Olympic Games to local matches on a Saturday afternoon, sport brings people together. It is a key part of creating safe, strong and sustainable communities.

Indeed, in some of Australia's regional and remote communities, the local tennis, football or basketball club that provides and susta.. community interaction.

(Kemp, 2006b)

The lead agency charged with implementing much of BASA and its successor BACTS, the Australian Sports Commission (ASC), is even more explicit in its belief of the place of sport in building communities, stating that 'sport provides a strong and continuous thread through Australia's diverse and widespread population (and) it is a binding element in our social and cultural fabric' (ASC, 2005: 2).

BASA marked a distinct shift in policy for the Australian Government (Stewart et al., 2004). Sport policy and related programmes from the 1990s that were designed to provide opportunities for participation in physical activity were replaced by an emphasis on participation in organized sport through the community club-based sport system. BASA emphasized the role of Australia's 26000 community sport clubs as the primary vehicles for increasing the talent pool from which elite athletes are drawn, as well as pivotal sites for community activity. The policy emphasized the role that sport plays in the development of social capital outcomes, specifically social cohesion and social connectedness rather than acknowledging that sport organizations might well require social capital stocks to facilitate their activities and thus contribute to the achievement of government policy objectives.

Canada

Government interest in the role played by sport in social development is not limited to the Australian context. As early as 1987 the Canadian federal government articulated a connection between involvement in sport and recreation activities and the creation of positive social or community benefits in the *National Recreation Statement* (Interprovincial Sport and Recreation Council, 1987: 2):

Recreation [including organised competitive sport] has an almost unlimited potential to develop life skills, to enhance communities and to promote and maintain healthy, independent lifestyles which contribute significantly to the quality of life in Canada.

These sentiments were reiterated 14 years later in a discussion paper on developing Canadian sport policy (Government of Canada, 2001). The discussion paper laid the foundations for contemporary Canadian sport policy and argued that 'sport occupies a special place in Canada's heritage and history, and contributes greatly to the health, well-being and identity of individuals, communities and the nation as a whole' (Government of Canada, 2001: 2). The role of sport in developing social capital was also highlighted:

> Sport is considered an essential tool for nation building and can lead to the promotion of national identity, and enhancing our sense of community and citizenship. Through sport, individuals learn to volunteer and to accept a sense of responsibility for civil society. … Organizing sport clubs and events is one of the great training grounds for social action in Canada. Learning to organize meetings, negotiate for use of shared facilities, and deal with expectations, triumphs and failures all build social capital.
>
> (Government of Canada, 2001: 5–6)

The role of a national sport policy in assisting Canada achieve a more inclusive society and the creation of social capital related outcomes was a focus of the proposals outlined in the concluding passages of the discussion paper. It specifically noted that participation and excellence in sport contributes to breaking down barriers to participation, developing a more inclusive society and that it fosters a shared sense of citizenship. Creating a national sport policy would also 'contribute to social cohesion … [and] … the social integration of marginalised and at risk groups' (Government of Canada, 2001: 20). Finally, the importance placed on the capacity of sport to deliver social capital outcomes was highlighted in a vision for Canadian sport that 'Canadian's shared sense of citizenship and quality of life will be strengthened through an increased participation in sport' (Government of Canada, 2001: 20).

In 2002, after a lengthy period of consultation, the Canadian Government produced the *Canadian Sport Policy* that drew heavily from the 2001 discussion paper. The idea that sport could contribute to building social capital was far from lost:

> Sport is an essential tool for building strong individuals and vibrant communities and for enhancing our collective pride and identity and sense of belonging. Through sport in their respective communities, Canadians learn to volunteer and to accept a sense of responsibility for a civil society. … Establishing sport clubs and organizing events are great training grounds for social action. Social capital is built by learning to organize meetings, negotiate for use of shared facilities, and deal with expectations, triumphs and failures.
>
> (Government of Canada, 2002: 5–6)

The assumption that participation in sport creates social capital, as illustrated by the similarity in the preceding passages from the discussion paper and the actual Canadian sport policy, would appear to be widely accepted by the sport policy community in Canada. This acceptance is also evident in the latest strategic plan of Sport Canada, the lead government agency responsible for implementing the majority of Canada's sport policy in conjunction with the National Sport Organizations (NSOs). The plan states that 'The Government of Canada's investment in sport is grounded in strong logic: Sport, as a tool for social development, has the ability to engage citizens and communities, surmount social barriers and contribute to building a healthier, more cohesive society' (Sport Canada, 2004: 3).

This acceptance also extends to the wider social policy community within Canada. In a publication from the Public Policy Forum and the Sport Matters Group, involvement in sport and physical activity was considered to be the pre-eminent example of 'citizen and community participation' (Bowen, 2004: 13). Citing the propensity of Canadians to volunteer in sport organisations over other forms of voluntary service, Bowen (2004: 13) argued that 'participation in sport organizations is a remarkable incubator for engagement, governance and democracy'. The link between sport and social capital was highlighted even further in a report published by the Conference Board of Canada in 2005 that stated:

Typically, community-based sport programs support civic engagement and social cohesion, thus building social capital, by: providing opportunities for volunteerism; reinforcing relationships between children and parents, within families, within neighbourhoods and across communities; establishing partnerships between community-based sport organizations and similar organizations in their area (such as local community service centres, school boards and schools); and strengthening relationships between various levels of government, out of which new programs that build civic engagement and social cohesion can develop.

(Bloom et al., 2005: 30)

In summary, the conviction that sport is able to create social capital appears to be even more prominent amongst Canadian policymakers and in Canadian sport policy than that of Australia. The Canadian sport policy places a similar emphasis on the role that sport plays in the development of social capital outcomes, specifically social cohesion and social connectedness, but also uses sports' assumed ability to create social capital as a justification for government investment in sport. The Canadian sport policy, much like its Australian counterpart, also considers sport to be a producer rather than a consumer of social capital, failing to acknowledge that sport organizations require social capital stocks to facilitate their activities and thus contribute to the achievement of government policy objectives.

England

The nation that has arguably attracted the most attention from sport policy researchers, England, has followed a similar path to Australia and Canada in its treatment of social capital within its sport policy. The number of national policy documents, strategy statements and frameworks produced in the last decade related to sport in England is quite staggering compared to other Commonwealth nations. This is due (in part) to the way sport is structured. The UK Government Department of Culture Media and Sport (DCMS) is the main policy agency for sport across the UK that works in conjunction with Sport England, an independent government funded organization that has undergone a number of major adjustments to its various roles as sport development agency, funding agency and strategic policy developer. The reliance of Sport England on DCMS funding means that it effectively acts as the agent for implementing government sport policy.

England's contemporary sport policy has its foundations in the 1997 publication *England the Sporting Nation* (English Sports Council, 1997) that identified a modest set of targets to improve the numbers of people playing sport and the achievements of elite athletes, but did not consider social capital in any meaningful way. This was followed by the *Government's Sport Strategy* where the instrumental value of sport being used for social development was identified through statements such as 'sport is one of the best ways of breaking down barriers in our society and we must use it to its full potential' (DCMS, 2000: 14) and 'sport can make a unique contribution to tackling social exclusion in our society' (DCMS, 2000: 39). The vision outlined in the *Government's Sport Strategy* was transformed into a detailed strategy through consultation with English sport's stakeholders and published as the *Government's Plan for Sport* (DCMS, 2001).

It was at this stage that tackling social inclusion became a prominent part of the overall agenda of the UK Government and sport had been identified as a key component of the policy mix that could tackle social inclusion problems. A new sport policy document *Game Plan* was produced by the DCMS and the UK Government's Strategy Unit (Cabinet Office, 2002). The rhetoric that sport can build stronger communities was maintained in this new policy: 'using sport to promote social inclusion can also help to build social capital through developing personal skills and enlarging individuals' social networks' (Cabinet Office, 2002: 60). There was also, however, an acknowledgement that perhaps the evidence base for such claims needed to be improved and that specifically, there was a 'lack of systematic and comprehensive evidence to demonstrate these linkages [between sport and social capital development] and help policymakers understand exactly how they work' (Cabinet Office, 2002: 7). Nevertheless two of the 14 goals for sport set out by DCMS in funding agreements between DCMS and Sport England were to 'use sport to improve the lives of the socially excluded' and to 'use sport-based activity/development as a means of regeneration' (Cabinet Office, 2002: 220). The *Game Plan* document also repeated the claims that governments should invest in sport in order to assist sport deliver 'greater social inclusion' (Cabinet Office, 2002: 42).

Two years after the publication of *Game Plan*, Sport England produced *The Framework for Sport in England* that outlined a vision for sport until 2020 that would see England as the most active and successful sporting nation in the world (Sport England, 2004). One of the key outcomes sought from the sport policy was the creation of stronger and safer communities through people's involvement in sport.

Emerging evidence is beginning to highlight the impact of sport in relation to creating stronger communities and addressing issues of community safety, including reductions in anti-social behaviour, reductions in the propensity to commit crime, and reductions in the 'fear' of crime amongst the wider community.

(Sport England, 2004: 30)

This focus on the use of sport for the achievement of wider social outcomes was highlighted a year later in a joint report produced by Sport England, DCMS and the Local Government Association, titled *Sport Playing Its Part* (Sport England, 2005). The CEO of Sport England highlighted the way in which sport and social policy had become linked in the introduction to the report:

We firmly believe that sporting outcomes and social policy outcomes however work hand in hand – involving more people in sport contributes to the achievement of a healthier, fitter nation, stronger communities which come together through sport and help young people develop, achieve and make a positive contribution through sport.

(Sport England, 2005: 2)

The report also neatly encapsulated the way in which sport is viewed by sport policymakers and the wider social policy community in relation to its potential to develop social capital:

Sport contributes to strengthening community cohesion, engagement and capacity building – sporting activities and events contribute to the development of stronger social networks and more cohesive communities. They provide opportunities for social engagement, often with alternative peer groups, which can create awareness of difference and break down barriers for individuals and communities. Sport can be used as an engagement mechanism to build relationships with hard to reach individuals or groups and can open up alternative channels that enable local people, in particular those who are alienated from mainstream services, to obtain advice and information on a wide range of health, social, education and employment issues.

(Sport England, 2005: 8)

In summary, the England sport policy as represented in the various documents of the DCMS and Sport England reviewed in this chapter, demonstrates a similar conviction to the idea that sport is able to create social capital that is found in the Canadian and Australian sport policies. It places a similar emphasis on the role that sport plays in the development of social capital outcomes, specifically social cohesion and social connectedness and also consistently uses sports' assumed ability to create social capital as a justification for government investment in sport. In a similar fashion to the Canadian and Australian sport policies, the policies of Sport England and DCMS conceptualize sport to be a producer rather than a consumer of social capital, failing to acknowledge that sport organizations require social capital stocks to facilitate their activities and thus contribute to the achievement of sport and wider social policy objectives.

New Zealand

The central tenets of contemporary New Zealand sport policy were developed from the recommendation of a Ministerial review of sport and recreation in 2001 known as the *Graham Report*. Social cohesion was identified as one of four public goods that result from involvement in sport and physical activity, the others being a healthier society, an enhanced sense of identity and image, and crime prevention. The report presented a comprehensive argument for increased funding for the sport and recreation sector in New Zealand that would 'play a critical role in a prosperous New Zealand – in health, physical well-being, social cohesion, self-esteem and national pride' (Ministerial Taskforce, 2001: 4). The belief that sport has the capacity to deliver social capital outcomes is, like the reviews that led to the development of the Australian, Canadian and England sport policies, repeated throughout the report. Examples of these statements include 'sport fosters intangible benefits, particularly social cohesion at the family and community level' (Ministerial Taskforce, 2001: 9) and 'recreation and sport plays a socially cohesive role at the family level' (Ministerial Taskforce, 2001: 41). This belief is also evident in the key principles developed by the report for the development of sport and recreation in New Zealand in the first quarter of the twenty-first century, including 'recreation and sport are essential to improving personal health, total well-being and self-esteem and fostering community and social interaction' (Ministerial Taskforce, 2001: 64), and 'recreation and sport provides a means of bridging social differences between people from widely varied backgrounds, personal orientations and cultures' (Ministerial Taskforce, 2001: 65).

The *Graham Report* resulted in the creation of Sport and Recreation New Zealand (SPARC), a new federal government agency responsible for developing and implementing sport and recreation policy. SPARC took over the responsibilities of the former Hillary Commission and the New Zealand Sports Foundation, as well as some elements of the Office of Tourism and Sport. A quote from the strategic plan of SPARC for 2003 is illustrative of how the principles relating to sport and social capital outcomes espoused in the *Graham Report* were transferred to the operations of SPARC:

Sport and recreation clubs are at the core of New Zealand communities, drawing individuals together, providing facilities and access to community services. Approximately one-third of all New Zealanders participate in organised sporting activities. This activity fosters cooperation and helps strengthen social ties and networks within communities.
(SPARC, 2003: 4)

In 2006, this belief in the role sport participation can play in developing social capital was undiminished: 'sport and recreation organisations around New Zealand are part of our social fabric' (SPARC, 2006: 2). Indeed, investment by SPARC to support high-performance sport was also justified on the basis that it 'helps create a strong sense of national identity, pride and social cohesion' (SPARC, 2006: 9). One of the wider government outcomes sought through the actions of SPARC is greater social cohesion: 'organised sport and physical recreation activities play an important role in furthering personal and social development for individuals and communities. They foster cooperation between individuals and help strengthen social ties and networks within communities' (SPARC, 2006: 14).

While not espoused in a specific sport policy document or statement, the intentions of government support of sport via SPARC includes a clear focus on creating social capital related outcomes. The strategies of SPARC demonstrate that New Zealand sport policy supports the notion that sport is able to create social capital in much the same way as the Australian, Canadian and English policies. It emphasizes the role that sport plays in the development of social capital outcomes, specifically social cohesion and social connectedness and not surprisingly, uses sports' assumed ability to create social capital as a justification for government investment in sport. Again, the sport policy conceptualizes sport to be a producer rather than a consumer of social capital.

Conceptualizing social capital

Some common themes are evident in the way social capital has been represented within the sport policies of Australia, Canada, England and New Zealand. It is clear that the policymakers for each nation implicitly believe that the concept of social capital captures something tangible in the community and that it is an accepted term in the halls of government. The inclusion of social capital in these sport policies reflects an acceptance by policymakers that social capital has some legitimacy and that it is relevant to sport. This legitimacy is arguably tied to the traditional way in which participation in sport is perceived to be character building, a focal point for learning life's lessons, and as a generally positive experience for individuals. The untested logic of the inclusion of social capital within these sport policies is that through being involved in community-based sport, an individual will be able to experience positive social benefits of belonging to a group, making friends and feeling part of a community. Sport clubs and organizations are viewed as overwhelmingly constructive spaces that generate social connections, social cohesion and social integration of increasingly multicultural communities. The policies fail to acknowledge that some sport organizations can be discriminatory, exclusive or unwilling to engage with all members of a community. In this context it appears that these sport policies have interpreted sport as being able to deliver bridging social capital outcomes that are always positive without considering the potentially negative social capital outcomes from involvement in voluntary groups and associations.

There is also a lack of conceptual clarity about the sources and benefits of social capital. In the Australian, Canadian and New Zealand sport policies there are clear links made between elite sport success and the creation of social capital. It is not clear, however, whether the source of social capital is the elite success of athletes at events such as the Olympic Games or World Championships, or it is the national identity and pride that results from such success. The policies make various claims that elite success is important in nation building, national identity, national pride, a shared sense of citizenship and for portraying a nation's image. It is unclear if the funding of elite sport programmes is justified on the basis that national pride leads to social cohesion or that the social cohesion leads to other social capital benefits, or, indeed, that national pride and social cohesion develop independently. If we accept, as discussed in Chapter 1, the common core of social capital theory is that social networks have value, it is difficult to understand how governments might conceive of a causal relationship between elite sport success and social capital, particularly as the policies do not mention that government should fund elite sport because people come together to watch, and in doing so build and extend their social networks. As a result the links are tenuous, but this perhaps has as much to do with the political expediency of legitimizing and justifying spending on elite sport and the imbalance between spending on elite and community (local or grass roots) sport, as it does with a lack of conceptual clarity. The conceptual confusion about the sources and benefits of social capital is exacerbated when the policies refer to community or local level sport. In these instances, of which there are many, the sport organization or club is often the source of social capital, as well as the vehicle for its use, and at various times a tool for broader social development, participation and action.

The sport policies examined in this chapter also consider social capital as something that is created through involvement in sport, or in other words, that the social interactions created through being involved in sport will lead to higher levels of trust within communities. This rather simplistic representation of social capital fails to acknowledge that the very existence of community- or club-based sport is almost entirely dependent on the maintenance of social capital stocks (i.e. social interactions) by communities that facilitate social capital outcomes, such as trust and increased social cohesion, that are the focus of these sport policies. Thus the sport policies portray sport organizations as producers of social capital rather than as consumers. The irony is that the policies provide no focus on how government sport agencies can go about supporting sport clubs and other voluntary associations produce these social capital outcomes – they are simply assumed to be automatically created.

The notion that sharing equates to the existence of social capital is common among the policies and review documents examined within this chapter. Identity is linked to social cohesion, as if two or more people sharing the same experience or feelings is akin to these people engaging in a social network. The assumption appears to be that a shared understanding of the nation's identity, or a shared experience of its strengthening through successful sporting competition with other nations, is sufficient to generate increased social cohesion and improved social outcomes. This notion of shared experience is also evident in the conceptualization of community sport organizations and clubs. The mere act of sharing in the sport experience (ill defined in itself) is sufficient to generate positive outcomes, such as greater social cohesion or community strength.

The issue of who receives a benefit from the generation or maintenance of social capital is also unclear throughout the sport policies examined within this chapter. Importantly, there appears to be little or no distinction made between social capital that might exist between individuals, families, clubs, organizations and groups, communities and nations. These categories either blend into one, in which case the term community is favoured, or the benefits of social capital are assumed to be easily transferable between the categories. For example, the policies assume that the benefits that accrue to an individual through the extension of their social networks are somehow captured by a stronger community. In essence the assumption within these policy documents is stronger social networks, at whatever level, are of benefit to all, which ignores the notion that some individuals or groups might be enjoying a greater share of resources as a result of their social network at the expense of others. Rather than make what is admittedly a difficult attempt at achieving some degree of clarity in terms of how social capital is created and used by individuals, families, groups, communities and nations, the policies allow these elements to coalesce into an amorphous whole.

The simplistic conceptualization of sport participation delivering social capital outcomes such as increased trust means that the policies do not consider how sport is related to other types of social capital such as bonding or linking social capital. Sport organizations are obvious sites for developing and utilizing bonding social capital, especially in team-based competitive sports, yet this is not a specific focus of the policies. The potential for sport organizations to facilitate links between individuals of different socio-economic backgrounds and between communities is also not an explicit focus of these sport policies. The policies are very clear in claiming that sport strengthens communities, enhances people's sense of community, makes communities more cohesive and encourages, improves and builds people's pride, identity and belonging. The policies, at the very least, appear to be implying that sport clubs or organizations are good at creating, developing and maintaining bonding social capital, in which the norms, networks and trust developed contribute to cooperation within the club or organization, as well as cooperation within the broader community. Participation in sport clubs and organizations in these terms is equivalent to community participation, particularly in regional, rural or remote communities.

Somewhat unexpectedly, the sport policies articulate bridging social capital even more clearly, and in this the political expediency of the link between sport and social capital is perhaps most evident. All four national sport policies refer to the ability of sport to bring diverse groups together, bridge social differences, break down barriers, promote social inclusion and reduce social exclusion, although it is clear that each country has a particular emphasis. The English sport policy in particular is focussed on using sport to minimize social exclusion and refers specifically to developing and growing the social networks of individuals and the ability of sport to access and then engage people experiencing social disadvantage. In general these policies ignore the possibility, as we noted in Chapter 1, that the composition of sport organizations and sport teams is just as, if not more likely than other community organizations to facilitate insular behaviour, values and norms that might engender strong bonding social capital, but limit bridging social capital. In all four national sport policies, but perhaps more so in the Australian, Canadian and New Zealand cases the notion that sport has the capacity to engender bridging social capital appears to be merely wishful thinking than a realistic goal supported by evidence, strategies and actions.

There is also agreement within the four national sport policies that social capital is not only created within sport organisations and clubs, but also through sport organizations and clubs. The Canadian sport policy documents are the most explicit in this sense, noting that through sport people learn to take responsibility for civil society. This is most often connected to people volunteering their time and resources within sport clubs to contribute to a broader good (although it is often unclear whether 'broader' refers to family, group or community). In this respect sport organizations are considered obvious vehicles for the creation of social capital. It is unclear, however, whether sport organizations and clubs have the capacity to become training grounds for social action, and whether the skills necessary for organizing, running and participating in sport events are directly transferable to other aspects or sectors of society. The notion that sport could be an incubator for social engagement, governance and democracy is perhaps the most attractive and least intuitive of the links between sport and social capital contained within the policy documents. This is particularly so when we consider that sport has often been regarded as an opiate of the masses, an institution that serves to quell rather than ignite social or political action. It is reasonable to suggest that the social networks gained, if not the skills learned, within sport organizations and clubs will have benefit beyond their boundaries, but without sufficient evidence the claim that participation within sport organizations will flow on to other forms of civic participation or political and democratic engagement seems without merit.

Rationales for social capital in sport policy

There are a number of reasons why governments might seek to make overt connections between sport and social capital. First, governments have a vested interest in using a conceptual framework that supports their arguments for funding elite sport more than the simple notion that it 'makes people feel good'. A number of governments use sport as a vehicle for national and international prestige and recognition, of which the four examined within this chapter are no exception. In order to counter claims of elitism and justify the funding imbalance governments have developed a range of rationales over time. For example, in Australia the funding bias to elite sport was (and still is) justified on the basis that gold medallists and world champions provide young people with role models to emulate and that elite sport success encourages not only more active organized sport participation but also more informal unstructured physical activity as a mass of people become inspired by the feats of a few (Stewart et al., 2004). It now appears as if the concept of social cohesion is favoured as one of the primary justifications for increased elite funding. Although it might be a cynical conclusion to draw, using social cohesion as part of an argument for funding elite sport has the advantage that although it seems intuitively possible, it is very difficult to measure and therefore critique.

Second, the social capital concept is also used to justify and legitimize funding to community or local sporting organizations and clubs. The governments examined as part of this chapter all realize that more participants at the community level means more winners at the elite level. The need to generate a greater pool from which to select talented athletes is becoming more important as countries such as China and India begin to capitalize on their significant human resources. At the same time, much research demonstrates that the broad trend is towards informal unstructured physical activity and away from structured organized sport in the club setting (Stewart et al., 2004). In this respect notions of social cohesion and community strengthening are used as a palatable political rationale to complement the more instrumental reasons for funding community level sport, which include enhancing the talent pool and supporting structured sporting activities that are more easily measured than participation in unstructured informal physical activity.

Third, as a significant component of the non-profit sector, with a broad reach across most countries and many communities, with high levels of public awareness achieved through the media, sport is in many respects an obvious choice for government policy in the area of social capital. More than most, sport organizations are well suited to the notion of the appropriable organization in that many participants are involved for fairly instrumental reasons, such as fun and fitness, but are likely to gain additional benefits through their participation, even if their exact nature and extent are not readily apparent. Perhaps government has rightly identified that as a result, sport organizations might be well positioned to attract people, such as those experiencing social disadvantage, for fairly instrumental reasons, who might then be able to build or enhance their social networks, which might in turn improve their well-being. This is clearly one of the key tenets that underpin the connection of sport and social capital in public policy – sport has the organizational and social infrastructure to contribute effectively and efficiently to achieving government policy goals. Furthermore, it appears that government is attracted to the notion that sport is a universal language and is able to act as an agent in assimilating or enfranchising people from diverse racial and ethnic backgrounds, despite the fact that sport has arguably as much potential to create divisions between communities.

Fourth, the sport policy documents identify that in absolute and relative terms sport volunteering is significant. As volunteering is often viewed as a central component of a civil society and organizations and communities with high social capital stocks, making the link between sport and social capital is natural, if not reasonable, for government. A high proportion of volunteers relative to other organizations and a high proportion of total volunteers indicate to governments that sport organizations have a significant capacity to facilitate collaboration and cooperation, as part of their regular activities, rather than the result of a newly created programme or 'bolt-on' activity. The assumed connection between sport, volunteerism and social outcomes is a distinct policy advantage for government, because rather than create new policies and programmes to ameliorate social disadvantage or increase social connectedness, the number of people involved in sport can be increased to gain the same outcome. This rationale for the connection between sport and social capital ignores the decline in sport volunteering over time, as well as the fact that many of these sporting clubs are member benefit organizations, in which volunteer motives are not exclusively altruistic.

Finally, and perhaps most importantly, it appears that the connection between sport and social capital in public policy is part of a broader attempt to build stronger and safer communities, with enhanced capacity and greater self-reliance. If sport organizations and clubs that facilitate sport participation can begin to ameliorate social disadvantage then it is likely that the social and financial burden on government will be reduced. In other words, the motivation of governments to include references to maintaining strong and sustainable communities in sport policy through the work of sport organizations is not entirely altruistic, but can be interpreted as part of a broader neo-liberal process in which responsibility for such tasks is increasingly transferred from government to the non-profit sector, communities, families and individuals. If people experiencing social disadvantage begin to build and enhance their social networks through sporting organizations, then it stands to reason, as far as government is concerned, that communities will be not only be more cohesive, but less people are likely to be on welfare and the communities are likely to be safer. Clearly there are social, political and financial benefits, yet it is often difficult to determine the priority. If, as discussed previously, sport is able to act as an incubator for additional and wider social action then the ripple effects of the social networks created for and through sport are likely to have broader ramifications and benefits. In this scenario sport might not only be responsible for a reduction in crime or anti-social behaviour among young people, but might be responsible for organizations outside of sport operating more inclusively and effectively. If it is possible that sport can engage individuals and communities in this way, then it is with good reason that government should link sport and social capital.

Conclusions

The most obvious shortcomings of these sport policies in relation to their references to social capital outcomes are the absence of any meaningful social capital targets, measurement strategies or evaluative criteria with which to judge the achievement of these outcomes. This is understandable given the well documented difficulties in defining and measuring social capital as noted in the English sport policy (Cabinet Office, 2002). The sport policies all identify social capital outcomes that sport generates: increased social cohesion at national and local levels, greater social connectedness, a heightened sense of citizenship, increased community well-being, overcoming social barriers, and strengthening social ties and networks. While all of the sport policies assume these are generated by individuals, groups and communities being involved in sport, none of them identify what they will do to assist sport organizations achieve these outcomes. They simply assume that sport organizations are generating social capital outcomes, that they are effective at generating these outcomes, that the outcomes are positive for all participants and that more people involved in sport will lead to greater levels of social capital.

It would be reasonable to surmise that social capital outcomes have not been explicitly identified by policymakers and that the reasons for this are two-fold. Firstly, it is very difficult to measure social capital and to establish a cause and effect relationship between the actions of individuals, groups and communities involved in sport and increased social capital stocks for specific communities. Secondly, social capital appears to have been used to assist in the justification of overall sport funding and support, rather than as a discrete policy goal to be achieved through sport. In this sense, social capital is not the prime concern of sport policymakers who are still enamoured with policies and programmes that deliver measurable elite sport performance outcomes, control the use of performance enhancing drugs in sport, facilitate the hosting of sport events for economic development and lead to more people engaging in sport and physical activity to combat increasing rates of obesity and other health issues among the population.

There are more commonalities than differences between these sport policies in their treatment of social capital. The supposed benefits for increased social cohesion and connectedness that can be delivered by sport are apparent in each policy. They all consider social capital to be created through sport rather than be used by sport, that the social capital is always positive and that sport's capacity is primarily in the delivery of bridging social capital at the expense of other forms of social capital. They are also remarkably consistent in their use of social capital to assist in justifying expenditure on elite sport programmes. This suggests a high degree of policy convergence, at least in terms of the conceptualization of social capital and its relationship to sport. This convergence can be explained by the similar processes each country used to develop their sport policies. Each used a formal policy review process that outlined similar social benefits that arise from involvement in sport (c.f. Commonwealth of Australia, 1999; DCMS, 2000; Government of Canada, 2001; Ministerial Taskforce, 2001). These reviews were also conducted during a similar timeframe, namely 1999 to 2001, that focussed on explaining the benefits to their respective nations for having a national sport policy.

Although a reasonably small sample, the sport policies of the countries investigated as part of this analysis reveal that the connection between sport and social capital is far more ideological and theoretical than other aspects of sport policy. On the one hand this is to be expected given that social capital is largely a theoretical concept that has only recently enjoyed a high level of political acceptance and currency. In this respect it might be overly optimistic to suggest or demand these sport policies conceptualize social capital in a more practical and realistic way when many authors and researchers have failed. On the other hand, the vaguely theoretical approach is in direct contrast to the more instrumental approach to other aspects of sport policy within these countries. Most notably, the elite sport and anti-drug policies of these countries are based far more in evidence, although admittedly they too have aspects of ideological development and implementation. In simple terms, however, the notion that more funding will mean better coaching, better talent identification, better facilities, better sport science and better equipment, and that these will lead to better international results is in stark contrast to the uncertainty of how and what can be achieved within the realm of social capital.

The absence of concrete measures to assess the outcomes achieved from connecting sport and social capital, the variety of rationales that might be used to explain the connection and the fluid conceptualization of social capital makes it difficult to determine the utility of including social capital within national sport policies. This analysis has demonstrated that governments are well placed to capitalize on sport's natural cultural, organizational and social advantages in developing social capital benefits, but it is unclear whether this is merely for political expediency. At worst, the connection between sport and social capital allows governments to justify funding decisions, abrogate (some of) its responsibility to directly address social disadvantage and convince people that sport organizations and clubs are inclusive environments on the basis of unproven assumptions and limited evidence. At best, the connection between sport and social capital is an acknowledgement that sport organizations and clubs are places where people build and enhance their social networks, that these social networks have value and that they might be used for a range of social purposes. In order to make the best scenario more than an acknowledgement, governments must at very least admit they are unsure about the connections between sport and social capital, that the social capital created within and through sport organizations is not necessarily positive and that the social capital created within and through sport organizations is of value in itself, rather than as a mechanism of justification for other policies and political agendas.

While the conceptualization of social capital may be relatively narrow within these sport policies, it should be noted that social capital has at least come to the attention of sport policymakers. Participation in sport and involvement in facilitating the involvement of others by administering, coaching, officiating or otherwise volunteering time and energy to assist in the operation of community-based sport are at the core of the relationship between sport and social capital. The next step for the sport policy community is to find ways to support the efforts of individuals and groups in both creating and developing social capital. In other words, sport policies should move to encompass a greater understanding of how social capital is both produced and consumed by sport clubs and associations, as well as the way in which government can support the creation of better social interactions in the context of sport participation and have a greater impact on social capital outcomes, such as increased perceptions of trust and safety in communities.

References

Australian Sports Commission (2005). *Enriching the Lives of All Australians Through Sport*. Canberra, Australia: Australian Sports Commission.

Bloom, M., Grant, M. & Watt, D. (2005). *Strengthening Canada: The Socio-economic Benefits of Sport Participation in Canada*. Ottawa, Canada: Conference Board of Canada.

Bergsgard, N.A., Houlihan, B., Mangset, P., Nodland, S.I. & Rommetvedt, H. (2007). *Sport Policy: A Comparative Analysis of Stability and Change*. Oxford: Butterworth-Heinemann.

Bowen, P. (2004). *Investing in Canada: Fostering an agenda for citizen and community participation*, Ottawa, Canada: Public Policy Forum. Available at www.ppforum.ca/common/assets/publications/en/bowen_layout_e.pdf

Cabinet Office. (2002). Game Plan: A Strategy for Delivering the Governments Sport and Physical Activity Objectives. London: Author.

Commonwealth of Australia (1999). *Shaping Up: A Review of Commonwealth Involvement in Sport and Recreation in Australia*. Canberra, Australia: Commonwealth of Australia.

Commonwealth of Australia (2001). *Backing Australia's Sporting Ability*. Canberra, Australia: Commonwealth of Australia.

Department of Culture, Media and Sport. (2000). *A Sporting Future for All*. London: Author.

Department of Culture, Media and Sport. (2001). *Governments Plan for Sport*. London: Author.

English Sports Council. (1997). *England the Sporting Nation: A Strategy*. London: Author.

Government of Canada. (2001). *Building Canada Through Sport: Towards a Canadian Sport Policy*. Quebec, Canada: Author.

Government of Canada. (2002). *Canadian Sport Policy*. Quebec, Canada: Author.

Green, M. & Houlihan, B. (2005). *Elite Sport Development: Policy Learning and Political Priorities*. London: Routledge.

Interprovincial Sport and Recreation Council. (1987). *National Recreation Statement*. Quebec, Canada: Author.

Kemp, R. (2006a). Funding Boost for Australian Sport: Media Release, Canberra, Australia: Author. Available at www.minister.dcita.gov.au/kemp/media/media_releases/funding_boost_for_australian_sport.

Kemp, R. (2006b). 2006 Sport Policy Summit, Canberra, Australia: Author. Available at www.minister.dcita.gov.au/kemp/media/speeches/2006_sport_policy_summit.

Liberal Party of Australia (2004). Building Australian Communities Through Sport, Canberra, Australia: Liberal Party of Australia.

Ministerial Taskforce. (2001). Getting set for an Active Nation: Report of the Sport, Fitness and Leisure Ministerial Taskforce. Wellington: The Taskforce.

Sport and Recreation New Zealand (SPARC). (2003). Statement of Intent 2003–2004. Wellington, New Zealand: SPARC.

Sport and Recreation New Zealand (SPARC). (2006). Statement of Intent 2006–2009. Wellington, New Zealand: SPARC.

Sport Canada (2004). Strategic Plan 2004–2008. Quebec, Canada: Author.

Sport England (2004). *National Framework for Sport: Making England an Active and Successful Sporting Nation – A Vision for 2020*. London: Sport England.

Sport England (2005). Sport Playing Its Part: The Contribution of Sport to Community Priorities and the Improvement Agenda. London: Sport England.

Stewart, B., Nicholson, M., Smith, A. & Westerbeek, H. (2004). *Australian Sport: Better By Design? The Evolution of Australian Sport Policy*. London: Routledge.

CHAPTER 5

Narrowing the gap through sport, education and social capital?

Grant Jarvie

Introduction

In addressing the promise and possibilities of sport, education and social capital this chapter begins by making a number of introductory remarks. First the notion that a relationship between sport and education may contribute to impacting upon people's life chances may be unfamiliar to some. At the heart of this approach is the simple recognition that individuals, groups and even nations located or born into different circumstances face different chances of enjoying desirable outcomes and differential life chances. In the UK one in five children is growing up in poverty and young people from different backgrounds continue to have unequal chances of enjoying good health, living in a secure environment or doing well at school. More than 11 million live in poverty. One of the most intransigent aspects of twenty-first century welfare reforms in Britain is that the poorest 15 per cent cannot afford to put cash aside to save for retirement – because they lack capital either in terms of savings or real estate (Rutherford & Shah, 2006: 11). Africa, the world's second largest continent, at the beginning of the twenty-first century contained 18 of the top 20 countries worldwide with the highest infant mortality rate. Sixteen African countries are in the top 20 poorest in the world, with 70 per cent of Africa's population surviving on less than $2 a day (Jarvie, 2007: 24). The first point then is that a gap exists both within countries and between countries in terms of life chances. The reasons for this gap are complex, differentiated, relational and in many cases unjust. Despite almost a decade of progressive policies in the UK the gap in life chances between disadvantaged children and their peers has failed to narrow significantly since 1997 (Fabian Society, 2006: xiv).

Second, with specific reference to the theme of this book both sport and education have historically been aligned with notions of social mobility, social capital and to some extent social transformation. The common denominator in all of these terms being the word *social*. The term is generally invoked to suggest a commitment to the broader welfare of society rather than the narrow interest of particular elites. Recently, radical versions of the notion of social forums and social empowerment for not only groups, or areas but also different parts of the world have been at the heart of a number of actions calling for a fairer more just world in which the gap between rich and poor is narrowed significantly. It is easy perhaps to be pessimistic about the future and it is important not to overestimate the power of education through sport but it is also vital not to ignore the potential capacity and possibility of the combined impact of sport and education to be a resource of hope for many people(s). It is also critical not to ignore the 'social' in either sport, education or 'social' capital.

The third introductory point builds upon the second one and that it is to highlight the potential for education through sport to be a catalyst for social change. It is self-evident that attempts to narrow the gap through sport, education and building any sustainable social capital must not only attempt to analyse or explain situations but ultimately change situations. What I am suggesting here is far from utopian or indeed new but while it is vital not to overestimate what sport can do, at the same time sport has helped to: (i) change some people's lives, (ii) symbolize change but also contribute to social change and (iii) work across societies and agencies to help or attempt make the world a better place.

In a general sense sport has contributed to different visions of what the world is and should be. Three are mentioned here and these might be referred to as: (i) the global neo-liberal view of sport in society in which the convergence of the opportunity gap between sport in the richest and poorest parts of the world might be possible (dependent upon a strict adherence to liberal policies); (ii) the hard third way view of sport in society that requires a more limited adherence to democracy but an enthusiasm for sporting partnerships funded between private/public sources, decentralization, arms length sports policy, an acceptance of global sporting values and less of a concern with sporting inequality, while still embracing certain egalitarian goals through provision for targeted or vulnerable sports groups and (iii) a softer but less likely third way in which sporting relief is used as part of an overall policy of managing capitalism's social contradictions with the typical role for sport being that of being a means to an end or a bridge builder of reconciliation in areas of conflict. Within this model, third world democracy and sport as a facet of social welfare come first, not last. In all of this it is valuable to have a notion of the sort of social change or vision of a better society that might be influencing the way in which sport might be a catalyst of social change.

Education through sport

Education through sport projects have long since been viewed as agents of social change. The following are some of the many popular answers that are given when the question 'what does education through sport provide us with' is posed: (i) it can increase knowledge and skills and in a broader sense contribute to the knowledge economy; (ii) it can help to provide opportunities for lifelong learning and sustain not just education but an involvement in sport and physical activity; (iii) the voluntary contribution to informal education through sport can make a positive contribution to helping young people; (iv) that education through sport can help foster and develop critical debate about key public issues; (v) programmes in different parts of the world which involve sport as part of an approach to tackling HIV education clearly view education through sport as an important aspect of international and humanitarian aid efforts and (vi) that education through sport helps to foster social capital through fostering relationships, networking and making connections. The effectiveness of this latter point is at the heart of the debate about social capital in the sense that associational activity through both education *and* sport can help people connect through a series of networks and these networks in themselves then constitute a form of social capital particularly where networks tend to share common values. These networks through education and sport therefore have the potential to act as a form of resource that can be seen, according to Field (2003: 1), as forming a kind of capital.

All of this tends to come alive when you look around the world and see some of the empowering things that are going on as a result of education through sport in some of the poorest areas of the world. There is no single agent or group or movement that can carry the hopes of humanity but there are many points of engagement through education and sport that offer good causes for optimism that things can get better.

Higher education, sport and international aid

Universities through sport and related activities are increasingly involved in forging partnerships which are adding value to the UK's own international development efforts. Narrowing the gap through education in sport is about the contribution that education in sport, in particular higher education, can make in relation to developing people, raising aspirations and being a real resource of hope. Education in and through sport has been making a difference as a result of UK Universities undertaking a significant amount of international work in sport in, for example, Zambia, India, Kenya, Israel and Palestine. In a simple sense narrowing the gap through education and sport initiatives that attempt to foster forms of social capital is about some or all of the following: (i) universities that have committed to a series of sports development projects in Zambia aimed at tackling HIV education; (ii) the ongoing efforts of universities to fund educational scholarships to bring talented African athletes to the UK; (iii) universities that have been involved in football coaching and physical education courses that have been helping to forge international relations between Jewish and Arab children on the West Bank or (iv) knowledge transfer helping to develop practical courses related to education, sport, and physical education role in promoting forms of development – in other words sport-in-development.

While sport at times reproduces the politics of contested national and other identities, it should not be at the expense of an acceptance of the possibility of internationality or focus upon common humanity. Living sporting identities are in constant flux, producing an ever-changing international balance of similarities and differences that may contribute to what it is that makes life worth living, and what connects us with the rest of the changing world. As such, the notion of international education through sport and new forms of internationality must remain part of the vocabulary of global and regional sporting debates not just because it is a more realistic way of explaining the governance of sport today, but because it tempers the all-consuming notion of globalization and provides grounds for explaining the many 'other' worlds of sport outside of the transnational corporation.

European Year of Education through Sport

Education in Scotland has historically always been associated with preparing people for life as equal citizens in a common culture of community. The 2004 National Debate on Education in Scotland identified that the very purpose of education in Scotland should be broad and wide ranging and should be concerned not just with providing skills but enabling people to become 'active citizens of a modern Scotland' (Scottish Executive, 2004b). It is interesting to compare the priorities for education which were identified by the then Scottish Executive with the aims outlined by the European Parliament for the European Year of Education through Sport. They both: (i) highlight social inclusion of disadvantaged groups to be a main priority, (ii) place emphasis on the development of appropriate attitudes and values and focus on active citizenship and community development, (iii) lay emphasis on lifelong learning and (iv) the European Parliament also places an emphasis on lifelong sports participation.

The data base informing the European Year of Education through Sport, the European survey on sport and physical activity, saw sport as contributing to the development of certain values such as team spirit (61 per cent), discipline (47 per cent), sense of endeavour (43 per cent) and friendship (42 per cent). What Europeans wanted most from sport was a more citizen focused, cleaner model. The former Secretary General for the Council of Europe, in defending sport in Europe, did not highlight the European Football or Athletic Championships or other high profile events, but rather she stated that the real value of sport and physical activity was the hidden face of sport, the tens of thousands of enthusiasts and volunteers who find in their football, rowing and athletics a place for meeting and exchange but above all the training ground for community life. Sport, for her, was seen par excellence as the ideal school for democracy (Sportengland, 1998). The Secretary General had an idea about sport that was informed by a set of values and ideas and that education through sport carried with it significant added value in terms of citizenship, democracy and building trust among Europeans.

Sports participation in Scotland tends to get headline news because sports participation is viewed as being important in health terms and yet the civil renewal argument is just as compelling. It is an argument that has a particular resonance for volunteers and non-governmental organizations (NGO). A 2005 Department of Culture Media and Sport Report which included Scotland in the aggregate UK data, evidenced the part played by sports participation and organization in being a catalyst to create civil renewal. The key messages were that: (i) the UK is above the European average for both membership of sports groups and sports participation, and average for volunteering; (ii) 26 per cent of the UK population were members of sports clubs; (iii) 21 per cent actively played sport in the context of a sports organization and 6 per cent volunteered in clubs – Scandinavian countries in general displayed higher levels of associational involvement but the UK was ahead of many European Countries; (iv) sport was found to be the most popular type of group activity in the UK and (v) British people were more likely than the average European to belong to sports club and participate in sport and are as about as likely as the average European to volunteer in sports.

Membership of sports clubs appeared to have a number of beneficial impacts, in that members were more likely than non-members to vote, contact an official and sign a petition. Countries with high levels of sports participation tended to have higher levels of social and institutional trust. The correlations were substantial for the level of sports participation in a country and levels of social trust. Life satisfaction was also strong although perhaps not as significant. Countries with high levels of membership of sports groups tended to have high levels of membership of cultural and social groups, suggesting that participation is cumulative. In short membership and participation of sports clubs was associated with being more satisfied with life, more trusting, more sociable, healthier and more positive towards state institutions. Sports members also tended to have slightly more liberal views about immigration.

Candle Who Brings a Ray of Hope

There is the reality of Maria Urrutia, the women from Colombia who lifted 245 Kilos to win Colombia's first ever Olympic Gold Medal at the 2000 Sydney Olympic Games. The country as you know usually hits the headlines for other reasons but speaking to her nation following her success she was clear about what sport had helped her to do:

'She hoped that her success would reach others like her poor, black and female' – she went on – 'I hope others see that you can make a living, see the world and get an education, through sports, or even in music and other arts'.

(Gillon, 2000: 18)

In a country where the average wage is less than an Euro or a dollar a day, the lucrative European and American road race circuits are attractive career options for Kenyan athletes. When Catherine Ndereba broke the world record in the Chicago Marathon in October 2001, she received a $75000 prize purse, $100000 for breaking the world record and a Volkswagen Jetta worth $26125. This was in addition to a not insignificant appearance fee merely for turning up (Shontz, 2002). A world championship gold medal has been estimated to be worth $60000, as well as opening other lucrative avenues in terms of qualification for appearance fees in big races (Nejenga, 2003). Money is perhaps more of a motivation to women due to the independence it buys them – 'Once a woman begins to earn her own money, she is valued immediately by her family and her community' (Shontz, 2002). The barriers for women acquiring wealth in Kenya are inherently unequal. For instance, women cannot inherit land and they often invariably live on land as a guest of their male relatives, but athletic wealth in some cases can help buy land. Therefore, as Kenyan women win road races and track meets, they can acquire control of substantial amounts of money which allows them to invest in their own land – a once unlikely prospect for women not born into wealthy families.

Founded in 1987, the Mathare Youth Sports Association (MYSA) in Kenya, lies in one of the countries poorest slum areas (Hogenstad & Tollisen, 2004). An area with a population of nearly one million people and with an average household income, for a family of eight, of about 63 pence a day. Here, sport is placed at the centre of a humanitarian aid programme precisely because it is a point of contact with young kids that can entice young people to learn. It is a vehicle for facilitating mutual self-help and education on a massive scale. Sports leagues far in excess of 14 000 children run on a 'pay it back' approach, in which in return for help with facilities and organization, players help keep the neighbourhood clean, plant trees, attend aids, pregnancy and drug awareness classes. Scholarships exist for photography, music and drama classes. Teams got points for their work as well as their sport. Reflecting back on the impact of MYSA one former goalkeeper said:

Older kids who have been involved since its beginning have become leaders and role models in the community and football has been the catalyst for their social, physical and intellectual development.

(Jarvie, 2006: 375)

The ethos here was pretty straight forward – ask kids what they want, and use sport and physical activity as a basis for developing economic and social capital, local solutions to local problems, education and a track record of success, all of which has been recognized internationally through a number of awards. The MYSA was short listed, indeed got down to the last five, for a Nobel Peace Prize in 2003 for its contribution to attacking poverty. Other nominees included Tony Blair, George Bush and Jacques Chirac.

There is Maria Mutola from Mozambique, the 2000 Olympic Women's 800 Champion, five time world indoor 800 metres champion and thrice outdoors world record holder and subject of an article entitled 'Candle Who Brings a Ray of Hope'. The article referred to the humanity of the athlete – what the athlete herself calls a moral duty to her country – in that athletic winnings from grand prix victories were often returned home to Mozambique to assist in the purchase of farms and small businesses, wells drilled, schools endowed, children sent abroad to University and in some cases life-saving surgery all dependent upon a track victory (Gillon, 2004). In 2003 when Mutola became the first athlete to collect $1 million for outright victory on the Golden League Athletic Grand Prix Circuit she routinely sent track winnings back to her country of origin. Chamanchulo, the suburb of Maputo in which Mutola grew up, is ravaged by HIV, passed on in childbirth or breast milk to 40 per cent of the children (Gillon, 2004).

Whether the current international arrangements for education through sport or education and sport are robust enough is open to question, but they continue to have the potential to provide pathways of hope for many people in different parts of the world. It is a partnership that if given the opportunities to thrive perhaps could light many candles of hope all over the world but more importantly provide opportunities for better life chances for some. What is clear from these and other examples is that active partnerships involving education through sport at all levels is desirable, perhaps inevitable and certainly a popular agent for bringing about change, but that the conditions need to be created to let social forces, social forums and social empowerment thrive through building new forms of social capital.

Following the national dream

In a relatively autonomous Scotland some of the richest and poorest sectors of society identify with forms of sport in different ways. Contemporary patterns of sports participation in Scotland are illustrative of the fact that sport in Scotland is socially differentiated. Sport's social and commercial power in Scotland makes it a potentially potent force for good and bad. Education through sport in Scotland is important because it can be a symbol of democratic change, it can promote internationality, it can contribute to different ideas of community but it can do all of this within a context that everyone has the right to education. Education in Scotland has historically always been associated with preparing people for life as equal citizens in a common culture of community (Paterson, 2003).

It is arguable that football is the national sport in Scotland but its popularity and potential attraction for young boys and increasingly girls in Scotland should not be underestimated. Football in Scotland has during 2002 undergone a national review and an audit of its structures, responsibilities and provision for youth footballers who do not make the grade of the professional footballer (Scottish Executive, 2004a). The following example is not atypical of the youthful cultural patriot who wanted to live the dream of Scottish football and found out that he was being released from a premier professional football league club? His mother worrying about the effect this would have on her son said:

I would have done anything for him not to experience the hurt, but I didn't have a choice because all he has ever wanted to be is a footballer. I wouldn't mind my son being a footballer, but it would be better if he was one with letters after his name and educational qualifications in his pocket.

(Rhodes, 2004: 17)

In 2002, Scottish football clubs released 350 players. That was 30 per cent of the workforce with the most common age being that of 19. Numerous developments have attempted to tackle the issue of youth football and education. There is the Johan Cruyff Academy that in conjunction with European institutions offers programmes in sports management direct to athletes. The Learning in Football Initiative launched at Hampden in 2003 was also aimed at helping footballers find a new career path (Scottish Government, 2003). The picture is not the same for women youth footballers. Indeed an essential addition to the 2002 review of Scottish football would have been to include women's football as part of the review. Stirling University research has found that women footballers in Scotland are by comparison with their male counterparts very well qualified whether it is in terms of standard grades, higher grades, further or higher education degrees (Macbeth, 2003). There were just over 1200 professional male footballers in Scotland but also according to 2001/2002 figures 786 registered women footballers playing in the senior leagues. In many cases this group of women footballers in terms of qualifications are higher than national adult population figures for Scotland as a whole with: (i) 32.9 per cent of women footballers having first or higher degree compared to 2001/2002 figures for the national adult population of 16 per cent of males and 15 per cent of females; (ii) 97.64 per cent of registered women footballers holding standard grades compared to national adult population figures of just over 67 per cent of males and 72 per cent of females and (iii) in terms of higher grades just over 64.18 per cent of women footballers holding higher grades compared to the national adult male population figure of 59 per cent and with the national adult female population of 52 per cent having higher grades in 2001/2002.

A critical comment about education through sport might reflect upon agents who may be the product of the Scottish education system, a system which itself has been critically reviewed but remains internationally respected. Scots have always been ambivalent about freedom but the story of what the education system has given to the Scottish people is the priceless ability to recognize the bigger questions, situate your own position in a wider context and think things out for yourself about what to do about it – Is it worth holding on to the idea that education through sport can contribute to this sense of what Paterson (2003) refers to as ordered freedom? It may be suggested that in many ways the partnership of education through sport can really make a difference to the quality of life. An effective partnership in action means that a country such as Scotland, which has often been cited as having a good education system, perhaps needs to do more to help sport with its challenges. It might be useful to evaluate whether the partnership of education through sport continues to provide pathways of hope for many people in different parts of the world, including Scotland. It is important not to let down or forget the boy or girl who wanted to live the Scottish dream, but look after them better, help to create the conditions to let the relationship of education through sport thrive – that would truly be a partnership in action worth trusting and striving for because education through sport has much to offer.

Narrowing the gap through education and sport?

Is education through sport about citizenship, social cohesion and social responsibility? When the former first Minister for Scotland, Jack McConnell, in his St Andrews day speech talked of talking Scotland up, about starting with Scotland's young people, about renewing democracy, about the importance of cultural activities, including sport, he could have almost been paraphrasing Tom Johnston the former Secretary of State for Scotland who in November 1942 charged the then Advisory Council of Education in Scotland with being a parliament of education and seeking how schools could ensure that young people were properly equipped to discharge the duties and exercise the rights of citizenship (Paterson, 2003).

The notion of citizenship, like the word community, is very slippery indeed. Both of these terms carry with them notions of trust and mutual obligation involving others. For the current Prime Minister the notion of citizenship is straight forward in that it implies that individuals owe a duty to one another and the broader society. The collective power of all should be used for the individual good of each. Gordon Brown has continually argued that in recognition of our inter-dependence upon one another, people must accept their responsibilities as individuals (Brown, 2002). Community action should never be allowed to be a substitute for personal responsibility to others. There is material to suggest that education through sport can help with some of this. Programmes such as First Tee Golf in America which had Tiger Woods playing golf with hundreds of inner city kids in New York is based upon nine core values, including trusting others, but also making golf more accessible.

103

Improving life chances requires a co-ordinated effort and as such any contribution that education through sport can make must also build upon a wider coalition of sustained support for social and progressive policies. The life chances approach to narrowing the gap between rich and poor has a key role to play in producing social change. It requires harnessing a strong political narrative and action plan that fits with many people's intuitive understanding that life should not be determined by socio-economic position and that people do have choices, whilst drawing attention to the fact that some people and places face greater risks and more limited opportunities. Equalizing life chances and focusing on areas such as poverty should sit together as part of a vision for a better society. In part the promise and possibilities of education through sport are encapsulated in the words of the former Olympic and Commonwealth athlete Kip Keino (2007) (Interview with the author 5 February 2007):

I believe in this world that sport is one of the tools that can unite youth – sport is something different from fighting in war and it can make a difference – we can change this world by using sport as a tool.

I've run a lot for water charities and children's charities. I believe we share in this world with members of our society who are less fortunate. This is important. We came to this world with nothing and we leave this world with nothing. So we can be able to make a better world for those who need assistance.

Concluding remarks

Current debates about social capital and social cohesion may, at one level, raise questions concerning the direction of sport within social policies. Sports have been at the heart of city life in many parts of the world for sometime and yet urban policy needs to address the issue of whether the role of sport remains that of entertainment or whether sport is a social right or both. If sport were to facilitate social capital then cities rather than using sport as a basis for attracting the national and international destination of major events or sports festivals might wish to resurrect the notion of sport as a social right rather than a spectacle or form of entertainment. Cities in all parts of the world are first and foremost places to live for millions of people and yet access to sport remains problematic for many vulnerable groups of people. The citizens who seem the most ignored are those with the fewest resources (Harvey, 2003). The Canadian Council on Social Development points out that more than 60 per cent of children in the poorest households almost never participate in organized sports, whereas the figure is 27 per cent for children from affluent homes. The Council also confirmed the theory that cities that give young people a voice in policy development are more inclusive than others. Thus it might be argued that if sport does help to facilitate notions of social capital and/or community then a pre-requisite of any such approach necessitates viewing sport as a social right rather than a form of entertainment. Harvey (2003) is insightful when he suggests that the sociability networks that may develop in and around community sport and recreation initiatives may help to strengthen social bonds and consequently be a potential source of social capital. If this is the case then sport as a social right for children and all vulnerable groups cannot be left to chance.

The concept of social capital carries with it a heavy burden of claims that it only recently has been subjected to critical review (Johnston & Percy-Smith, 2003). At it heaviest, as typified by writers such as Putnam the presence of absence of social capital is used as an explanatory factor for economic and political performance. More modest claims are also made for social capital in that it allegedly contributes to the formation of strong formal and informal networks, shared norms and trusting social relationships. In relation to communities it is asserted that high trust communities typically experience less crime, anti-social behaviour and social fragmentation. For individuals, it is suggested that social capital contributes to better health, higher levels of educational attainment and access to employment. Social capital, it is maintained, is a factor that contributes to higher levels of civic and voluntary activity and in turn such activity enhances democracy by offering citizens greater choices and opportunities.

On the other hand Portes (1998) has identified at least four negative consequences associated with social capital. First, the exclusion of outsiders as a result of strong ties that exist within a particular group or community. Second, group or community closure which inhibits the economic success of its members as a result of free riding on the part of some group members. Third, conformity within the group or community resulting in restrictions of personal freedom and autonomy. Finally, social capital is partly responsible for a downward levelling as a result of group solidarity that arises out of opposition to mainstream society and inter-generational experiences of exclusion and discrimination. In all of these ways social capital is viewed as excluding outside influences and enforcing damaging group norms if you do not belong to a community or group. Thus it is important to be aware that the notion of social capital has a dark side as well as a positive side and that discussion of sport, education and social capital must be sensitive to both the positive and negative aspects of social capital in action.

This chapter has looked at some of the arguments and some evidence which would support the fact that sport and education or education through sport provides a potential resource of hope which can make a difference to people's lives. Historically sport and education have been key avenues of social mobility and an escape from poverty for some. It has been suggested that rather than capital the emphasis should be on the 'social' in social capital and aligned to that it is necessary to think of ways in which the 'social' in social science, social change and social empowerment may contribute to alternative practices and ways of thinking about sport and education. Thinking systematically about emancipatory alternatives and the part played by sport and education is only one way or element in the process by which the limits of the possible can expand and the promise and possibilities of the power of education through sport can become more of a reality for more people. It is important to remember that around the world many new proposals are continually being tried.

The social challenge is enormous and the promise of education through sport should not detract from the fact that increasing competition within some of the poorest areas of the world often depletes social capital and leaves its potential fragmented. The informal sector sometimes dissolves self-help networks and solidarities essential to the survival of the very poor and it is often women and children who are the most vulnerable. An NGO worker in Haiti describes the ultimate logic of neo-liberal individualism in a context of absolute immiseration (Davis, 2006: 184):

Now everything is for sale. The women used to receive you with hospitality, give you coffee, share all that she has in her home. I could go get a plate of food at a neighbour's house; a child could get a coconut at her godmother's, two mangoes at another aunt's. But these acts of solidarity are disappearing with the growth of poverty. Now when you arrive somewhere, either the women offers to sell you a cup of coffee or she has no coffee at all. The tradition of mutual giving that allowed us to help each other and survive – this is all being lost.

Narrowing the Gap through Education in Sport is about the enormous, almost unique contribution that education in sport, in particular higher education, has made in relation to developing people, raising aspirations and being a real resource of hope, nationally, internationally and locally. Yet the relationship between social capital and education in a recent review calls for an increasing awareness of not only the need for alternative conceptualizations of social capital but an awareness of the diverse number of ways in which this relationship is examined, defined and operationalized (Dika & Singh, 2002). The conceptual umbrella of social capital is often stretched to include a variety of social factors that do not always coherently hang together. Problems with the conceptualization and measurement of social capital have resulted in a body of research that does not always acknowledge the differential access to social networks and social resources. Thus, much remains to be done of the *social* in social capital is to be fully realized.

The promise of education through sport to narrow the gap or forge new forms of social capital should not be overestimated. A penultimate issue might be the right of all people to have access to education and/or sport and the small contribution that education through sport can make to this goal. With the international campaigns against world debt in abeyance new ideas and progressive ideas are needed to cure the problems in part caused by international finance institutions attempting to solve the debt problem of the global South and other places. Football is popular in places such as Brazil where it is estimated that some 250 million children work and a further 250 million who are not working are in school. The need to raise money for the family unit through the informal economy means that children often do not have access to education and the failure to study only serves to maintain poverty (Landman, 2004). Yet some of the projects illustrated in this chapter highlight the promise, possibilities and limits of education through sport to make a difference, be a ray of hope. Sport cannot do this on its own but swapping international debt for education, including education through sport, may be one of the possible strategies open to a progressive, humanitarian international approach to education through sport which could challenge the very values at the heart of global sport. It may assist in creating the conditions that may allow education through sport to thrive. In short swapping debt for education including education through sport may assist millions of children and others to gain substantive education, transferable skills and enable some ultimately to become more active participants in a national economy, secure better life chances and escape a cycle of poverty.

Finally, globalization is a good example of a contested concept or idea. It is contested along two dimensions – explanatory and normative. Global sport is also a contested idea in that there is no agreement or consensus about what global sport actually is. All too often the alternatives to global sport also remain silent in accounts of global sport. As a result key silences about sport's role within alternative debates about education, internationalism, anti-globalization, anti-capitalism, social movements and the power of the social within the world past and present also remain under researched. Neo-liberalism some have suggested is dead but the values often associated with neo-liberalism seem to be alive and well. Freedom is often reduced to the right to buy and sell and reduces solidarity to privatized individualism. Historically the potential of education through sport lies not with the values promoted by global sport or particular forms of capitalism. The possibilities that exist within education through sport are those that can help with radically different views of the world perhaps based upon opportunities to foster trust, obligations, redistribution and respect for sport in a more socially orientated humane world. Possibilities do exist to provide resources of hope within a world that is left wanting on so many fronts. To ignore the capacity of education through sport to assist with social change, to foster forms of real *social* capital is not an option that can be left to chance.

References

Brown, G. (2002). *Maxton*. Edinburgh: Mainstream Publishing.

Davis, M. (2006). *Planet of Slums*. London: Verso.

Dika, S. & Singh, K. (2002). Applications of social capital in educational literature: A critical synthesis. *Review of Educational Research*, 72(1), 31–60.

Fabian Society (2006). *Narrowing the Gap: The Fabian Commission on Life Chances and Child Poverty*. London: Fabian Society.

Field, J. (2003). *Social Capital*. London: Routledge.

Gillon, D. (2004). Candle who brings a ray of hope. *The Herald*, 24(November), 12.

Gillon, D. (2000). Maria strikes unlikely gold. *The Herald*, 7(October), 18.

Harvey, J. (2003). *Sports and Recreation: Entertainment or Social Right?* http://policyresearch.gc.ca/page.asp?pagenm=v5n1_art_07.

Hogenstad, H. & Tollisen, A. (2004). Playing against deprivation: Football and development in Nairobi, Kenya. In: G. Armstrong & R. Giulianotti (Eds.), *Football in Africa: Conflict, Conciliation and Community* (pp. 210–219). London: Palgrave.

Jarvie, G. (2006). *Sport, Culture and Society*. London: Routledge.

Jarvie, G. (2007). The promise and possibilities of running in and out of east Africa. In: Y. Pitsiladis, J. Bale, C. Sharp &

T. Noakes (Eds.), *East African Running: Towards a Cross-Disciplinary Perspective* (pp. 24–39). London: Routledge.

Johnston, G. & Percy-Smith, J. (2003). In search of social capital. *Policy and Politics*, 31(3), 321–334.

Keino, K. (2007). Interview with the author, 5 February.

Landman, T. (2004). *Swapping Debt for Education*. Available at http://www.fabianglobalforum.net/forum/article027.html.

Macbeth, J. (2003). *Women's Football in Scotland: An Interpretative Analysis*, unpublished PhD thesis. Scotland: University of Stirling.

Nejenga, P. (2003). Kenya: Runners invest their money in real estate. *East African Standard*, 17(November), 2–3.

Paterson, L. (2003). *Scottish Education in the Twentieth Century*. Edinburgh: Edinburgh University Press.

Portes, A. (1998). Social capital its origins and applications in modern sociology. *Annual Review of Sociology*, 24, 1–24.

Rhodes, M. (2004). Fantasy football. *The Scotsman Magazine*, 10(June), 16–18.

Rutherford, J. & Shah, H. (2006). *The Good Society; Compass Programme for Renewal*. London: Lawrence and Wishart.

Scottish Executive (2004a). *Action Plan for Youth Football*. Available at http://www.scotland.gov.uk/pages/news/2004/03/p_SETCS230.aspx.

Scottish Executive (2004b). Education for Excellence: Choice and Opportunity. Available at http://www.scotland.gov.uk/library5/education/ndser-08.asp.

Scottish Government (2003). *Playing the Learning Game*. Available at http://www.scotland.gov.uk/pages/news/2003/08/SET-CS205.ASPX.

Shontz, L. (2002). *Fast Forward: The Rise of Kenya's Women Runners*, post-gazette.com sports, 22 October, Pittsburgh.

Sportengland (1998). *The Social Value of Sport*. London: Sportengland.

Part Two

Clubs and Community Sport Organizations

Community sport networks

Alison Doherty and
Katie Misener

Community sport is characterized by networks of individuals who come together to volunteer their time for community sport organizations (CSOs), as well as external stakeholders who have an interest in the operation and/or performance of the CSOs (CSOs are synonymous with local voluntary sport clubs or associations.). Social capital is a purported benefit of social networks by virtue of the social trust and reciprocity that may be produced, and reproduced, when individuals and groups work together. The chapter begins with an overview of the nature of CSOs and a working definition of social capital. This is followed by a discussion of social capital in relation to the community sport networks of volunteers and stakeholders, including evidence of the potential for, existence of, and barriers to social capital in and through these networks. The chapter concludes with a discussion of directions for research and implications for practice.

Community sport organizations

CSOs are non-profit, voluntary organizations that provide many of the recreational and competitive sport opportunities we enjoy in our communities. The local soccer club, the pee-wee baseball league, the minor ice hockey association, and so on, provide accessible and affordable pathways for children and adults alike to participate in organized sport and physical recreation (Cuskelly, 2004). As a result, they play a key role 'in developing sport and in meeting community expectations regarding physical activity and sporting competitions' (Tower et al., 2006: 167). CSOs constitute the grassroots level of a sport system that extends through to high performance and elite sport. At the wide base of what has traditionally been seen as the 'sport pyramid' the focus of CSOs is primarily on participation, including both competitive and more recreational or non-competitive forms. Recently, there has been a move to a more integrated model of sport that emphasizes the mutually enabling connection between high performance and 'sport for all' as a part of lifelong physical activity (e.g. Canadian Sport Centre, 2005; Barnes et al., 2007).

CSOs are a substantial fixture in our communities. In many Western countries sport and recreation organizations comprise the largest proportion of non-profit voluntary organizations (Seippel, 2006). For example, in Canada, which has one of the largest voluntary sectors in the world (Hall et al., 2005), sport organizations comprise 21 per cent of all non-profit voluntary organizations, and 71 per cent of those organizations operate at the community level (Hall et al., 2004). Furthermore, there are relatively high levels of participation in CSOs. According to the 2002 European Social Survey, 21 per cent of the population of the UK reported active sports participation in the context of sport clubs (Delaney & Keaney, 2005). From that survey, the highest rate of participation was reportedly in the Netherlands, at 25 per cent (Delaney & Keaney, 2005). In Canada, findings from the 2004 Physical Activity Monitor indicate that over three-quarters (76 per cent) of Canadians who reported regular participation in sport were involved in a community-based sport club of some type (CFLRI, 2005).

As membership-based, non-profit organizations, CSOs have a mandate to provide their members with opportunities to participate in recreational and competitive sport. Despite their magnitude, CSOs continue to be operated almost exclusively by sport volunteers who undertake roles 'to support, arrange and/or run organised sport and physical activity' (Australian Bureau of Statistics (ABS), 2002: 39). The network of volunteers within a CSO comprises three key groups: executive board members, coaches, and general volunteers. Executive volunteers are elected or appointed to the CSO's board. The roles and responsibilities of these volunteers include long-term and strategic planning for the club, developing policies and procedures, financial management, relations with external stakeholders, and coordinating the programmes and services the CSO provides (Doherty & Carron, 2003; Cuskelly et al., 2006; Hoye & Cuskelly, 2007). Coaches are another critical part of the CSO, and are typically involved on a volunteer basis as well. With some exceptions in certain sports (e.g. figure skating, gymnastics), most community level coaches receive no more than a small honorarium for their time and services (Cuskelly et al., 2006). Coaches are charged with teaching skills, designing training programmes and competition plans, selecting and preparing individuals and teams for competition, and evaluating athletes' progress.

General volunteers comprise a group of individuals who provide support to the CSO in many ways that may be considered more peripheral than the core roles of the executive board and coaches (Cuskelly et al., 2006). General volunteers are involved in such tasks as fundraising ventures, player registration, managing team equipment, assisting with event planning and implementation, and driving players to out of town competitions. General volunteers play an integral role in supporting the operation of the CSO, taking their direction from the board and/or coaches. Of course, board members and coaches may also be involved in these supporting roles, and data indicate that sport volunteers often take on multiple roles within their CSO (e.g. LIRC, 2003; Delaney & Keaney, 2005; Doherty, 2005a, 2005b; Cuskelly et al., 2006; Welch & Long, 2006). Together, the board members, coaches, and general volunteers work to ensure there are accessible, affordable, and quality opportunities for recreational and competitive sport participation in the community.

Despite the involvement of this network of volunteers, no organization is totally self-sufficient but rather must establish linkages with other organizations and people in order to achieve its goals (Pugh & Hickson, 1989). A CSO has relationships with various external stakeholders upon which it is dependent for important resources. Similarly, these stakeholders become involved with the CSO because doing so provides some valued return. Our focus here is 'primary' stakeholders who have a direct, utilitarian relationship with the CSO (Clarkson, 1995), and who can influence or be influenced by the actions of an organization (Freeman, 1984). CSO stakeholders include, but are not limited to, participants (and parents), facility providers and other suppliers, corporate sponsors, media, other CSOs, municipal government, and regional, provincial/ state, and national sport governing bodies. The relationships range from, for example, participants who register for CSO programmes, to local facility providers who contract the use of playing fields and gymnasia, to corporate sponsors who provide financial or in-kind support to CSOs, and the local media who provide promotion and coverage of CSO programmes and competitive results. Each of these stakeholders has a relationship with a CSO because the sport organization has something the stakeholder needs or wants; for example, participants gain access to coaching, facilities, and/or competitions, facility providers generate revenues from rental fees, corporate sponsors hope to generate goodwill and a higher profile in the community by supporting local sport clubs, and the media works towards its mandate of providing coverage of current events in the community. This network of CSO stakeholders is fundamental to the successful delivery of community sport.

Social capital

In addition to their critical role in community sport, these CSO networks of volunteers and stakeholders may be important sources of social capital. The notion of social capital represents an attempt to objectify or embody the non-material social effects (in contrast to more material, economic effects) that are generated through 'the structure and functioning of the social world' (Bourdieu, 1986: 242). In simpler terms, 'the core idea of social capital theory is that social networks have value' (Putnam, 2000: 19). Thus, social effects may be expected even when the primary purpose of a relationship is more economic or utilitarian.

To develop a working definition of social capital as a framework for this chapter, we begin with Bourdieu's (1986: 248) conceptualization of social capital as 'the aggregate of the actual or potential resources which are linked to possession of a durable network of more or less institutionalized relationships of mutual acquaintance and recognition – or in other words, to membership in a group'. The notion of a durable network suggests that social capital accrues over time as social relationships are developed. The notion of institutionalized relationships suggests that a network that engenders social capital is one of organized or systematic connections or affiliations; this may range from a family to a corporate entity, or from a youth sport team to a professional sport franchise.

However, not every group or network engenders social capital. Social capital is not merely a function of nominal membership in a network, but rather active engagement there (Putnam, 2000). In other words, social capital is only generated as a result of meaningful interaction with others. Bourdieu (1986: 253) suggests that 'the transformation of economic capital into social capital presupposes a specific labour, that is, an apparently gratuitous expenditure of time, attention, care, concern, which, as is seen in the endeavor to personalize a gift, has the effect of transfiguring the purely [utilitarian] import of the exchange and, by the very same token, the very meaning of the exchange'. That is, social capital accrues in relationships that go beyond basic material transactions, with the presumption that there must be some effort or 'specific labour' on the part of those in the relationship to invest further in the connection. We may presume that in utilitarian relationships, social capital is more likely to develop where there is effective communication, cooperation, and further collaboration within the group or network; what Putnam (2000: 58) refers to as 'active and involved membership'. It is surprising, then, that social capital is often measured in terms of the numbers or proportion of participants in a group or network (e.g. Coalter, 2007), rather than the nature of the relationships among those participants, as participation itself is not enough to declare the existence of social capital.

The resources that are associated with networks of engaged members are capital which Bourdieu (1986: 241) defines generally as 'social energy in the form of ... living labor'. 'Social energy' may accrue to individuals within the network and to the network itself. More specifically, this energy is conceived as the social trust (in each other, rather than necessarily trust in government or other social institutions) and norms of reciprocity and cooperation (give-and-take, mutual obligation) that may develop from meaningful, durable, and relatively institutionalized connections among individuals or groups (Putnam, 2000).

Seippel (2006: 171) reminds us that, as a resource, '[social] "capital" is something that might give future benefit ... with implications for action in and postures towards other social actors or arenas'. Thus, social capital may be expected to benefit individuals or groups in the focal network, benefit other relationships or networks, and benefit the community or society as a whole. One perspective is that social capital is a potential means to a further return in the marketplace, such that the trust and reciprocity developed in a relationship is expected to pay future economic and/or social benefits (e.g. Bourdieu, 1986); 'I'll do this for you now, in the expectation that you (or perhaps someone else) will return the favor' (Putnam, 2000: 20). From this perspective, social capital may be seen as more utilitarian and even self-serving. Putnam (2000: 20) refers to this as 'specific reciprocity'. Another perspective is that the social energy (capital) derived from a social network enhances the likelihood of increased civic engagement or participation in one's community in any one or more of a variety of forms, such as volunteering or voting (e.g. Putnam, 2000); the social trust and sense of reciprocity developed in one relationship will 'pay it forward' as people engage with and for others in other settings. Still a further perspective is that social capital enhances the ability of people to work together (e.g. Putnam, 2000), through more effective communication, cooperation, and collective action that results from norms of trust and reciprocity. Putnam (2000: 20–21) describes these latter two perspectives as 'generalised reciprocity'.

These two perspectives suggest that social capital may continue to be reproduced or strengthened over time within the relationship (Bourdieu, 1986), and may be manifested beyond the original relationship as individuals and the group itself become connected with other individuals and groups. This dynamic process is illustrated in Figure 6.1. Social capital may be generated within an interpersonal or intergroup relationship where there is meaningful interaction in the form of communication, cooperation, and even collaboration. The social energy generated there may be further reproduced within the relationship, strengthening the ability of the actors to connect

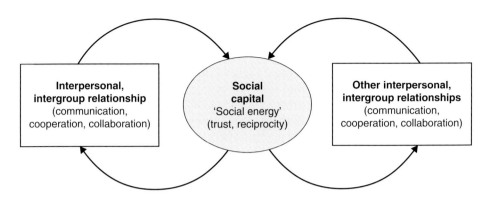

Figure 6.1
The (re)production of social capital

and work together because of a deepening sense of social trust and reciprocity. That same social energy may be manifested in other relationships with which the original actors become involved; providing, perhaps, the impetus for their engagement in those relationships, and at least a baseline of social trust and a sense of reciprocity for communication, cooperation, and collaboration there. These perspectives are consistent with the notion that social capital contributes to the well-being of a community (Woolcock, 2001); that, because of social capital, people are more likely, and better able, to work with and for each other to deal with communal issues and problems. As Putnam (1995: 67) notes, 'life is easier in a community blessed with a substantial stock of social capital'.

Our working definition of social capital may be further enhanced by the consideration of two ways that social capital can be constructed (Putnam, 2000): bonding social capital and bridging social capital. Bonding social capital exists when social networks are among demographically similar, like-minded people. It refers to the trust and reciprocity that is created and expressed within dense or closed networks (Tonts, 2005). The social capital generated by this type of group is characterized by a greater ability to mobilize the solidarity in the group, which is consistent with the easier communication, understanding, and trust that comes from being with others who are similar to oneself (Doherty & Chelladurai, 1999). However, bonding (exclusive) social capital can be limiting in its tendency to reinforce narrow ideas of identity (Putnam, 2000), and further segregation and exclusionary practices (Coalter, 2007). In other words, the further effects of social trust and reciprocity may be limited to those within the group, or others like them. Seippel (2006) refers to this as 'closing' of social networks.

In contrast, bridging social capital exists when social networks are among less similar individuals with different backgrounds and demographics. As a result, interaction within the network can pave the way to new ideas and sources of information (Centre for Citizenship and Human Rights, 2007), and generate a broader identity of the group (Putnam, 2000). The social trust and reciprocity developed in this type of network may be expected to have broader effects, beyond the group. Seippel (2006: 171) refers to this as 'opening up of new social relations'. The social capital generated in bridging networks may be associated with social inclusion and acceptance of diversity (Doherty & Chelladurai, 1999). Nonetheless, bridging social capital is likely more fragile than bonding social capital that develops in dense and closed networks (Tonts, 2005). A further aspect of bridging social capital is a vertical dimension that refers to the alliances or linkages formed to 'leverage resources, ideas, and information from formal institutions beyond the [focal network]' (Woolcock, 2001: 13). This 'linking social capital' (Woolcock, 2001: 13) expands our understanding of the potential social effects of even wider, overlapping networks that bring groups or institutions together and that generate broader reciprocity.

Sport is increasingly cited as a public policy issue because of its presumed contribution to individual and collective social capital (e.g. Coalter, 2007). There is a similar trend outside of sport, in the context of non-profit voluntary associations for the most part, where social capital is hypothesized to contribute to everything from positive community relations, to the social inclusion of traditionally excluded groups, to bridging political and religious divides (e.g. Williamson & Acheson, 2006). Indeed, social capital may be evident nowhere more than in the context of volunteerism, and specifically voluntary organizations where individuals volunteer 'with' rather than just 'for' others (e.g. Putnam, 2000; Smith, 2000; Field, 2003; Bowen, 2004; Isham, Kolodinsky & Kimberly, 2006; Seippel, 2006). Volunteering is a form of 'social citizenship' that involves 'active participation in the life of a city' (Body-Gendrot & Gitell, 2003: ix). It *is* an expression of social trust and reciprocity. A discussion of whether social capital is generated through volunteerism may seem tautological, however Bourdieu (1986: 249) reminds us that 'the [social] profits which accrue from membership in a group are the basis of the solidarity which makes them possible [in the first place]'. As Field notes, voluntary organizations are an important vehicle for both the creation and expression of social capital. As noted in Figure 6.1, social capital generated in one relationship may continue to strengthen that relationship, and it may show itself in other forms of civic engagement, including other relationships where social trust and reciprocity may in turn be developed within the group. An example of this may be evident in the sport setting where the opportunity to give back to (one's) sport is a common and particularly important motive for CSO volunteers (e.g. LIRC, 2003; Doherty, 2005a, 2005b; Cuskelly et al., 2006; Welch & Long, 2006); seemingly a reflection of social capital generated in their playing days.

Foley and Edwards (1998) note that the extent to which social capital is created, is equal for all members, and is more positive or negative, depends on the context of the relationships. It is of interest, then, to consider whether there are particular, and unique, elements of the CSO networks of volunteers and community sport stakeholders that are associated with social capital. To do this we draw on existing literature and data pertaining to CSO volunteer and stakeholder networks. Our underlying assumption is that social capital is a potentially important, positive resource for individuals, groups, and the community as a whole, however, we do acknowledge that it can be a negative force such as when it supports antisocial, exclusionary, discriminatory, or corruptive behaviour (e.g. Putnam, 2000). Our focus is whether CSO networks appear to be likely sites for the (re)production of that social energy according to the nature of engagement in those networks.

It is important to note that our interest is in social capital as a by-product of the more functional work of CSOs, whose mandate is to provide substantive programmes and services for their members. Bourdieu (1986: 249) notes that, although social capital resources may develop (further) from involvement in a group, 'this does not mean that they are consciously pursued as such'. Rather, social capital is, 'to a large extent probably the unintended consequences of instrumental, normative and/ or expressive actions' (Seippel, 2006: 171). This perspective is consistent with sport itself where developing a sense of fair play, cooperation with others, and social trust may be a by-product of the primary focus on playing the game (Uslaner, 1999; Cuskelly et al., 2006).

The community sport network of volunteers

As noted earlier, CSOs comprise one of the largest subsectors of non-profit and voluntary organizations in many developed countries. As may be expected, then, sport is served by one of the highest proportions of volunteers. In Canada, for example,

18 per cent (1.17 million) of all Canadians who volunteer, or 5 per cent of the entire population, give their time to sport (Doherty, 2005a). There are even higher rates of sport volunteering in Australia, New Zealand, and England, where at least 26 per cent of all volunteers in these countries are involved in sport (approximately 10 per cent and 15 per cent of the population of Australia and England, respectively) (Cuskelly et al., 2006).

In this chapter we are interested in whether the nature of volunteers' involvement in CSOs is consistent with the creation and expression of social capital. According to our working definition, social capital is a function of more or less institutionalized relationships that are a recognized part of a durable network; these relationships must be characterized by meaningful interaction in order for social trust and norms of cooperation and reciprocity to be (further) developed there. Our discussion draws on existing literature and data regarding various aspects of the nature of community sport volunteerism as an indication of the potential for and evidence of social capital in that context.

We begin by considering the extensive commitment of volunteers in the sport setting, which has been consistently noted (e.g. LIRC, 2003; Tonts, 2005; Doherty, 2005a, 2005b; Cuskelly et al., 2006; Welch & Long, 2006). As indicated earlier, sport volunteers comprise one of the largest components of the voluntary sector in many countries. They also reportedly contribute a substantial number of hours to formal organizations where they are, by definition, volunteering *with* others (rather than just *for* others); a condition which is fundamental for (re)producing social capital (Putnam, 2000). Due to different sampling and data collection methods there is mixed evidence from different countries (Cuskelly et al., 2006), however it appears that sport volunteers contribute on average between 98 (Australia) and 208 (England) hours per year to their CSO (Cuskelly et al., 2006). There is likely variability in the concentration of those hours during the year, and by volunteer role in the club. For example, Cuskelly et al. cite data from the Australian Bureau of Statistics which indicates that executive volunteers and coaches tend to be involved for a longer period of the year (over 40 weeks or more) while general club volunteers are likely to participate on a more seasonal basis. Furthermore, in a study of sport volunteers in England, Shibli et al. (1999) reported that general club volunteers contributed on average 2.7 hours per week, while committee members contributed an average of 4.6 hours per week. We may expect that coaches provide even more hours on a weekly basis, given the nature of their involvement in training, instruction, and competition.

Data also indicate that sport volunteers tend to take on several roles within the organization (Shibli et al., 1999; LIRC, 2003; Sharpe, 2003; Delaney & Keaney, 2005; Tonts, 2005; Doherty, 2005a, 2005b; Cuskelly et al., 2006; Welch & Long, 2006). In Canada, the majority of sport volunteers are involved in organizing and supervising activities or events (71 per cent), and teaching or coaching (60 per cent) (Doherty, 2005a). About half are involved with the CSO's executive committee or board (46 per cent) and in fundraising activities (45 per cent), and/ or other capacities such as administrative work for the club (32 per cent), driving (27 per cent), and miscellaneous activities (16 per cent). Australian data reveals comparable proportions of involvement in these activities (Cuskelly et al., 2006). Thus, for example, it would not be unusual for a coach to also be on the CSO's board of directors, or to help out in a general way with fundraising or event planning. Board members are very likely to help out with various activities and events as well, beyond their formal role as executive members. Thus, in addition to their considerable involvement, the (multiple) roles that sport volunteers take on and the very nature of those roles suggest the potential for substantial contact and interaction with others in the CSO network of volunteers. We may presume, for example, that individuals interact directly with others to at least some extent when organizing and supervising programmes and events. However, further empirically based insight into the extent and nature of interactions is required.

There is some evidence of the durability of that involvement and interaction, which is fundamental to the development of social capital over time (Bourdieu, 1986), based on volunteers' tenure with their organization. Canadian data indicate that sport volunteers tend to be involved with their CSO an average of three to five years, and over half (57 per cent) are involved three or more years (Doherty, 2005a). The extent and nature of volunteer involvement in CSOs, based on substantial hours, (multiple) roles where there is likely to be interaction, and extended involvement over time, suggest that CSO volunteer networks are a likely site for the (re)production of social capital. However, participation rates and levels alone are not sufficient to indicate social capital (Field, 2003). As noted earlier, it is the nature of relationships in a network that determines the extent to which social energy in the form of trust, cooperation, and reciprocity are engendered.

In an effort to go beyond participation rates and levels, Harvey, Levesque and Donnelly (2007) examined the social capital that accrues to community sport volunteers as a result of the number and nature of connections one has in a club.

They measured the number of people in different occupations with whom each volunteer connects through a CSO's network of volunteers, and the volunteers' perception of the extent to which other volunteers in that network could help them. Thus, Harvey et al.'s focus was specific reciprocity, a form of social capital where an individual acquires social resources in a relationship that he or she may expect to pay off in the future (Putnam, 2000). Harvey et al. found that men had greater access to this form of social capital than women, in terms of both number of connections and the perceived value of those connections. They also reported that the value of those connections was positively associated with years of volunteering, although they could not confirm the direction of that relationship (Harvey et al., 2007). Although the focus of their study was limited to specific reciprocity vs. a broader consideration of generalized reciprocity that may benefit the group and wider community, the findings indicate that volunteers do feel a sense of reciprocity associated with their involvement in a CSO.

With regard to the nature of those connections, certainly we may expect that board members work closely together to oversee the planning and management of their CSO. In *Sport Governance*, Hoye and Cuskelly (2007) devote a chapter entitled 'Teamwork' to a discussion of working relationships in non-profit voluntary sport organizations. Some research has been undertaken in this area. For example, in a case study of one CSO, Sharpe (2003: 435) found that 'although each [executive volunteer] had his or her duties, there was overlap between what each member did, and they generally made plans and decisions as a collective'. A few studies have focused on the nature of group dynamics in CSO executive committees or boards. In this context, Doherty and Carron (2003) reported that cohesion or integration of the group with regard to both task and social aspects was fairly high, although task cohesion was significantly higher. This particular dynamic was characterized by, for example, a strong sense that 'the committee is united in trying to reach its goals ... committee tasks pull members together [and there is a] feeling of cooperation among members regarding tasks' (Doherty & Carron, 2003: 128); characteristics that are consistent with social capital. Further, task cohesion was most meaningful to the volunteers themselves and to the perceived effectiveness of the committee as a whole, likely reflecting the task-oriented focus of the group (Doherty & Carron, 2003). In a further study, Doherty et al. (2004: 109) found that CSO board members perceived there to be very strong norms or 'expectations about how to treat each other (social norms) and how to work together (task norms)'.

The norms of participation (e.g. doing one's share, contributing), cooperation (e.g. assisting each other, working together, acknowledging others' efforts), and individual performance (e.g. doing what was promised, coming prepared for meetings), in particular, appear to parallel the concept of social capital. All of the norms were, perhaps surprisingly, only modestly associated with member behaviour, including attendance and effort. Doherty et al. noted that the findings may have been limited by the measurement of the quantity rather than quality of member behaviour, and suggested that 'perceived norms may have a stronger association with the quality of members' contributions to the committee ... such as initiative, cooperation or performance' (2004: 128). Taken together, the research on CSO board dynamics suggests they are meaningful sites for the creation and expression of social energy (capital) in terms of the trust and reciprocity that exists and is valued in those networks.

Beyond the work of Harvey et al. (2007), there does not appear to be any research that has specifically examined the relationships between board members, coaches, and/or general volunteers; although, as noted earlier, we can assume there is also meaningful interaction, in terms of communication, cooperation, and even collaboration among those volunteers. The results of a qualitative study of volunteer management in CSOs, undertaken with 90 CSO volunteers across a variety of sports, provides some evidence of the reciprocity among club volunteers (Doherty, 2005b). Doherty (2005b) found almost unanimous acknowledgement of the support that club volunteers perceive they have in order to do their work. Specifically, the volunteers talked about:

- Providing support to coaches, in terms of other volunteers looking after such things as athlete registration, booking facilities and referees, organizing equipment, and relaying regular information regarding resources and rule changes from the provincial sport governing body.
- Helping each other out, in terms of picking up the slack for other volunteers, spreading tasks around and, specifically, coaches helping each other and executive volunteers helping each other.
- Support from the club president and executive to coaches and general volunteers in terms of ensuring open communication, being available, helping deal with parents, and providing direction and encouragement in the volunteers' tasks.

Doherty (2005b: 45) concluded that there appears to be a 'culture within the clubs that reflects an expectation that volunteers will help each other out'. This is consistent with the findings of the study of CSO executive committee norms noted earlier (Doherty et al., 2004). It was noted that such a working environment, where volunteers are committed to their work and to helping each other out, and can be trusted to do what they say they will do, was described by the volunteers as one of the 'best things' (Doherty, 2005b: 60) about volunteering in the CSO, and a key factor in why they stay involved. Paralleling that, the 'worst things' (Doherty, 2005b: 62) were reportedly a lack of volunteers to do the work and volunteers who do not carry through on their commitments. Social capital was seemingly present and valued in the networks of these CSO volunteers.

As noted earlier, there are differences in the levels of involvement by different groups of volunteers, with executive committee volunteers and coaches engaged for longer periods of the year and for more hours on a weekly basis. We also may expect some variation in the degree of interaction among different types or groups of volunteers, and we have already discussed group dynamics in CSO executive boards. For example, coaches may be quite autonomous in their CSO involvement, as their main activity is with the participants on the playing field. However, there may be meaningful interaction among coaches within a club, because of their similar roles and responsibilities, and CSO efforts to ensure head coaches do not work alone but have help from assistants (Doherty, 2005b). In fact, social capital associated with volunteer coaches may be (re)produced to the greatest extent in the coach–player network. With regard to general sport volunteers, because of their relatively lesser involvement in the club, we may expect less social capital to accrue to and through these more peripheral volunteers. Thus, there may be subgroups of volunteers within CSOs that have more meaningful, durable relationships than all volunteers together. The nature and extent of these interrelationships, and any variation in social capital there, should be explored.

Finally, we can consider the notions of bonding and bridging social capital. The demographic profile of the network of sport volunteers provides some insight into the CSO as a site of social capital. There is consistent evidence of a relatively narrow profile of CSO volunteers (e.g. Shibli et al., 1999; LIRC, 2003; Doherty, 2005a, 2005b; Cuskelly et al., 2006). Sport volunteers are typically men (64 per cent), 35–44 years of age (41 per cent), college or university graduates (53 per cent), and employed full-time (82 per cent) (all data based on Doherty, 2005a). This profile suggests that CSOs are supported by a network of volunteers who are very similar to each other, and thus may be sites for bonding social capital. Such a dense network may be particularly conducive to the CSO culture of helping out described earlier; however, it may be enough only to aid the group with 'getting by' rather than 'getting ahead', which is purported to be facilitated by bridging social capital (Putnam, 2000; Coffe & Geys, 2007). A homogeneous group is not able to reap the task benefits of greater diversity (e.g. different ideas, challenges to the status quo; Doherty & Chelladurai, 1999) and, we would argue, the broader social capital benefits associated with the opening of social networks (Seippel, 2006). The bonding social capital that may be evident among sport volunteers is also purported to be consistent with exclusionary practices and the closing of social networks where trust and reciprocity is limited to those in the group, or those like them (Putnam, 2000; Seippel, 2006; Coalter, 2007). Collins and Nichols (2005: 123) question whether 'the strength of informal networks between 'stalwarts' [may] act as a barrier to new volunteers'. Indeed, sport volunteer networks have been criticized for their closedness to certain groups of individuals who remain underrepresented there (e.g. women, younger and older individuals, those not in the labour force) (Doherty, 2005a). This may reflect a narrow 'recruitment niche' (Nichols & King, 1999) that constrains the ability of CSOs to expand their volunteer base, and limits the opportunity for others to become engaged in the community through service to sport. Sharpe (2003: 446) notes that 'one of the most desirable qualities of grassroots associations [like CSOs is] its accessibility to a broad spectrum of volunteers'. However, the reality is that there is a fairly narrow, exclusive profile of sport volunteers, which in turn limits bridging social capital that is purported to be associated with broader effects of social trust and reciprocity (Putnam, 2000; Collins, 2005).

To summarize, the network of volunteers in a CSO appears to be a likely site for the creation and expression of social capital by virtue of the extent and nature of volunteer involvement there, the nature of executive volunteer board dynamics, and the broader culture of helping out. The narrow profile of sport volunteers suggests that the network may be characterized by bonding social capital. Regardless, trust, and reciprocity can be, and evidently are, (re)produced there, and are important to the CSO and to individual volunteers.

The community sport network of stakeholders

We turn now to a discussion of the nature of relationships in the CSO's network of stakeholders upon which it is dependent for certain valued resources. Although we refer to the CSO *network* of stakeholders, we are in fact using the term fairly loosely as our focus is on the CSO and its dyadic linkages rather than a more complete view of the connections between and among all actors in the community sport network. We acknowledge that interorganizational networks can be much more complex than the simplistic view we are taking here, with a potential multiplexity of ties (Stern, 1979); ties that may also be sources of social capital.

As noted earlier, CSOs may be involved with a number of different stakeholders with whom they have a direct, utilitarian relationship. CSOs establish linkages with other organizations and individuals in order to achieve their goals. These relationships may be an important means for CSOs to acquire needed resources, while providing a valued return for the stakeholder. CSO stakeholders include, for example, participants (and their parents), and such groups as facility providers, municipal government, sport governing bodies, corporate sponsors, media, and other community sport providers. The relationships are based on exchange; for example, the CSO needs participants to meet its mandate and justify its existence as a sport provider and participants (and their parents) are looking for a recreational or competitive programme; the CSO may need access to facilities to run its programmes and the municipality or a commercial venue needs to have people and programmes in its buildings and on its fields; and, the CSO may need the credibility and support of a higher-level sport governing body while that organization needs community level clubs to help with sport development.

There is evidently variation in the respective stakeholders' interests in the CSO (and vice versa), and in turn how important they (and the resources they provide) are to the CSO. Given that, we may expect that the character of the relationships varies as well. The nature of the linkages between the CSO and its various external stakeholders is central to our discussion of this network as a source of what is probably best described as linking social capital. The connections between various organizations involved in the delivery of sport and recreation at the community level and their external stakeholders have been the focus of several studies (e.g. Vail, 1993; Thibault & Harvey, 1997; Thibault et al., 1999; Frisby et al., 2004; Cousens et al., 2006; Tower et al., 2006; Barnes et al., 2007). These relationships are most frequently referred to as 'interorganizational linkages' or 'partnerships' in the literature, despite their often dramatically different nature. As a result, these terms are imprecisely defined (Lindsey, 2006).

Cousens et al. (2006) suggest that it is useful to examine the nature of these relationships according to Faulkner's (1995) continuum of ascending ties. Faulkner notes that interorganizational relationships vary by level of integration, which is a function of such factors as: the degree of interdependence of the two parties and the extent and type of resources that are exchanged or shared (e.g. goods, services, and/or information); the degree of cooperation and emotional investment in the relationship; and, the duration of the interactions and the relationship itself. Accordingly, interorganizational relationships range from basic market transactions or exchanges that require little investment of time or effort, to partnerships where people in the organizations work together to at least some extent to achieve their respective and often mutual goals, to further strategic alliances such as joint ventures, mergers, or acquisitions (see Figure 6.2). Each type of relationship reflects different objectives and outcomes for the organizations involved (e.g. simple economic exchanges, complex collaborative ventures). It is worth emphasizing here that each type of relationship is based on the degree of interaction between *people*. Thus, as further indicated in Figure 6.2, we can expect that social capital builds as a result of increasing integration within the network.

Given that the generation of social capital is dependent on meaningful and durable interaction, we may expect variation in the amount of social energy that is (re)produced in these different types of utilitarian relationships. Greenhalgh (2001) notes that partnerships and strategic alliances are consistent with increased commitment, trust, loyalty, shared expectations, and reciprocal access to resources; 'Being partners is very different from being conventional buyers and sellers. Partners

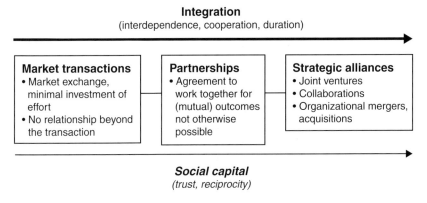

Figure 6.2
Organizational network relationships and social capital (Faulkner, 1995; Child & Faulkner, 1998)

feel like they are part of a common group. This gives them a sense of identity and common purpose' (Greenhalgh, 2001: 102). This phenomenon is consistent with the (re)production of social capital. Indeed, with reference to interorganizational relationships, Cousens et al. (2006: 49–50) note that, 'intangible capital … emerges when individuals develop collective understandings that facilitate continued, cohesive joint activities'. Again, interorganizational networks are consistent with the notion of linking social capital which results from the establishment of additional alliances with other organizations in order to access and leverage resources (Woolcock, 2001).

The sport literature is replete with recommendations for more 'partnership' vs. mere transactional types of relationships as a more effective form of linkage among sport stakeholders (e.g. Thibault & Harvey, 1997; Thibault et al., 1999; Cousens et al., 2006; Misener & Mason, 2006; Tower et al., 2006). Partnerships are advocated as a strategic way for sport providers, be they CSOs, municipalities or private facilities, to maintain and enhance sport delivery (Thibault & Harvey, 1997; Thibault et al., 1999; Cousens et al., 2006; Cuskelly et al., 2006; Barnes et al., 2007). For example, Tower et al. advocate a relationship marketing approach to partnerships in the community sport setting, where CSOs would focus on the interaction rather than just the transaction in a relationship, with the ultimate intent of building increased value for both partners. In turn, sport providers are aware of the need for increased integration with new or existing partners as a means to overcome resource scarcities (Allison, 2001; Cousens et al., 2006; Tower et al., 2006; Barnes et al., 2007).

Of course, not all stakeholder relationships will be partnerships; each relationship varies by its objectives and level of integration. Some may be a source of strategic resources, based on longer-term partnerships or alliances (e.g. CSO relationship with its provincial/state governing body), while others may be 'temporary remedies for resource scarcity' (Cousens et al., 2006: 33), such as short-term facility access arrangements. However, CSOs are cautioned against an over-reliance on the latter type of relationship (e.g. Allison, 2001), because they lack the integration, interdependence, and cooperation that are associated with greater continuity in and success of interorganizational linkages (e.g. Thibault & Harvey, 1997; Tower et al., 2006). While the focus of recommendations and strategies for effective CSO partnerships is the exchange of needed resources, it is likely that social capital will be engendered in these relationships as well. Furthermore, the trust and partnership created by a vibrant society of organizations that work in cooperation is important for creating a stable environment for broader business and economic growth (Jurbala, 2006). This, too, is consistent with the broader effects of linking social capital (Woolcock, 2001).

While there appears to be potential for the generation of social capital in and through the CSO network of stakeholders, evidence suggests the necessary type of relationship is not realized to any great extent in the sport system (e.g. Vail, 1993; Allison, 2001; Cousens et al., 2006; Tower et al., 2006; Barnes et al., 2007). In fact, in a study of CSOs in Scotland, Allison found that clubs operate quite autonomously; only about one-quarter even had links with such stakeholders as schools and other community organizations, while less than one-fifth had relationships with commercial companies such as corporate sponsors. The most common stakeholder organization with which the CSOs had links was sport governing bodies (85 per cent), followed by other sport clubs (50 per cent), and local government (41 per cent) (Allison, 2001). Given the dense and relatively closed network reflected in the narrow profile of sport volunteers, Collins and Nichols (2005: 123) wonder whether, the 'attitudes of stalwarts influence the willingness of clubs to accept external support'.

When considering the degree of CSO-stakeholder integration, Barnes et al. (2007: 566) found that actors involved in the Canadian sport system at large were characterized by 'a very loosely coupled sport system wherein the type of linkages binding organizations together, the frequency of interaction and the amount of resources shared were viewed as inadequate by its stakeholders'. More specifically, in a qualitative study of the nature of organizational linkages in sport and recreation delivery in two communities, Cousens et al. found that the sport provider and stakeholders referred to all interactions as partnerships, regardless of the degree of integration in the relationships. In fact, Cousens et al. concluded that the linkages they described were more like market transactions involving the exchange of financial or physical resources. Very few of the relationships involved long-term commitments beyond the original exchange transaction, and there was little effort towards formalizing partnerships with these or other organizations (Cousens et al., 2006). In one community, Cousens et al. found that 'partnerships' tended to be informal and based on long-time social ties. Similarly, Allison found that management practices in sport clubs, including interorganizational relations '[were] generally seen as a much more organic and intuitive process based on trust and experience rather than formal contracts' (2001: 78). While the social capital associated with these relationships can be very real and very positive, it may also be detrimental to an organization when formal processes are neglected, and there is an over-reliance on informal, personal relationships that cease to exist if personnel change; for example, the club president is a long-time friend of the school principal and access to the gyms is based on a handshake, an arrangement that may end immediately when either or both retire. Nevertheless, Adams and Deane (2005: 73) suggest that apparent CSO 'self-sufficiency suggests that deep-seated and sophisticated informal support systems operate at the level of community sport clubs'. The nature of these informal networks warrants further investigation to better understand the management of CSOs, external relationships, and social capital that may be associated with these linkages.

We turn now to a discussion of the nature of relationships between CSOs and particular stakeholders. In an early study, Vail (1993) noted that the links between schools and CSOs tend to be limited in their number and degree of cooperation. Rather than integrated, reciprocal partnerships there 'appears to be some duplication of programmes and services and little sharing of human and physical resources' (Vail, 1993: 25). Interestingly, Sharpe (2003) and Barnes et al. (2007) echoed these same sentiments 10–15 years later. In contrast, more effective linkages that are consistent with partnerships are more likely to exist between CSOs and municipalities, where they work together to achieve their unique and shared goals: 'Local organisations' access to municipal recreation facilities allows them to develop and promote their sport while municipalities benefit from the maximum use of their facilities by citizens' (Thibault & Harvey, 1997: 56). Nonetheless, in a study of CSOs in the UK, Adams and Deane (2005) found the relationships to be one-sided where the local (government) authority was much more strategic and proactive than the clubs. They noted a reluctance on the part of the club to get involved because of a concern – even a fear – of lost autonomy, lack of trust, and increased workload associated with such partnerships (Adams & Deane, 2005; also Sharpe, 2003). Similarly, in a qualitative study of sport facilities and local sport associations, Tower et al. (2006) found that participants representing these groups felt challenged to work more cooperatively together because of the power imbalance inherent with a shortage of facilities in a community. They also admitted that 'they did not always know what they should be doing in order to make the partnership work; they also did not focus their efforts [there]' (Tower et al., 2006: 178).

Corporate sponsors are another group of potential stakeholders in the CSO network, yet there is little or no published research on the nature and extent of these relationships. At the national sport organization level, there is evidence that even relatively small organizations are strategically pursuing and managing corporate partnerships or joint ventures (Doherty & Murray, 2007), although this is generally undertaken by paid staff. It may be safe to assume that corporate sponsorship makes up a very small proportion of revenues for most CSOs; nevertheless, this is one network where there is a particular demand for careful attention to meaningful, and accountable, partnerships (e.g. Thibault & Harvey, 1997; Misener & Paraschak, 2006; Doherty & Murray, 2007).

The CSO-sport governing body/government network has received some attention because of the increasingly formal relationships related to government funding (e.g. Nichols et al., 2003). Specifically, provincial/state and national sport governing bodies have become a government conduit for potentially major sources of CSO funding in several countries, with stringent expectations about the fulfillment of certain requirements in exchange for those funds; for example, club accreditation schemes, adherence to child protection legislation guidelines, and introduction of particular sport development programmes (Nichols et al., 2003). However, clubs perceive a power imbalance in this relationship, where funding is strictly tied to compliance with government-driven legislation and initiatives (Nichols et al., 2003). This may create a barrier to building interdependent, cooperative partnerships that are further characterized by trust and reciprocity. As sport is used as a government policy instrument in many countries, with funds channelled to the community sport level to serve government purposes, the relationships among key stakeholders in this particular community sport network, and the social capital that may be a byproduct of the relationships, merits further consideration.

Finally, a few studies have examined the relationship between CSOs and parents of participants. De Knop and colleagues (De Knop et al., 1998; De Knop et al., 1999) conclude that the nature of the relationship varies from no interaction (or a mere market transaction associated with registration), to 'thinking', and ultimately to 'acting (rendering services), and deciding (shared management)' (De Knop et al., 1999: 104). 'Acting' and 'deciding' are consistent with volunteering in the club and represent the likely more interactive and integrated involvement that was discussed earlier with respect to the CSO network of volunteers. At this level, parents are internal to the club and involved in its operations in some way. It is worth noting here that, although CSOs are very dependent on parents as volunteers (e.g. Doherty, 2005a), only a very small percentage of parents – De Knop et al. (1999) cite 12.2 per cent – are actively involved in their child's club. The 'thinking' involvement of parents who remain external stakeholders takes them beyond the simple transaction of registration to a heightened interest in what programmes and services the CSO offers, and how. While they may not be CSO partners according to Faulkner's (1995) definition, these individuals ask questions, demand answers, and generally try to stay on top of what is going on in, and around, the club. Sharpe (2003) cites the example of parents associated with one CSO who became increasingly concerned about, and in some cases intolerant of, the informality and increasing disorganization that characterized the management of this particular CSO. While she doesn't provide further insight into the specific nature of the dynamic between the CSO and parents, Sharpe does conclude that CSOs must take into account the perceptions of stakeholders, and particularly parents, who evaluate what the club is doing. We may speculate that social trust and reciprocity can be developed over time to the extent that the network is characterized by meaningful social interaction, including communication, cooperation, and even collaboration in support of each actor's goals and needs; for example, regarding such issues as registration fee levels, pre-season competition schedules, or the purchase of new uniforms. Participants, and their parents, may be considered CSOs' most important stakeholder – their raison d'etre – and thus further research into the nature of the relationships, including the (re)production of social capital, should be undertaken.

To recap, while there seems to be great potential, and need, for CSOs to link and develop more integrated partnerships with various stakeholders, this does not appear to be played out to any great extent in community sport so far. Thus, not only is the utilitarian basis of (potential) CSO stakeholder networks likely compromised (i.e. the exchange of valued resources), so too is the opportunity for linking social capital that accrues to, and through, CSO networks based on alliances with other groups and organizations. CSOs may be reluctant to engage in more integrated partnerships because of the time required to develop and maintain these types of linkages, when volunteers are already stretched in their day to day operations (Allison, 2001), and when CSOs need resources urgently. As well, with increased integration there is likely to be decreased autonomy for the club, a possible power imbalance, and even different levels of commitment which, rather than generating social trust and norms of reciprocity, engender caution, fear, and mistrust on the part of the club (e.g. Sharpe, 2003; Adams & Deane, 2005).

Concluding comments

The focus of this chapter has been social capital that is a function of the interpersonal relationships that may exist in more economic or utilitarian networks in the community sport setting; specifically, the network of CSO volunteers and the network of CSO stakeholders. These networks are fundamental to the successful delivery of community sport. A social capital perspective highlights the trust and norms of reciprocity and cooperation that may be an additional, non-material return on investment in the relationships among volunteers and between CSOs and their stakeholders (c.f. Bourdieu, 1986; Seippel, 2006). The more utilitarian or 'working' aspect of these relationships will likely always be the primary focus, however social capital may be a valued by-product (Bourdieu, 1986), with potential benefits for individuals (e.g. specific reciprocity), as well as for the group itself, other linkages, and the community at large (generalized reciprocity).

According to the literature reviewed here, CSO networks appear to be potential and actual sites for social capital and the social energy it engenders, although this phenomenon is currently more evident among volunteers than among the network of stakeholders that interact with the CSO. This variation may not be surprising given that the potential for social capital is dependent on personal or social interactions which may be inherently limited beyond the CSO, and may decrease over time as the relationship 'takes care of itself', requiring less direct involvement. According to Silverman (2004: 128), 'the durability of social capital decreases as personal relations become less regularised. As a result, the role of social capital is more pronounced in the internal operation of an organisation than it is in interorganisational networks.' Nevertheless, there appears to be potential for the development of (more) social capital among stakeholders, especially given the call for the cultivation of partnership types of relationships. However, several barriers and limitations to both CSO volunteer and stakeholder networks that, by extension, present challenges to the (re)production of social capital in and through these networks have been discussed.

In addition to providing some evidence of (the potential for), and limitations to, social capital in community sport networks, the chapter highlights the need for further insight into the social effects associated with these networks, and several areas for investigation have been noted. In particular, future research should examine the extent and nature of interactions among CSO volunteers, with a specific focus on the (re)production of social capital. In addition, any variation among the key groups of executive volunteers, coaches, and general volunteers should be explored, as we may expect some differences based on, for example, the extent and nature of their respective contributions. This will help expand our understanding of the working relationships within CSOs, and particularly their social effects. The impact of these effects (i.e. trust, reciprocity, cooperation) on individuals, the group, further CSO linkages, and the community at large should also be examined so that we may better understand the influence of social capital that is (re)produced among CSO volunteers. It would also be of interest to empirically examine bonding and bridging social capital in the community sport volunteer network (c.f. Coffe & Geys, 2007), to determine whether the network is more consistent with one form of social capital or the other, and whether that makes a difference in terms of impact on individual volunteers, and the group and CSO as a whole.

Future research should also focus on the extent and nature of interactions between CSOs and various stakeholders; again, with a specific focus on the (re)production of social capital. Further, any variation based on the stakeholder (e.g. schools vs. parents vs. sport governing bodies) and type of relationship (i.e. transaction vs. partnership vs. strategic alliance, vs. more informal linkages) should be explored. Existing literature indicates that CSO linkages with stakeholders are limited in number and degree of integration; thus, it would be useful to gain a further understanding of factors that limit these utilitarian relationships and, specifically, the potential for social capital.

There are implications for policy and practice that may be directed towards addressing the barriers and limitations to CSO networks that create challenges to social capital. Social capital appears to be associated with CSO volunteer networks, as indicated by the substantial involvement of volunteers, integration around group tasks, and a culture of helping out. Thus, to the extent that the narrow profile of sport volunteers is consistent with a dense and closed network that limits the involvement of a broader cross-section of society, and limits the broader effects of social capital, CSOs should be encouraged to expand their recruitment niche (Nichols & King, 1999) and open up to new social relations (Seippel, 2006). However, such a recommendation likely needs to be framed in the context of the utilitarian advantages for the CSO, in terms of helping it meet its goals. Thus, the intent is not necessarily to 'construct' social capital but rather to support the structure and mechanisms that engender social capital in the CSO volunteer network (c.f. Coalter, 2007). The benefits to the CSO include a more diverse task group, that is more representative of its community, and that may generate a wider variety of ideas and, as such, is more likely to help the organization with 'getting ahead' vs. just 'getting by' (Putnam, 2000; also Doherty & Chelladurai, 1999). The potential benefits to the community include the involvement of a wider cross-section of society, and generalized reciprocity that may be developed through CSO volunteer involvement.

In addition to policy and practice that highlight the utilitarian advantages of (more effective) interorganizational linkages in community sport (e.g. Thibault & Harvey, 1997; Cousens et al., 2006; Tower et al., 2006; Barnes et al., 2007), the benefits of social capital that may be associated with more integrated partnerships can also be emphasized. In fact, Cousens et al. (2006: 43) found that community sport stakeholders in their study did have 'a heightened awareness of the trust, commitment, loyalty, and time duration typically associated with enduring, mutually advantageous, collaborative relationships'. With a general understanding of the broad benefits, efforts should be further directed towards encouraging, educating, and assisting both CSOs and (prospective) stakeholders to develop these types of relationships, that must be manageable given the voluntary nature of CSOs, and that are not limited by power imbalances, mistrust, and varying commitment of the parties involved (c.f. Sharpe, 2003; Adams & Deane, 2005; Tower et al., 2006). The broader effects of linking social capital suggest that the trust and reciprocity that may be engendered through interorganizational linkages in the community sport setting can be expected to benefit the parties involved, and the community at large as that social energy contributes to the development of a connected society.

References

ABS (2002). *Involvement in Organised Sport and Physical Activity, Cat. No. 6285.0*. Canberra: Commonwealth of Australia.

Adams, A. & Deane, J. (2005). Local authorities' support networks for sport volunteers. In G. Nichols & M. Collins (Eds.), *Volunteers in Sports Clubs* (pp. 57–82). Eastbourne: LSA.

Allison, M. (2001). *Sports Clubs in Scotland*. Edinburgh: Sportscotland.

Barnes, M., Cousens, L. & MacLean, J. (2007). From silos to synergies: A network perspective of the Canadian sport system. *International Journal of Sport Management and Marketing*, 2(5/6), 555–571.

Body-Gendrot, S. & Gitell, M. (2003). *Social Capital and Social Citizenship*. Lanham, MD: Lexington Books.

Bourdieu, P. (1986). The forms of capital. In J.G. Richardson (Ed.), *Handbook of Theory and Research for the Sociology of Education* (pp. 241–258). Westport, CN: Greenwood Press.

Bowen, P. (2004). Investing in Canada: Fostering an Agenda for Citizen and Community Participation. Retrieved November 8, 2006 from http://www.sportmatters.ca.

Canadian Sport Centres (2005). *Long-Term Athlete Development – Canadian Sport for Life*. Vancouver, BC: Canadian Sport Centres.

Centre for Citizenship and Human Rights (2007). *Tracking What Works: Voluntary Activity, Community Strengthening and Local Government*. Melbourne: The Municipal Association of Victoria.

CFLRI [Canadian Fitness and Lifestyle Research Institute] (2005). *Local Opportunities for Physical Activity and Sport: Trends From 1999–2004*. Ottawa, ON: CFLRI.

Child, J. & Faulkner, D. (1998). *Strategies of Cooperation: Managing Alliances*. Oxford: Oxford University Press.

Clarkson, M.B.E. (1995). A stakeholder framework for analyzing and evaluating corporate social performance. *Academy of Management Review, 20*, 92–117.

Coalter, F. (2007). Sports clubs, social capital and social regeneration: 'Ill-defined interventions with hard to follow outcomes'. *Sport in Society, 10*(4), 537–559.

Coffe, H. & Geys, B. (2007). Toward an empirical characterization of bridging and bonding social capital. *Nonprofit and Voluntary Sector Quarterly, 36*(1), 121–139.

Collins, M. (2005). Voluntary sports clubs and social capital. In G. Nichols & M. Collins (Eds.), *Volunteers in Sports Clubs* (pp. 105–118). Eastbourne: LSA.

Collins, M. & Nichols, G. (2005). Summary – An emerging research agenda. In G. Nichols & M. Collins (Eds.), *Volunteers in Sports Clubs* (pp. 119–125). Eastbourne: LSA.

Cousens, L., Barnes, M., Stevens, J., Mallen, C. & Bradish, C. (2006). "Who's your partner? Who's your ally?" Exploring the characteristics of public, private, and voluntary recreation linkages. *Journal of Park and Recreation Administration, 24*(1), 32–55.

Cuskelly, G. (2004). Volunteer retention in community sport organizations. *European Sport Management Quarterly, 4*, 59–76.

Cuskelly, G., Hoye, R. & Auld, C. (2006). *Working with Volunteers in Sport: Theory and Practice*. London: Routledge.

De Knop, P., Buisman, A., De Haan, M., Van Iersel, B., Horvers, C. & Vloet, L. (1998). Parental participation in their children's sports club. *International Scientific Journal of Kinesiology and Sport, 30*, 5–13.

De Knop, P., De Martelaer, K., Van Heddegen, L. & Wylleman, P. (1999). Parents as volunteers in sports club. *European Journal for Sport Management* [Special Issue], 104–112.

Delaney, L. & Keaney, E. (2005). *Sport and Social Capital in the United Kingdom: Statistical Evidence from National and International Survey Data.* London: Institute for Public Policy Research.

Doherty, A. (2005a). *A Profile of Community Sport Volunteers.* Toronto: Parks and Recreation Ontario. Retrieved from http://www.prontario.org/PDF/reports/FinalReport_ExecutiveSummary_PhaseOne.pdf.

Doherty, A. (2005b). *Volunteer Management in Community Sport Clubs: A Study of Volunteers' Perceptions.* Toronto: Parks and Recreation Ontario. Retrieved from http://www.prontario.org/PDF/SportVolunteerPhseIIExecutiveSummary.pdf.

Doherty, A.J. & Carron, A.V. (2003). Cohesion in volunteer sport executive committees. *Journal of Sport Management, 17*(2), 116–141.

Doherty, A. & Chelladurai, P. (1999). Managing cultural diversity in sport organizations: A theoretical perspective. *Journal of Sport Management, 13,* 280–297.

Doherty, A. & Murray, M. (2007). The strategic sponsorship process in a non-profit sport organization. *Sport Marketing Quarterly, 16*(1), 49–59.

Doherty, A., Patterson, M. & Van Bussel, M. (2004). What do we expect? An examination of perceived committee norms in non-profit sport organizations. *Sport Management Review, 7*(2), 109–132.

Faulkner, D. (1995). *Strategic Alliances.* London: McGraw-Hill.

Field, J. (2003). *Social Capital.* London: Routledge.

Foley, M.W. & Edwards, B. (1998). Beyond Toqueville: Civil society and social capital in comparative perspective. *American Behavioral Scientist, 42*(1), 5–20.

Freeman, E.R. (1984). *Strategic Management: A Stakeholder Approach.* Marshfield, MA: Pitman.

Frisby, W., Thibault, L. & Kikulis, L. (2004). The organizational dynamics of under-managed partnerships in leisure service departments. *Leisure Studies, 23*(2), 109–126.

Greenhalgh, L. (2001). *Managing Strategic Relationships: The Key to Business Success.* New York: The Free Press.

Hall, M.H., de Wit, M.L., Lasby, D., McIver, D., Evers, T., Johnston, C., McAuley, J., Scott, K., Cucumel, G., Jolin, J., Nicol, R., Berdahl, L., Roach, R., Davies, I., Rowe, P., Frankel, S., Brock, K. & Murray, V. (2004). *Cornerstones of Community: Highlights of the National Survey of Nonprofit and Voluntary Organizations. Catalogue no. 61–533-XIE.* Ottawa: Statistics Canada.

Hall, M., Barr, C., Easwaramoorthy, M., Sokolowski, S. & Salamon, L. (2005). *The Canadian Nonprofit and Voluntary Sector in Comparative Perspective*. Toronto: Imagine Canada.

Harvey, J., Levesque, M. & Donnelly, P. (2007). Sport volunteerism and social capital. *Sociology of Sport Journal*, 24, 206–223.

Hoye, R. & Cuskelly, G. (2007). *Sport Governance*. Oxford: Elsevier.

Isham, J., Kolodinsky, J. & Kimberly, G. (2006). The effects of volunteering for nonprofit organizations on social capital formation: Evidence from a statewide survey. *Nonprofit and Voluntary Sector Quarterly*, 35(3), 367–383.

Jurbala, P. (2006). *Sport, the Voluntary Sector, and Canadian Identity*. Toronto: Community Active.

Lindsey, I. (2006). Local partnerships in the United Kingdom for the new opportunities for PE and Sport Programme: A policy network analysis. *European Sport Marketing Quarterly*, 6(2), 167–184.

LIRC [Leisure Industries Research Centre] (2003). *Sports Volunteering England 2002*. Sheffield: LIRC.

Misener, K. & Paraschak, V. (2006). Fundraising capacity in Canadian national sport organizations: Relationship-building and gender. *Third Sector Review [Special Issue: Sport and the Third Sector]*, 12(2), 41–61.

Misener, L. & Mason, D. (2006). Creating community networks: Can sporting events offer meaningful sources of social capital. *Managing Leisure*, 11, 39–56.

Nichols, G. & King, L. (1999). Redefining the recruitment niche for the Guide Association in the United Kingdom. *Leisure Sciences*, 21, 307–320.

Nichols, G., Taylor, P., James, M., King, L., Holmes, K. & Garrett, R. (2003). Pressures on sport volunteers arising from partnerships with the central government. *Society and Leisure*, 26, 419–428.

Pugh, D.S. & Hickson, D.J. (1989). *Writers on Organizations*. Newbury Park, CA: Sage Publications.

Putnam, R.D. (1995). Bowling alone: America's declining social capital. *Journal of Democracy*, 6, 65–78.

Putnam, R.D. (2000). *Bowling Alone: The Collapse and Revival of American Community*. New York: Simon and Schuster.

Seippel, O. (2006). Sport and social capital. *Acta Sociologica*, 49(2), 169–183.

Sharpe, E. (2003). 'Its not fun anymore:' A case study of organizing a contemporary grassroots recreation association. *Society and Leisure*, 26(2), 431–452.

Shibli, S., Taylor, P., Nichols, G., Gratton, C. & Kokolakakis, T. (1999). The characteristics of volunteers in UK sports clubs. *European Journal for Sport Management*, 1(Special Issue), 10–27.

Silverman, R.M. (2004). Community development corporations (CDCs) in the deep south: The interaction of social capital, community context, and organizational networks. In R.M. Silverman (Ed.), *Community-Based Organizations: The Intersection of Social Capital and Local Context in Contemporary Urban Society* (pp. 125–146). Detroit: Wayne State University Press.

Smith, D.H. (2000). *Grassroots Associations*. Thousand Oaks, CA: Sage.

Stern, R.N. (1979). The development of an interorganizational control network: The case of intercollegiate athletics. *Administrative Science Quarterly, 24*, 242–266.

Thibault, L., Frisby, W. & Kikulis, L. (1999). Interorganizational linkages in the delivery of local leisure services in Canada: Responding to economic, political, and social pressure. *Managing Leisure, 4*, 125–141.

Thibault, T. & Harvey, J. (1997). Fostering interorganizational linkages in the Canadian sport delivery system. *Journal of Sport Management, 11*, 45–68.

Tonts, M. (2005). Competitive sport and social capital in rural Australia. *Journal of Rural Studies, 21*, 137–149.

Tower, J., Jago, L. & Deery, M. (2006). Relationship marketing and partnerships in not-for-profit sport in Australia. *Sport Marketing Quarterly, 15*(3), 167–180.

Uslaner, E. (1999). Democracy and social capital. In M. Warren (Ed.), *Democracy and Trust* (pp. 121–150). Cambridge: Cambridge University Press.

Vail, S. (1993). Schools and community sport clubs: Are they on the same team? *CAHPER Journal, 49*(2), 22–25.

Welch, M. & Long, J. (2006). *Sports Clubs: Their Economic and Social Impact*. Leeds: CCPR.

Williamson, A. & Acheson, N. (2006). *Voluntary and Community Organizations and Their Potential to Contribute to Improved Community Relations*. Paper presented at the annual meeting of ARNOVA, November 16–18, Chicago.

Woolcock, M. (2001). The place of social capital in understanding social and economic outcomes. *ISUMA Canadian Journal of Policy Research, 2*(1), 11–17.

Voluntary sport clubs: The potential for the development of social capital

Chris Auld

Introduction

Sport is a central element and a prominent dimension of popular culture within many countries (Mewett, 1999; Kirk, 2000). The centrality of sport is evident in the saturation level of media coverage of sport, the making of heroes of sport champions, the high level of public funding for sport and the high salaries of elite athletes. Congruent with the prominence of elite and professional sport, there has been a continuing fascination by governments in many jurisdictions with the role of sport in delivering a wide range of social outcomes and benefits to communities (Coalter, 2007). Such benefits are frequently encapsulated within the term social capital. This is especially the case as communities face increasing pressures from global economic, social and cultural changes that some have argued are eroding traditional community life (Atherley, 2006). Middleton et al. (2005: 1711) argued that the absence of social capital 'is thought to be a key factor in neighbourhood decline'. While the potential for individuals to benefit from sport involvement is well documented, for many policymakers the more fundamental and important concern is with the potential for such benefits to be aggregated to the broader community or social level. Coffé and Geys (2007) indicated that interactions in voluntary organizations are assumed to have positive externalities on the community as a whole and as suggested by Long and Sanderson (2001: 187), there is a 'belief that benefits accrue beyond the individual in ways that support community development and regeneration'. Sport is thus frequently portrayed as an institution with a high degree of potential for social cohesiveness which contributes to community resilience (Cairnduff, 2001).

One of the reasons sport is perceived as having the potential to impact positively on communities is its broad appeal and high level of market penetration. For example, the Australian Bureau of Statistics (ABS, 2007) reported that nearly two-thirds (66 per cent or 10.5 million people) of Australians aged 15 years and over indicated that they had participated in sport and physical recreation at least once in 2005–2006. Males and females (both 66 per cent) exhibited similar participation rates. Furthermore, Australia has approximately 30,000 community level sports clubs (Cuskelly et al., 2006) and although the number participating in non-organized activities (8.6 million or 54 per cent) was almost double that for participation in organized activities (4.4 million or 28 per cent), the extent of involvement with voluntary sport associations is still significant. The number of voluntary sport clubs is complemented by a significant sport volunteer workforce. According to Cuskelly et al. (2006), the scale of sport volunteering in Australia is extensive with between 1.1 and 1.4 million people volunteering for sport organizations annually. Sport volunteer participation rates are similar internationally (5 per cent in Canada, 8–10 per cent in Australia and 5.1 per cent in England). Furthermore, in Australia around one-quarter of all volunteers are involved as sport volunteers and this figure is similar in England (26.5 per cent), Canada (18 per cent) and New Zealand (27 per cent). Consequently, numerous government agencies have based sport and recreation interventions on underlying (and somewhat comforting) assumptions that sport and recreation programmes have a positive impact on social and economic problems. Such a view is based on a traditional functionalist perspective. Pringle (2001) argued that a functionalist approach assumes that sport helps to contribute to social order and therefore, the strengthening of both elite and grass roots sport structures results in a more cohesive society.

However, despite a significant level of widespread support for the view that positive community outcomes are generated by sport, the actual evidence is sparse and/or lacking in rigour. This position is not new. For example, almost 20 years ago Glyptis (1989) argued that most sport and recreation programmes had been provided on the basis of both assumed need and benefit. Coalter and Allison (1996 cited in Coalter et al., 2000) later added that it was difficult to find evidence to substantiate claims that sport played a significant role in community development and much of the evidence tended to be anecdotal or based on short-term case studies. Furthermore, many policy-makers and sport management professionals seem to accept that it is axiomatic that sport produces positive individual and social benefits thereby rendering redundant any need for research in this area. Consequently, the dearth of evidence about sport outcomes may be related to the lack of willingness to rigorously address both the potential and actual results of community programmes. It is perhaps not coincidental, therefore, that Haywood (1995) argued that only sport providers with an educational emphasis have examined their underlying aims and conducted a public debate about them. On the other hand, recreation providers have largely been silent on this issue.

Taking this perspective even further, Pringle (2001: 63) argued that functionalist views of sport:

problematically romanticise the benefits of sport while tending to ignore how sport can act as a conservative force through supporting inequitable power relations and social divisions. Thus, although there may be evidence to support the existence of certain social benefits associated with high performance sport, functionalist justifications misrepresent sport as a panacea for a range of social ills while ignoring the possibility that all members of the community may not share equally in its benefits or costs.

Conceptualizing social capital

One of the problems facing those who seek a better understanding of the relationship between sport and social capital is despite its wide use, the concept is poorly conceptualized and operationalized (Harvey et al., 2007). Debate about social capital tends to be based on assertion rather than evidence (Middleton et al., 2005). Weisinger and Salipante (2005: 52) concluded that 'we seem to know surprisingly little about the formation of bridging social capital' and Tonts (2005) argued that social capital is not static and may vary across space and time. Furthermore, Middleton et al. (2005: 1712) reported the UK Office of National Statistics referring to the 'justifiable confusion' about the nature of social capital and also lamented that such a poorly defined concept 'has moved to the heart of neighbourhood regeneration'. Forrest and Kearns (2001) also expressed concerns about the indiscriminate application of the term social capital and more recently, Leonard (2004: 929) suggested that 'at the empirical level, social capital has been defined more by its absence than its presence'.

Despite these concerns, there have been many attempts to define social capital but they vary considerably and largely reflect the purposes of the different disciplines involved. Onyx and Bullen (1997: 23) suggested that social capital is about 'immediate and personal connections between people and events, rather than the more distant and formal relationship with government institutions and policy'. Social capital is 'the raw material of civic society' and community development at the grass roots level. The production of social capital requires 'dense, lateral networks involving voluntary engagement, trust, and mutual benefit' (Onyx & Bullen, 1997: 24). In less complex terms, Badcock (2002) suggested that social capital is the glue that helps communities stay together. In summary, social capital is considered to be the raw material that is the basis of community development. One definition of community development is the enhancement of the whole community and its citizens through social interaction, voluntary engagement and trust; purported to be the very seat of creation of further social capital (Onyx & Bullen, 1997).

Although social capital can be produced anywhere, its production is most commonly associated with the third sector of which sport is a significant component. Third sector organizations can act as vehicles for individuals to connect with each other and display behaviour that often (but not always) has elements of altruism and social responsibility associated with it. In the sport context, such involvement is usually manifested in the day-to-day (rather than periodic event-based) contributions of parents and other supporters who turn out each week to coach, administer, manage, maintain and promote grass roots community level sport. Badcock (2002) argued that social capital is formed by informal networks and community support mechanisms found in a range of settings, including school committees, resident associations and sporting clubs.

Sport and community benefits

Despite the contrary perspectives of Pringle and others outlined earlier, Coffé and Geys (2007: 121) argued the 'abundance of affirmative outcomes has incited a belief that social capital is a normatively positive thing'. According to a review by Long and Sanderson (2001), the most commonly claimed positive externalities arising from sport and recreation interventions include collective identity, increased cohesion, social integration and co-operation, and improving the capacity of the community. Other themes frequently identified in the literature include community image and pride, and social capital. These themes are synthesized and explored in the following sections.

Identity, integration and community cohesion

According to Badcock (2002: 177), most identities are not fixed but are 'fluid, many-faceted and interchangeable' and depend on the circumstances of a particular interaction (e.g. who with, time and place). In the sport setting, Cronin and Mayall (1998: 6) argued that the 'creation of identity through sport takes place at many different levels' and may include individual, local and regional, ethnic and national identity. They further elaborated that sport is a significant channel for the expression of a range of different types and levels of identity and that there was overwhelming evidence to support such an argument.

Heinemann (1993) argued that due to the integrating nature of sport, it had the potential to overcome the problematic context of identity formation resulting from the fragmentation of cultural identities and subsequent problems reconciling these with potential multiple roles (e.g. parent, partner, citizen, employee, neighbour). Furthermore, Figler and Whitaker (1995: 30) suggested that communities have 'come to rely on sports as a measure of our psychic stability' and subsequently perceive sports as rituals which alleviate anxieties and uncertainties. Figler and Whitaker (1995) presented a number of examples in which they indicated sport has played a vital role in the USA during times of crisis including the Kennedy and King assassinations and the 1989 San Francisco earthquake. They argued that the ritual of Sunday Football and World Series Baseball was 'preserved because a shaken nation needed the sense of stability' and assurance they provided (Figler & Whitaker, 1995: 30).

While sport has been advocated as an integrating force by some, others have suggested that this is not the case and this is especially so when sporting contests highlight ethnic and/or geographic-based rivalries. Weisinger and Salipante (2005) argued that a major concern for the overall voluntary sector was the extent to which associational activity either builds or erodes bridging social capital in interethnic contexts. Again, this is not a new issue. Arbena (1993) citing Luschen (1984) suggested that sport had the potential to assist with identity building and it could also lead to conflict. Arbena (1993: 156) argued that while there was evidence to support arguments that sport may help in diffusing social disputes, on the other hand sport may 'stimulate emotions that provoke social tensions'. Tonts (2005) found that there were varying patterns of ethnic participation in different sports with some sports seen as being a white only domain.

Sport and ethnic identity was also explored by Hay (1998, cited in Cronin & Mayall, 1998). Hay examined the role of soccer in assisting with the assimilation of Croatian migrants in Australia. Hay's research indicated that while the activities of the soccer clubs facilitated integration and reduced opportunities for conflict, conversely, the strengthening of the Croatian identity may have also impeded integration 'by the resultant enmity and distrust from other groups' (Cronin & Mayall, 1998: 8).

However, it also seems that sport can play a role in the 'more paradoxical, ambiguous and multi-layered aspects of identity' according to Cronin and Mayall (1998: 9). They argued that individuals can simultaneously have pride in a national sports team and hold an internationalist perspective or display a distinct ethnic identity through support of a particular sports team, but also seek to assimilate and lose their sense of separate identity. Madan (2000), who examined the relationship of World Series Cricket and Australian diasporic Indian identity, echoed this view. Madan (2000: 27) asserted that collective identity is related to 'blood, soil or language' and because diasporas can no further claim their nationalism through soil or in many cases, language, cricket provided the vehicle for expressions of their diasporic nationalism. However, such manifestations are 'not about desiring a return to the homeland or rejecting the country of citizenship' (Madan, 2000: 34). The power of sport to elicit strong diasporic nationalism is further supported by Werbner (1996: 104) who examined the Pakistani experience in Britain. After a Pakistani victory over England in cricket, a Pakistani born in Britain indicated that, while proud to be British, 'when it comes down to the hard core, I'm really Pakistani'.

Community image and pride

These types of benefits seem to mainly accrue through sporting success – the vicarious pleasure and pride of success by 'your' team or individuals that you may perceive to be part of your 'imagined' community. Bale (1993) cited in Rowe and McGuirk (1999: 135) suggested that sport can provide 'the major focus for collective identification' partly though stimulating a strong sense of place and thus reinforcing feelings of pride attached to a specific geographic locale. Such benefits are frequently cited as justifications for government investment in sport. However, Bale (2003) also later argued that some inappropriate manifestations of sport are essentially masculine celebrations of community, frequently involving strong local identification and also a vigorous tendency to denigrate opposing communities.

Rowe and McGuirk (1999: 125) asserted that 'having a successful sports team has been seen widely either to confirm the exalted status of a "boom" city or partially to compensate for that city's decline'. Furthermore, they suggested that in the USA, the 'winning and losing of sports franchises have a symbolic civic significance seemingly out of proportion to any strictly economic measure of their importance' (Rowe & McGuirk, 1999: 125). It may be that the 'inflated' importance of sports teams has something to do with the capability of the team to communicate and embody the city culture and geographic identity. As suggested by Rowe and McGuirk (1999: 126), urban centres try to secure:

sports mega-events in order to ... attract national and international media attention and signify the global status which it is believed accompanies the capacity to 'win' and successfully stage a complex (post) modern sports spectacle. Sport then continually grows in importance as a social institution, which, in various urban sites, is believed

capable of: … promoting the image or 'brand identity' of the city, especially through the deployment of an appealing homology between the
notions of the sports team qua city representative symbol, and of host
city qua successful sports team; functioning as a locus of community
affect and identity which, among other articulations, reproduces the
concept of spatially constructed identity.

Swindell and Rosentraub (1998: 6) indicated that 'the potential for intangible benefits from (sport) teams cannot be …
dismissed in a cavalier fashion by the academic community'.
Their research focused on the outcomes accruing to a community from the presence of sports franchises and events and
involved a survey of 1500 residents of Indianapolis. Swindell
and Rosentraub (1998: 7) found that sports teams are 'clearly
critical in establishing a sense of pride' and a sports event
(the Indianapolis 500) was ranked highest in determining the
area's reputation. Similarly, Rowe and McGuirk (1999: 137)
concluded after their analysis of the impact of sporting success on the City of Newcastle (Australia) that 'it is apparent
that sport's impact on civic "brand identity" and community
affect is not inconsiderable'. Furthermore, Wann et al. (2001: 181)
argued that sport events can 'help combat the pernicious
effects of apathy and the cessation of motivation, a condition
that can prove fatal to any social system'.

Swindell and Rosentraub (1998) also found that while residents enjoyed substantial positive externalities from the presence of sport franchises in Indianapolis, there were different
patterns between residents in terms of the extent to which civic
pride was generated. These differences were attributed to frequency of attendance and visitation to the sports events. Quirk
and Fort (1992) argued that increases in civic pride may accrue
to 'non-fans' as also suggested by the findings of Swindell
and Rosentraub (1998). Quirk and Fort concluded, after citing
extensive economic evidence, that the most important benefit
provided by the stadiums and teams is the common identification symbol especially associated with a successful team –
the team brings the city together. This conclusion was later
echoed by Rowe and McGuirk (1999) and in a rural context
by Tonts (2005). Quirk and Fort (1992) further suggested that
although difficult to quantify, this does not mean these types
of benefits for communities do not exist. It is likely that such
benefits are the real justification for the large subsidies paid to
sports teams rather than the more mundane and also difficult
to measure expenditure benefits.

However, despite the level of support for positive community
outcomes, some writers have suggested that such benefits are

usually short term and may be somewhat illusory. For example, Klein (1984 cited in Pringle, 2001: 63) argued that 'the sense of unity ... does not help individuals from diverse ethnic or religious backgrounds, negotiate better long-term social relationships or change wealth-gaps between people' and the feel-good factor 'is of little real value in helping to create a more equitable society'. Furthermore, Coakley (1994: 364–365) argued that such positive feelings provide only 'momentary relief' and the 'unity associated with sports almost never gets converted into collective action that might transform society and make it more democratic and economically fair'.

Social capital

Despite a lack of conceptual and empirical clarity and the concerns expressed by a number of observers, it appears to be well accepted by policymakers that sport can contribute to a sense of community and a sense of place, mainly through its potential to build social capital. Middleton et al. (2005) argued that social cohesion occurs informally through interactions between friends and neighbours and also more formally through local organizations. An often aired view (Putnam, 1995; Badcock, 2002) is that in recent times, the focus on individual rights and self-reliance has resulted in the loss of social capital with a consequential reduction in community cohesion. Furthermore, Putnam has argued that secondary and tertiary networks (e.g. sports fans) do not provide effective opportunities to build social capital. In a contrasting view, Wann et al. (2001: 187) suggested that Putnam's dismissal of the possibility of sports fandom contributing to social capital 'was perhaps a hasty judgment on his part'. Wann et al. (2001) also argued that at least in America, social capital may be moving into a new form as Americans turn to less intimate and more public locations to connect with each other. This development has been influenced by such factors as urbanization, technology, individualism and geographic mobility which have reduced opportunities for traditional forms of sociability. Wann et al. (2001) subsequently argued that through sport events, fans are aware of each other and share a quasi-intimacy and social connectedness.

A further argument that sport has the potential to play a significant role in the development of social capital is the extent to which personal leisure occurs via interactions with other people. A significant proportion of leisure takes place in a social context with family and friends and frequently reported motivations for engagement in sport are socializing and social interaction. Iso-Ahola (1980) argued that social interaction is a strong and unambiguous leisure motive, is a leading reason for engagement in leisure and concluded that 'social interaction is the main ingredient' in leisure (Iso-Ahola 1980: 7). Auld and Case (1997) also argued that social motives in leisure were prominent and this finding was later reinforced in the specific sport context by Tonts (2005). A study of the quality of life of 571 residents of Brisbane (Australia) found that leisure satisfaction and participation were significant predictors of perceived quality of life (Lloyd, 2000). Lloyd suggested that it was the role of social leisure in integrating people into new groups and networks through which shared symbols and identities were created that contributed to its importance. It seems therefore that sport and other leisure participation is 'frequently a context for social integration and for activity that brings us together in common activity that fosters communication and intimacy' (Kelly, 1987: 37). Kelly's research indicated that leisure was important for social integration. It therefore seems that sport can provide the context which develops stronger social bonds through shared symbols and identity as well as common goals, purposes and a sense of actualization, all of which may be important conditions for promoting social capital.

On the other hand, the actual evidence to support these views is sparse and, in addition, conflicting evidence also exists. Long and Sanderson (2001: 195) in a study of Directors of Leisure Services in the UK suggested that enhanced social cohesion was not a 'necessary consequence' of sport and quoted one respondent as saying:

I can give plenty of examples (of social integration), but then there are plenty of examples when they just go home afterwards. ... I suppose sport can be really good just as sport can be really bad.

Furthermore, after conducting a case study of rugby union in New Zealand, Pringle (2001: 70) concluded that rather than enhancing social cohesion, some sporting events 'achieve quite the opposite'. This view reinforces the earlier work of Argyle (1996) who argued that positive in-group attitudes are often accompanied by negative attitudes to the out-group. Argyle found that amongst a range of leisure groups (e.g. social, sporting, musical, religious), sporting groups were much less likely to express a high degree of acceptance of out-groups. Coffé and Geys (2007) also argued that there are no guarantees that social capital will produce positive externalities on society. In contrast to Argyle, their research found that different types of voluntary organizations demonstrated varying levels and types of social capital. Hobby clubs, arts activities, sport associations and humanitarian associations (e.g. Red Cross) were more likely to exhibit bridging social capital whereas retiree associations, women's groups and youth organizations were among the most bonding groups.

The nature of social capital

Often missing in these assertions about the potential for sport to build social capital and community capacity is a rigorous examination of the nature and quality of any social capital that may result. A number of authors have argued that many community-based organizations tend to produce bonding as opposed to bridging or linking social capital (Putnam, 2000; Dekker & Uslaner, 2001; Paxton, 2002; Wollebaek & Selle, 2002; Seippel, 2006). Furthermore, this is seen as problematic because in simple terms the 'bonding form of social capital is exclusive, whereas the bridging form is more inclusive' (Weisinger & Salipante, 2005: 33) and importantly, that this distinction focuses directly on the issues of similarity and difference. However, Coffé and Geys (2007) suggested that any theoretical distinction between bonding and bridging social capital remained underdeveloped.

Despite these concerns most observers agree that bonding social capital occurs amongst homogenous groups, is often parochial and only benefits those with internal access to the groups (Leonard, 2004). Weisinger and Salipante (2005) further argued that bonding social capital relies on strong ties within groups with similar backgrounds that work against weaker bridging ties. On the other hand, bridging social capital results from relationships and ties between heterogeneous groups. Such groups have members from a cross-section of society involving, for example, different religions, ethnicities and income levels. These individuals may not normally be affiliated apart from their interaction through the organization. Such social connections are more likely to deliver linkages that are more outward looking and made up of individuals from a broad array of social backgrounds. Thus individuals connected through bridging capital have the potential for a wider range of interactions and subsequently enhanced opportunities for broader community engagement (Frank & Yasumoto, 1998; Paxton, 1999). Bridging social capital can thus assist communities to build capacity and resilience in the face of dynamic and rapid change. However, Weisinger and Salipante (2005) argued that the presence of bridging ties will not produce bridging social capital unless the social ties engender mutual respect and the maintenance of tangible ties.

There is also a third type of social capital, identified as linking social capital. It consists of vertical bonds between less affluent individuals and those with more powerful positions – usually in formal organizations (Middleton et al., 2005). Indeed, one of the important attributes of sport organizations is their potential to bring together people from different vertical strata of the community. However, the potential beneficial impact of local sport clubs on linking social capital production could be diluted by those clubs that develop as 'defensive communities' (Coalter, 2007) with memberships that reflect relatively homogenous groupings (e.g. by income and occupation).

Coffé and Geys (2007) argued that bonding and bridging social capital are not mutually exclusive but rather are dimensions along which the different forms of social capital can be compared. Nonetheless, there is a perception that organizations can move from one to the other and according to Leonard (2004: 928):

The notion that social capital can be potentially converted into other forms has greatly appealed to policy makers anxious for quick-fix solutions ... without a corresponding focus on the complexity of the 'certain conditions' under which such a process become possible. This has led to an emphasis on building or rebuilding social capital in disadvantageous areas.

Weisinger and Salipante (2005) further argued that even when significant opportunity and motivation are present, a lack of shared experiences and relevant skills can constrain the production of bridging social capital. Despite the focus on sport and the intuitive and widely held comforting sense that it must be good for communities, it is not axiomatic that social capital results from the actions of community organizations or indeed that social capital always has positive impacts on communities. On the other hand, such organizations may actually have deleterious impacts on their members and those with whom they interact, especially in the context of inner and outer groups.

Social capital and local sport clubs

As indicated earlier, the 'associational nature of sports participation (and particularly sporting clubs) is sometimes seen as a forum for the creation of social capital' (Tonts, 2005: 139).

However, it is also apparent that although sport has the potential to develop social capital in local communities, the nature of the social capital produced is the key to the extent to which this process realizes positive outcomes for communities. Tonts (2005) argued that there is evidence that sport helps to develop both bonding and bridging social capital. Citing Harris (1998) he indicates that sport can facilitate new friendships that cut across social boundaries and this process extends beyond players to include non-participants such as parents, officials, coaches and spectators. The local sport club context is an obvious site for this process to occur. However, Tonts also cautioned against romanticising the role of sport.

According to Middleton et al. (2005) social capital may be divided among different sub-communities within local areas who subsequently may perceive each other as rivals or threats competing for limited resources (e.g. members). There is little doubt that such tensions frequently exist between different sports clubs. Coffé and Geys (2007: 132) argued that membership of voluntary associations does not necessarily produce positive externalities for the community and refer, as do other authors, to the 'dark side' of social capital. Summarizing material from a number of sources they suggested that most individuals receive most of their social support through bonding ties and that such ties may create in-group bias that can consequently foster out-group hostility. Coffé and Geys (2007: 124) concluded that:

inward-looking social relations may … generate an us-versus-them way of thinking in which a group develops strong social connections and levels of generalized trust among its members but generally distinguishes itself from other groups or even avoid or distrust members from these other groups.

The result is that clubs may be unwelcoming of those that exhibit some type of difference to the dominant group (Tonts, 2005) and there is a real danger that many local sports clubs typify (and may even encourage) such practices. Tonts (2005) further argued that in some areas in rural Australia, sport participation was sharply divided based on class, ethnicity and status. Furthermore, Paxton (2002) found that sport (as well as religious and union) organizations typically had lower levels of external connections than did other types of voluntary associations such as human rights and environmental associations. Demonstrating this viewpoint, Taylor and Toohey (2001) argued that to improve cultural diversity, Australian sport had to change the way it was structured. They stressed that 'sport providers need to open their doors to all members of the community and actively encourage inclusive practices, rather than just acting as passive purveyors of sport' (Taylor & Toohey, 2001: 212). This approach is reinforced by Coffé and Geys (2007) who suggested that establishing links between dissimilar groups can help generate an identity that both diminishes in-group bias and encourages inclusion of former out-group members. Similarly, Weisinger and Salipante (2005) added that social capital resides in social networks rather than individuals and thus the practices and norms of voluntary associations related to interpersonal interactions are critical to whether within that organization bridging social capital was likely to be eroded or created.

Leonard (2004) suggested that social capital is not benign and people can be excluded as well as included in networks. Weisinger and Salipante (2005: 30) argued that 'it is well known that much associational activity is exclusionary'. While many have advocated that the answer to concerns about the potential exclusivity of bonding social capital is the development of bridging and linking social capital, this view is not universally shared. For example, Leonard (2004) argued that for bridging social capital to emerge, the conditions supporting bonding social capital will be undermined and even by doing so does not ensure the development of social capital. The 'fragile' (Tonts, 2005) nature of social capital is illustrated by Coleman (in Middleton et al., 2005) who argued that social capital was transitory and could be adversely affected by rising affluence and public policy intervention. If this is the case, then as suggested by Middleton et al. (2005), it raises questions about the sustainability of social capital created by the interventions of policymakers.

Middleton et al. (2005) also found that social capital was linked to economic capital. Local sports clubs may have restricted potential to ameliorate this relationship. For example, it costs money to join a club and other costs such as equipment and clothing are also normally incurred. In addition, participation usually requires expenditure on transport and sometimes entry and court fees. Middleton et al. added that the expectation of reciprocity was a further cost barrier to participation. Some individuals will not be able to reciprocate. For example, if someone buys a round of drinks others may consequently avoid this type of interaction, thus reducing the opportunity for interactions to take place. Local sports clubs should be cognizant that while costs may not exclude participation, they may act as a barrier.

Given these constraints and the potentially problematic process of shifting from the production of bonding to bridging social capital, how then might local sports clubs modify their actions and cultures to ensure they have the potential to do so? As discussed earlier, sport seems well positioned to have an impact on social capital production given the extent of its broad appeal and levels of involvement. Furthermore, sport is typically perceived as involving social ties that are typically bridging in nature albeit given the qualifiers raised previously (Coffé & Geys, 2007). One key opportunity for sport clubs is that bridging social capital may be developed as a by-product of the organizational mission. Weisinger and Salipante (2005) in a study of the racial composition of Girl Scout troops found that bridging social capital is likely to be insufficient to sustain interactions between diverse members. They therefore suggested that voluntary organizations should initially rely on bonding social capital to increase diversity and then actively 'structure mission-relevant interactions among diverse members to create bridging social capital, and sustain pluralistic diversity' (Weisinger & Salipante, 2005: 29).

Using the earlier work of Adler and Kwon (2002) Weisinger and Salipante (2005: 34) argued that voluntary associations require three elements to be present before social capital can be produced:

1. Opportunity – a network of social ties creates the opportunity for social capital to be developed.
2. Motivation – actors must be motivated to use their social ties to produce collective activity.
3. Ability – actors must have the 'collective ability to leverage social ties towards purposeful action'.

While it appears that the local sport club context is not an unlikely source of both opportunity and perhaps to a lesser extent motivation, it is not clear that these resources are matched by ability. This statement is not aimed at sport volunteers but rather at a sport system increasingly under pressure to deliver more social outcomes. As suggested above, the production of social capital and even more so, a shift from the production of bonding to bridging social capital is not automatic and frequently requires sustained and targeted effort. Unfortunately, policymakers continue to place further expectations on an already stretched voluntary sector which is under increasing pressure from changing levels of volunteer commitment, the perceived time squeeze, increasing professionalized expectations, and escalating compliance, standards and accountability requirements.

Conclusion

One dominant issue in the social capital literature is the lack of conceptual and empirical clarity regarding the meaning and outcomes of social capital. This situation is exacerbated by the dearth of strong evidence about both the production and impacts of social capital generally and also more specifically in the sport setting. This agenda still has some considerable way to move forward considering comments by Glyptis (1989) almost 20 years ago in which she argued that any claims for the community benefits of sport were rarely supported by appropriate evidence. It should also be noted however that there is generally a similar lack of strong evidence to support some of the neutral or negative views concerning the links between sport and social capital.

While there is some empirical evidence available that is very positive about the community benefits of sport supposedly generated through the development of social capital, many of the claims are anecdotal in nature, based on self-reported data, small and non-representative samples and/or involve short-term context specific case studies. This situation is changing however and recent work by Coalter (2007), Harvey et al. (2007) and also Atherley (2006) and Tonts (2005) in the Australian rural context are encouraging examples of more rigorous and systematic examinations of the relationships between sport and social capital. Furthermore, much of the literature reflects traditional male sports and male involvement in sport, including that of spectators, and there is also a bias in the data towards westernized sporting cultures. Despite the research shortcomings, however, a large number of sport management professionals, policymakers and academics are quick to generalize about the assumed universal benefits of sport. This is a fundamental problem and tends to promulgate the assumed intuitive assumptions about the 'public good' nature of sport via the production of social capital. Just as many of the strongly proclaimed economic benefits of sport have been demonstrated to be frequently exaggerated, there is a danger that without rigorous research input into policy and programme decisions, the promise of social capital will also prove to be equally nebulous.

Having said that, however, it is interesting to reflect on what communities would be like without local sport programmes. It is argued that given the generally positive perceptions about sport and its contributions to the community, most observers and residents would feel that community life would suffer in the absence of local sport clubs. Perhaps then the generally optimistic position adopted by decision makers, but frequently criticized as naïve and uniformed by some commentators, is not an unrealistic strategy. However, this view does not suggest the need for rigorous scholarship can be ignored. Policymakers, without overselling the merits of sport, should continue to support carefully planned and professionally led sports programmes while at the same time, encouraging and funding the research that is much needed in this area.

As indicated above, it seems evident that despite a considerable level of available literature, the amount, level and sophistication of the actual evidence contained therein are somewhat lacking. It is suggested that one reason for this may be the overall positive dispositions towards sport of those working in the field and their advocacy of its beneficial role in the lives of individuals and communities. Perhaps one reason for people being motivated to work in the sports industry may be because they inherently believe in the fundamental 'goodness' of sport. If this is the case it may be that they do not feel there is a need for strong evidence because the benefits of sport are 'obvious' for all to see, especially when they personally observe these in practice in a small number of specific situations or individual cases. Support for this viewpoint is provided by Long and Sanderson (2001: 193) who, in their study of Leisure Directors in the UK, indicated that some respondents 'took offence that we were questioning these claimed benefits'. If so, the profession should not be so defensive, begin to openly reassess this issue and willingly confront the challenge of developing and disseminating the appropriate evidence to build a case based on empirical evidence rather than emotive assertion.

However, it is incumbent on researchers, policymakers and sport programme delivery personnel to remind ourselves of the context in which we work. While it seems there can be instrumental community benefits from sport, the intrinsic outcomes should not be discounted, that is, the justification of sport as an end in itself. Therefore, perhaps government can and should reinforce this message as a justification for its investment and the programmes ensuing from this investment. The literature clearly suggests that under the right conditions, the enjoyment derived by both participants and spectators, and indeed to volunteers, may be one of the most important community benefits provided by sport. Consistent with this view, Gratton and Taylor (1991: 193) suggested that it is 'the inability of the government agencies involved in sport to specify clearly what it is they are trying to provide that is the major element of government failure in the market for sport in the recent past.' There is no substantial evidence to suggest that this situation has changed. Subsequently, there also needs to be more rigorous and well-informed policy support for local sport clubs that is cognizant of their specific milieu (e.g. the increasing pressures on the voluntary sector and how this may impact on their capacity to deliver social outcomes) and which reflects realistic expectations about the role of sport in the production of social capital.

As suggested above, there are numerous issues related to the social capital and sport relationship that should prove to be potentially very fruitful avenues for future research initiatives. Research evidence needs to influence the views of policymakers so that they become more sophisticated and analytical in their approach and move beyond the 'natural' outcome assumptions underpinning much public policy debate in this area.

A central issue in the Australian context is the role of volunteer sport organizations in the creation of social capital in rural and regional communities. This is especially the case as these communities are under particular stress from rural restructuring with many communities facing declining populations with concomitant pressures on community vibrancy and resilience. Therefore researchers could focus on how the internal dynamics, policies and actions of voluntary sport organizations influence community capacity building through the production and maintenance of both bonding and bridging social capital. The interactions between these different types of social capital should also be investigated as well as to the extent they have differential impacts on marginality and exclusion, and whether the social capital produced in sport clubs resonates in the wider community.

While it is often assumed that the social capital is a natural outcome from community engagement in sport, as suggested by Weisinger and Salipante (2005) three antecedents are required. While opportunity and motivation are more likely to be relatively easy building blocks to establish, a more challenging issue for local sports clubs is one of ability. While many volunteers are committed and work hard and long hours, the specific problems facing contemporary communities and the associated pressures on the voluntary sector require more than this. Researchers may also want to focus their attention on the means by which the skill and ability capacities of voluntary sport clubs can be developed in order that these organizations have enhanced potential to contribute to social capital. For example, do different type of sport and sport club cultures produce different types and levels of social capital and further, is there a relationship between club cultures and the potential of sport clubs to shift between bonding and bridging social capital production?

Finally, given the increasing externally driven pressures on local sport clubs, a further research agenda could investigate the links between changing patterns of volunteer participation (e.g. sustained vs. short term/episodic; core vs. peripheral volunteering) and the nature and fragility of social capital. This may be especially crucial for rural and regional communities.

References

Arbena, J.L. (1993). International aspects of sport in Latin America. In E.G. Dunning, J.A. Maguire & R.E. Pearton (Eds.), *The Sports Process: A Comparative and Developmental Approach* (pp. 151–167). Champaign: Human Kinetics.

Argyle, M. (1996). *Social Psychology of Leisure*. London: Penguin.

Auld, C.J. & Case, A.J. (1997). Social exchange processes in leisure and non-leisure settings: A review and exploratory investigation. *Journal of Leisure Research*, 29(2), 183–200.

Atherley, K.M. (2006). Sport, localism and social capital in rural Western Australia. *Geographical Research*, 44(4), 348–360.

Australian Bureau of Statistics (2007). *Sports and Physical Recreation: A Statistical Overview, Australia, 2007*, Edition 1, Cat no. 4156.0. Canberra: Commonwealth of Australia.

Badcock, B. (2002). *Making Sense of Cities: A Geographical Survey*. London: Arnold.

Bale, J. (1993). *Sport, Space and the City*. London: Routledge.

Bale, J. (2003). *Sports Geography* (2nd edition). London: Routledge.

Cairnduff, S. (2001). *Sport and Recreation for Indigenous Youth in the Northern Territory*. Canberra: Australian Sports Commission.

Coakley, J.J. (1994). *Sport in Society: Issues and Controversies*. St Louis: Mosby.

Coalter, F. (2007). Sports clubs, social capital and social regeneration: 'Ill-defined interventions with hard to follow outcomes'. *Sport in Society*, 10(4), 537–559.

Coalter, F., Allison, M. & Taylor, J. (2000). *The Role of Sport in Regenerating Deprived Urban Areas*. Edinburgh: The Scottish Office Central Research Unit.

Cronin, M. & Mayall, D. (1998). *Sporting Nationalisms: Identity, Ethnicity, Immigration and Assimilation*. London: Frank Cass Publishers.

Coffé, H. & Geys, B. (2007). Toward an empirical characterization of bridging and bonding social capital. *Nonprofit and Voluntary Sector Quarterly*, 36(1), 121–139.

Cuskelly, G., Hoye, R. & Auld, C.J. (2006). *Working with Sport Volunteers: Theory and Practice*. London: Routledge.

Dekker, P. & Uslaner, E. (2001). Introduction. In P. Dekker & E. Uslaner (Eds.), *Social Capital and Participation in Everyday Life* (pp. 1–8). London: Routledge.

Figler, S.K. & Whitaker, G. (1995). *Sport and Play in American Life: A Textbook in the Sociology of Sport*. Madison, WI: Brown & Benchmark.

Forrest, R. & Kearns, A. (2001). Social cohesion, social capital and neighbourhood. *Urban Studies*, *38*(12), 2125–2143.

Frank, K.A. & Yasumoto, J.Y. (1998). Linking action to social structure within a system: Social capital within and between subgroups. *American Journal of Sociology*, *104*, 642–686.

Glyptis, S. (1989). *Leisure and Unemployment*. Milton Keynes: Open University Press.

Gratton, C. & Taylor, P. (1991). *Government and the Economics of Sport*. Harlow: Longman.

Harvey, J., Levesque, M. & Donnelly, P. (2007). Sport voluntarism and social capital. *Sociology of Sport Journal*, *24*, 206–223.

Haywood, L. (1995). Community sports and physical recreation. In L. Haywood (Ed.), *Community Leisure and Recreation*. Oxford: Butterworth-Heinemann.

Heinemann, K. (1993). Sport in developing countries. In E.G. Dunning, J.A. Maguire & R.E. Pearton (Eds.), *The Sports Process: A Comparative and Developmental Approach* (pp. 139–150). Champaign: Human Kinetics.

Iso-Ahola, S.E. (1980). *The Social Psychology of Leisure and Recreation*. Dubuque, IA: Wm C. Brown.

Kelly, J.R. (1987). How they play in Peoria: Models of adult leisure. In G.A. Fine (Ed.), *Meaningful Play, Playful Meaning* (pp. 35–44). Champaign: Human Kinetics.

Kirk, D. (2000). Gender association: Sport, state schools and Australian culture. In J.A. Mangan & J. Nauright (Eds.), *Sport in Australian Society* (pp. 49–64). London: Frank Cass Publishers.

Leonard, M. (2004). Bonding and bridging social capital: Reflections from Belfast. *Sociology*, *38*(5), 927–944.

Lloyd, K. (2000). *The Relationship Between Place-Centred and Person-Centred Leisure Attributes and Quality of Life, unpublished Doctoral Dissertation*. Griffith University, Brisbane.

Long, J. & Sanderson, I. (2001). The social benefits of sport: Where's the proof?. In C. Gratton & I. Henry (Eds.), *Sport in the City: The Role of Sport in Economic and Social Regeneration* (pp. 187–203). London: Routledge.

Madan, M. (2000). 'It's not just cricket!' World series cricket: Race, nation, and diasporic Indian identity. *Journal of Sport and Social Issues*, *24*(1), 24–35.

Mewett, P.G. (1999). Fragments of a composite identity: Aspects of Australian nationalism in a sports setting. *The Australian Journal of Anthropology, 10*(3), 357–375.

Middleton, A., Murie, A. & Groves, R. (2005). Social capital and neighbourhoods that work. *Urban Studies, 42*(10), 1711–1738.

Onyx, J. & Bullen, P. (1997). *Measuring Social Capital in Five Communities in NSW: An Analysis.* Centre for Australian Community Organisations and Management (CACOM) Working Paper Series No. 41. Sydney University of Technology.

Paxton, P. (1999). Is social capital declining in the United States? A multiple indicator assessment. *American Journal of Sociology, 105*, 88–127.

Paxton, P. (2002). Social capital and democracy: A cross-national study. *American Sociological Review, 67*, 254–277.

Pringle, R. (2001). Examining the justifications for government investment in high performance sport: A critical review essay. *Annals of Leisure Research, 4*, 58–75.

Putnam, R.D. (1995). Bowling alone: America's declining social capital. *Journal of Democracy, 6*(1), 65–78.

Putnam, R. (2000). *Bowling Alone: The Collapse and Revival of American Community.* New York: Simon & Schuster.

Quirk, J. & Fort, R.D. (1992). *Pay Dirt: The Business of Professional Team Sports.* Princeton, NJ: Princeton University Press.

Rowe, D. & McGuirk, P. (1999). Drunk for three weeks: Sporting success and city image. *International Review for the Sociology of Sport, 34*(2), 125–141.

Seippel, Ø. (2006). Sport and social capital. *Acta Sociologica, 49*(2), 169–183.

Swindell, D. & Rosentraub, M.S. (1998). Who benefits from the presence of professional sports teams? The implications for public funding of stadiums and arenas. *Public Administration Review, 58*(1), 11–20.

Taylor, T. & Toohey, K. (2001). Sport and cultural diversity: Why are women being left out?. In C. Gratton & I. Henry (Eds.), *Sport in the City: The Role of Sport in Economic and Social Regeneration* (pp. 204–213). London: Routledge.

Tonts, M. (2005). Competitive sport and social capital in rural Australia. *Journal of Rural Studies, 21*, 137–149.

Wann, D.L., Melnick, M.J., Russell, G.W. & Pease, D.G. (2001). *Sport Fans: The Psychology and Social Impact of Spectators.* New York: Routledge.

Weisinger, J.Y. & Salipante, P.F. (2005). A grounded theory for building ethnically bridging social capital in voluntary organizations. *Nonprofit and Voluntary Sector Quarterly, 34*(1), 29–55.

Werbner, P. (1996). 'Our blood is green': Cricket, identity and social empowerment among British Pakistanis. In J. MacClancy (Ed.), *Sport, Identity and Ethnicity* (pp. 87–111). Oxford: Berg.

Wollebaek, D. & Selle, P. (2002). Does participation in voluntary associations contribute to social capital? The impact of intensity, scope and type. *Nonprofit and Voluntary Sector Quarterly, 31*(1), 32–61.

Community sport/recreation members and social capital measures in Sweden and Australia

Kevin M. Brown

Introduction

To what extent are sport and social capital linked and in which ways? While this area is arguably under researched at present, there have been indications that such an association may be negative. For example, some of my previous work has pointed to the apparent propensity for bonding but not bridging forms of social capital in Australian community sport organizations (Brown, 2006a, b). This chapter initially extends those analyses theoretically by revisiting Putnam's discussion of tolerance and social capital (Putnam, 2000: 355) and develops from this an argument that points to the potential importance of the concept of active citizenship. Analysis of data from a recent study of comparative active citizenship is then presented through an assessment of samples of community organization members in the cities of Lund (Sweden) and Ballarat (Australia). The results present a more optimistic picture of community sport/ recreation members in comparison to members of a range of other community organizations on measures of trust, tolerance and civic activity, and it is concluded that some previous studies need to be reconsidered in the light of these findings.

Though the idea of the importance of civic activity/engagement can be traced back to the Athenian city state (Held, 1987: 17–19; Burchell, 2002: 90), current usage is strongly linked to Putnam's (1993, 2000) popularized (in academic, political and policy circles) and highly influential work on social capital in which he uses a range of social indicators to argue that there has been a decline in social participation from the 1960s to the present day across a wide range of activities. He shows decline in 'thick' (within-group) and 'thin' (generalized across-group) trust, horizontal ties, religious attendance and a wide range of group memberships. Putnam regards this as a decline in social capital and while his data relate to the USA, the general thesis is by extension applicable to all western societies. Stone (2000, 2001) illustrates the dominant broad definition of social capital as: 'networks of social relations characterised by norms of trust and reciprocity' (Stone, 2000: 10, 2001). Likewise, the Organization for Economic Co-operation and Development (OECD) use: 'networks together with shared norms, values and understandings that facilitate co-operation within or among groups' (OECD, 2001: 41). Social capital has been applied at small group to national scales and key discussions have centred on questions of measurement (how to) and causality (to what extent do high levels of social capital promote trust and mutuality and to what extent is social capital produced by interactions based in trust and mutuality?). Generally speaking, the term has developed to encompass the constituents of generalized reciprocity and involvement in social networks (Coleman, 1988, 1990; Fukuyama, 1995; Paxton, 1999; Onyx & Bullen, 2000; Szreter, 2002; Begum, 2003).

Clearly, social capital requires citizens to be active network participants. If social capital relates to the cumulative networking/cementing effects for society as a whole that result from the sustenance of generalized reciprocity, then active citizenship is perhaps best seen as (a crucial) part of the building blocks of that reciprocal system. Simply put, without active citizens engaged in a whole range of give and take relations, the conditions for social capital accumulation could not exist (Powell & Edwards, 2002; Cattell, 2004). While activity per se has not received primary focus in Putnam's work, more attention has been paid to the potential and limits of activity in political and policy debates. The development of the concept under British Conservative governments of the 1980s was part of a populist push which ultimately relied on the idea of talented and successful citizens showing others the way forward and acting as role models (Ignatieff, 1989; Flint, 2002: 251–252). Since its embrace by New Labour, active citizenship has been broadened in constituency to describe all manner of things voluntary, particularly those involving partnership participation of all kinds (Dahrendorf, 2001; Marinetto, 2003). Turner's development of the passive/active division as part of his reformulation of Marshall's theory of citizenship arguably provides a stronger theoretical framework within which social capital can be understood (Turner, 1992, 1993). In particular, Turner stresses that active forms of citizenship are produced from 'below' by active political agents (Turner, 1992: 40–47, 1993: 9). To date, however, thoroughgoing theoretical analyses of these kinds have not generally been forthcoming within the literature on active citizenship with some exceptions such as Janoski and Gran (2002).

Putnam's earlier work (Putnam, 1993) has been criticized on at least three grounds: firstly that he under-stresses the capacity of social capital to create 'inward looking' social capital networks whether they be the Ku Klux Klan or the Okalahoma bombers (e.g. Paxton, 1999); secondly, that Putnam fails to consider that (in the USA at least) the period of social capital decline has been accompanied by increasing tolerance and decreasing social equality thereby raising the possibility that social capital may be associated negatively with the former and positively with the latter; and thirdly that social capital as a concept shares a measure of the romanticization often attached to earlier constructions of community (Levi, 1996: 51–52;

Leonard, 2004: 929) leading Putnam to regard it as prima fascia, a social good, the glue of society which binds together otherwise disparate individuals and groups. Certainly, Putnam's strong focus on social solidarity links his work to the long tradition of pluralism, de Toqueville's focus on the democratic potential of civic membership and the role of intermediary groups in countering possessive individualism (Brown et al., 2000: 44–47).

Putnam attempted to address these critiques in *Bowling Alone* (Putnam, 2000). His perceived over-emphasis on social solidarity is here tempered by the inclusion of the concepts of bonding and bridging social capital. In addition, Putnam reasserts that social capital can be positively associated with both tolerance and equality. He devotes a chapter to the 'dark side' of social capital and develops a typology (Putnam, 2000: 355) of societies based on levels of social capital and tolerance. Given this emphasis on tolerance as a key constituent in understanding social organization, it is worth looking directly at his typology here (see Figure 8.1).

Taking into account the concepts of bonding and bridging social capital developed by Gittell and Vidal (1998: 8) and applied by Woolcock and Narayan (2000), Putnam's typology suggests that of the four ideal types, only 'civic community' can be considered positive. Both 'anarchic' and 'sectarian community' types represent perceived regressive features of bonding social capital (this is a development from the earlier notion of 'thick' trust). Here, high levels of bonding social capital combine with intolerance of 'others' to produce potentially regressive social milieus where strong in-group identification precludes forms of bridging social capital (which rely on levels of generalized trust and tolerance of difference typically found in relations of shared collective activity) in an inward turning dynamic. The 'individualistic' and 'civic community' types represent the dominance of bridging social capital and for Putnam, the typology's importance lies in the suggestion

	Low social capital	*High social capital*
High tolerance	'Individualistic' [You do your thing and I'll do mine]	'Civic community' [Salem without 'witches']
Low tolerance	'Anarchic' [War of all against all]	'Sectarian community' [Salem with 'witches']

Figure 8.1
Types of society. Adapted from Putnam (2000: 355)

that 'civic community' with high social capital and tolerance is theoretically possible. Though Putnam's typology is explicitly set at a societal level, this could equally apply at the level of organizations seen as aggregates of their members' standing on social capital and tolerance measures. The possibly caricatured view of a highly bonded sport organization membership focused on inward rather than outward links would in this scheme fit the type of 'sectarian community'.

While the recognition of the 'dark side' of social capital represents an advance on his earlier work, problematic issues remain. In particular, while Putnam's discussion of tolerance focuses attention on the fact that social capital production relies on activity to create conditions of enhanced trust and democratic practices, his argument is not wholly satisfactory. He bases his claim that tolerance and social capital are associated on the assumption that more active individuals possess heightened qualities of tolerance: 'social joiners and civic activists are as a rule *more* tolerant of dissent … than social isolates are' (Putnam, 2000: 355) and: '… individuals who are more engaged with their communities are generally *more* tolerant than their stay-at-home neighbors' (Putnam, 2000: 355). This optimistically assumes an underlying gravitational pull towards the light side of social capital. His argument does slip at times to the acknowledgement that: '… not all studies have found a positive correlation [between social capital and tolerance] but none have found negative' (Putnam, 2000: 496). The existence of such a link therefore remains an empirical question. Nevertheless, measures of (relative) tolerance, civic activity, trust and connectedness remain potentially useful tools in assessing whether differences exist between members of different types of community organizations including sport and relating this back to the question of social capital. Putnam's additional argument that the US experience since the 1960s can be partly attributed to generational change (in which post-baby boomers are no more tolerant than their preceding generation) merely begs the question of what forces determine this surface pattern? (Putnam, 2000: 356–357). Putnam backs his claims about civic activists being more tolerant partly by reference to US State scores on tolerance and social capital indices (SCI) (Putnam, 2000: 355–356). This shows a positive relationship between social capital and tolerance on a state basis but it should be noted that this is a general SCI and not an activity index per se. The SCI includes attitudes and state statistical measures on voter turnout, organizations per 1000 population, etc. as well as activity components. The composite nature of the SCI may in fact serve to artificially inflate social

capital differences between states by counting higher potentials and actualities in the same index. For example, it is easier
to be a member and attend meetings in states where organizations are greater in number. In addition, see Rotolo and Wilson
(2004) who demonstrate that longitudinal data fail to support
Putnam's thesis of generational change.

Community sport/recreation

I have argued elsewhere that the relatively large incidence
of sport/recreation organization members has not been
accompanied by a corresponding level of attention within
sociological and third sector literature (Brown, 2006a). There
are signs that this situation is being addressed and two main
themes can be identified in the discussions so far: the most
dominant of these comprises work that draws connections
between inequality in general and sport participation in particular. Keogh (2002: 2) cites Australian Bureau of Statistics (ABS)
from 2001 that show persons born in Australia to have more
than double the participation rate in sport than those born
overseas (27–10 per cent). Lareau (2003) indicates the ways
in which middle-class North American parents use their children's participation in sport to deepen class and race advantages. Other studies have noted that sport participation and
attendance is positively correlated with education, occupation
and other socio-economic status (SES) measures (Lascu et al.,
1995; White & Wilson, 1999; Scheerder et al., 2002: 232, 2005).
In addition, the tendency for sport per se to help maintain or
deepen social divisions has been noted. Cashman (1995: 208)
refers to Australian sporting culture as racist and sexist and
Harris (1998: 146) refers to the masculinist nature of much
sport. Burdsey and Chappell (2003) and Bairner (2003) discuss
how sport in Northern Ireland and Scotland has contributed
to nationalism through the construction of us/them divisions
and the development of ideas of outsiders. Similarly, Rowe
(2003) argues that sport encourages strong forms of inward
looking identification. Jarvie explicitly contrasts the communitarian view of sport with the potential for social disconnec-
tion inherent in increasing individualism and notes that some
sports or aspects of sport (he gives the example of golf) have
reproduced exclusivity and privilege (Jarvie, 2003: 146).

The second theme focuses rather on the potential of community sport to cultivate forms of social cohesion. Cunningham
and Beneforti (2005) discuss this in a policy related context
of the potential benefits to health and education that sport

participation may bring to indigenous communities in the Northern Territory, Australia. Both Arai and Pedler (2003: 187) and Jarvie (2003) consider favourably the communitarian view of community sport as having the potential to promote social inclusion and increase the *common good*. Harris (1998) notes the possible correspondence between sport teamwork and stronger collective communities and Smith and Ingham (2003: 259) compare the artificiality of imposed professional sport in a US case study to the more authentic community drivers of 'civic rituals'. Ultimately, these arguments are based within social capital and community studies debates.

Analysis of data from the 2003 Australian Survey of Social Attitudes [AuSSA] (Gibson et al., 2004) indicated that it was the first of these two themes that best described sport/recreation membership (Brown, 2006a, b). In terms of social capital measures sport/recreation members scored below average across a range of community organizations and were grouped with religious organizations in a low trust, low civic activity classification (Brown, 2006b). While the survey data confirmed the numerical importance of sport/recreation membership in Australia, it also showed that sport/recreation members were underrepresented in those born outside Australia and the main English-speaking countries, women and metropolitan area residents (Brown, 2006a: 26). It concluded that it was likely that the activities of sport/recreation members were geared towards inward looking social capital activities rather than wider bridging relationships outside their groupings (Brown, 2006a: 33–34). However problems of measurement were noted in the AuSSA data. In particular, the conflation of sport/recreation and social club memberships was likely to create inaccuracies when attempting to study community sport/recreation members per se (Brown, 2006a: 34).

The comparative active citizenship research project

An opportunity to revisit some of these issues arose in the analysis of data from a larger project funded by the Australian Research Council that looked at comparative active citizenship in six countries: '*Comparative Dimensions of Active Citizenship: An Analysis of Indicators of Inclusivity and Exclusivity in Civil society*' (Chief Investigators – S. Kenny, K.M. Brown, J. Onyx and T. Burke). The method was a comparative cross-sectional random sample survey design of members of community organizations in Australia, Russia, Spain, Sweden, the Netherlands and the UK. The study was delimited by drawing third sector organization databases from two locations in each country and then sampling from those frames. The first level of stratification was by country. The second level was by location to identify one larger and one smaller town/city (by population). Specifically: one larger city/ town (60 000–130 000 population) per country. This town had to be a non-capital city (national, or state) and have a mixed economy: one smaller (hinterland) town (5000–10 000 population) per country. This town had not to be dominated by a single major industrial, service or tourism base. Purposive sampling was used at stages one and two. A listing of all community organizations in each location was attempted using available sources. Twenty community organizations in the larger towns and 10 organizations in the smaller towns were randomly selected within a third level of stratification to ensure that the following areas of organizational focus would be represented in the sample: youth/education; health/welfare; arts/culture; sports/ recreation; human and social rights and displaying a mix of the following functions: member serving; public serving and service delivery. The 11 locations were: Australia (Ballarat and Blayney); Russia (Mytischi); Spain (Logrono and Sabinanigo); Sweden (Lund and Tomelilla); the Netherlands (Warmond and Zwolle) and the UK (Norwich and Downham Market). Self-administration questionnaires were distributed to members of each organization in the final samples. The questionnaire measured a mix of social capital items including three dimensions of trust: 'generalized trust' using the standard measure as used in the World Values Surveys [variable V27], *Generally speaking, would you say that most people can be trusted or that you can't be too careful in dealing with people? 1. Can't be too careful. 2. Most people can be trusted* (Inglehart et al., 1999); 'trust of neighbours' and 'trust of government. A civic activity scale was also computed comprising answers to questions about how frequently respondents: contacted their local council about community issues; were participants in community programs; had joined local actions to defend services and did favours for their neighbours. A summary indicator of tolerance was also included through a question measuring attitudes (agreement or disagreement) towards refugees' rights to access resources (*Refugees to Britain/Sweden should have access to society's resources equal to that of British/Swedish citizens*). This design was supplemented by qualitative interviews with community organization workers and members in all sites in order to achieve a level of triangulation (see Devine & Roberts, 2003). In focusing here on possible differences between sport/recreation group members and other community organization members, the two locations with the largest samples have been chosen (Lund, Sweden and Ballarat, Australia). This ensures the samples are large enough to allow basic statistical tests of significance. Across the 11 locations, sport/recreation members varied as a proportion of the total sample from 3 per cent (Zwolle, $n = 2$) to 28 per cent (Lund, $n = 71$). There were 188 respondents (all locations) classified as members of sport/recreation organizations which was 12.6 per cent of the total combined sample. The analysis presented here was not part of the original research design that instead focused on the measurement of comparative active citizenship patterns using location as the smallest aggregated level (e.g. see Brown, 2006c). Respondents self-defined the organization to which they belonged in terms of its major focus of activity (arts/culture, health/welfare, human rights, social rights, sport/recreation and youth/education). A strength is that this likely alleviates the problem of conflating sport and social club memberships noted above in relation to previous Australian studies (Brown 2006a, b). However, the data provided no indication of the types of sport/recreation organization in terms of their specific sport/activity or whether they were involved in active/passive or competitive/non-competitive pursuits.

Lund

Lund (population 102 000) is a regional city in southern Sweden. Six hundred kilometres south of Stockholm and 250 kilometres from Gothenburg, it is geographically closer to the Danish capital Copenhagen (35 kilometres). The Lund sample comprised 252 respondents connected to organizations involved with activities concerned with sport/recreation (28 per cent, $n = 71$), arts/culture (20 per cent, $n = 50$), health/welfare (19 per cent, $n = 48$), youth/education (18 per cent, $n = 46$), social rights (8 per cent, $n = 21$) and human rights (3 per cent, $n = 7$).

Over 70 per cent of the sample were in the middle aged and 65 plus categories and a small proportion (10 per cent) were aged under 25 years, mostly students. Just over half of the sample lived in couple families and a similar proportion was in paid work. Education attainment was relatively high with over 60 per cent having a university degree. This is a close match to the population of Lund in which 64 per cent of the population aged between 20 and 64 years have completed university education. Over 90 per cent were involved with the community organization as a member or volunteer, just over half were involved in the organization's decision-making processes and almost all had been involved with another community organization in the past.

Women made up 60 per cent ($n = 146$) of the Lund sample. The median age range was 45–64 years and 42 per cent ($n = 104$) of respondents were aged in this category. Sixty per cent (148) of the sample lived in couple families, one-third of them (19 per cent, $n = 47$) with dependent children, with the next largest group people living alone (28 per cent, $n = 70$). Over half the Lund sample was employed with 39 per cent ($n = 97$) in full-time work and 15 per cent ($n = 37$) in part-time or casual work. Another 30 per cent of the sample ($n = 75$) were retired or pensioned. There was a majority of students among the 13 per cent ($n = 32$) who gave their employment status as 'other'. A relatively high proportion of the Lund respondents (62 per cent, $n = 153$) had completed a university degree. Half (53 per cent, $n = 131$) of all respondents were members of the organization they completed the survey through and another 38 per cent ($n = 94$) were unpaid workers with the organization. Fifty-five per cent ($n = 136$) were involved in the decision-making processes of the organization. Over two-thirds (70 per cent, $n = 174$) were currently involved in one or more other community organizations and 80 per cent ($n = 199$) had been involved with another organization in the past.

Ballarat

Ballarat (population 65 000) is the second largest regional centre in the state of Victoria, Australia, 110 kilometres north-west of the state capital, Melbourne. The Ballarat sample comprised 394 people involved in organizations concerned with a range of activities specified as: youth/education (31 per cent, $n = 121$), health/welfare (22 per cent, $n = 86$), arts/culture (19 per cent, $n = 76$), sports/recreation (10 per cent, $n = 39$), human rights (7 per cent, $n = 29$) and social rights (6 per cent, $n = 25$).

The Ballarat sample was characterized by a high ratio of women to men, predominantly middle-aged home owners in full- or part-time employment with just under half having university qualifications. Just over half the sample was connected to their organization as a volunteer or member and a relatively large proportion (73 per cent) were involved with at least one other community organization. Past connection to organizations was also high at 88 per cent. Two-thirds were involved in decision-making in their organization.

The Ballarat sample had the highest proportion of women to men of all the location samples (76 per cent female). The median age category was 45–64 years old (41 per cent). Ballarat's other age categories were 25–44 years (31 per cent), 65 and over (18 per cent) and under 24 years (10 per cent). Main household types were: related adults (which include the situation of parents living with an adult child or children, 26 per cent); couples with dependent children (23 per cent); living alone (20 per cent) and couples with no children (17 per cent). Sole parents with dependent children made up 6 per cent of the sample. The modal housing tenure was owner-occupier (51 per cent) with an additional 32 per cent owning with a mortgage. Private rental was 14 per cent and public housing 1 per cent. Forty-one per cent were full-time employees, 29 per cent, part-time or casual, 22 per cent retired/pensioners, 4 per cent carer/home duties and 2 per cent unemployed. While secondary school (30 per cent) was the modal category for highest education level completed, the spread was fairly even across other categories: trade/diploma (21 per cent); university degree (26 per cent) and postgraduate qualification (22 per cent). The connection to the organizations was as follows: full- or part-time worker (34 per cent); member (30 per cent); volunteer (24 per cent) and manager (7 per cent). Sixty-seven per cent ($n = 258$) were part of the decision-making process in their organization, 73 per cent (285) were also involved in at least one other community organization and 88 per cent ($n = 342$) had been connected to another community organization in the past.

The correlational data yielded several significant associations at weak to moderate levels. Across locations and organizational types, level of education was significantly positively related to expressed connection to neighbours ($r = 0.222$, $p < 0.01$), civic activity ($r = 0.181$, $p < 0.01$), tolerance ($r = 0.145$, $p < 0.01$) and generalized trust ($r = 0.117$, $p < 0.01$). Of the other potential independent variables, gender indicated that women were significantly associated with trust for neighbours ($r = -0.135$, $p < 0.05$) and connection with neighbours ($r = -0.104$, $p < 0.01$), while age was significantly negatively associated with both connection with neighbours ($r = -0.222$, $p < 0.01$) and civic activity ($r = -0.128$, $p < 0.01$). The data confirm the assumed nexus discussed above between generalized trust and trust for neighbours ($r = 0.194$, $p < 0.01$) and government ($r = 0.114$, $p < 0.01$). As well, generalized trust was positively associated with both civic activity ($r = 0.181$, $p < 0.01$) and tolerance ($r = 0.145$, $p < 0.01$). The data support Putnam's assumption indicating that civic activity was positively associated with tolerance ($r = 0.176$, $p < 0.01$).

Table 8.1 Zero-order correlations for pooled data: all community organization members, Lund and Ballarat ($n = 605$)

Variables	1	2	3	4	5	6	7	8	9
1. Gender	—								
2. Age	−0.080*	—							
3. Education	−0.026	−0.030	—						
4. Trust general	−0.063	−0.002	0.117**	—					
5. Trust neighbors	−0.135*	0.060	−0.058	0.194**	—				
6. Trust government	−0.065	0.036	0.014	0.114**	−0.229**	—			
7. Connect neighbour	−0.104**	−0.207**	0.222**	0.259**	0.029	−0.042	—		
8. Civic activity	−0.052	−0.128**	0.181**	0.170**	0.128**	−0.141**	0.198**	—	
9. Tolerance	−0.059	−0.037	0.145**	0.182**	0.056	0.022	0.174**	0.176**	—
M								3.54	3.60
SD								1.82	1.30

*$p < 0.05$. **$p < 0.01$.

Coding key for variables used in zero-order correlations

1. Gender 1 = Female 2 = Male

2. Age 1 = <45 years 2 = 45 years and older

3. Education 1 = Trade/diploma and below 2 = Completed university

4. Trust general These days you can't trust most people.
1 = Strongly agree, 2 = Agree, 3 = Unsure, 4 = Disagree, 5 = Strongly disagree

5. Trust neighbours Do you trust your neighbours to act in your best interest?
1 = No not at all, 2 = No, 3 = Unsure, 4 = Yes, 5 = Yes definitely

6. Trust government Do you trust government officials to act in your best interest?
1 = No not at all, 2 = No, 3 = Unsure, 4 = Yes, 5 = Yes definitely

7. Connect neighbour A good neighbour is someone who always minds their own business.
1 = Strongly disagree, 2 = Disagree, 3 = Unsure, 4 = Agree, 5 = Strongly agree

8. Activity Scale (range = 1–8) lo = less active hi = more active

9. Tolerance Refugees to this country should have access to the full set of rights as all other citizens
1 = Strongly disagree, 2 = Disagree, 3 = Unsure, 4 = Agree, 5 = Strongly agree

Sport/recreation and other organizations compared by location

To test the proposition that members of sport/recreation organizations may score differently to other group members on the range of social capital measures discussed above, the sample was collapsed into members of sport/recreation organizations and members of all other organizations combined. This meant combining the following organizational types into the 'other group' category: human rights; social rights; youth/education; health/welfare and arts/culture. Table 8.2 and Table 8.3 show the comparison in mean scores for the two groups in Lund and Ballarat.

The results for Lund and Ballarat were similar. In both samples, sports/recreation members scored higher on social capital measures than other group members combined with the exception of the civic activity scale and neighbour connection in Lund. In summary, Ballarat sport/recreation scored more highly than the combined other group members on the key measures of generalized trust, tolerance and civic activity while in Lund the same was true in relation to the first two measures of generalized trust and tolerance.

Independent samples t-tests were conducted to test the significance of these differences in mean scores on the social capital measures for sports/recreation (SR) and other group (OG) members. In Lund there was a significant difference in scores for the groups on the measures:

- connection to neighbours
  (SR = 4.02, SD = 0.92, OG = 3.51, SD = 1.17;
  $t[164.610^*] = 3.61, p = 0.000$);
- tolerance
  (SR = 4.09, SD = 1.07, OG = 3.66, SD = 1.32;
  $t[155.817^*] = 2.6, p = 0.01$);
- government trust
  (SR = 2.73, SD = 0.88, OG = 2.43, SD = 0.93;
  $t[240] = 2.37, p = 0.018$).

*Equal variances not assumed.

In Ballarat there was a significant difference in scores on the measures:

- neighbour trust
  (SR = 3.67, SD = 1.06, OG = 3.22, SD = 1.14;
  $t[369] = 2.36, p = 0.019$);
- government trust
  (SR = 2.51, SD = 1.00, OG = 2.19, SD = 1.01;
  $t[368] = 1.96, p = 0.05$).

Table 8.2 Type of organization member by social capital measures, Lund ($n \leqslant 252$)

Lund		Generalized trust	Connection to neighbours	Civic Activity Scale	Tolerance	Do you trust government officials to act in your best interest?	Do you trust your neighbours to act in your best interest?
Sports/recreation	Mean	3.27	4.02	3.04	4.09	2.73	2.41
	N	71	71	68	70	71	71
	Standard deviation	1.08	0.92	1.59	1.07	0.88	1.10
Other groups	Mean	3.08	3.51	3.14	3.66	2.43	2.44
	N	172	172	167	172	171	171
	Standard deviation	1.05	1.17	1.75	1.32	0.93	1.05
Total	Mean	3.14	3.66	3.11	3.79	2.52	2.43
	N	243	243	235	242	242	242
	Standard deviation	1.06	1.12	1.70	1.26	0.92	1.06

Table 8.3 Type of organization member by social capital measures, Ballarat ($n \leqslant 394$)

Ballarat		Generalized trust	Connection to neighbours	Civic Activity Scale	Tolerance	Do you trust government officials to act in your best interest?	Do you trust your neighbours to act in your best interest?
Sports/recreation	Mean	3.50	3.90	4.28	3.76	2.51	3.67
	N	38	38	39	38	39	39
	Standard deviation	1.18	1.23	1.73	1.30	1.00	1.06
Other groups	Mean	3.49	3.57	3.81	3.47	2.19	3.22
	N	335	336	329	333	331	332
	Standard deviation	1.18	1.15	1.81	1.33	1.01	1.14
Total	Mean	3.49	3.59	3.86	3.50	2.22	3.26
	N	373	374	368	371	370	371
	Standard deviation	1.18	1.16	1.81	1.32	1.02	1.13

Therefore in both locations sport/recreation members scored significantly higher on some of the social capital measures and on the remaining measures there was no significant difference between the groups. Possible multivariate effects deserve consideration but the data were not wholly suitable for multiple regression due mainly to considerations of sample size (Tabachnick & Fidell, 2001: 117). The data may also present a problem of singularity if the three variations of trust measurement were to be used in the model.

From the combined zero order correlations shown in Table 8.1, level of education had significant positive associations with connection to neighbours ($r = 0.222$, $p < 0.01$), civic activity ($r = 0.181$, $p < 0.01$), tolerance ($r = 0.145$, $p < 0.01$) and generalized trust $r = 0.117$, $p < 0.01$). In Lund, more sport/recreation members had completed university education (79 per cent) than members of other groups (66 per cent). The significant difference found in the Lund sample between the two groups of members on tolerance may therefore have been partly a function of this differential. However in Ballarat, the proportion of university educated members is equal between the two groups and so education cannot have had a separate effect on the social capital scores of sports/recreation members and members of other groups.

Table 8.1 also illustrates that gender was significantly associated with trust for neighbours ($r = -0.135$, $p < 0.05$) and connection with neighbours ($r = -0.104$, $p < 0.01$) with women more likely to score positively on these measures. There was a small percentage difference in Lund between sport/recreation members and other members in terms of women (+6 per cent) and this may have affected the significant difference found between the two groups on connection with neighbours. Ballarat had a larger difference in gender balance (sport/recreation members containing 9 per cent more women).

Age was significantly negatively associated with both connection with neighbours ($r = -0.222$, $p < 0.01$) and civic activity ($r = -0.128$, $p < 0.01$). In the Lund sample, there were small percentage differences in the youngest and oldest age categories between groups with sport/recreation members having 4 per cent more members aged under 25 years and 8 per cent more members aged over 65 years. This is likely to have only small effects on the social capital scores by groups. In Ballarat, however, the age profiles between sport/recreation members and members of other groups were more differentiated with other group members having 43 per cent under 44 years compared to 18 per cent of sport/recreation members.

This is likely to effect measured group scores on connection with neighbours and civic activity but in a direction favoring measured higher scores on those indicators for members of other groups.

Discussion and conclusion

Following discussion of Putnam's treatment of tolerance and social capital, a mix of indicators measuring aspects of trust, connectedness, civic activity and tolerance was outlined as a potentially useful instrument for measuring broad aspects of comparative social capital. This analysis of the data from Lund and Ballarat shows that for both samples, members of sport/recreation organizations compared to all other types of community organization members scored significantly higher on some social capital measures. In addition they were not significantly different on the remaining measures. In Lund, the significantly higher scores for sport/recreation members were found on measures of connection to neighbours, tolerance and government trust. In Ballarat significant differences in this direction related to the measures of neighbour trust and government trust. Though a full multivariate analysis was not considered due to sample size restrictions, scrutiny of the distributions of the potentially important independent variables of gender, age and education suggested that at the very least, there was no measurable significant difference between sport/recreation organization members and members of other community organizations in either location on social capital measures.

In light of this, some previous work may need to be qualified. In particular, analyses using AuSSA data may be questioned given the Ballarat sample was surveyed at approximately the same time (2003) and within the same geographical context (Brown, 2006a, b). The present study lends weight to the proposition that the methodological problem noted (conflation of sport/recreation members and social club members) in the AuSSA analyses might have indeed resulted in artificially lower social capital measure scores for sport/recreation members in the AuSSA data. Therefore a more optimistic view of sport/recreation organization members emerges in terms of them demonstrating equal or higher social capital indicator scores compared to all other community organization members surveyed.

It must also be noted that the present study contains its own limitations. Firstly, the nature of the sample meant that respondents self-identified the organization to which they belonged but were not required to give further details. Therefore the samples are not able to indicate the focus or type of the sport/recreation organization. Clearly, the type of organization in terms of its governance (Hoye & Inglis, 2003) and the sport pursued (Scheerder et al., 2002, 2005) may have significant consequences for the profile of the member base and the social capital potential of group activities. Secondly, there was no control group in the research design so we do not know if the measured social capital indicator levels of organization members were the same, higher or lower than for non-members. On one hand, this is not a problem when addressing the question of possible differences between members of types of organizations that has been the main focus here. On the other, it means that we cannot test the idea that such organizations are boosters of social capital using these data (Arai & Pedler, 2003: 187; Jarvie, 2003). Thirdly and following on from the last point, the question of causality remains untouched. That is, to what extent does community organization membership attract those citizens who may already score higher than average on social capital measures and to what extent does membership increase or decrease those scores?

Within the limitations set out above, the study indicates that for the Lund and Ballarat samples community sport/recreation members achieved the same scores (no significant difference) or higher scores (significant difference) on the social capital measures considered. Replication of this kind of study may be one useful way forward as would research using case study designs. This latter strategy would complement cross-sectional studies by potentially providing more in-depth and triangulated data that would aid understandings of the potentials and limits of particular community sport/recreation organizational types and organisational forms in terms of community strengthening and social capital.

References

Arai, S. & Pedlar, A. (2003). Moving beyond individualism in leisure theory: a critical analysis of concepts of community and social engagement. *Leisure Studies, 22*, 185–202.

Bairner, A. (2003). Political unionism and sporting nationalism: An examination of the relationship between sport and national identity within the Ulster unionist tradition. *Identities: Global Studies in Culture and Power, 10*, 517–535.

Begum, H. (2003). Social Capital in Action: Adding Up Local Connections and Networks – A Pilot Study in London. London: Centre for Civil Society.

Brown, K.M. (2006a). The position of Australian community sporting organisations in the third sector: membership profiles, characteristics and attitudes. *Third Sector Review, 12*(2), 17–39.

Brown, K.M. (2006b). Attitudinal characteristics of community group members in Australia: trust, maintenance and change. In L. Alice, J. Barbara, K.M. Brown, P. Connors, M. Kelly & S. Kenny (Eds.), *Community Development in a 'Global Risk Society'*. Melbourne: Deakin University.

Brown, K.M. (2006c). Aspects of comparative active citizenship. In: J. Baulderstone, P. Saj (Eds.), *Navigating New Waters: Proceedings of the Australia and New Zealand Third Sector Research Eighth Biennial Conference*, Adelaide, 26–28 November 2006 [electronic format], Flinders University: Adelaide, 1–28.

Brown, K.M., Kenny, S., Turner, B.S. & Prince, J.K. (2000). *Rhetorics of Welfare: Uncertainty, Choice and Voluntary Associations*. New York: St Martins Press.

Burchell, D. (2002). Ancient citizenship and its inheritors. In E.F. Isin & B.S. Turner (Eds.), *Handbook of Citizenship Studies* (pp. 89–104). London: Sage.

Burdsey, D. & Chappell, R. (2003). Soldiers, sashes and shamrocks: Football and social identity in Scotland and Northern Ireland. *Sociology of Sport Online, 6*(1). [http://physed.otago.ac.nz/sosol/v6i1/v6i1.html].

Cashman, R. (1995). *Paradise of Sport: The Rise of Organized Sport in Australia*. Melbourne: Oxford University Press.

Cattell, V. (2004). Having a laugh and mucking in together: Using social capital to explore dynamics between structure and agency in the context of declining and regenerated neighbourhoods. *Sociology, 38*(5), 945–963.

Coleman, J.S. (1988). Social capital in the creation of human capital. *American Journal of Sociology, 94*(supplement), 95–120.

Coleman, J.S. (1990). *Foundations of Social Theory*. Cambridge: Harvard University Press.

Cunningham, J. & Beneforti, M. (2005). Investigating indicators for measuring the health and social impact of sport and recreation programs in Australian indigenous communities. *International Review for the Sociology of Sport, 40*(1), 89–98.

Dahrendorf, R. (2001). *The Arnold Goodman Lecture 17 July, 2001*. Tonbridge: Charities Aid Foundation.

Devine, F. & Roberts, J.M. (2003). Alternative approaches to researching social capital: A comment on Van Deth's measuring social capital. *International Journal of Social Research Methodology, 6*(1), 93–100.

Flint, J. (2002). Return of the governors: Citizenship and the new governance of neighbourhood disorder in the UK. *Citizenship Studies*, 6(3), 245–264.

Fukuyama, F. (1995). Trust: The Social Virtues and the Creation of Prosperity. New York: The Free Press.

Gibson, R., Wilson, S., Meagher, G., Denemark, D. & Western, M. (2004). *The Australian Survey of Social Attitudes, 2003*. Canberra: Australian Social Science Data Archive, The Australian National University.

Gittell, R. & Vidal, A. (1998). Community Organisation: Building Social Capital as a Development Strategy. London: Sage Publications.

Harris, J.C. (1998). Civil society, physical activity and the involvement of sports sociologists in the preparation of physical activity professionals. *Sociology of Sport Journal*, 15, 138–153.

Held, D. (1987). *Models of Democracy*. Cambridge: Polity.

Hoye, R. & Inglis, S. (2003). Governance of nonprofit leisure organizations. *Society and Leisure*, 26(2), 369–387.

Ignatieff, M. (1989). Caring just isn't enough. *New Statesman and Society*, 2(35), 33–37.

Inglehart, R. et al. (1999). *World Values Surveys and European Values Surveys, 1981–1984, 1990–1993, and 1995–1997* [Computer file] ICPSR version, Ann Arbor, MI: Institute for Social Research [producer], Ann Arbor, MI: Inter-University Consortium for Political and Social Research [distributor].

Janoski, T. & Gran, B. (2002). Political citizenship: Foundation of rights. In E.F. Isin & B.S. Turner (Eds.), *Handbook of Citizenship Studies* (pp. 13–52). London: Sage.

Jarvie, G. (2003). Communitarianism, sport and social capital. *International Review for the Sociology of Sport*, 32(2), 139–153.

Keogh, V. (2002). *Multicultural Sport: Sustaining a Level Playing Field*. Melbourne: Centre for Multicultural Youth Issues.

Lareau, A. (2003). *Unequal Childhoods: Class, Race and Family Life*. Berkeley, CA: University of California Press.

Lascu, D., Giese, T., Toolan, C., Guering, B. & Mercer, J. (1995). Sport involvement: A relevant individual difference factor in spectator sports. *Sport Marketing Quarterly*, 4, 41–46.

Leonard, M. (2004). Bonding and bridging social capital: Reflections from Belfast. *Sociology*, 38(5), 927–944.

Levi, M. (1996). Social and unsocial capital: A review essay of Robert Putnam's making democracy work. *Politics and Society*, 24(1), 45–55.

Marinetto, M. (2003). Who wants to be an active citizen? The politics and practice of community involvement. *Sociology*, 37(1), 103–120.

OECD (2001). The Well-being of Nations: The Role of Human and Social Capital. Paris: OECD.

Onyx, J. & Bullen, P. (2000). Measuring social capital in five communities. *Journal of Applied Behavioral Science*, 36(1), 23–42.

Paxton, P. (1999). Is social capital declining in the United States? A multiple indicator assessment. *American Journal of Sociology*, 105, 88–127.

Powell, J. & Edwards, M. (2002). Policy narratives of ageing: The right way, the third way or the wrong way? *Electronic Journal of Sociology*, 6(1). [http://sociology.org/content/vol006.001/powel-edwards.html].

Putnam, R.D. (1993). Making Democracy Work. Civic Traditions in Modern Italy. Princeton, NJ: Princeton University Press.

Putnam, R.D. (2000). Bowling Alone. The Collapse and Revival of American Community. New York: Simon and Schuster.

Rotolo, T. & Wilson, J. (2004). What happened to the 'Long Civic Generation'? Explaining cohort differences in voluntarism. *Social Forces*, 82(3), 1091–1121.

Rowe, D. (2003). Sport and the repudiation of the global. *International Review for the Sociology of Sport*, 38(3), 281–294.

Scheerder, J., Vanreusel, B., Taks, M. & Renson, R. (2002). Social sports stratification in Flanders 1969–1999. *International Review for the Sociology of Sport*, 37(2), 219–245.

Scheerder, J., Vanreusel, B. & Taks, M. (2005). Stratification patterns of active sport involvement among adults. *International Review for the Sociology of Sport*, 40(2), 139–162.

Smith, J.M. & Ingham, A.G. (2003). On the waterfront: Retrospectives on the relationship between sport and communities. *Sociology of Sport Journal*, 20, 252–274.

Stone, W. (2000). Social capital and social security: Lessons from research. *Family Matters*, 57(Spring/Summer), 10–13.

Stone, W. (2001). *Measuring Social Capital: Towards a Theoretically Informed Measurement Framework for Researching Social Capital in Family and Community Life*, Research Paper No. 24. Australian Institute of Family Studies, Melbourne: AIFS.

Szreter, S. (2002). The state of social capital: Bringing back in power, politics and history. *Theory and Society*, 31(5), 573–621.

Tabachnick, B.G. & Fidell, L.S. (2001). *Using Multivariate Statistics* (4th edition). Mahway, NY: HarperCollins.

Turner, B.S. (1992). Outline of a theory of citizenship. In C. Mouffe (Ed.), *Dimensions of Radical Democracy: Pluralism, Citizenship, Community* (pp. 33–62). London: Verso.

Turner, B.S. (1993). Contemporary problems in the theory of citizenship. In B.S. Turner (Ed.), *Citizenship and Social Theory* (pp. 1–18). London: Sage.

White, P. & Wilson, B. (1999). Distinction in the stands. *International Review for the Sociology of Sport*, 34(3), 245–264.

Woolcock, M. & Narayan, D. (2000). Social capital: Implications for development theory, research and policy. *World Bank Observer*, 15(2), 225–249.

Volunteering in community sport organizations: Implications for social capital

Graham Cuskelly

Local sports clubs are an important component of the formal and informal social networks that underpin the creation, development and maintenance of social capital. Local community based sport clubs provide opportunities for community members to come together on a regular basis to play, facilitate and watch sport as well as enabling club members to participate and engage in the wider social networks that are connected through various formal and informal mechanisms to sport. The collective term community sport organizations (CSOs) is used in this chapter to describe local sport clubs which have been variously labelled as voluntary sport organizations, amateur sport clubs, community amateur sport clubs and grassroots sport organizations. Sport England (2005a) adequately captured the concept of CSOs when it defined community amateur sports clubs as:

properly constituted as a not-for-profit organisation, with no provision for payment to members during the life of the club or upon dissolution. It can be either unincorporated (i.e. an association of members with unlimited liability) or incorporated as a company limited by guarantee (not shares). The club must operate an open membership policy that allows anyone, within reason, to join and use its facilities.

This chapter focuses on volunteers because it is individuals who are engaged in the operation of CSOs who are more likely to impact on the development of social capital than those who are simply members by virtue of being players or being related to a player (e.g. parent of a junior player). Volunteering and participation in voluntary organizations are important components in the comprehensive measurement of social capital. Putnam (2000: 291) used a number of independent measures to compile what he defined as a social capital index. Of the 14 independent measures that comprised the social capital index, half were associated with volunteering and voluntary organizations, most of which correlated highly with the index score overall. While none of the independent index measures were exclusively in the domain of sport, they encompassed CSOs and the types of activities that occur frequently within them. The seven social capital index components most closely associated with CSOs were measures of community organizational life and volunteering and included:

- Percentage of individuals who served on a committee of a local organization in the last year (correlation with social capital index = 0.88).
- Percentage of individuals who served as an officer of some club or organization in the last year (0.83).

- Number of non-profit organizations per 1000 population (0.82).
- Mean number of club meetings attended in the last year (0.78).
- Civic and social organizations per 1000 population (0.78).
- Mean number of group memberships (0.74).
- Mean number of times did volunteer work last year (0.66).

Of the three general forms of sport engagement identified in Chapter 1 – playing, facilitating and watching – this chapter focuses on facilitating sport. It draws on publicly available statistics on volunteering to explore the nature and extent of volunteer engagement in sport. It does not take a particular philosophical stance on sport volunteering and social capital, nor is it informed by a particular theoretical framework. Rather, questions such as who volunteers in sport, how and why they become involved, the nature and extent of sport volunteering and how these statistics compare to other sectors are addressed in order to consider possible implications for the development and maintenance of social capital. In focusing on volunteer involvement statistics, this chapter does not empirically examine important components of social capital such as reciprocity, trust, and social norms or the structures of social networks. However, some of the possible consequences of volunteer involvement for social capital are explored.

Before moving into an analysis of sport volunteering it is important to clarify the meaning of the term sport volunteer. The Australian Bureau of Statistics (ABS) encapsulated the notion of facilitating engagement in sport when it defined a volunteer as 'someone who willingly gave unpaid help, in the form of time, service or skills, through an organisation or group' (ABS, 2001: 44). The reference period was the 12 months prior to the survey and the ABS further defined sport volunteering as 'roles undertaken to support, arrange and/or run organized sport and physical activity' (ABS, 2002: 39) and included coaches, instructors or teachers; referees or umpires; committee members or administrators; scorers or timekeepers; medical support people and other roles. In contrast, Sport England (2005b: 9) included informal volunteering when it defined sport volunteers 'as individual volunteers helping others in sport and receiving either no remuneration or only expenses. This includes those volunteering for organisations (formal volunteers) and those helping others in sport, but not through organisations (informal volunteers)'. Beyond the context of sport, Volunteering Australia (2005) defined formal volunteering as 'an activity which takes place through not for profit organizations or projects and is undertaken: to be of benefit to the community and the volunteer; of the volunteer's own free will and without coercion; for no financial payment; and in designated volunteer positions only'. These definitions share some commonalties such as volunteering being an unpaid helping activity which, in sport, facilitates the participation of others. However, these definitions also serve to highlight the dangers of making direct comparisons between statistical information from different nations.

Rates of sport volunteering

Volunteering in the community through formal organizations is an important contributor to the development and maintenance of social capital. Those involved in volunteering represent a substantial proportion of the population and sport volunteering, in turn, accounts for a large proportion of volunteers (see Table 9.1). The overall rate of volunteer participation as a percentage of the total population varies from about one-quarter in Canada (26.7 per cent) to almost half of the population in England (48 per cent). Sport volunteers represent between 18 and 27 per cent of all volunteers and as a proportion of the population, the rate of sport volunteering is between 5 and 15 per cent. The wide variance in sport volunteer rates as a proportion of the total population is likely to be a function of methodological differences as well as social and cultural differences between the nations studied. However, any particular

Table 9.1 Sport volunteer participation rates

Volunteer participation	Australia[a]	Canada[b]	England[c]
Total volunteers	4 395 000	6 513 000	22 000 000
Total volunteer participation to total population (rate)	31.8%	26.7%	48.0%
Sport volunteer participation	1 141 000	1 170 000	5 821 000
Sport volunteer participation to total population (rate)	8.2%	5%	14.8%
Sport volunteer participation to total volunteers (rate)	26.0%	18.0%	26.5%

Note: Volunteer and population statistics for persons aged 15 years or older (Canada), 16 years or older (England) and 18 years or older (Australia).

Source: [a] ABS (2003), [b] Doherty (2005), [c] Sport England (2003).

form of activity that involves 5 per cent or more of a population, such as sport volunteering does, represents a substantial amount of capacity for the coordination and delivery of sport participation opportunities in community sport. Such levels or rates of activity not only contribute to the total stock of social capital in the community, they also offset what might otherwise be higher costs for sport participation. Just as there is variance in overall rates of sport volunteer participation in the population there are likely to be variations in the degree to which different population groups volunteer, why they volunteer and how much and for how many years they volunteer.

Who is involved in sport volunteering?

Aggregated volunteer numbers and rates of volunteering provide a broad overview of the scope of volunteer activity in the population and in CSOs. Profiling the demographic characteristics of sport volunteers, however, provides an opportunity to understand who volunteers and may provide some insights to understanding how and why social capital is developed and maintained in CSOs and in what forms – such as bonding, bridging or linking social capital. The statistics that describe the demographic characteristics of sport volunteers can also be compared to other (non-sport) volunteers and the population in general to provide a perspective on the broad social groups that are either under- or over-represented amongst sport volunteers. However, national statistics tend to mask the nature and scope of sport volunteering at a local CSO level. Aggregated statistics conceal what are likely to be high degrees of variance in the demographic profiles of particular CSOs or groups of CSOs in different geographic regions, states or provinces.

Sex

Studies of sport volunteers in Canada, England and Australia reveal that sport volunteers are more likely to be male than female by a proportion of at least three to two. Statistics from Australia (ABS, 2003) showed that males accounted for 60 per cent of sport volunteers. This statistic was lower than but consistent with Canadian (64 per cent male) (Doherty, 2005) and British (67 per cent male) (Sport England, 2003) sport volunteers. In contrast, other (non-sport) volunteers were more likely to be female in Australia (57 per cent), Canada (54 per cent) and presumably England. These statistics are consistent with those reported by Gidengil et al. (2003) (in Stolle & Cruz, 2005: 93) who found that 'men are more involved than women in sports teams, business associations, and labour unions, while women tend to have higher participation rates than men in community service groups and women's associations'. Whether by individual choice or social processes, networks and institutions in sport are, to a large extent, male dominated. As a consequence the social networks and connections that develop are likely to reflect more masculine norms of trust and reciprocity in which male volunteers are likely to feel a stronger sense of identity, further promulgating the male dominance of volunteering in CSOs. The situation in sport volunteering is almost opposite to volunteering in other sectors where female volunteers are dominant.

Age

Sport volunteering tends to be dominated by adults in the 35–54 years age group as a proportion of sport volunteers, and in comparison to both other (non-sport) volunteers and the population. In Australia the 35–44 age group accounted for almost one-third (31 per cent) of all sport volunteers (ABS, 2003) which is six percentage points higher than the 25 per cent of other (non-sport) volunteers in the same age group. As a participation rate in the population no fewer than one in eight (12 per cent) 35–44 year olds volunteer in sport compared to the average sport volunteer participation rate in the population of 8 per cent. This pattern of volunteer involvement is also evident amongst the Canadian population. Sport volunteers aged 35–44 years account for 41 per cent of sport volunteers which is substantially higher than 24 per cent rate of the same age group amongst other (non-sport) volunteers. The rate of sport volunteering amongst 35–44 year olds was almost twice that of the 21 per cent of the Canadian population in the same age group (Doherty, 2005). In England 35–59 year olds were the dominant age group accounting for 40 per cent of sport volunteers (Sport England, 2003). Age group patterns are less clear amongst younger and older age groups. In Australia, volunteers aged 18–24 years accounted for 13 per cent of all sport volunteers. Even though the data were aggregated for larger age group categories in Canada and England, 19 per cent of Canadian sport volunteers were aged 15–24 years and in England 16–24 year olds accounted for more than a quarter of all sport volunteers (28 per cent), both substantially higher than the comparable Australian statistic. Perhaps reinforcing the perception that sport volunteers tend to be younger than other (non-sport) volunteers, the relatively older age categories accounted for small proportions of sport volunteers. For example, 14 per cent of Australian sport volunteers were aged 55 years and over, which was half the size of the other (non-sport) volunteers in the same age group (28 per cent). Similar patterns were evident amongst Canadian volunteers. Amongst those aged 55 years and over, one in five were sport volunteers (20 per cent) whereas those aged 55 and over accounted for 30 per cent of other (non-sport) volunteers (Gumulka et al., 2005).

These statistics suggest volunteers in CSOs exhibit a substantially different demographic profile than other (non-sport) volunteering. Sport volunteering is clearly dominated by a middle adulthood age cohort. Volunteers from relatively younger age cohorts (less than 25 years) and older age cohorts (55 years or older) represent relatively small proportions of sport volunteers. These statistics are also reflected in rates of volunteering in the population. The rate of volunteering amongst the population aged 35–44 years is much greater in sport organizations than it is in other (non-sport) organizations. The development and maintenance of social capital in CSOs is largely dependent upon the continued involvement of the middle adulthood age cohort. The reason that this age group is dominant in CSOs could be explained either by the involvement of their children in sport or because volunteering is a way of extending participation beyond playing and spectating. Parents who sign their children up for sport may feel a sense of duty, whether through reciprocity or obligation, to help a CSO facilitate the participation of their child and the children of others. Volunteering is also a way of extending involvement in sport when a playing 'career' is drawing to a close. Sport participants, particularly in team sports, tend to develop bonds of trust and friendship through local sport clubs and may be reluctant to cut themselves off from a social network when their playing 'career' ends. Drawing on continuity theory (Atchley, 1989, 1999), Cuskelly (2004) described this change of involvement as a transition-extension process amongst sport participants. Irrespective of the social processes at play, the middle adulthood age cohort has a substantial influence on the social capital of CSOs. However, the dominance of this age group could be impacting negatively on the involvement of volunteers from more diverse age groups, thus reducing the development of bridging forms of social capital.

Education and labour force status

Statistics on labour force status showed that sport volunteers were more likely to be employed full or part time than were other (non-sport) volunteers. For Canadians, 84 per cent of sport volunteers were employed compared to 67 per cent of other (non-sport) volunteers and 63 per cent of the Canadian population (Doherty, 2005). Amongst Australians, 84 per cent of sport volunteers were employed compared to 66 per cent of other (non-sport) volunteers who were employed (ABS, 2003). Canadian data reveal that the highest level of education for sport volunteers is not remarkably different to that of other (non-sport) volunteers (Doherty, 2005). However, compared to the Canadian population, volunteers (sport and other) tend to have higher levels of education. For example, 53 per cent of the Canadian population have completed post-secondary education whereas 65 per cent of sport volunteers were reported as having completed some post-secondary education. These statistics imply that the development and maintenance of social capital in CSOs is associated with labour force status and educational attainment. To the extent that individuals undertake or complete post-secondary education and are employed they are more likely than less highly educated individuals and those not in the labour force (e.g. stay at home parents, retired or unemployed) to be part of the volunteer networks that manage and operate sport.

The association of level of education and labour force status and sport volunteering is either a function of individual choice or organizational constraints. Community members who are less educated and not in the labour force do not have the networking benefit of being employed and may believe that they do not have the skills or confidence to volunteer for a CSO. Even if they are a member of a club by virtue of their participation in sport or through the participation of another family member, they may feel inhibited about becoming a volunteer. From an organizational perspective, CSOs are tending to become increasingly bureaucratic in response to their external environment including the demands imposed by national and state/provincial sport bodies for great professionalism, government policy and legislation (e.g. privacy and child protection) (Cuskelly et al., 2006). As CSOs develop along these lines they become more formalized in their operations and possibly more demanding of their volunteers. Perhaps unintentionally, these actions reinforce the view that volunteers need the skills, confidence and experience that are developed though education and employment, leading to the exclusion of particular groups within the population.

Why do volunteers get involved in sport?

Rates of volunteering provide a broad overview of the scope of volunteer activity in the population. However, understanding the reasons volunteers become and stay involved in sport provides insights to their motives and the attraction process. It also provides a perspective from which to make observations about the social networks which are likely to be influential in decisions to initially volunteer and motives to continue volunteering. Using a focus group method, Sport England (2003) reported that the most frequently cited attractions to volunteer in sport clubs were social benefits including friendship, camaraderie and being part of the club (40 per cent of 48 focus groups), giving something back (38 per cent) and parent involvement with own children (34 per cent).

Using data from the National Survey of Giving, Volunteering and Participating (NSGVP) (Statistics Canada, 2000), Doherty (2005) reported that Canadian sport volunteers first became involved through their children's involvement (40 per cent), because someone in the organization asked them (21 per cent) and because they were a member of the organization (13 per cent). Amongst other reasons 26 per cent of sport volunteers were responding to a public appeal, being nominated to a position or a friend outside the organization asked them to volunteer. A further question on the Canadian survey focused more on motives by asking respondents why they volunteered. Almost all sport volunteers were involved to help a cause in which they believe (94 per cent), to use their skills and experience to help the organization's cause (87 per cent), because someone they know is personally affected by the organization or its activities (e.g. child or adult partner) (76 per cent), to explore their own strengths (57 per cent) and because they have friends involved (30 per cent).

The most frequently cited reasons for volunteering in Australian sport were personal or family involvement (43 per cent), personal satisfaction (42 per cent), helping others or the community (38 per cent), doing something worthwhile (22 per cent) and social contact (20 per cent) (ABS, 2003). Cross-national comparisons between data collected using different methods and for potential differing purpose need to be made with caution. However, these statistics suggest that individuals are, to a large extent, attracted to sport volunteering predominantly through existing social networks. This includes personal involvement in the sport or through the involvement of their children, membership or the camaraderie and social contact which are part of being in a club.

Sport volunteers compared to volunteers in other sectors

The Canadian and Australian studies reported statistics comparing sport volunteers to volunteers in other community

sector organizations. Labelled 'other volunteers' to differentiate them from sport volunteers, other (non-sport) volunteers
included community and welfare/social services; health; education, research and training; emergency services; environment and animal welfare; and religious organizations. These
statistics have been summarized in Table 9.2 and the reasons
categorized as 'personal involvement or social connection',
'personal fulfilment and altruism', and 'developing or using
skills'. Simple percentage mean and difference scores have

Table 9.2 Reasons volunteers become and continue to be involved in sport and other organizational forms of volunteering (Australian and Canadian statistics)

Reason (ABS[a] and NSGVP[b])	Sport volunteers (%)	Other volunteers (%)	Difference (%)[c]
Personal involvement/social connection			
Believe in cause supported by the organization[b]	94	95	−1
Personally affected by the cause that organization supports[b]	76	69	7
Personal/family involvement[a]	43	27	16
Through children's involvement[b]	40	12	28
Friends volunteer[b]	30	30	0
Someone in the organization asked[b]	21	30	−9
Social contact[a]	20	17	3
Member of the organization[b]	13	15	−2
Mean %	*42*	*37*	*5*
Personal fulfilment/altruism			
Explore own strengths[b]	57	57	0
Personal satisfaction[a]	42	43	−1
Help others/community[a]	38	50	−12
Do something worthwhile[a]	22	32	−10
Be active[a]	15	10	5
Mean %	*35*	*38*	*−4*
Develop or use skills			
Use skills/experience[a]	87	81	6
Use skills and experience[b]	12	13	−1
Learn new skills[a]	6	7	−1
Mean %	*35*	*34*	*1*

[a]ABS: Australian Bureau of Statistics (2003), [b]NSGVP: National Survey of Giving, Volunteering and Participating (NSGVP) (Doherty, 2005), [c]Percentage differences may not tally exactly due to rounding.

been computed to compare sport and other volunteers. Clear trends are difficult to distinguish, however, sport volunteers seem to be more likely than other (non-sport) volunteers to become or stay involved in volunteering through a personal or social connection (mean 42 per cent vs. 37 per cent). In contrast, sport volunteers are less likely than other volunteers to give altruistic or personal fulfilment reasons for volunteering, 35 and 38 per cent, respectively. Both groups are about equally likely to volunteer to use or develop their skills (1 per cent difference). Large differences between sport and other volunteers are evident in relation to being involved in sport volunteering through children (40 per cent vs. 12 per cent) or personal/family involvement (43 per cent vs. 27 per cent).

Implications for social capital

The statistics presented here suggest that initial engagement and ongoing involvement in sport volunteering tend to reinforce the maintenance and development of bonding social capital. This inference is based on the observation that sport volunteers' reasons for initially becoming involved or continuing to volunteer are tied to their personal connection to sport, whether through their own involvement or the involvement of children or family members. Further evidence that sport volunteers are more likely to contribute to the development of bonding rather than bridging social capital is provided by the less frequent reporting of personal fulfilment and altruism as reasons for volunteering. Sport volunteers are not as motivated by helping others or the community as they are to serve a cause in which they or their family members are involved and personally affected. It appears that sport volunteers first become involved in sport organizations through personally playing or watching the game, often through their family members' involvement, before becoming more engaged in an organization as a volunteer. Volunteering in sport seems to be a secondary level of involvement behind playing and watching. As a consequence the social capital that has been created and developed through other forms of sport involvement is maintained rather than created anew through sport volunteering.

The nature and extent of volunteering

Statistics that describe the nature and extent of volunteering provide an opportunity to extend our understanding beyond who volunteers and why they volunteer. Summary statistics such as hours contributed by volunteers, how many years people volunteer, the number of organizations for which individuals volunteer and their roles within them allow us to examine the behavioural aspects of volunteering and to speculate about the implications for the social capital in CSOs.

Years volunteering

An important aspect of the development and maintenance of social capital is the average number of years that individuals volunteer. Volunteers who stay with one organization for many years are likely to contribute more to the development and maintenance of social capital than those who stay for short periods of time and have relatively little opportunity to engage with other volunteers. But how are years volunteering distributed amongst volunteers and to what extent are sport organizations different in this regard from other (non-sport) organizations? The ABS (2003) reported that more than half of all sport volunteers (61 per cent) had commenced their involvement less than six years ago. There was little difference between sport and other (non-sport) volunteers. About the same proportion of other (non-sport) volunteers, 59 per cent, had commenced their involvement less than six years ago. These statistics reveal no more than four out of every ten volunteers have six or more years experience in one organization. It might be reasonable to assume that longer-term volunteers are more likely to hold leadership and decision-making positions which are more influential in the development and maintenance of norms such as reciprocity and trust. However, sport and other volunteer organizations are faced with the constant challenge of renewing social capital as new volunteers take the place of those who leave.

Number of organizations

Individuals who volunteer for more than one organization in their community are presumably more widely connected to their community. Multiple organization volunteers are therefore likely to contribute more to the development and maintenance of bridging and linking forms of social capital than those who volunteer for only one organization. ABS (2003) statistics revealed that sport volunteers were more likely than other (non-sport) volunteers to undertake voluntary work for more than one organization. Even though more than half of sport volunteers (55 per cent) undertook voluntary work for only one organization over a 12-month period, over two-thirds of non-sport volunteers (69 per cent) were involved in only one organization. Similar involvement patterns were reported for Canadian volunteers (Doherty, 2005). Sport volunteers were more likely to volunteer for two or more organizations (62 per cent) than they were for one organization (38 per cent). Whereas other (non-sport) volunteers' pattern of involvement was almost the direct opposite with 59 per cent volunteering for only one organization. These findings raise the issue of the seasonal nature of sport as a possible influence in sport volunteers seeking more than one volunteer opportunity. Because most CSOs operate on a seasonal basis (summer vs. winter sports) most sport volunteers have about a six-month break from their organization each year. This allows sport volunteers to return to their organization with a renewed sense of enthusiasm for the next season as well as releasing them from ongoing volunteer commitments to contribute their time to another organization. Having the opportunity to volunteer for more than one organization contributes to the development of social capital through access to other local community and social networks.

Volunteer hours

Another indicator of the stock of social capital is the volunteer hours contributed to CSOs and other voluntary organizations. Isham et al. (2006) provided support for the proposition that volunteer hours in non-profit organizations increase social capital, but reported that the effect was small. The ABS (2003) reported that sport volunteers contributed a total of 130 million hours in the year prior to interview, which they estimated as equivalent to 70 000 people working full time for a year. With more than 1.1 million sport volunteers, there was a mean 98 hours per volunteer for sport involvement. This was slightly less than the mean of 108 hours contributed per year for other (non-sport) volunteers. Canadian statistics (Doherty, 2005) report higher mean annual hours per volunteer than the Australian statistics with a mean of 189 hours for sport volunteers and 162 hours for other (non-sport) volunteers. Because of the seasonal nature of most sports, it is not surprising that sport volunteers contributed less hours on average than other volunteers. If Australian sport volunteer hours were spread over a six-month period rather than a year the mean would be 3.8 hours per week. For Canadian sport volunteers the mean hours per week over a six-month sport season would equate to 7.3 hours.

Median scores represent a more stable measure of central tendency than mean sores and were reported by the ABS

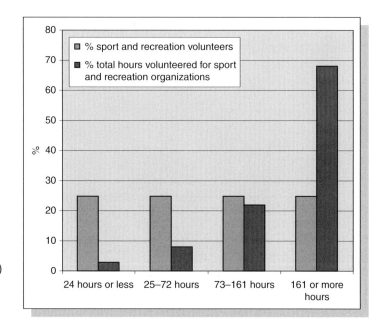

Figure 9.1
Percentage of
total annual hours
volunteered by
percentage of total
volunteers (NSGVP)
Source: Adapted
from Gumulka et al.
(2005)

(2003) as 40 hours and 43 hours for sport and other (non-sport) volunteers, respectively. Median scores which are substantially lower than mean scores indicate a non-normal distribution with a positive skew. This distribution pattern is evident in the Canadian sport volunteer statistics (see Figure 9.1) where 3 per cent of total volunteer hours are contributed by one-quarter of Canadian volunteers. In contrast, 68 per cent of total volunteer hours in sport are contributed by a similar proportion of sport volunteers. If one were to assume a linear relationship between hours contributed and the production of social capital in CSOs, it is evident that a relatively small proportion of volunteers are responsible for the development and maintenance of social capital in sport. The more highly involved volunteers are the ones most likely to spend more hours communicating and networking with club members, other volunteers and the wider community, thereby benefiting their CSO. Indirectly, highly involved volunteers are also likely to benefit more so than those who are less involved as they build up feelings of trust and reciprocity amongst the individuals and voluntary and business organizations with whom they regularly interact.

Conclusion

This chapter has summarized, described and analysed the nature and extent of volunteering in CSOs and has attempted to identify implications for the development and maintenance of social capital from an empirical perspective. To the extent that it has not taken a particular theoretical approach factors such as the structural and relational aspects of social connections have not been considered. Structural factors which influence social capital include network size, density (Coleman, 1988) and types (e.g. horizontal and vertical networks (Putnam, 1995) and homogenous and heterogeneous networks (Stolle & Rochon, 1998)). Relational aspects are more qualitative factors that cannot be captured in the statistics reported here and include norms of trust and reciprocity. These norms are multidimensional and exist at various levels from social groups, both familiar and unfamiliar, to institutions including nonprofit, government and private sector organizations and society in general. With these limitations in mind it can be concluded that volunteer engagement, involvement and behaviour vary a great deal in relation to characteristics of volunteers, their motivations for volunteering and the CSOs for which they volunteer. Volunteering in CSOs, therefore, involves a wide array of volunteers who contribute to and benefit from the development and maintenance of social capital to varying degrees.

The predominant characteristics of sport volunteers (male, employed and 35–54 years of age) suggest that bonding social capital is likely to be prominent in CSOs. The population group most involved in sport volunteering is often time poor, balancing work, family and volunteer commitments, resulting in social capital development that is erratic and ephemeral rather than ordered and enduring. Moreover, to the extent that the development of social capital is dependent upon the qualitative aspects of social relations, it is difficult to see how high levels of trust and reciprocity are developed when the majority of sport volunteers are time stressed. The observation that the longer hours of volunteer work are carried by a small proportion of volunteers suggests that the development of social capital in CSOs tends to be concentrated within a relatively small group of sport volunteers. While many club members and their families enjoy the benefits of being involved in playing, and watching sport, relatively few members are sufficiently involved to develop the rich social networks needed to fully realize the benefits of good quality social capital. Given that the predominant group of CSO volunteers are time poor it is likely that the characteristics of those who are most engaged are dissimilar to the predominant male, employed full time, 35–54-year-old volunteer. The existence of a dominant group within a CSO could lead to the exclusion of some groups from volunteering. Individuals from less well represented groups may feel intimidated by the strong organizational culture in some CSOs or not feel as though they have the competence to participate as a volunteer. Excluding different groups, whether intentional or unintentional, reduces opportunities to develop bridging and linking forms of social capital in CSOs and may ultimately be detrimental to these organizations if they fail to adjust to the changing characteristics and expectations of their surrounding communities.

The social networks through which people connect to their communities are probably similar to the networks that connect many of the same people to the volunteer opportunities that exist within CSOs. Those already involved in the community through family and organizational connections are more likely to be known to other community members and asked or invited to volunteer for a CSO before less networked individuals. Individuals without some type of personal connection to other community members or the sport itself seem less likely to actively seek opportunities or accept invitations to volunteer, which implies that sport volunteering is more likely to reinforce the development and maintenance of bonding capital.

References

Australian Bureau of Statistics (ABS) (2001). *Voluntary Work, Australia, Cat. No. 4441.0.* Canberra: Commonwealth of Australia.

Australian Bureau of Statistics (ABS) (2002). *Involvement in Organised Sport and Physical Activity, Cat. No. 6285.0.* Canberra: Commonwealth of Australia.

Australian Bureau of Statistics (ABS) (2003). *Australia's Sports Volunteers 2000.* National Centre for Culture and Recreation Statistics: Commonwealth of Australia.

Atchley, R.C. (1989). A continuity theory of aging. *The Gerontologist, 29,* 183–190.

Atchley, R.C. (1999). *Continuity and Adaptation in Aging: Creating Positive Experiences.* Baltimore, MD: Johns Hopkins University Press.

Coleman, J. (1988). Social capital in the creation of human capital. *American Journal of Sociology, 94,* 95–120.

Cuskelly, G. (2004). Volunteer retention in community sport organisations. *European Sport Management Quarterly, 4,* 59–76.

Cuskelly, G., Hoye, R. & Auld, C. (2006). *Working with Volunteers in Sport: Theory and Practice.* London: Routledge.

Doherty, A. (2005). *A Profile of Community Sport Volunteers.* Ontario: Parks and Recreation Ontario and Sport Alliance of Ontario.

Gidengil, E., Goodyear-Grant, E., Nevitte, N., Blais, A. & Nadeau, R. (2003). Youth civic engagement in Canada: Implications for public policy. In Stolle, D. & Cruz, C. (2005). *Social Capital in Action: Thematic Policy Studies*. Canada: Government of Canada.

Gumulka, G., Barr, C., Lasby, D. & Brownlee, B. (2005). *Understanding the Capacity of Sports and Recreation Organizations*. Toronto, ON: Imagine Canada.

Isham, J., Kolodinsky, J. & Kimberly, G. (2006). The effects of volunteering for nonprofit organizations on social capital formation: Evidence from a statewide survey. *Nonprofit and Voluntary Sector Quarterly, 35*(3), 367–383.

Putnam, R. (1995). Bowling alone: America's declining social capital. *Journal of Democracy, 6*(1), 65–78.

Putnam, R.D. (2000). *Bowling alone: The collapse and revival of American community*. New York: Simon and Schuster.

Sport England (2003). *Sports Volunteering in England 2002*. Sheffield: Leisure Industries Research Centre.

Sport England (2005a). *Tax Breaks for Community Amateur Sports Clubs*. London: Sport England.

Sport England (2005b). *Sport England's Policy on Volunteers in Sport*. London: Sport England.

Statistics Canada (2000). *National Survey of Giving, Volunteering and Participating*. Ottawa, Canada: Statistics Canada.

Stolle, D. & Rochon, T.R. (1998). Are all associations alike? Member diversity, associational type, and the creation of social capital. *American Behavioral Scientist, 42*(1), 47–65.

Volunteering Australia (2005). *Definitions and Principles of Volunteering* (Information Sheet), Melbourne: Volunteering Australia. Available at http://www.volunteeringaustralia.org/files (accessed 11 June 2007).

Part Three

Sport and Social Capital in Action

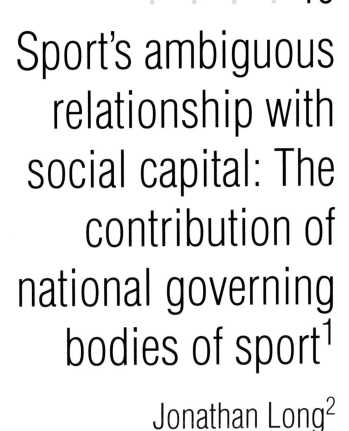

Sport's ambiguous relationship with social capital: The contribution of national governing bodies of sport[1]

Jonathan Long[2]

[1] An earlier version of this paper was presented at a Leisure Studies Association conference on *Leisure and Social Capital* and appears in the proceedings edited by Kirsten Holmes.
[2] With grateful thanks to my CRI colleagues who also worked on the CCPR project, Mel Welch and Paul Robinson.

Introduction and context

An alternative title for this chapter might be 'My ambiguous relationships with sport and social capital'. Perhaps I need not chastize myself for this as both sport and social capital represent multi-dimensional and elusive concepts – Hall's (2005) contribution to the Office for National Statistics (ONS) web site describes social capital as a multi-faceted concept that embodies networks and norms.[3] Moreover, these are ambiguities that are emphasized by the common presumption that promoting social capital is a means of addressing social inclusion and cohesion. Further complications arise from there being at least three identifiable academic traditions (though with earlier roots) that have addressed social capital: Coleman (1961), closely linked to his interest with education and human capital; Bourdieu (1984), linked to his ideas of cultural capital and symbolic capital and Putnam's work (2000), underpinned as it is by communitarianism, which is the strand adopted most enthusiastically in the USA and the UK at least.

Despite arguments that the decline in social capital observed by Putnam in the USA has not occurred in the UK (e.g. Johnston & Jowell, 1999), the social capital thesis has been embraced here. Indeed, the status 'social capital' has achieved in the policy world is intriguing. How this eminence, and the project itself, are interpreted depends on the political position of the analyst. For some it is an attempt to appropriate older established notions of community and solidarity and render them subservient to the interests of capital through financial accounting systems. For others it is to take back in the interests of social welfare some of the ground lost to the economics of the bottom line during the period of pre-eminence enjoyed by neo-liberal economics. Nonetheless, for leisure scholars it comes as something of a relief to find a big idea accepted in government and academic circles that allows us such ready access to the debate. From relatively early writings (e.g. Bellah et al., 1987) the potential contributions from sport and leisure have been stressed. Indeed, Siisiäinen (2000) has suggested that it is only really in relation to sport and leisure associations that Putnam's idea of social capital has any purchase.

Putnam's initial proposition that social interaction is declining is a concern that has exercised leisure scholars for some time, producing discussions of increasingly privatized lifestyles. And many have felt in tune with civic communitarians

---

[3] See the ONS Social Capital Project at http://www.statistics.gov.uk/socialcapital/.

who have embraced Durkheim's (1902) emphasis on social solidarity as a way of realizing social cohesion, having long argued that leisure and sport have an important contribution to make in that regard.

Following Putnam's line (2000), most authors in sport see the main source of social capital as residing in civil society (where people engage in sport), rather than in the state and political institutions. Moreover, Putnam's association of social capital with civic virtue links well with Stebbins' (1982) notion of serious leisure that has been deployed by many leisure scholars. Still operating in this realm of civil society I want to use this chapter to bring together some of the concerns previously expressed about the social capital thesis with an attempt to examine just how sporting institutions (in this case national governing bodies of sport (NGBs) and other national sports organizations (NSOs)) might deliver various elements of social capital (Welch & Long, 2007). In so doing I shall set on one side the bigger political issues typically associated with critiques of the communitarian base (Blackshaw & Long, 2005). I recognize that this might leave me open to the very criticism we previously directed at Jarvie's (2003) functionalist invocation of social capital, but I do so in part to try to focus attention on the responsibilities of sporting institutions.

The social capital thesis

In conventional economic theory capital might be seen as wealth used to produce more wealth, or exchange. It rests in the accumulation of goods previously produced that are used in the production of other goods and services, including further capital goods. Ideally in sport there should be a virtuous cycle in which the capital used to produce participation sustains, renews and refreshes capital so it does not get worn out and depleted. Being not-for-profit organizations NGBs (and most of their member organizations – regions, counties, leagues, clubs) are free to use their financial and non-financial capital to generate future capital as there is no requirement to extract a surplus to pay shareholders.

In discussions of social capital, the focus of attention is most commonly on social connectedness, and hence the discussions around 'bonding', 'bridging' and 'linking'. The Organization for Economic Co-operation and Development (OECD) definition of social capital involves 'networks together with shared norms, values and understandings that facilitate co-operation within or among groups' (http://www.esds.ac.uk/government/docs/

soccapguide.pdf). Sabatini, editor of the Social Capital Gateway (http://www.socialcapitalgateway.org/index.htm), prefers a different emphasis, seeing social capital as 'the set of trust, institutions, social norms, social networks, and organizations that shape the interactions of actors within a society and are an asset for the individual and collective production of well-being'. However, it is interconnectedness that is most commonly taken as the starting point for promoting shared values and generating trust that will encourage the reciprocity essential to a productive society. In Putnam's formulation this is not a one-to-one reciprocity, but one in which people are moved to do things for someone else in the expectation that others unconnected with this transaction will do something for them.

Even unreconstructed Marxists know that the revolution will not happen as a result of people acting in isolation, and that the first step is to come together in recognition of shared interests. Some time ago at a BSA/LSA study group in 1980, Long was moved to suggest that leisure, as well as promoting social control might perform transformative functions through bringing people together (after Marcuse, 1964). Although the potential power of the aesthetics of art (Marcuse's interest) cannot be directly translated into the world of sport:

[I]f we assume that community development should increase social cohesiveness and collective responsibility, producing less self-centred networks and orientations, reduce the likelihood of loneliness, increase personal and social skills, transform the opportunities available in the neighbourhood and increase the community's political power, it would seem that, at the very least, leisure is capable of facilitating such change.

(Long, 1981: 164)

The spotlight once again fell on Putnam more recently when he gave an interview to John Lloyd of the Financial Times suggesting that the Harvard study of social capital in America indicated that ethnic diversity had an adverse effect on social capital:

In the presence of diversity, we hunker down. We act like turtles. The effect of diversity is worse than had been imagined. And it's not just that we don't trust people who are not like us. In diverse communities, we don't trust people who do look like us.

(Lloyd, 2006: 1)

The Commission for Racial Equality felt obliged to respond by welcoming the research and suggesting that it reflected the Commission's own concerns that separateness is becoming more entrenched in parts of our society.

> We now have to find ways of meeting this challenge and reap the benefits that diversity brings; we need to acknowledge what we have in common and be open to new ideas. In working towards this goal the CRE continues to promote and fund projects which encourage people from different communities to meet and understand one another, such as *sporting initiatives* and cross-cultural mentoring schemes [italics added].
>
> (Johnson, n.d.)

What seems to have attracted rather less attention is Putnam's supplementary observation reported in the Lloyd article that: 'What we shouldn't do is to say that they [immigrants] should be more like us. We should construct a new us.'

An alternative take

Part of Putnam's thesis is that social capital is both a private and a public good such that the community as well as the individuals concerned benefit from their participation. To be fair, some nuance is attached to this by recognizing that what is good for those inside the network may not be good for those outside it, and he also introduces the idea of 'dark capital', which is exploited for anti-social purposes (Putnam, 2000: 21–22)[4] as in the case of urban gangs, NIMBY ('not in my backyard') movements, and power elites. Parallels might be drawn with the fiercely exclusionary practices of some sporting groups in which exclusivity is celebrated in the name of group/team solidarity and collective identity (Jarvie, 2003). However, these caveats are no sooner identified than Putnam lays them aside.

Blackshaw and Long (2005) suggested that the Putnamesque social capital thesis revolves around a very particular understanding of freedom, choice and identity. Our generalized proposition (derived from Bauman, 2001) was that the thesis seems to take the form that in post-modernity identity comes through the pattern of consumption that is chosen, so as you choose, choose wisely. And of course, the wiser choices are like those 'we' choose, hence the power of the community to limit the freedom of social actors.

Social capital is supposed to be for the general good, but capital is acquired in order to realize benefits, and those benefits are usually for the self. One of the important distinctions between the Putnam school and Bourdieu (1993) is the

---

[4] He also notes that an era of much higher social capital in the USA in the 1950s and 1960s was not so good for those marginalized because of their ethnicity, gender, social class, sexual orientation or, he might have added, political belief.

conviction of the former that social capital, although created by the free will of individuals, is of mutual benefit, whereas the latter sees it as a positional good that only has value insofar as others lack it. Social capital is related to the extent, quality and quantity of social actors' networks *and* their ability to mobilize these. For Bourdieu capitals are resources to be exploited, combined to constitute the categories of distinction which both produce and reproduce social class divisions (being a member of an exclusive golf club, being on the 'right' committee, etc.). So 'the profits of membership' of civic associations and social networks are not available to everybody.

It is not uncommon among leisure writers to presume that social capital contributes to the democratic project's presumed search for accommodation. True, this is sometimes challenged. For example, Hemingway (1999) is alert to the undemocratic potential of participation that needs both money and time to increase utility, so he tries to resolve which forms of leisure might stimulate trust, co-operation and connectedness. Despite offering some ways in which sport can be used in social protest, Jarvie (2003: 142), like the bulk of commentators on the role of sport, returns to the idea that through sport 'people learn to take responsibility, to follow rules, to accept one another, to look for consensus and take on democracy'.

Let me also register two operational problems that concern me. First, the like us/unlike us separation that lies at the heart of the distinction between bonding and bridging is hard to appreciate given the multi-dimensionality of any individual (sex, age, class, occupation, ethnicity, sexual orientation, political belief, abilities, interests, etc.). And indeed, the data that even Putnam draws upon are incapable of sustaining this distinction whatever its intuitive appeal. Second, the research techniques do not have the power to distinguish between presumed cause and effect (whether people derive social capital from their participation or are able to participate because they already enjoy a certain level of social capital).

The Central Council of Physical Recreation project

The Central Council of Physical Recreation (CCPR) is the umbrella organization for 270 national governing and representative bodies of sport and recreation in the UK. It is an advocate that aims to promote and develop the interests of all levels of sport and physical recreation and provide services to participants and administrators. It is independent of government but does receive public funding; its member organizations, in addition to being funded by their members also receive public funding. In light of that it is all too easy for the government to see NGBs as a cost to the exchequer, perhaps not fully appreciating the return secured on its investment. This is more evident for sport than for other parts of the voluntary sector that are seen to be providing for others while sport is seen to be providing for itself. CCPR has, therefore, been keen to demonstrate wider social benefits.

Given the prominence of the idea of social capital it is hardly surprising that an organization like CCPR should want to claim 'a piece of the action'. We were commissioned to look behind the frontline participation statistics to review the levels of social, intellectual and technical capital generated by or inherent in the NGBs of sport and other voluntary NSOs and their members (Welch & Long, 2007). At this level the concept of social capital may have more to offer than when used at the macro level to drive policy.

Within our project one of the big challenges naturally lay in the measurement of this 'ambiguous' and 'multi-faceted' concept; even indicators of civic engagement are difficult to operationalize empirically. The Saguaro Seminar (the project fronted by Putnam in the USA) initially developed a Social Capital Community Benchmark Survey that typically took 25 minutes to administer, though this has now been distilled into a shorter form with 5–10 minutes of questions (http://www.ksg.harvard.edu/saguaro/measurement.htm). In the UK the ONS identified the key dimensions that underpin social capital:

- views about the local area (satisfaction with living in the area, problems in the area, fear of crime, etc.);
- civic participation in local and national issues (propensity to vote and take action);
- reciprocity and trust (trusting other people, trusting institutions);
- social networks and support (contact with friends/relatives and having people to turn to);
- social participation (involvement in groups and voluntary activities).

On the basis of those they have constructed a 'Social Capital Harmonised Question Set' to be administered in large scale public surveys (ONS, 2005).

Whether or not it is possible (methodologically justifiable) to modify this harmonized question set and administer it to people within the ambit of NSOs, we lacked the funding to do so. We had to find an alternative, making use of data more readily available.

Social capital was taken to be represented by the ties between people, and in the ways in which organizations organize themselves and reproduce themselves into the future with social capital becoming inherent to them irrespective of the individuals involved. Immediately this heralds a number of challenges:

- Typical of analyses of social capital is the problem of whether it resides with individuals (sports participants) or organizations (NGBs).
- What can be used to measure social capital?
- Do the data exist for those measures?
- How much of anything recorded can be attributed to the actions of NGBs as opposed to any other sporting agent?

The project was addressed through three phases.

1. Review

An initial review of the research literature and available data provided a frame for our efforts to assess the non-financial elements of capital being generated by NSOs. Bonding capital (links with like people) is valuable in and of itself, insofar as bringing people together increases opportunity for participation, and those bonded together in sport are likely to participate more frequently than they would do otherwise. Sport is generally recognized as playing a significant role in building bonding capital. By encouraging frequent participation bonding capital may also deliver other outcomes, like getting healthy. Less clear are the opportunities for bridging capital (links between different groups), and linking capital is likely to be more limited (connections with other parts of the power hierarchy), though clearly what CCPR itself tries to facilitate. Individuals may contribute to different forms of capital by operating at different levels of the NGB.

The contribution of NGBs is through providing the organizational infrastructure that allows opportunities for participation. Their framework of governance provides continuity and coherence to sport through ethics, rules, accountability, self-regulation of fair play through an enclosed judicial system, and reinvestment in the sport – the essence of capital.

2. Expert analysis

We called together a panel of experts in the subject area for a workshop to review and refine that initial framework: Professor

Tony Bovaird, University of the West of England; Professor Fred Coalter, University of Stirling; Professor Margaret Talbot, CCPR (now Association for PE); Professor Peter Taylor, University of Sheffield (now Sheffield Hallam University); Professor Jonathan Long, Mel Welch and Paul Robinson, Carnegie Research Institute. As set out in the report (Welch & Long, 2007: 29–30), this process identified the key elements of these different forms of capital and indicative data (see below).

3. Consultation with NGBs

While we did not expect to get a standard set of data from each NSO, we needed to find some way of involving the sporting institutions that were the subject of the exercise. So we selected a variety of NGBs as exemplars and reviewed with them their contribution in terms of non-financial capital. The set of NGBs we chose represented different scales of membership/operation, and a spread of sport and recreation. To do this we considered: size in terms of membership/participants and number of paid staff; wealth; international success; Olympic/non-Olympic; competitive/recreational; primarily participation/participation and spectating; professional element/purely amateur; team or individual sport; dependent on natural resources or built facilities; proportion of junior/adult/senior membership; male and female participation rates. This might have produced any number of combinations, but we arrived at the following mix:

- British Canoe Union (BCU);
- British Mountaineering Council (BMC);
- British Orienteering Federation (BOF);
- English Table Tennis Association (ETTA);
- Rugby Football League (RFL);
- Sheffield and Hallamshire County Football Association (SHCFA) – although a sub-national body it is a similar size to many NGBs and larger than many more;
- The Fitness League (formerly Women's League of Health and Beauty) (TFL).

Interviews were arranged with senior officers, who were sent a pro forma identifying the information needed for the project and a meeting was then arranged to collect raw data and officers' views. Follow-up phone calls were used to gather supplementary information and check records.

The search for indicators

We tried initially to dissect what might be encompassed by each form of non-financial capital and consider where we might find useful data. This review of the existing material produced an initial framework that considered non-financial capital in terms of social, intellectual and technical components (see Figure 10.1).

The review by our expert panel confirmed the impossibility, or at least arbitrariness, of establishing a pound equivalent for these elements of social, intellectual and technical capital, and also recognized the shortcomings of the standard data sets (large scale surveys and audits) in terms of providing appropriate measures. Consequently, much of the emphasis had to be on exploring with individual NGBs what data they held that might be capable of demonstrating the nature and scale of these elements.

Social and human capital (reproducible and sustainable) might be evidenced in:

- Volunteers (helping; self-determination) – the number of people and the hours they contribute could be used to produce hypothetical delivery costs
- Paid staff
- Clubs and leagues – clubs offer bonding capital, and also have some bridging capital, but the latter is not easy to identify
- + Inter-club competition beyond leagues
- Events – drawing people together, including spectating
- NGB continuity and history
- Symbolic value, reflected in ability to attract participants, spectators and financial support as well as pride and status (a major reason for reinvestment) – indicated in part by international success/medals

Intellectual capital (diffusion/passing on of knowledge) might be evidenced in:

- Knowledge of the game
- Communications systems
- Education in the form of badges, award schemes and coaching
- Advocacy/campaigning around issues like: child protection; disability discrimination; health and safety; ethics and fair play
- Performance development (all levels) – for example, through talent ID schemes
- Sports science – programmes operated and projects funded
- Commercial value/products that operate as 'invisible' exports, like databases, TV/media rights and copyright

Technical capital which reinforces the primary sporting purpose

- Governance, for example, fair play framework
- Management of competitions and leagues
- Event management
- Facilities and equipment (ownership, management of, knowledge base)
- Insurance cover offered to membership

Figure 10.1

Indicators of social, Intellectual and technical capital generated by National Sports Organizations

In accord with the framework provided by Figure 10.1 we took intellectual capital to lie in the sporting ethos and moral authority provided by the NGBs and the values they establish. Technical capital was taken to be represented by the rules and mechanics of the sport that are codified and transmitted by the NGBs which are the repositories of the skill sets and procedures that make participation possible. There is also a symbolic dimension to these elements. This symbolic capital derives from belief systems, values and commitment that help to promote collective identity and civic pride. Some of the elements identified in the CCPR project as constituting intellectual and technical capital might otherwise be seen to be important elements of social capital. So insofar as they address connectedness (e.g. communications and training events) and common values (e.g. through guardianship of the game, education, advocacy and campaigning) those elements will be included in this chapter when appropriate. Our examination of possible indicators and their contribution to the assessment of social capital quickly highlighted some fundamental challenges to the original project.

Active participation

For those following Putnam, active participation is valued above passive consumption (again linking with Stebbins' (1982) conception of serious as opposed to casual leisure) in terms of presumed contribution to social capital (e.g. Arai & Pedlar, 2003), but this may not be appropriate. Sport is regarded as being sociable, which in large part is why participation in sport is supposed to promote social connectedness. However, some sports are lonely and demanding of time (not just the loneliness of the long distance runner), especially when practised at a high level. When compared with this kind of participation, there may be more social capital to be derived from being a habitual supporter of a team – the capital that comes from physical interaction and conversational exchange.

Measurement

For many of the indicators we identified it was impossible to locate data that would be consistent across all sports/organizations. Even in those instances where apparently good quality data do exist we found confusion over exactly what is being measured and different quantities indicated by different measures or by apparently similar measures in different surveys. For those who have been involved in research for any length of time this comes as little surprise, but it makes the estimation of a quantity of social capital even more elusive.

Differentiation and meaning

As already noted, participation in sport may contribute to bonding by bringing similar people together, but its contribution to bridging capital is less clear. We should acknowledge too that bringing people together physically may not do so socially; aggressive competitiveness may divide. Moreover, we know from a series of reported events and research studies that these encounters may promote misogynist, racist, xenophobic and other divisive attitudes. So what is this connectedness generating? In recent years NGBs have been distinguished by their differing efforts to counteract such damaging divisiveness so that sport can fulfil its potential for promoting social cohesion.

Attribution

Even at the basic level of participation it is not clear how much of what is measured can be attributed to NGBs (especially as walking accounts for so much of the participation). Some NGBs have individual members, some operate through the affiliation of a club, and some have a hybrid system.[5] The Football Association (FA), for example, insists that all football teams are affiliated to the FA through leagues and competitions, but this is not quite what happens in practice with many less formal and impromptu games. It might be argued that even the most casual sporting involvement can be attributable to NGBs because they have constructed the game that people recognize. In some sports non-members may be even more indebted to the NGB, as is the case, for example, among climbers who generally benefit from the legal access agreements negotiated by the BMC, irrespective of whether they are members. Essentially what we need to try to do is to address Wacquant's (1998: 28) distinction between informal and formal social capital, in which the latter consists of 'the set of resources and values that individuals may draw upon by virtue of membership of, or connection to, formal organizations'. While NGBs no longer provide the sole organizational structure in sport, they are still the only people doing it primarily for the sport rather than for some other interest. Moreover, the framework of governance supplied by NGBs provides continuity and

---

[5]The Fitness League is organized in a different way again; it is the tutors who affiliate and then run their own classes.

coherence to sport through ethics, rules, accountability, self-regulation of fair play through an enclosed judicial system, and reinvestment in the sport – the essence of capital.

Interconnectedness

As indicated above, connectedness is the most common starting point for considerations of social capital, and participation in sport self-evidently encourages people to come together in significant numbers around the country. Without that social interaction other social benefits would not accrue; it is the sine qua non. But to be productive in creating social capital this needs to promote reciprocity, understanding, compassion and an inclusive concept of community (Wilson, 1997). The people involved in these links include the staff of the NGB, the volunteers (at national, regional, county and local level) and the members participating in the sport. A significant part is played also by coaches who may be full-time staff (but most often are not), who may be paid or volunteers. Whereas the measurement of effectiveness in other leisure areas (e.g. the arts, museums, entertainment) is largely or wholly based on viewers or visitors (i.e. consumers rather than participants) the principal recognized measure of the success of NGBs is an increase in the number of participants. The provision of non-participatory benefits – for example, live spectator audience, television viewing, news media consumption (printed and electronic), reading of literature – and their consequent impacts (including economic, social, community and literacy) are usually ignored when evaluating NGB performance.

At the most basic level the data from the General Household Survey (GHS) and now the Taking Part Survey (conducted by British Market Research Bureau (BMRB) on behalf of the Department for Culture Media and Sport) or the Active People Survey (conducted for Sport England by Ipsos MORI) give an indication of the social force potentially represented by participation in sport generally (and broadly defined). Just over half of all adults (aged 16 and over) take part in sport or active recreation on at least one occasion in four weeks.[6] However, even these base measures offered by attempts to estimate the numbers involved are uncertain; different quantities are

---

[6] 54 per cent of adults (aged 16+) on at least on occasion in the past four weeks according to the Taking Part Survey in 2005/2006; 59 per cent (28 per cent when walking is excluded) according to the General Household Survey in 2002/2003 – the difference is at least as likely to be to do with differences in methodology as any real change.

recorded at every turn. For example, according to the GHS (2002) some 125 000 had canoed in the preceding four weeks, while six times that number took part over the previous year, and the BCU claims 1.2 million participants on the not unreasonable basis of including those under 16 (not part of GHS) who canoe.

It may be one step too far to suggest that whatever social capital is gained by all participants can be attributed to NGBs. Perhaps it is more appropriate to consider those who participate through sports clubs; with the exception of the recent spate of private health clubs most of these are affiliated to an appropriate governing body. Moreover, as Putnam holds, people are more likely to increase their social interaction by being a member of a club than by being an individual participant. The club structure usually provides for inter-club activity, which brings their members into contact with those of other clubs so that they experience what happens elsewhere; an opportunity for cross-fertilization and identifying good practice.[7] Different affiliation procedures mean it is possible to get accurate records of the number of clubs within some sports, but not others. However, the CCPR estimates that there are over 100 000 voluntary sports clubs in England alone. Our own research revealed that just one county FA had 1100 affiliated football clubs, the RFL 480, the BMC 300 and the ETTA has 8000 teams in its affiliated leagues.

Adams (2006) suggests that voluntary sports clubs are distinct from other voluntary associations in their ability to generate capital that sponsors forms of collective action, and that this effects a link to decision-making processes. To claim all this as the product of NGB action may be to exaggerate the process, but on the basis of Adams' arguments NGBs may play a valuable role in providing a structure that helps to ensure that this capital does not dissipate. The clubs do not exist for purely altruistic purposes; though many individuals do contribute altruistically, clubs are self-help organizations that provide an essential contribution to the quality of life of their membership. Among other social benefits this can offer meeting places for isolated people to come together in friendship, who might otherwise not have associated because of ethnic, social, religious or lifestyle reasons. Any club, though, can be off-putting to outsiders. Even those that are not 'exclusive' may exclude simply because they are good at bonding members together as this can deter others who do not feel they are a part of what is going on.

---

[7] It is not unusual for there to be some level of resentment towards any central body, so for some clubs this contribution to social capital might seem to be despite rather than because of the NGB.

Examining the GHS data is a salutary reminder that within the general patterns there are big variations in participation by class, sex, age, etc. And it is the less advantaged groups in the population that are least likely to be involved. What purpose then is served by the social capital generated? Overall we are obliged to question whether sport is likely to be the force for renewal and a more equitable society that its apologists suggest. Nonetheless, according to the GHS in 2002, 17 per cent of adults (aged 16+) were a member of a sports club for an activity in which they took part in the four weeks before interview.[8] This amounts to 38 per cent of participants when walking is excluded (despite the Ramblers' Association little walking is formally organized through club membership), almost 7 million people. Overall, health and fitness clubs and sports clubs were equally popular amongst adults but there was a large gender difference with men almost twice as likely to be a member of a sports club as women (22 per cent compared to 12 per cent). The GHS also records those who take part competitively in sport and those who receive tuition in sport, two groups who might be benefiting more directly from NGB activity – 28 per cent of participants had competed in the past year (over 5 million people), and 37 per cent had had tuition in that time (some 6.7 million). Gender differences are even more evident among those who take part competitively in sport and physical activity (20 per cent men compared to 5 per cent women). However, it was women who were more likely to have received tuition. Measures of more formal involvement increased between 1996 and 2002 among those who participated in any activity (excluding walking and darts); club membership, competitive participation and tuition, were all found to have risen significantly.

Delaney and Keaney (2005) estimated that membership of a sports club had an impact on well-being equivalent to a £3600 increase in income per year. They also found that countries with higher levels of membership in sports groups among their citizens have higher levels of social trust. A similar relationship between sporting membership and trust in society and its institutions was found at the level of the individual. Members of sports organizations are also slightly more likely to be politically involved than the average citizen and, perhaps surprisingly, more likely to express the view that immigration enriches the cultural life of the nation. Of course, these correlations may have more to do with the type of people who participate in sport rather than the participation itself.

---

[8] This at a time when the two major political parties in Britain are struggling to maintain a membership of no more than half a million between them.

Some of the social capital generated through participation and even club membership may be only indirectly related to NGBs; the link for those employed by NGBs is far more direct. NGBs are increasingly likely to employ staff at their headquarters, as regional development officers, and as coaches and performance directors. The larger governing bodies have also developed a network of administrative staff at region/county level. In addition, through their partnerships NGBs may oversee, facilitate or encourage employment opportunities via local authorities, educational institutions and other publicly funded bodies (e.g. county sports partnerships) or in the private sector. These staff not only create opportunities for social connection between sports participants but also derive social capital themselves through their employment (Barros & Barros, 2005). Their study again showed the different facets of social capital. For example, it was found to have a positive effect on earnings, thereby conferring advantage on those in possession of it at the expense of others, whereas we were more concerned with its contribution to the common good.

Beyond the NGB employees is a vast array of members, clubs, coaches and volunteers. There is, however, no consistent formula at work. Our seven governing bodies had ratios of staff to members varying between 1:193 and 1:5250, with substantial variations in the ratios for clubs and participants as well. The work NGBs and their various components undertake can never be effectively delivered solely by paid employees; the contribution of the volunteer is critical to the organization of virtually every sport in Britain. They provide both the governance and the workforce and do a wide range of tasks: committee work, fundraising and handling money, helping to organize and run events, etc. The skills deployed in these roles do not just benefit the sports world, but are transferable to other areas. The NGB structures thereby bring together an extensive network of people who may be from a wide variety of backgrounds, but share the common interest and cause of their sporting activity.

Once again the data sets that seem to hold the key to assessing the contribution to social capital lead to rather different estimates. While the *European Social Survey* (2002) estimates that 6 per cent of the UK population volunteers through sport, the Home Office figures from the *Citizenship Survey* (Attwood et al., 2003) suggest it is 10 per cent.[9] The CCPR estimates are

[9] Interestingly the estimate from the UK's Citizenship Survey of the people who are formal volunteers on a monthly basis (27 per cent) is the same as the figure calculated by the Corporation for National and Community Service (2007) in the USA for those who volunteer at least once in the year.

higher still at nearly 15 per cent of adults in the UK volunteering in sport (Nichols, 2003). Even using a stricter definition of volunteering in a formal organization to provide sport the estimate was between 12 and 13.4 per cent, over 6 million people, 'the vast majority in NGBs and their clubs'. On the basis of this last estimate 26 per cent of all 'formal' volunteering takes place in sport and recreation, which would make this the most popular area for providing voluntary help. That same study calculated that the time given by 'formal' volunteers in sport and recreation is at least 187 million hours a year, 169 million of which are within the clubs, events and competitions/leagues of the NGBs. That would amount to the equivalent of over 100 000 full-time workers, or c. £1 billion even if paid only at the rate of the minimum wage. (To this army of volunteers can be added a proportion of coaches – the MORI report for Sports Coach UK (2004) estimated that 400 000 of the 1.2 million coaches in the UK are provided by NGBs.)

To assess the contribution to social capital this needs to be more than just a numbers game. What they get from their volunteering (Kemp, 2002; talks a bit mechanistically about output variables) determines the nature of the social capital involved. The bulk of the responses provided in the Sport England study (Taylor et al., 2003) did identify satisfactions that relate to social capital: social benefits like friendship and being part of the club; fulfilment from helping others and giving something back; pride in helping the club; satisfaction from seeing youngsters improve; sense of belonging. Young volunteers, though, were more ego-centred, often motivated by building their CV.

Values

In the social capital thesis all this participation and meeting is inextricably linked with the production and maintenance of a set of shared values, and the thesis is further predicated on the belief that the sharing promotes harmonious relationships and trust mechanisms to allow society to be more productive. The social case for sport appears to be underpinned by a presumption that the core values are of fair play, team spirit, respect and discipline. But for others sport is associated with gamesmanship, winning at any price, top-down domination, exclusion, sexism, racism, homophobia, xenophobia … This is the dark side of sport that matches the dark side of social capital. So there is not just an issue of whether people want to participate and be included, but one of whether that inclusion is likely to generate the kind of social capital that will encourage trust and reciprocity.

Existing members of clubs and their NGBs may want to maintain the essence of the sport they know and love, while potential members may be more likely to be attracted (or encouraged by their parents) if the sport is safe (as possible), maintains a code of ethics and fair play, and appears accessible and welcoming. For NGBs, the core values are typically their first priority; without them the NGB might be seen to have failed in its fundamental purpose to safeguard the essence of the sport. However, this may mean that the 'welcome' is restricted to people who are 'like us' (wittingly or unwittingly). Indeed, some may be persuaded to join for that very reason. This extends beyond the 'players' to the volunteers. Most NGBs, and their regional and county sub-divisions, admit that they have not been very successful in extending their volunteer base from the traditional white, middle aged, middle class and, in most of the established team sports, male stereotype (the same might be said of clubs). While many NGBs are enjoying an influx of paid development officers, generally a younger and more eclectic mix, information about volunteers suggests that the age profile is increasing.

The responsibility for enforcing procedures, regulations and disciplinary codes can lead to a distancing between those who play the sport and those who administer it. However it may also lead to more inclusive initiatives like formulating anti-discrimination regulations, promoting participation by people from minority ethnic groups and people with a disability, and working with programmes to help disaffected young people. Our case study governing bodies provided many examples of initiatives to extend participation to sectors of the population, for example:

- SHCFA runs a regional centre of excellence for disabled players; has set up a summer league for asylum seekers; and has worked with people running projects to reduce youth crime.
- Recognizing that orienteering is largely a rural activity and that the opportunities to participate tend to rule out the socially and economically deprived, BOF is now trying to introduce activities to inner-city schools and communities.
- ETTA has an extensive programme for people with a disability.
- The Canoe Foundation (a registered charity) has been set up by BCU to encourage young people and people with a disability to take up the sport.
- TFL is providing physical activity for (increasingly) older women, who might otherwise not take any exercise.

It is this kind of initiative that is required if sport's contribution to social capital is to benefit more than those who are already included in society's institutions.

The value systems help to shape a set of shared sporting symbols that promote collective identity and civic/national pride. International success (or failure) by British (or English/Scottish/Welsh or Northern Irish) competitors has been assuming a higher level of political significance, and has increasing influence on government decisions about funding NGBs, thereby potentially distorting their overall priorities. In some sports the respect for the work of NGBs enhances the UK's international standing. Because of the significance of such symbols political analysts might interpret them as being used as a means for those with power to continue to exercise power.

If people want information or a definitive ruling on some aspect of the sport they look to the governing body. Hence, one of the fundamental roles of NGBs is to disseminate knowledge and enhance understanding of their sport. They do this both within their membership and for the wider community by providing a repository of knowledge on issues such as:

- rules of play/performance;
- construction of calendars of events and fixtures;
- technical knowledge on performance enhancement, including coaching.

They also provide a neutral point of reference for the resolution of disputes, misunderstanding or uncertainty. It is not just the number of person years contributed to these functions annually, but the accumulated knowledge base passed from one staff/committee member to another that ensures capital is maintained and developed.

At an even more fundamental level the very history and continuity of NGBs exerts an undertow that contributes to the shaping of social capital. While things go well it lends credence to the sporting ethos they establish, the common values they promote and safeguards relationships that contribute to trust and reciprocity. As institutions that have survived since the Victorian era, NGBs and their member clubs carry a certain status, a status from which people can derive social capital through association. That status may be strengthened by others sharing it, but is dependent on not too many doing so (many clubs were set up to provide for the minority who had completed their education through school or military establishments and local authority provision for all came much later). The structures of governance, too, in serving to ensure historical continuity also serve to exclude some groups. For example, SHFCA is not unusual in having nobody from a minority ethnic group and no woman on its Council.

To participate in sport means to share these legacies, and crucially here, the historical development of NGBs shapes what they are today. Fired by tradition governing bodies try to maintain standards and ethical positions. As the keepers of the keys to the past they are responsible for the preservation of their sports' values. Armed with the authority of history they are sport's natural advocates, promoting it and its benefits. In order to do so, NGBs spend considerable time, money and expertise in publicity, communication with members and other interested parties. Modern IT has increased the scope for NGBs to interact with their (potential) membership, communicating not just knowledge and information but also value sets. Most NGBs and many of their affiliated clubs have their own web sites (the RFL's three web sites receive over 80 000 hits a month), sometimes with a 'members only' section and sometimes allowing interactive data input by members. In themselves these communications constitute further forms of participation and interaction. The government benefits too from not having to worry about communicating with individual members to articulate policy or finding out what is required by sport; they have a ready conduit in the NGBs. NGBs have an advocacy and campaigning role to play among their own members. This is particularly important in building an ethical and equitable sporting body, one that campaigns against child abuse and racism and promotes inclusive practices. NGBs have to be successful in this if they are to avoid what Putnam refers to as dark capital, the kind that may be very beneficial to a small group, but highly damaging to outsiders.

Conclusions

While our CCPR project was concerned to illustrate the part played by NGBs in shaping social capital, it is clear that they in turn are shaped by social processes: shifting government policies and interests; legislation like that for health and safety or child protection; economic drivers like those leading the private sector to play a greater part in providing for some aspects of active leisure; declining provision elsewhere through work-based sport and recreation clubs; a growing litigation culture; and increased media coverage that concentrates on fewer sports.

Part of the problem for sports professionals operating in policy circles is the lack of weight afforded sporting arguments because sports bodies are seen as mutual self-help (self-interest) organizations rather than altruistic ones. It is not surprising then that an opportunity has been seized by advocates of sport and leisure of adopting social capital arguments. The association with social capital has been useful to Sport England in rationalizing its Active England programme, and has rejuvenated the interest of the CCPR in volunteering. Collectively they have marshalled arguments like those in the Denham report (2001: 28), which concluded that:

Sporting and cultural opportunities can play an important part in re-engaging disaffected sections of the community, building shared social capital and grass roots leadership through improved cross-cultural interaction.

Sport does have the potential to communicate across those cultural boundaries that divide communities in a way that is at the same time respectful of the differences that separate them. But that is it; the potential exists, but there can be no simplistic reduction to: 'being involved in sport increases social capital, therefore sport is a good thing'. Nonetheless, quite independent of wider social benefits it seems reasonable to claim that:

- NGBs do help to promote social capital if only among part of the population.
- The social capital that resides in NGBs does provide socially valued goods to those involved.
- If NGBs did not fulfil their various roles, there would be pressure on the government to finance some alternative.

However, if the world of sport simply reproduces itself through these processes, such forms of capital may be seen to be of little value unless they have social relevance.

We know from the GHS that not only are women less likely to participate in sport, but they are less likely to have done so as a member of a club or part of an organized competition, those aspects of sport most likely to be attributable to NGB activity. Similar differentials exist for social class, ethnicity, disability and age (we lack information on religion and sexual orientation). This clearly affects not only who benefits from the social capital generated by NGBs, but also the nature of that capital. Remember that part of the value associated with the social capital may be derived from some people not having it (Bourdieu, 1993). Clearly the relationships producing this capital are not static. As indicated above, the NGBs are subject to changing socio-political processes, like shifting tastes and legislative constraints; and the NGBs can also act themselves, like the way some have done to promote equity, thereby increasing bridging capital.

Our project again drew attention to the issue of where social capital resides, whether at the individual or collective level (Uphoff, 2000). Like Putnam, Bullen and Onyx (1998) follow Coleman in presenting it as a bottom-up process, a natural consequence of the focus on connectedness, but our case study examples suggest that there is social capital that resides at an institutional level irrespective of the particular individuals involved. As the guardians of the sport those organizations have a major part to play in sustaining the imagined and imaginary communities (Bauman, 2001; Spracklen, 2001) through continuation of the historic legacy and the sport's ethos. This they achieve through law setting, education, and communications that present 'knowledge' to members.

At this stage we know nothing of associated opportunity costs. Much youth provision is founded on the presumption that occupying time in sport will at least prevent young people engaging in activities deleterious to society. It is also plausible that if many participants were to direct their activity elsewhere (arts, conservation, politics, community, etc.) they might generate greater levels of social capital. We lack the research evidence to get anywhere near that calculation.

This project was a salutary experience (we knew it was not a trivial exercise from the outset). However, if reviewed sensibly it does help to focus attention on some of the key dilemmas. Attempts to calculate the overall amount of social capital produced using a standard metric are likely to be less productive than analyses of how positive contributions to social capital are engineered. The latter serve to focus attention on action needed to ensure that negative processes are challenged. So what might be expected of NGBs?

Certainly, there is currently an expectation that NGBs will play their part in increasing participation in sport, thereby, so the argument goes, improving the nation's health and tackling social exclusion. This would also be likely to increase connectedness, but NGBs might have a bigger impact on social capital by promoting pro-social values through sport rather than some of the divisive ones sometimes evident. NGBs might also be encouraged to negotiate the paradox of maintaining the spirit of their respective sports whilst not simply welcoming but encouraging the participation of different groups and inviting them to bring their ideas with them. However, we should not be disingenuous in our expectations. As already identified, sports clubs and NGBs are mutual aid organizations. They are there to ensure that members have the opportunity to play their sport rather than to operate as social welfare organizations.

It is not the fault of NGBs, but in policy discourses there is an implicit reprimand in the way in which increasing social capital is advocated as a means of turning around disadvantaged communities (or nations) – 'If only you people would …' The main thing that most people who live in localities suffering the worst excesses of deprivation have in common is their poverty. In these localities there is often little in the way of the 'norm', solidarity or trust, and it may be eminently sensible to keep yourself to yourself. Bauman (2004) argues that it is often the case that trust is recast as naivety and is replaced by suspicion and 'let's wait and see how they work' joint alliances, which tend to be entered into with a 'cancellation option' in mind.

I have been critical of some of the presumptions underpinning the social capital thesis, but implicit in part of what I have said is the suggestion that bridging (and linking) capital is preferable to bonding capital. This may in part be what lies behind recent efforts in Australia to outlaw the use of ethnic identifiers in the names of sports clubs in the belief that any show of ethnocentrism encourages clubs to be inward looking rather than building bridges to others (similar debates have been rehearsed in the UK, particularly around the establishment in England of 'Asian' cricket clubs and leagues). Whatever the details of such pronouncements, it seems to penalize those who are excluded rather than those who are already incorporated in established structures; nothing is said about the many clubs that retain military or educational connections. At first sight there is an intuitive appeal to encouraging maximum mixing through participation in sport, but in a different context in the 1980s many left wing organizations established black sections and women's sections as a mechanism for increasing participation. The argument then was that through the solidarity of bonding people acquired the skills and confidence to take on challenges they would otherwise have found daunting.

So my position is that social capital, certainly as incorporated into policy development, is a flawed concept, but it might be possible to use it to highlight what sporting institutions need to do to increase the chances of delivering whatever positive aspects the advocates of social capital might want to claim for sport (or perhaps social benefits I might want to see). I remain sceptical though that social capital shows the pathway to address social exclusion and those involved in sports policy should beware the tenuous links.

References

Adams, A. (2006). The Political Opportunity Structure for Voluntary Sports Clubs in England, a paper presented to the annual conference of the European Association of Sport Management, Nicosia, 6–9 September.

Arai, S. & Pedlar, A. (2003). Moving beyond individualism in leisure theory: A critical analysis of concepts of community and social engagement. *Leisure Studies*, 22(3), 185–202.

Attwood, C., Singh, G., Prime, D., Creasey, R. & others (2003). *2001 Home Office Citizenship Survey: People, Families and Communities.* Home Office Research Study 270. London: Home Office.

Barros, C.P. & Barros, C. (2005). Human and social capital in the earnings of sports administrators. *European Sport Management Quarterly*, 5(1), 47–62.

Bauman, Z. (2001). *Community: Seeking Safety in an Insecure World.* Cambridge: Polity Press.

Bauman, Z. (2004). *Wasted Lives: Modernity and Its Outcasts.* Cambridge: Polity Press.

Bellah, R., Madsen, R., Sullivan, W., Swidler, A. & Tipton, S. (1987). *Habits of the Heart.* Berkeley: University of California Press.

Blackshaw, T. & Long, J. (2005). What's the big idea? A critical exploration of the concept of social capital and its incorporation into leisure policy discourse. *Leisure Studies*, 24(3), 239–258.

Bourdieu, P. (1984). *Distinction: A Social Critique of the Judgement of Taste.* London: RKP.

Bourdieu, P. (1993, trans. 1999). *The Weight of the World: Social Suffering in Contemporary Society.* Cambridge: Polity Press.

Bullen, P. & Onyx, J. (1998). *Measuring Social Capital in Five Communities in NSW: Overview of a Study.* Available at http://www.mapl.com.au/A2.htm.

Coleman, J.S. (1961). *Adolescent Society: the Social Life of a Teenager and Its Impact on Education.* New York: Free Press.

Corporation for National and Community Service (2007). *Volunteering in America: 2007 State Trends and Rankings in Civic Life.* Washington, DC: Corporation for National and Community Service.

Delaney, L. & Keaney, E. (2005). *Sport and Social Capital in the United Kingdom: Statistical Evidence from National and International Survey Data.* London: IPPR.

Denham, J. (2001). *Building Cohesive Communities: A Report of the Ministerial Group on Public Order and Community Cohesion.* London: Home Office.

Durkheim, (1902). *The Division of Labour in Society.* New York: Free Press.

Hall, C. (2005). *Social Capital: Introductory User Guide*. Newport: ONS. Available at http://www.esds.ac.uk/government/docs/soccapguide.pdf.

Hemingway, J. (1999). Leisure, Social Capital and Democratic Citizenship. *Journal of Leisure Research, 31*(2), 150–165.

Jarvie, G. (2003). Communitarianism, Sport and Social Capital: Neighbourly Insights into Scottish Sport. *International Review for the Sociology of Sport, 38*(2), 139–153.

Johnson, N. (n.d.). *Commission for Racial Equality Director of Policy and Public Sector*. Available at http://www.cre.gov.uk/Default.aspx.LocID-0hgnew0lo.RefLocID-0hg00900c002.Lang-EN.htm.

Johnston, M. & Jowell, R. (1999). Social capital and the social fabric. In R. Jowell, R. Curtice, A. Park, & K. Thomson (Eds.), *British Social Attitudes. The 16th Report. Who Shares New Labour's Values* (pp. 179–200). Aldershot: National Centre for Social Research/Ashgate.

Kemp, S. (2002). The hidden workforce: Volunteers' learning in the Olympics. *Journal of European Industrial Training, 26*(2/3/4), 109–116.

Lloyd, J. (2006). Harvard study paints bleak picture of ethnic diversity. *Financial Times*, 9 October, 1.

Long, J. (1981). Leisure as a tool for community development and the opiate of the masses, In A. Tomlinson (Ed.), *Leisure and Social Control* (pp. 161–165). Brighton: Chelsea School.

Marcuse, H. (1964). *One Dimensional Man: The Ideology of Industrial Society*. London: Routledge and Kegan Paul.

MORI for Sport Coach UK (2004). *Sports Coaching in the UK*. Available at http://www.sportscoachuk.org/NR/rdonlyres/4CC9B752-610A-4060-895E-D6C7BDEDCAB9/0/SportsCoachingUKFinalReport.pdf.

Nichols, G. (2003). *Citizenship in Action: Voluntary Sector Sport and Recreation*. London: CCPR.

Office for National Statistics (ONS) (2005). *Social Capital: Harmonised Concepts and Questions for Social Data Sources, Version 2.0*. Newport: ONS.

Putnam, R.D. (2000). *Bowling Alone: The Collapse and Revival of American Community*. New York: Simon & Schuster/Touchstone.

Siisiäinen, M. (2000). *Two Concepts of Social Capital: Bourdieu versus Putnam*, A paper presented at the ISTR Fourth International Conference The Third Sector: For What and For Whom? Trinity College, Dublin, 5–8 July.

Spracklen, K. (2001). 'Black pearl, black diamonds': Exploring racial identities in rugby league, In B. Carrington & I. McDonald (Eds.), *'Race', Sport and British Society* (pp. 70–82). London: Routledge.

Stebbins, R. (1982). Serious leisure: A conceptual statement. *Pacific Sociological Review*, 25(2), 251–272.

Taylor, P., Nichols, G., Holmes, K., James, M., Gratton, C., Garrett, R., Kokolakakis, R., Mulder, C. & King, L. (2003). Sports volunteering in England, 2002. London: Sport England. Available at http://www.sportengland.org/volunteer_full_report.pdf.

Uphoff, N. (2000). Understanding social capital: learning from the analysis and experience of participation. In P. Dasgupta & I. Serageldin (Eds.), *Social Capital: A Multifaceted Perspective* (pp. 215–252). Washington, DC: The World Bank.

Wacquant, L.J.D. (1998). Negative social capital: State breakdown and social destitution in America's urban core. *Netherlands Journal of Housing and the Built Environment*, 13(1), 25–40.

Welch, M. & Long, J. (2007). *Beyond the Bottom Line: An Analysis of the Social, Technical and Intellectual Capital Provided by National Governing Bodies of Sport*. London: CCPR, http://www.ccpr.org.uk/dyncat.cfm?catid=4262.

Wilson, P. (1997). Building social capital: A learning agenda for the twenty-first century. *Urban Studies*, 34(5/6), 754–760.

Public policies, social capital and voluntary sport

Ørnulf Seippel

Introduction

'Sport for all' is the overall goal for Norwegian public policies towards sports. The most important policy tool (in economic terms) for reaching this goal is an arrangement of public grants for construction and maintenance of sport facilities. These grants are based on money from national lotteries, and half of the public resources spent on sport at the state level are devoted to these facility grants. The question behind the research project on which this chapter is based is how this policy tool – grants for facilities – affects or influences how the policy goals justifying the policy tool are actually reached. In other words, how does this arrangement for grants for facilities contribute to the policy goal of 'sport for all'? On the one hand it seems straightforward to determine the effects of these policies: counting sport facilities, and to be more precise, counting active athletes at these facilities. On the other hand, the processes where these policy tools are applied and realized are complex and not easily understood. Accordingly, to really understand what happens in these processes and how various outcomes come about, relevant questions are: How are the arrangements institutionalized? What kinds of resources are required to succeed in these arrangements? What are the interests of the actors involved? What are the outcomes of these arrangements when specific actors with their respective interests and resources act within the institutional frames given? In short, the main question of this chapter is how different actors' possession and employment of various forms of resources – and for this chapter especially social capital – carry importance for their outcome. Whereas others have been asking how participation in sport somehow results in some kind of social capital (as for example trust, cohesion, community, political interests and attitudes, see Jarvie, 2003; Seippel, 2006), this chapter asks how (non-sportive) social capital carries importance for sport policies.

The outcome of these arrangements, and the role of social capital and other resources as influential factors, have to be studied relative to some specific types of outcome, and the challenge then becomes how to operationalize 'sport for all' as an outcome. I will discuss the outcomes of sport policies towards facilities along three dimensions. The first, and the most direct operationalization of the sport-for-all-policy-goal, is the *effectiveness* of these policies: To which extent is the intended objectives actually achieved? Secondly, a question is whether this is an *efficient* way to organize these policies: How is the balance between benefits and costs? Third, the case studied here is interesting because it is placed at the intersection of the voluntary and political sectors both claiming to be democratically organized, and this raises interesting normative questions of legitimacy: Where and when do the actors involved in these processes challenge each others roles as legitimate actors?

The chapter is structured as follows. The next section will introduce a theoretical framework used to describe and explain the outcome of policy processes with a special focus upon the role of social capital within these processes. Thereafter methods and the case will be presented. The substance of the chapter contains one part showing how this policy process is institutionalized, and one part discussing how the actors involved actually manoeuvre within this institutional set up. Three types of outcomes – efficiency, efficacy and legitimacy – are discussed. The chapter concludes with a discussion aiming at a more general contribution to the theories on governance and the question of how policy networks actually work at the intersection of public and voluntary politics.

Public policies, social capital and voluntary sport:
A theoretical approach

As a general background, it should be noticed that the case in question is an instance of what is commonly described as 'governance': a policy arena with less clear and hierarchical authority structures and more dependence on cooperation, negotiation and social networks than is often thought to characterize public policies. The case is also a good example of governance in the respect that there are two sets of substantially different actors – public authorities and voluntary organizations – interacting (Pierre, 2000; Pierre & Peters, 2000; Salamon, 2002; Kjær, 2004; Kooiman, 2005). The governance concept – being a sensitizing concept (Blumer, 1969) – makes it possible to see developments within sport policies as part of larger societal shifts, to lead attention towards interesting research questions, and to relate the findings from this chapter to a more general discourse on governance and public/voluntary interactions. The perspective does not, nevertheless, suffice for more analytical descriptions or explanations of our case, and the more concrete challenge is to find a perspective useful for understanding how the many actors involved act within this institutional opportunity structure.

For the actors taking part in these arrangements and applying for grants, the aim is to generate resources, and they do this by employing what they have of available resources in light of their interests, knowledge and what they see as the opportunity structure. As this research will show, what makes for success in these grant seeking processes is, first, possession of different forms of capital, and economic and material resources are most obviously of importance. Second, we found both human and social capital to be of uttermost importance to succeed in the process running. Next, the interviews also indicated that some kind of affinity (cultural capital) for sports in general, specific sports in particular and incomprehension for others because of specific aspect commonly recognized as negative (e.g., violence, doping and eating disorders) were at work. A final type of resources of use for the actors in this study is what could be called political capital: the extent to which sports and sport facilities are prioritized by politicians.

This constellation of actors with interests and resources facing an institutional framework is close to a theoretical perspective proposed by Hedström (2005), where the point is simply that resources are spent in light of actors' belief and interests (desires) given an opportunity structure facing the actors. Given that most of the actors involved in the study had a common goal – to work toward the construction and/or maintenance of sport facilities to produce sport activities – the challenge becomes to identify what makes a difference to their participation in the grants arrangement and what thereby might explain why some succeed and others fail. The crux of this analysis then turns out to be a search for what kind of resources the actors are able to raise in order to invest and employ in the process and how this affects the outcomes of the grants process.

A second requirement for a theoretical framework is, in this case, to deliver a better understanding of how social capital as one type of resource might matter in such policy processes. Basically, social capital is about relations and networks between actors, that is: social structures. Two types of social structures are at the core of social capital discussions: bridging and bonding (Putnam, 2002) or, very much the same distinction in different terms, brokerage and closure (Burt, 2005). There are of course variations with respect to both types of structures, and especially when it comes to brokerage, there have been discussions about how various brokerage roles function (Gould & Fernandez, 1989). Among the most famous role of brokerage is the one covering structural holes (Burt, 1992). A second side of the social capital concept is how these network structures actually matter. Again there are two sides to the social capital discourse of relevance. For some, the most important thing is that social capital produces (or reflects) trust between actors (Putnam, 1992, 2000; Hardin, 2006; Tilly, 2005). For others, the focus is more upon exchange of information and thereby some kind of influence (Lin, 2001). In the bonding case, trust does make for some kind of community, but bonding is weaker as a source for new information or influence than bridging since 'all know all' already. In the bridging case the result is less community and trust and more information and influence. In an approach combining the strong sides of the two, Coleman (1990) emphasizes how social capital helps overcome collective action problems by providing trust through information. This is obviously a conceptual ideal. Empirically there will be instances where the two overlap, where information might build trust, and trust is a prerequisite for influence (in contrast to power).

Method and cases

The purpose of this study is not primarily to say something in general on how these kinds of processes occur, but to provide a more thorough and deeper understanding of how they tend to take form: how actors experience the opportunities given by the institutionalization of sport policies, how they tend to approach them and act and how outcomes are produced. To achieve this aim, two types of data were collected. First, documents of three kinds were studied: (1) public documents like the Report to the Storting (Parliament) laying out the main goals of the public sport policies and tools applied to achieve these goals; (2) general policy documents belonging to the central part of national sport federations (NSFs) and setting out their main goals; and (3) documents of various kinds central to the specific sport federations representing the sports selected for the study. The second type of data were interviews with actors central to these processes. At the national level, a selection of representatives of the department and central persons in the national sports confederation were interviewed. Furthermore, six representatives of specific NSFs were interviewed. Then two counties (of 19 in total) and two sports were chosen, and representatives of the county, regional sport confederation (RSC) (both employed and elected) and regional sport (both employed and elected) were interviewed. Then six municipalities were visited (of which two were within our selected counties) and central actors interviewed. Finally, six leaders of sport clubs and six representatives of the sport councils were interviewed (see Figure 11.1).

	Public sector	Voluntary sector
National level	Department of sport policies (DPS)	NIF – joint administration of all sports in Norway NSF – national sport federations
County level	Counties	RSF – Regional sport confederation: Joint administration of all sports in the county or region Members: regional sport federations
Municipality level	Municipalities	Sport Councils: Coordinating body for all clubs within a municipality Members: Sport clubs
Local level		Sport clubs

Figure 11.1
Norwegian sport structure

Institutional framework as opportunity structure

In this section the institutional framework in which the actors perform will be sketched: From the actor's point of view this is the opportunity structures they are facing: Which actions are (im)possible? Which actions are (not) invited? Two components make up the most important parts of what I call the institutional framework: (i) the actors taking part in the processes with their goals, resources and the structural relations between these actors and (ii) the rules, norms and knowledge guiding the interaction in this field (Scott, 1995).

The NSF comprises 12 000 member clubs of which 5000 are so called 'company clubs' with links to companies. The 7000 clubs analysed relevant in this study are voluntary sport organized as voluntary organizations where the members are in charge of the clubs through open and democratic elections of officials. The most important direct resources for these voluntary sport clubs are voluntary work and member fees. These local sport clubs are in turn organized in two lines which add up to the national Norwegian Sport Federation (NIF). One organizational line follows sports such that for example all clubs organizing football are affiliated to the regional and national football federation. All sport federations have a national office, but only the larger sports do also have regional offices. The other organizational line is regional so that all clubs are member of the RSC (county level): all clubs in Oslo are also member of Oslo Sport Confederation.

The public authorities involve four actors of special importance for this case. At the top, the Parliament sets the basic though rather general goals for public sport policies. The most important administrator at the national level is the Department of Sport Policy (DSP) in the Ministry of Culture and Church Affairs. Then there are those working with sport at the county level. Finally, municipalities have their more or less developed, explicit and prioritized sport policies (Mangset & Rommetvedt, 2002). At municipal level there is also an interesting institutional set up, Sport Councils, where the local clubs meet with the municipalities, a true public/voluntary arena. In essence public national policies towards voluntary sports could be said to comprise four main areas: (1) sports facilities as is the topic of this chapter; (2) financial support to the sport federations; (3) financial support from local authorities; and (4) something called 'support for local activity'.

The rules for applying for financial support for sport facilities are outlined by the DSP. A first rule of interest for the purpose of this research is the actors allowed to apply for these grants including sport clubs, municipalities, counties or actors being part of the NIF-system. It should be noted that there is also an opening for other actors, but they have to be approved by the ministry before entering the process. Thereafter it is essential to note that applications have to be directed through and integrated in municipality plans. Municipalities then pass the applications to the counties, which set up a list of applications, which are in turn passed to the DSP. The department decides on the 'amounts' distributed to the counties and the counties in turn distribute the resources. The amount granted should constitute one-third of actual costs. Furthermore, there are several provisions regarding the level of grants and exceptions from the rules intended to, for example, prioritize development of urban facilities, provide funding for costly facilities' and 'smaller' technologies falling outside the arrangement. Facilities funded through this arrangement have to be open to the public for at least 40 years, and should not generate profits for the owners.

On the one hand, these rules open up many ways to apply for these resources: the initiative might come from different actors, there are many possible coalitions between actors to achieve funding and there are many factors influencing how various actors are able to participate in these processes. On the other hand, there is a more or less clear expectation, and tradition, that the initiatives should be local or at least include local actors. There is also an expectation that there must be some kind of local funding for the facilities, which is roughly expected to be one-third through a club (voluntary work) and one-third from the municipality (and one-third applied for). So, on the one hand, these state grants are indeed important and most of the informants reported that without them there would have been no facilities, but they do at the same time only constitute one-third of the total funding.

In this case, the goals behind the institutionalization of the field are as already indicated, 'sport for all', and this is then specified to be more important for some groups of the population – children and youth – than others. The state actors are also explicitly concerned with sport and physical activity for those not participating in organized sport. Moreover, there are visions related to the organizational forms of voluntary sport organizations: open and democratic organizations with voluntary work as an important resource. Other actor's visions are then mostly more 'myopic' versions of these general goals: sport x for all that want to do sport x, sport for all in the municipality.

Acting (with social capital) in an institutional field

The following will describe how different actors see their institutional opportunity structure and how they actually tend to act when it comes to winning public grants for building and maintenance of sport facilities. The focus will be on the two streams of interaction – horizontal, linking local actors, and vertical, where actors from different levels network – which appear as the most pertinent for an understanding of how resources, and especially social capital, matters in a specific institutional setting for the outcome of the arrangements under study.

Horizontal interaction at the local level: Sport clubs, sports councils and municipalities

A first hindrance for succeeding in the grant arrangements involves economic capital. First, there is a question both of the amount of resources required to succeed in the grant seeking process, and to actually construct or maintain facilities. Second, clubs differ when it comes to types and amounts of material capital they actually possess and how they are able to employ what they have. Basically, a prosperous club (property, savings, income) is obviously better positioned for winning grants than a club without.

When informants were asked about a basic premise for success with facility grants, they unanimously answered some kind of local enthusiasm, local competencies (human capital) and local networks (social capital). Thus, a club with persons of enthusiasm and competencies necessary to submit good applications will obviously fare better in these processes than those without, and knowing the right actors – in the club, other clubs, public official, private investors, sport officials – does also pave the way for alliances/coalitions and success in the arrangement. Finally, representing a sport which many people – or at least some of those involved in the process – appreciate (cultural capital) makes it much more likely to succeed in these processes.

A second set of local actors are Sport Councils, a forum at the intersection of voluntary sport clubs and municipalities. On the one hand they are supposed to work in 'both' directions: both to communicate from the sport clubs into the local political system and to effect sport policies from the local polity to the clubs. The task most often emphasized in the interviews conducted for this research, however, was sport councils as a channel for political influence and pressure from the clubs into the political system: turning human and social capital into political capital.

Beside the clubs, the most important actor at the local level are municipalities. There are huge differences (size, organizational structure prosperity) between Norwegian municipalities, and the role they play in the arrangements under study in this chapter. A formal and decisive role of municipalities is to ingrate building of sport facilities into general municipality plans and, in cooperation with sport councils, to pass applications onto the counties. Moreover, they are 'expected' to contribute financially to the process of building and maintaining. This might involve financial support – or at least some kind of financial guarantees – which makes it easier to succeed with grants and construction, or, in other cases, particularly with a rural bias, they might be able to provide property. They often also play important roles as the owner, maintainer or financial supporter of facilities. A factor emphasized in previous research (Mangset & Rommetvedt, 2002) and mentioned in many of the interviews, is the extent to which municipalities are able and willing to employ people in positions devoted to sport. This is not legally required, but several informants said there is direct link between having people employed in such position and the quality and quantity of the applications coming from specific municipalities. For sport clubs this implies that there is an experienced person in the local polity who has decisive knowledge of both how to work out a good application (human capital) and knowledge on how to reach others of use to get ahead in the process (social capital).

Besides the more obvious functioning of economic and human capital, social capital as both bonding and bridging is shown to matter. First, the need to base these processes in local initiatives and the requirement of some kind of local funding (often as voluntary work), leads to and depends upon some kind of bonding. This community building depends on trustful relations at the local level; knowing that contributing time and efforts is worthwhile. Such cooperation is made possible because social interaction within a club shows people that others are willing to make an effort to succeed, and makes it possible to mobilize voluntary work.

Second, there is a need to link these local resources and initiatives to the larger society – to other clubs, municipalities, market actors, actors in the sport policy system – and here we find bridging – linking hitherto unknown actors – to provide information on how to proceed, what to do and how to do it. These processes do involve circulation of information, but might also produce trust. Social networks between clubs, municipalities and other local actors also help to overcome collective action problems: the clubs will see the municipality really has something to offer and public agents might see that local clubs do represent a proper need for facilities and have a potential for really completing a process of facility construction.

It is also of interest to note the many ways it is possible to convert forms of capital. The research revealed that social capital increases human capital, making it possible to mobilize economic capital. In one case a club was paying (economic capital) consultants to work out the application (human capital). In other cases having links to certain actors (social capital) resulted in political support (political capital) or help to work out the application (human capital). In this way information and trust might be produced, and successful development and application of social capital might turn into political capital, in turn conducive to the economic capital related, more or less directly, to the grants arrangements. Taken together, at least one kind of capital is necessary to get these processes started, and the whole arrangement is based on merging some constellations of resources with public resources. Yet, differences in these resources will heavily influence which clubs, and thereby which sports, which regions and which people in the end succeeding in these processes.

In between: Counties and RSCs

In the institutional framework set up above, the role of the counties is to bring together and coordinate the processes of applications from the many municipalities within the county. The counties themselves do seldom have or contribute to grants for facilities. Yet, the counties did, however, report that they have a say in the prioritizing of facilities passed onto the Department, and they emphasized a certain responsibility for their region as a whole and tried to secure a certain diversity of types of facilities. In sum, counties have very little economic capital with respect to these arrangements, but have a certain role to play and do important work with respect to human and social capital. RSCs role in these processes is, formally, to 'look over' the recommendation being sent from the county to the DSP. The informants were in agreement that there were not many conflicts and not much politics to be executed in these arrangements, and RSCs seem to be of rather marginal importance with respect to grants to facilities.

Vertical policy networks: RSF and NSF

A first significant difference between NSFs regards finances. A few are able to provide some kind of direct funding for certain facilities, and some do help with sponsors. Second, the same differences show up for human capital (and there is of course an overlap). Whereas the larger federations have people employed both at national and regional levels, other federations have no people with competencies at all. Some have more ad hoc arrangements. Third, some sports are very good at and conscious of actively linking actors at various levels to promote their standing, and, as part of this, some sports report that they have easy access to important political and administrative actors, and thereby are able to connect actors. Finally, sports are reporting differences on how they are met by other actors (politicians, sponsors, etc.): one sport with a clearly healthy image reported that even though people where not particularly interested in their sport, they were always met with a positive attitude. Other sports were met with a more hostile attitude, especially at local levels. So, there are important differences in cultural capital: some have to build cultural capital before they can even come into consideration, whereas others are able to walk right in and convert their existing cultural capital to economic capital.

The differences between sports and their national federations are significant, and are mostly repeated or even strengthened at the regional level. First, most of the sports with large affiliations do have representation at the regional level – regional sports federations (RSF) – whereas small sports are without. Of the two RSFs interviewed, one was very keen to emphasize the importance of facilities whereas the other gave few and vague indications as to how to contribute in this field. Neither of the sport regional federations were directly able to fund sport facilities substantially themselves, but the larger were representing a sport federation able to provide funding for certain types of facilities centrally, and to link local, regional and national actors. The large RSF has consultants within the regional federation working only with facilities and is able to help in many ways: having courses, providing material. The other RSF says that this – helping local clubs wanting to initiate the process toward facilities – is impossible, even though the central federation wants us to do so: 'facility projects have to be based on local initiatives coming from vital clubs'. What they could do, at best, was to establish contact between actors. The larger federation is also active in what one would have called lobbying: they send their central representatives to meetings in the municipality to convince local authorities that building sport facility is a wise investment. Thus, they were better in using their social capital and especially at converting social capital into political capital. They also have an explicit aim to link actors in ways that promote their abilities to construct and/or maintain facilities.

In sum it is important to see the variation among sport federations when it comes to helping out with sport facilities. Many (small) sports have weak NSFs and are without regional representation, whereas other (large) sports dispose of huge resources of most kinds – economic capital (indirectly), human capital, social capital, political capital – at this level. This means that there are vertical streams of resources differentiating local actors by sports and that matters decisively for how the arrangements for sport facilities actually function.

National level

The clear impression gained from the interviews was that the Norwegian Olympic Committee and Confederation of Sports (NIF) does not have a central role with respect to facility policies and further that there exists a kind of division of labour: NIF mainly working with sport activity, *DSP* with facilities. NIF is nevertheless involved in some of the larger and often controversial questions where issues are sent to the NIFs board. DSP is obviously important as the main financial contributor and as the actor that sets the rules of the game. Even though DSP is an extremely influential actor for facility policies in general, it is, when the rules are set, up to the actors involved to make up the applications and DSP is not significantly involved in the concrete processes.

I have identified two streams of policy networks of special importance for how the arrangements for public funding for building of sport facilities functions. On the local level, clubs, sport councils and municipalities are the main actors, and building social networks both within clubs and local communities to strengthen the enthusiasm and competencies appear vital. Links between local actors above club level is also important to integrate these projects in the larger local environments and thereby to involve more kind of resources is a must. Vertical networks between specific clubs and sport federations are also important channels of resources and seem very helpful for actors related to specific sports to go ahead with their applications and to succeed with them.

Policy outcomes (and social capital): Efficiency, efficacy and equity

So far I have described how the arrangements for grants for construction and maintenance of sports facilities are institutionalized, and I have showed how actors having different interests and possessing various amounts and kinds of resources lead to success (or failure) in these processes. On the background of the above descriptions, I will systematically discuss the question of policy outcomes related to the three dimensions presented in the introduction. Again, I will do this with a special eye to how social capital matters in these cases.

Efficiency

A key question is whether this is a way to institutionalize the arrangement for grants for construction of sport facilities that is cost effective, that is: what is the balance between costs and benefits? From most involved actors' point of view, the answer to this is positive: they get as a rule of thumb three times as much out of this process compared to what they put into it. This happens through a state-funded framework providing incentives for potential actors supposed to take part in the arrangement: if they contribute, others will and together all will be better off; resources will be generated. And most, if not all, of the informants confirm that this is an arrangement generating resources. The number of applications, clearly outnumbering available grants also proves this. There are differences when it comes to opinions on how effective it is: some actors say that the arrangement leads to the same sum as the grants being invested locally (doubling) whereas other seems to assume that the grant sum is quadrupled. This aspect of the efficiency of the process – different actors (voluntary and political) sharing, pooling and getting access to each other's resources – is the crux of the whole arrangement, and without this crossover of resources, Norwegian sport policies would have looked very different. It generates resources, spreads the risks and links the actors together in a way conducive for collective action (Jones et al., 1997).

It is an arrangement not only making it possible but also legally required to merge resources from various levels and types of actors. In this way, the arrangement is also effective in the way that it makes it possible to contribute with different forms of capital, and to transform forms of capital into other forms of capital, thereby making it possible to generate more resources than if only one capital form were allowed (Coleman, 2000). The other side to this arrangement and its dependency on local competencies is that entrepreneurial work done locally at times probably suffers from lack of experience and the need for each one to negotiate products and projects anew, even though similar projects are carried out elsewhere. The success of some of the large federation's central negotiation with contractors seems to indicate that there is a kind of local under-achievement going on.

The success of this arrangement is dependent upon the capability of mobilizing local resources, and to achieve this social capital is of uttermost importance. Social relations between the actors at the local level do: (i) bond together local actors directly concerned, thereby enabling the local enthusiasm necessary to get applications started; and (ii) bridge different actors that have to be involved to succeed in the process. This is an example of the strength of the weak ties (Granovetter, 1973), the need to involve different groups of people, not necessarily those already knowing each other. These links provide information on how to proceed and succeed in these arrangements and build trust between the members in a way that makes the process overcome collective action situations where no one alone has a convincing reason to invest the resources required to start the process. It also makes the process work smoother. In this way social capital is a prerequisite for extracting the resources involved, and thereby fulfilling all the visions related to the social capital concept. It provides the links between new actors and makes them work together as a group: Granovetter's weak ties fill in Burt's structural holes with Putnam's trust solving Coleman's collective action problems. Part of the efficiency of social capital results from its capacity for merging different types of capital and thereby functioning as a catalyst for the generation of resources.

The case is also an interesting example of the kind of increasingly common (new) governance – networks modes to do politics. It shows how these kinds of networks and policy implementations, based on public resources, are dependent upon specific local resources such as social capital, but also how it is thereby able to generate resources. In sum, this is basically an arrangement with a high efficiency and is probably the main reason for the continued existence of the arrangement where all actors involved lose some of their autonomy and influence in the return for other actor's resources.

Effectiveness

The next question is how this arrangement for public grants for construction of sport facilities influences the extent to which the policy goal of 'sport for all' is reached. A truly effective policy presumes that the overall policy goal of 'sport for all' follow directly from applying the chosen tool (grants for facilities). As shown, the outcomes of these arrangements are dependent upon various actors' interests and resources and it seems close to wishful thinking to believe that the distribution of these interests and resources add up in a way that do not discriminate along any dimensions, thereby precluding the extent to which sport for all is reached.

The reason it is difficult to secure sport to all to the same extent is that the whole arrangement of grants is based on local initiatives to secure sufficient resources and funding, and even though the interests of these local actors do not really contradict the overall policy goals, they each have biases that might add up to systematic biases in the overall system. The interviews indicate that inequalities in particular are produced along geographical and sportive lines. The situation is that the goals of local actors are more specific versions of the general aims: 'sports for all' turns into 'sport x for all' or 'sport for all people in area y', then 'sport x for all living in region y', and finally 'sport x (and y) for all members (which could be only old men) of club z'. Moving from the national level towards local levels implies a movement in goals from the most general towards more local versions of the general goal, and these moving goals will have repercussions for the outcome of the processes. The point is that even though these are rather strongly state-based policy tools, there is an autonomy in the local policy networks that makes it possible to adjust them to local interests (Hudson et al., 2007).

The situation found is a typical principal–agent (Petersen, 1993; Aghion & Tirole, 1997; Shapiro, 2005) situation where there are discrepancies – not very outspoken, not very serious taken one by one – between two actors, where the one (principal) tries to make the other (agent) fulfil the principal's goals. The principal has the power to state the goals, but has to rely on the second actor – the agent – to implement the goal. The challenge is the extent to which the principal has control over the agent. In the case examined within this chapter, there is a certain control inherent in the formal rules and the funding, but within these limits, there is a possibility for action that agents might use, and this provides enough scope to produce outcomes deviating somewhat from the overall aim of sport for all.

In social capital terms what happens is that two types of social capital are in play, and contributes to different types of bridging and bonding. First, local actors are horizontally bonded to each other, and hence bonds between local actors are strengthened. Even though these local networks makes possible to mobilize resources as, for example, voluntary work without having financial resources and thereby have an equality-making effect, it does also favor local communities already strong on social capital. Second, local actors at the municipality level are linked, and there are clear differences when it comes to municipalities' willingness and competencies for prioritizing sports. Third, local groups are vertically linked to sport federations in cases where sport federations are strong enough to provide help and resources; that is, bonding and bridging based on sport. In this way, social capital is important in bridging actors and thereby generating resources, but at the same time this involves a kind of bonding excluding others and leading the interests of those involved in specific regional or sportive directions. The challenge for political steering is exactly that social capital does both: bridging actors easing policy implementations and bonding actors making them prioritize particularistic goals at the cost of general goals.

This discussion shows that there is a dilemma built into this arrangement when it comes to the questions of efficiency and effectiveness because the two dimensions at times appear agonistic and thereby have to be balanced. Clearer public policy aims will probably lower the local enthusiasm whereas the other way around, an even more open process could have initiated even more local initiatives but decreased the effectiveness.

This study found two ways that specific interests seem to dominate aspects of the facility arrangement, but also found other examples of how those involved promoted and articulated interests that could bias the arrangement. Some actors were concerned with competition from what they considered non-sport actors, or sport actors that they did not really consider proper sports. Several sports addressed the elite – participation question, others were concerned with gender, age, ethnicity and social origin. Some public actors were worried about the lack of priority given to sport at the cost of other issues (mostly culture). And some were concerned with construction of facilities being pursued at the cost of maintenance. All institutional actors 'above' club level were concerned with service provision for the disabled.

One of the most apparent findings when interviewing actors in these fields is the cumulative character of resources: there seems to be a 'Matthew' effect operating where those given shall have more, and social capital helps this process. Even though there could be an equalizing effect in the possibility of converting different forms of capital, it is also the case that having different kind of capital and being able to convert them in the most profitable form, partly through social capital, also could make those already strong stronger.

A second goal of public sport policies is to motivate and stimulate for democracy and voluntarism. Again, on a first and quantitative level it seems clear that this arrangement in demanding private and local resources almost forces clubs to mobilize volunteers, and thereby strengthens the civic aspects of voluntary sports. Furthermore, voluntary work releases public resources and the outcome for those involved – devoting voluntary labour – will be a feeling of efficacy important for keeping up the voluntary work. On the negative side, working with facilities might be exhausting and burn out some of the potential for voluntary work. There is also a paradox built into the tendency to build increasingly more complex and high quality sport facilities because this is technologies requiring special competencies to be run and maintained. The result of voluntary efforts then might be professionalisation which in turn might produce new challenges for the organization.

Addressing the question on manageability makes it possible to see more in detail how these problems come about. According to Salamon (2002) there are four specific factors of special importance for an actor's ability to manage governance processes: coerciveness, directness, automaticy, visibility. Public authorities have a certain control over this grant arrangement, and they do so to speak *coerce* the involved actors to adhere *directly* to the rules they have set, and in the end they approve of projects that are granted support. In this way they have a certain control, at the same time as it is indeed limited because the whole incentive structure is based on local knowledge and interests merging with public goals. Yet, a less open public approach, both more coercive and more direct, could probably damage this incentive structure. In short, there is a steering paradox built into this model, and the possibility to improve on the effectiveness without seriously damaging efficiency seems to impose ad hoc extra arrangements (as is at present the dominant strategy) rather than to change the manageability of the process through a more direct or coercive approach.

There are several actors – with different interests and varying resources – involved in the process and many are only involved once (building only one facility), so there is, at least for clubs, a relatively low level of what Salamon calls *automatity*: one cannot trust those involved to do what they are used to and thereby improve on the predictability of the process by convention. In some cases municipalities or sport federations with some experience are involved, and in these cases the outcomes of the process are more foreseeable. But standardization among the experienced actors does easily lead to further differences in the abilities to take part in such processes.

The last factor is *visibility*, and to a certain extent sport facilities do have a high visibility: it is not easy to not build a publicly funded sport facility and get away with it. Yet, it is not easy to document how they actually are used and by whom. Accordingly several actors in the research sample – of different types, and at different levels – were concerned with contributing to more minute visibility: how are various sport facilities actually used? Thus, the challenge is to take the step from confirming that the facility is set up, to find out how they actually are used. Heightening visibility – that is, increased knowledge on how various forms of facilities are used – would strengthen the normative pressure (which is part of the rationale for governance networks (Jones et al., 1997)) for specific uses and the potential for ad hoc adjustments improving efficiency and equity. Having and sharing more precise understandings of how these processes might have systematic biases could produce adjustments in the arrangements which do not disturb the efficiency of the process.

When it comes to the question of social capital, coercion and directness are some kind of opposites. The whole arrangement where social capital is employed to generate other resources is fundamentally based on – when the rules of the games are accepted – the fact that the local actors are trusted and free to develop plans according to local needs and interests and not, to large extents, along lines decided strictly by others or under control from others. Thus, again, the ambiguity resulting from the weak central steering of local interests and resource generation makes the level of manageability rather low. Higher visibility would heighten the stream of information running through the system, and – even though this requires trustworthy knowledge – should not threaten the trust on which the system is based. Even though the knowledge might be to the disadvantage of some, they will be forced to accept it if it they see it as legitimate (Habermas, 1984).

In this section I have shown how grant arrangements are built on the assumption that a lack of proper control of the coordination of these interests leads to a problem with the quality of the process in the meaning that there is a lack of security, control and knowledge of the extent to which the goals of sport for all and not only some selection of the population actually is reached. Some of the biases resulting from these problems are acknowledged and the Department for Sport Policies has set up special arrangements for some social groups/activities/ facilities – immigrants groups, handicapped, people being physically active outside organized sports, new sports, expensive facilities – and has countered some of these biases to a large extent. The meta-question then is obviously the extent to which the balance between having an arrangement generating resources and the need for adjusting the biases of the arrangement. If there is a quest for more research resulting from this discussion, it is the need for knowledge of the actual use of sport facilities.

Legitimacy

That all actors involved in these arrangements are also democratically organized – either as part of the political system or as part of the sport organizational system – also raises the question of legitimacy. The situation is not only that two sets of actors with partly diverging interests cooperate on common projects, but also that both need to legitimate their actions and the (lack of) success they experience in these arrangements. I will present three discourses that either contests the legitimacy of other actors or discloses a need for legitimating own actions and then interpret these discourses in light of the question of the role of social capital in these processes.

On an overall level, the actors responsible for the institutional aspects of the arrangement are keen to legitimate the whole process both through its efficiency and effectiveness: the extent to which resources are generated and the goal – sport for all – is reached. They legitimate their own actions as well: as being only the administrator of politically designed goals and themselves being thereby without significant influences in the process. Both these claims were contested by other actors. It was claimed that this was a closed system that should be more open and that the DSP should accept, if they really want NIF as a democratic autonomous organization, that some of the grants given could be spent otherwise than DSP wants. Some claimed that sport policies needed a clearer political foundation and articulation, others that the DSP is far too influential. Of interest here is the fact that there is a process going on in Norwegian sports where the justification of having a regional confederation is very much in focus. An interesting question then is whether this organizational unit has a role in the process of facilities that justifies its existence. As far as we can see their role in these processes is rather marginal. That is, there are several actors that would like to see the foundation of the arrangement somewhere else: either upwards making it 'more political', or downwards increasing the influence of 'sport democracy'.

A second set of discourses contesting the legitimacy of the arrangement occurred among those losing out in the sport facility arrangement. Among the complaints was that representations in local Sport Councils blocked possibilities of getting a foothold in regions. Others claimed that those in charge in various institutions – for example, municipalities – simply disliked them or their sports. A further question was whether the state should actually support facilities for activities outside the 'sport systems' and thereby organizations not reflecting the traditional sport values. Some also stated, as above, that there should be a clearer political steering of the process, indicating that too much was left to the political administration.

A third set of discourses addressed the fairness of the arrangement and were presented by those with success in the process feeling a need to justify the outcome of the arrangement: that their success was not unfair or at the cost of others and more deserving actors. This was, of course, partly because they were attacked or accused for being too dominant.

What is interesting to note is that all these discourses concerned with the legitimacy of the arrangement basically address aspects of the social capital operating in the process. They show very clearly the ambiguity of social capital and the role it plays in policy processes and why identical social capital processes have two names: bonding (as a positive term) and closure (as a negative term). In the three cases outlined above the situation is that social bonding which for some enables mobilization of resources for others is experienced as a constraint – as a closure – excluding participation from someone that should have had a say in the discourse. In the first discourse this is about a shift in political accentuation, in the second a more inclusive discourse at the local level, and thirdly about closed discourse linked to specific sport. It is difficult from this research to say for sure how justified these critical points are, but they do all point toward a dilemma posed by network arrangements of the kind studied here: successful bridging bonds new actors making some kind of action possible but at the price of excluding others from taking part in the goods produced.

In this section I have shown how the arrangements studied seem a success when it comes to efficiency, and faces several dilemmas when it comes to efficiency and legitimacy. Moreover, I have pointed out how both this success and these dilemmas to a large extent could be interpreted as resulting from the dependency of these processes' on social capital: social capital bridges actors and releases enormous amounts of resources, but social capital also bonds social actors in a way that closes them off from the outer world and thereby restricts access to goods.

Conclusions and discussions

The purpose of this chapter was to study Norwegian public policies toward construction and maintenance of sport facilities. Leading questions have been: what are the institutional frameworks within which the many actors operate?; which opportunities do the different actors face within these institutional set ups?; how do they actually try to reach which goals, what resources do they possess, and how do they employ these resources?; what are the outcomes of these arrangements?; and why does social capital matter?

The overall policy goal for Norwegian sport policies is 'sport for all'. To reach this goal, sport facilities have to be constructed and maintained, and the arrangement under study is the central policy tool for reaching this goal of 'sport for all'. The arrangement is based on a complex set of rules and involves actors from both public and voluntary sector operating at several geographic levels. There are relatively detailed rules for how to take part in these arrangements, and the actors and the rules together comprises what I have called the institutional framework for the arrangement, and from the involved actors points of view these actors and the rules are the opportunity structures they act towards.

The chapter then described more in detail how various actors act within these opportunity structures, and the chapter focuses particularly on two sets of policy networks. First, the horizontal interaction between clubs, sport councils and municipalities at the local level were in focus. Second, vertical interaction between sport federations (both at national and regional levels) and clubs were covered. It became clear that these policy networks bridge actors in ways that enable them to generate the resources necessary to succeed in these processes. Taken together, these two policy networks reveal how there is a tendency for specific outcomes to be produced under this arrangement, and three sets of outcomes are discussed more thoroughly: efficiency, effectiveness and legitimacy.

For efficiency, this is, apparently for all actors involved, a good arrangement because, for each main type of actor involved, it raises roughly two times what each invests. For effectiveness, the arrangement also functions reasonable well, but does have some biases that affect the outcome. Looking at these two dimensions together reveals a tension in the arrangement: the openness of the arrangement is necessary to mobilize resources but involves a principal–agency situation that makes it difficult to control the outcome of the process directly.

Social capital has been shown to matter in these processes. Locally, social bonding is needed to mobilize the enthusiasm and reciprocal trust necessary to get the process started. Linking local actors as clubs, municipality, sports federation and market actors is also required to provide the information needed to succeed in grant seeking. Finally, actors belonging to specific sports (in some cases) were linked vertically and were thereby able to help mobilize resources. Social capital was, in this way, both a precondition for winning out in the process, but also one of the main reasons for some of the inequalities emerging from the process.

On a more general level the research explored within this chapter is an interesting case of what is commonly described as 'new governance': a less hierarchical and more network-based way to implement policies. This case showed clearly some of the social mechanisms involved in such governance policies and how the autonomy of the networks involved is a precondition for making local actors take the responsibility necessary for good implementation. But, at the same time this autonomy is a source of trouble within such processes. In this case, where both actors are democratically committed, it could be possible to steer the process by making the processes more transparent by inducing new and trustworthy information about what takes place.

References

Aghion, P. & Tirole, J. (1997). Formal and real authority in organizations. *Journal of Polical Economy*, *105*(1), 1–29.

Blumer, H. (1969). *Symbolic Interactionism*. Berkeley: University of California Press.

Burt, R.S. (1992). *Structural Holes. The Social Structure of Competition*. Cambridge, Mass.: Harvard University Press.

Burt, R.S. (2005). *Brokerage and Closure. An Introduction to Social Capital*. Oxford: Oxford University Press.

Coleman, J.S. (1990). *Foundations of Social Theory*. Cambridge, MA: Belknap Press.

Coleman, J.S. (2000). Social capital in the creation of human capital. In E.L. Lesser (Ed.), *Knowledge and Social Capital*. Boston: Butterworth & Heinemann.

Gould, R.V. & Fernandez, R.M. (1989). Structures of mediation: A formal approach to brokerage in transaction networks. In C. Clogg (Ed.), *Sociological Methodology* (pp. 19, 89–126). Oxford: Blackwell.

Granovetter, M. (1973). The strength of weak ties. *American Journal of Sociology*, *78*(6), 1360–1380.

Habermas, J. (1984). *The Theory of Communicative Action* (vol. 1). Reason and the Rationalization of Society. Boston: Beacon Press.

Hardin, R. (2006). *Trust*. Cambridge: Polity Press.

Hedström, P. (2005). *Dissecting the Social: On the Principles of Analytical Sociology*. Cambridge: Cambridge University Press.

Hudson, J., Lowe, S., Oscroft, N. & Snell, C. (2007). Activating policy networks: A case study of local environmental policy-making in the United Kingdom. *Policy Studies*, *28*(1), 55–70.

Jarvie, G. (2003). Communitarism, sport and social capital. *International Review for the Sociology of Sport*, *38*(2), 139–153.

Jones, C., Hesterly, W.S. & Borgatti, S.P. (1997). A general theory of network governance: Exchange conditions and social mechanisms. *The Academy of Management Review*, *22*, 911–945.

Kjær, A. (2004). *Governance*. Cambridge: Polity Press.

Kooiman, J. (2005). *Governing as Governance*. London: Sage.

Lin, N. (2001). *Social Capital. A Theory of Social Structure and Action*. Cambridge: Cambridge University Press.

Mangset, P. & Rommetvedt, H. (Eds.), (2002). Idrett og politikk – kampsport eller lag-spill? [Sport and Politics – Fighting Sports or Team Sports?] Bergen: Fagbokforlaget.

Petersen, T. (1993). Recent developments in the economics of organization: The principal–agent relationship. *Acta Sociologica*, *36*(3), 277–293.

Pierre, J. (Ed.) (2000). *Debating Governance*. Oxford: Oxford University Press.

Pierre, J. & Peters, G.B. (2000). *Governance, Politics and the State*. London: MacMillan.

Putnam, R.D. (1992). *Making Democracy Work*. Princeton: Princeton University Press.

Putnam, R.D. (2000). *Bowling Alone. The Collapse and Revival of American Community*. New York: Simon & Schuster.

Putnam, R.D. (2002). Introduction. In R. Putnam (Ed.), *Democracies in Flux*. Oxford: Oxford University Press.

Salamon, L.M. (2002). The new governance and the tools of public action: An introduction. In L. Salamon (Ed.), *The Tools of Government*. Oxford: Oxford University Press.

Scott, R.W. (1995). *Institutions and Organizations*. Thousand Oaks: Sage.

Seippel, Ø. (2006). Sport and social capital. *Acta Sociologica*, *49*(2), 169–184.

Shapiro, S. (2005). Agency theory. *Annual Review of Sociology*, *31*, 263–284.

Tilly, C. (2005). *Trust and Rule*. Cambridge: Cambridge University Press.

CHAPTER **12**

Race equality and
sport networks:
Social capital links

Kevin Hylton

Introduction

This chapter is based on a study of the Black and Ethnic Minority Sports pressure group BEMSport[1] (Hylton, 2003). BEMSport is committed to equality and antiracism in sport for black people and others suffering the limiting outcomes of racism in Yorkshire. This commitment was in recognition of issues such as the disparity in the representation of black people as administrators and senior managers in sport, as opposed to purely participants (Jarvie 1991a; Sports Council, 1994; Hylton, 1999; Long et al., 2000). The initial rationale for BEMSport came from recognition by many in sport that black people were being excluded through processes that resulted in their historical marginalization in sport's administration and policy development. In effect pressure was brought by regional actors to initiate a forum that would strengthen the networks and bonds of agents passionate for change in the opportunities for black people within Yorkshire sport. The Forum was also established to act as a support network for alienated black sports development professionals, most of whom were working in local authorities. According to Hain (1976) an organization with the social and community drives of BEMSport draws towards it individuals who in the past have been isolated by the organization and structure of their working or personal experiences. He suggests that organizations like these enable people to take some control of their own destiny by affecting and effecting change. This was clearly the case for the black professionals linked to the emergent pressure group as they saw the sum of BEMSport as being far more influential than its parts. Consequently the Forum members made a point to those established organizations in the sports policy network that they were failing and it was time that there was a critical black voice amongst them. Whatever the motivation for the Forum members to be involved the increased level of agency and capital achieved were important factors for them to join. Discussions with the key members evidenced that their ability to influence policymakers and practitioners in their new position as BEMSport executive members was a common reason for involvement.[2]

---

[1]The term 'Black and Ethnic Minority' was not universally accepted by the Forum members due to the negative connotations surrounding 'ethnic minority'. However, there was recognition that the term was used in a comfortable way by many diverse groups of people who the Forum did not want to exclude due to semantics.
[2]My role as observer as participant changed early on in this study to participant observer due to being co-opted onto the BEMSport executive. This opened up a unique insider position in the study.

In focusing on BEMSport and social capital it was sensible to construct a provocative question for this chapter to consider as an introduction to this topic; is it possible to establish that social capital was actually stimulated by BEMSport and if so, how? As a starting point this was clearly testing because social capital itself does not have a hard and clear definition. In addition, the original study was an ethnographic study of BEMSport as an action research study on racial equality in local government sport policy implementation (Hylton, 2003). This examination of BEMSport is intended to outline how institutional structures have systematically and summarily excluded black people from the policymaking and implementation processes in sport. In addition, social capital as a concept and contributor process of community development is used to examine how sport can be used as a tool for resistance. BEMSport's experiences acted as a barometer of success for sport professionals in the region through following their concerns and agendas in the research period from 1996 to 2000. This opportunity to appreciate the black client-eye view of racial equality issues allowed the original study to temper the normative proclamations of progress in race equality from established professionals in local government. Further, the significance of social capital is made clear by the presence or deficit of the tangible or relational capital that reinforces inclusion/exclusion for black communities (see Lin, 2001). Views from BEMSport's experiences critically challenge what is and should be happening across the region. The alternative discourse presented here is one that leisure and sport studies writers have argued is little known and is therefore worthy of further exploration in the academy (Henderson, 1988; Hemingway & Wood Parr, 2000; Johal, 2001). The findings suggest that the outcomes of local authority practices have meant that accounts 'inside' local authorities have been less critically reflective than more enthusiastic individuals and groups on the 'outside'. BEMSport occupies a space in regional sport networks that is paradoxical; BEMSport's existence contests the discourse of equality within the public sector, which presents local government sport as equitable in terms of the development and implementation of sports policy/practice. The historical developments that led members of a multicultural sports network to challenge the cumulative negative outcomes of public sector activity are illustrated here. BEMSport's story is a counter-story, a competing discourse, an alternative paradigm that situates the black experience of sport in a process that constrains as it liberates, empowers as it disempowers, includes as it excludes (Goldberg, 1993; Ladson-Billings, 1998; Nebeker, 1998; Delgado, 2000).

Social capital 'defined'

Although there is consensus in some areas it is useful to plot a path through some of the more popular debates around social capital to lead to a working definition for this chapter. A clear sign of social capital as a concept of some import in the UK emerged in 2001 when the Office for National Statistics (ONS) found it necessary to establish a coherent review of the literature for policymakers and practitioners (ONS, 2001). Like social exclusion, social cohesion, and the resurgent notion of the quality of life, commentators on social capital have described and interpreted it inconsistently and to this end it is worth revisiting some of the more persuasive arguments. Social capital constitutes part of a conceptual framework from which to understand the accumulation of 'currencies of worth' in society. To complicate matters, these currencies are both tangible and intangible. In the case of financial capital (money available for investing in sport) and physical capital (building and related sporting infrastructure) we can audit the capital available to agents in any sports network or other setting for sport across all levels of the sports development continuum (Silverman, 2004). Human capital can be tangible in terms of our ability to audit education and professional experience or qualifications. However, intangibles such as developing skills and interests, personalities, and more acute political acumen as a result of inclusion in networks are much more slippery to audit in real terms. Additionally, the concept of cultural capital most closely associated with the work of Bourdieu (1989) describes the accumulation or attribution of higher level social skills and status that constitute and are constitutive of elite and closed social and economic networks. It is clear that these versions of social capital are not mutually exclusive and further, any analysis of social capital must accept these conceptual slippages that will occur in its explanation.

Putnam (2000) supports the ONS in agreeing that social capital as a concept has a plethora of definitions and a clear outcome of this is his decision to define social capital in this 'lean and mean' way:

Social capital is ... social networks and the associated norms of reciprocity and trustworthiness.

(Putnam, 2007: 137)

Insofar as a succinct definition, as Putnam's, leads to a less problematic version of social capital I am more persuaded by Wilson's (1999) pragmatics that argues for an acceptance of social capital as a concept *and* process that work symbiotically with other forms of capital. Wilson argues for example that social capital is constituted by other forms of capital such as human capital because it emerges from these social relationships and networks. In addition social capital has been used interchangeably with social energy, community spirit, social bonds, civic virtue, community networks, extended friendships, good neighbourliness and social glue (ONS, 2001: 6). As the highest profile writer on social capital, Putnam posits that of the prominent themes among its various conceptions the outcomes of increased and therefore strengthened social ties have featured most (see also Field, 2003; and Halpern, 2005). The positive aspects of these social ties include mutual support, cooperation, trust and institutional effectiveness (Putnam, 2000: 22). However, the most important distinctions within the analysis of social capital for Putnam and of significance to the development of grass roots sport is the difference between bonding and bridging social capital. Bonding and bridging processes can be stimulated and occur at the same time although it is worth distinguishing both processes as markers for a more sophisticated understanding of how BEMSport stimulated social capital. Traditionally sport has been greatly valued by policymakers as they posit that it has many positive benefits. Sport has been purported to have properties that enable it to contribute to the smooth running of society as a form of 'cultural glue' which helps to hold it together (Hylton & Totten, 2007). Social capital is described in these terms often as an indicator of 'social glue' although Putnam extends the DIY metaphor to unpack the two forms of social capital when he argues that bonding social capital is the societal equivalent of superglue and bridging social capital is akin to our society's WD-40 (Putnam, 2000: 23).

For the purposes of this chapter I embrace a pragmatic version of social capital that considers two positions, one posited by Nahapiet and Ghoshal (1998) and another that makes more explicit racialized power relations in the institution of sport and sport networks (Hero, 2007). Nahapiet and Ghoshal (1998: 243) define social capital as:

The sum of the actual and potential resources embedded within, available through, and derived from the network of relationships possessed by an individual and social unit.

A corollary to the social capital debate comes from Hero (2007: xiii) who argues that social capital tends to emphasize civic association and engagement to the detriment of social structures and institutions. This is further supported by Lin (2001) who contends that we should consider how different social groups have different access to social capital, often related to privileges of structural positions or social networks. The consequence of the marginalization of racialized relations in theorizing social capital is that historical power relations and inequalities are marginalized or ignored thus leaving some analyses narrow, colour-blind and pluralistic in nature. This chapter aims to consider BEMSport's ability to stimulate social capital but still locating it as a racialized agent within a regional sport network.

Governance, sport networks and social capital

BEMSport was initially concerned with raising the profile of the inequalities and racism in sport that were becoming prevalent themes in public policy. By acting as a bridge between the regional black sporting community and established sport networks BEMSport attempted to fill the void in representation for black people in sport. John and Cole (1995) point out that due to the way local state decision-making has become more fragmented the emergence of the practice of extended governance has caused them to use networks at a local level to illustrate and explain the relationships between policy actors and the dynamic behind policy decisions. Network analysis, like social capital, emphasizes the principle of social networks and resource dependency between key decision-making actors in a dynamic relationship. The phenomena, in recent times, that have caused John and Cole to emphasize the prominence of governance and fragmentation in the UK revolve around the contract culture in local government. Compulsory Competitive Tendering, Best Value and Trusts have been engendered via the new managerialist discourse initiated in the 1980s and continuing into the New Labour Agenda in the 2000s. With the changing of Governments the discourse of the late 1990s and early 2000s was that of 'community' and community development which emphasized more the notion of active citizenship and civic participation in the light of a new 'Third Way' emerging from the New Labour administration. This was clearly a response to the outcomes of a destructive process of individualism for grass roots and community sport under the outgoing Conservative government that forced the public sector to roll back the state provision that supported mass participation in sport (McDonald, 1995; Hylton & Totten, 2007). This resulted in leaving more vulnerable groups at the mercy of market forces while resources were being released for other developments concerned with school and elite sport (Clarke, 1994;

Department of National Heritage, 1995; McDonald, 1995; Hylton & Totten, 2007). Inequalities, heightened as a result of the decentring of 'sport for all'/mass participation ideals, became part of the context for a reaction by the new sports pressure group – BEMSport.

Marsh and Rhodes (1992) and Rhodes (1997) have developed and utilized the policy communities and issue networks concepts in a bid to augment the emerging interest around policy networks and governance:

Policy network analysis develops the notion of insiders and outsiders by examining the mechanisms used for inclusion and exclusion and the impact they have on policy.

(Smith, 1993: 3)

Policy networks are a very useful analytic tool in this consideration of social capital and sport due to the interconnectedness of individuals and organizations in sport networks. Networks can be seen to be evolved institutional responses to complex social problems (Blom-Hansen, 1997). Here the key links and relationships beyond set decision-making systems are emphasized in what some might see as a more realistic reflection on the way 'things happen' in sport. The use of network analysis in investigations enables researchers to recognize that even on a sub-national, regional level there are a myriad of actors who may influence the nature of provision and therefore racial equality in a variety of settings in sport. At the same time a critical lens on networks can be used as a simple heuristic conceptual tool to illustrate social capital processes in sport. The dialectical nature of networks and therefore network analysis facilitates a more complex understanding of social capital as the acquisition of any combination of capital facilitates more efficient and advantageous privileges in social, economic and other sports developments terms. The acquisition of capital can also become interchanged or, as Silverman (2004) would suggest, they metamorphosize into each other.

Sport networks and 'race'

Marsh and Rhodes' (1992) questions of (i) 'Do interpersonal links have an impact on institutional ones? and (ii) Does the existence of a network affect policy outcomes?' are well debated questions by sociologists such as Giddens and Gramsci whose concepts of duality of structure, structuration and hegemony explain the dialectics and the intended and unintended outcomes of individual agents and institutions.

The under-representation of black people as senior officers in local authorities in Yorkshire meant that influential regional sport network members were effectively reproducing the same hegemonic relations, structures of power and racial exclusions from their feeder authorities that Brownill et al. (2000) observed in their analysis of urban development corporations. Observations of local authority ethnic disparities in Yorkshire authorities reflecting those in the network give further weight to these views (Hylton, 2003). It is no surprise that sport practitioners for these influential committees therefore reproduced a process of privileging white professionals and participants which recreated the hegemony of public sector providers. So a closer reading of BEMSport's relative position of influence on these committees must also be tempered with an understanding that their context reveals other processes at work. In particular, recognition of the dialectics of networks is likely to see the network reproducing BEMSport's marginal structural position within society, as indeed BEMSport modifies the sport network's practices (Blom-Hansen, 1997; Marsh, 1998b). Due to the connectedness of individuals and organizations in policy networks in sport the pattern of policymaking becomes essentially elitist (Marsh & Rhodes, 1992; Hylton, 2003). This may go some way to explaining Schaap and van Twist's (1997) view that closedness *within* and *of* networks is an essential characteristic for them to be able to operate effectively. For BEMSport to make any impact on race equality in the region it had to move from its relative outsider state to becoming a more established member of this sport network.

In his analysis of social capital, Field (2003) agrees that networks can promote inequality due to their restrictive access to the means of accruing social capital through association. Sport networks have been seen to operate with a noticeable inability to include others from an ethnically diverse background, thus reinforcing the marginalization and power differentials black people face in other social arenas. Some connections are clearly more useful than others in terms of their ability to build bridges and open up opportunities. This has become particularly emphasized by the emerging literature on racial exclusions, racism and sport (Lyons, 1991; Verma & Darby, 1994; Long et al., 2000; Carrington & McDonald, 2001; Hylton, forthcoming). Marsh's (1998a) conclusion that policy networks reflect the structured inequalities in society whilst reflecting their member's interests raises a point about exclusion and inclusion in sport policy networks that is rarely considered. Social capital can be viewed in this chapter as an asset that is unequally distributed in sport as well as a process that reinforces racialized inequality (Field, 2003). In this chapter BEMSport's progress as a notable actor in Yorkshire is outlined in relation to social capital. BEMSport's achievements in terms of its goals are highlighted as they provoke regional governing organizations to increase their efforts to develop sport for black people. Here the impact of the outcomes of local authority interventions in sport for, and with, black people emerge out of the lived experiences of BEMSport as 'outsider'. BEMSport contributed a reliable perspective on sport in local authorities from black sports professionals and community activists which came as a result of them working and networking with established 'insiders'. Further, BEMSport's eventual inclusion and prominence in its regional sport networks was analogous to the development of its variegated social capital as its bonds and bridges strengthened over the years. Consequently, BEMSport's longevity, links and associations were a clear barometer of how equalities work was developing in specific authorities and the region whilst it accrued recognition for the service it provided and consequently forms of social capital in terms of trust, knowledge, financial, human and cultural. After four years the study was concluded from its inception in 1996 when BEMSport became a significant agent within Yorkshire's sport network in 2000.

Black self-help and (anti)racism in sport

Polsby (1963: 4) asked three questions: (i) Who participates in decision making? (2) Who gains and who loses from alternative possible outcomes? and (3) Who prevails in decision making? Given the literature concerning 'race' and sports administration it is generally not black professionals who decide and not black people who generally gain from the eventual outcomes (West Midlands Council for Sport and Recreation, 1990). Consequently, ROTA (Race on the Agenda, 2001) confirm that due to the levels of inequality and racism in many areas in England it is necessary to recognize and fund independent black-led organizations as they are well placed to provide culturally sensitive services to their communities. Generally voluntary groups concentrate on the interests of their users and members, although in many cases black-led groups have been set up as a result of social injustice (Solomos & Back, 1995; Torkildsen, 1999; Home Office, 2001a). In support, McLeod et al. (2001) argue that the earliest documented forms of black self-help in England came as a result of black people recognizing that mainstream services were unable to provide adequately for their needs. This included housing, health, education, community and advocacy services. Sport and leisure were also factors addressed through black self-help and even in 1996 racialized problems in the provision and control of sport were the reasons for BEMSport to be formed.

The necessity for groups like BEMSport to come into existence can be demonstrated further through research by Sport England (2000: 4) which showed clearly for the first time that there are more unmet needs amongst minority ethnic groups in comparison to their white peers. For instance, 54 per cent of Pakistanis to 81 per cent for the 'Black Other' categories wished to take up a sport that they do not participate in, which was above the national norm. Curiously the survey only 'touched upon' experiences of racial discrimination even though in some categories one in five experienced racism (p. 6). This 'silence' on racism is symptomatic of institutional responses to such issues and even in the midst of such groundbreaking research on ethnicity the hegemonic values and assumptions underpinning public sector sport can be unpacked and criticized. Similarly in 1999 Sport England's research into its own activities found that minority ethnic communities in Derby, Leicester and Nottingham did not have equal access to them. To counter this problem they identified a need for greater coordination of sports opportunities, a need for community groups to work together and a need for racial equality support for local governing bodies of sport/sports clubs (Wheeler, 2000). Although not explicitly considered by Wheeler (2000), key social capital deficits were being identified using the discourse of community development (Hylton & Totten, 2007). This recognition of a dearth in relational and structural support in these recent experimental active communities projects is an indicator of emergent ideas on the need to oppose racism and support social justice in sport and improve the capacity of those in sport to develop it more equitably.

At a more political level the Department for Culture Media and Sport (DCMS), in fulfilling the social inclusion strategy of the Government, has developed a strategy that draws on the discourse of valuing diversity, active communities, partnership and devolution (DCMS, 2001). On many levels the voice of organized black voluntary groups is being courted to provide knowledgeable points of reference for public bodies. Further, the Home Office recognize that policy analysts and policy-makers need to consider more fully the structural constraints and power dynamics pressing upon black groups and black participation in society. An area for concern for the Home Office (2001a) was a need to recognize that there needs to be a 'race'-centred approach to policy, as a 'colour-blind' approach only reinforces racial disadvantage in policy formulation. Otherwise, marginalizing 'race' and ethnicity causes inconsistencies and fragmentation in service delivery (Gardiner & Welch, 2001). This has been underlined by the emphasis placed upon the importance of working with black communities by the Home Office (2001b) and ROTA (2001). Paul Boateng, the Home Office Minister of State, said of his compact with the black and minority ethnic voluntary sector:

The black and minority ethnic voluntary sector has a role to play in achieving our aim of a fair, more inclusive society. By empowering black and minority ethnic groups, we can work in partnership to tackle the social exclusion experienced by too many black and ethnic communities.

(Home Office, 2001b: 2)

Increasing social capital?

To develop a sense of how BEMSport has generated social capital it is useful to use Nahapiet and Ghoshal's (1998) typology which describes social capital in three dimensions: structural dimension, relational embeddedness and cognitive dimension. A structural view of social capital relates to some of the earlier descriptions of social capital, as patterns of connections between agents, but in particular the presence (or lack of) network ties. Relational embeddedness is more concerned with the quality of these ties as trust, respect, cooperation and support are conditional upon the quality of relationships we have within networks. The cognitive dimension refers to the intellectual processes that lead to shared norms, values and influential ideals amongst network members. Although not the purpose of this chapter, these intellectual processes lead us to insights into the everyday opinions, attitudes and ideologies that make up the 'assumptive world' of network actors that writers such as Rosenberg (1989) and Young (1992) have considered at more length.

Like many voluntary groups BEMSport was established on a wave of enthusiasm and a collective set of skills and experiences that accumulated into its greatest asset – its human capital. These disparate black sports development professionals were central to the setting of the nine objectives for the Forum which on examination emphasize a deficit for some in the provision and services of sport in the region (see Figure 12.1). The deficit relates to various forms of capital that are exchanged in a complex process to the advantage of the 'holders'. The nine objectives can be further explored at three levels (macro, meso and micro) to further explore the complex currencies required for BEMSport to gain success and therefore social capital amongst sport policymakers, practitioners and the black community.

Macro objectives

Delgado's (2000) argument that 'in-groups' create their own stories applies here to the general public commitments to equality by local authorities. These stories emanate from the symbolic pledges that typify local authority standpoints (Hylton, 2003). Often, these minimalist dispositions reflect the in-group's shared values and solidarity in networks that Fukuyama (2001) suggests is a characteristic of elites. 'Out-groups' like BEMSport aim to subvert that reality, hence its forceful macro objectives that place racism (1) and sports participation for black and minority ethnic (BME) individuals (2) and BME groups (3) at the centre of what they do. Where Fukuyama (2001) argues that social capital cannot be easily created or shaped by public policy he negates the negative effect of differential provision

---

Macro

1. To oppose racism in sport at all levels.
2. To promote sport and physical recreation in Yorkshire for Black and Ethnic Minorities (BEM)
3. To promote the development of sport for local BEM groups in the region.

Meso

4. To enhance consultation processes between sports providers and representatives of BEM.
5. To promote equality of opportunity and outcome for BEM in:
   - Sports participation including administration officiating and coaching.
   - The pursuit of excellence.
   - Representation in sports management and administration in local authorities, governing bodies and the voluntary sector.
   - Media Coverage.
6. To bring together BEM community representatives, recreation and leisure services officers, community sports development officers and officials of sports governing bodies to discuss sports race equity issues and other related matters in the context of BEM participation.
7. To raise the awareness and develop an understanding among sports providers of racism in sport and its impact on the ability of members of BEM to access opportunities in sport.

Micro

8. To give participants the opportunity to share experiences of good practice.
9. To encourage the provision of educational and training opportunities in sport and recreation for BEM.

Figure 12.1
BEMSport's nine objectives

and access to resources in sport brought about by weak policy and practice in sport. The importance of sport and other cultural activities as vital elements of inclusive and cohesive communities has been brought into sharp relief recently with the civil disturbances in the North of England. On a broader scale there is evidence of communities in the UK becoming more stratified and segregated on racial and ethnic lines (Phillips, 2005). In attempting to identify good practice in the provision of public services the Community Cohesion Review Team (Cantle, 2002) and an inter-departmental Ministerial Group on Public Order and Community Cohesion (Denham, 2001) identified a number of factors seen as contributory root causes for a breakdown in community cohesion and an increase in racial tension over recent years that make clear links between 'race', sport and social capital. Some of the main points have a direct relevance to sport and its organizations and they include a lack of adequate social, recreational, leisure, sporting and cultural activities; situations where communities exist in isolation one from another and in ignorance of one another's culture and values; situations where irresponsible media coverage of events is biased against race equality issues; weak political leadership, resulting in an absence of an agreed vision; discrimination and fear of racist victimization and a decline in traditional employment opportunities and obstacles preventing some BME communities from successfully engaging in the labour market (Neighbourhood Renewal Unit, 2005: 3).

In 2002 BEMSport was recognized in Sport England's review of good practice for its range of activism and in relation to mainstream provision a radical experimental approach (Sport England, 2002: 2). Sport England reported that:

Finally, there are organisations such as BEM[sport] in Yorkshire which aim to empower communities and to help develop the capacity of black and ethnic minority sports organisations, including assisting with management, training and help with funding. These schemes can be viewed as a mix of business development and community development, working at a more strategic level.

In this document focused on active communities, active citizenship and community development, Sport England reflected upon the need for organizations like BEMSport at a time when mainstream sport had become myopic in its approach to policy and provision. This sharing of social goals is redolent of Nahapiet and Ghoshal's (1998) concept of a cognitive dimension to social capital. The Sport England (2002) findings and the Cantle and Denham reports set a backdrop to Nahapiet and Ghoshal's (1998) 'regional systems of meaning making' on racial equality and community development as national and local policy concerns meld. Community development necessitates social transformation and anti-discriminatory action against broader social inequality (Hylton & Totten, 2007). One consequence of practitioners and policymakers not considering community development principles was outlined by Ledwith (2005) who describes the pitfalls of 'thoughtless action' and 'actionless thought'. 'Thoughtless action' would include attempts at sports development which failed to engage with underlying social issues. 'Actionless thought' would be recognition of social issues but no plan for change. Clearly when it comes to community development, sports professionals need to consider a form of 'thoughtful action'. Thoughtful action is clearly energized when sport is planned in a holistic way that incorporates the needs of all parties without recourse to short-term gains. In relation to Nahapiet and Ghoshal's (1998) structural dimension of social capital Sport England criticized the potential for change for the infrastructure of sport and described its actors as defensive, protectionist and insular in approach. In relation to BEMSport's objectives Sport England posited that:

It also means that some of the schemes, e.g. [...] BEM[sport], by their very nature will not gain easy support from other sports providers including local authorities. At best they will be seen as competitors for scarce resources, at worst threatening. Sport England will need to have the courage of its convictions. This will involve supporting the projects and advocating the benefits that arise from the projects.

(Sport England, 2002: 7)

BEMSport's 'story' is one that reflects their experiences and presents them in a way that offers some exposure to a black experience of social capital and 'the system'. It is in many ways about social capital deficits but specifically the result of this for BEMSport is revealed as inequality, social injustice, institutional racism and exclusion. What we get from BEMSport reframes the narrative of racial equality in public sector sport from those who experience it (Smith, 1999). To reiterate, this view of BEMSport's inception and development is a reflective account of responses to the cumulative outcomes of public sector sport provision. These experiences stand as a testimony to contested racialized spaces, alternative accounts of racial equality in sport and offer a counter-narrative to those in the mainstream of the academy and in sport policy and practice.

Meso objectives

On a meso/organizational level there are many examples of how BEMSport raised its profile and currency in the regional sport network through its relational embeddedness (Nahapiet & Ghoshal, 1998) (see Appendix). The milestones in the Appendix are a selection of the range of activities undertaken by BEMSport. BEMSport's impact on racial equality in sport should not be underestimated as its adaptation of the Commission for Racial Equality (CRE) Standards (CRE, 1995) for local authorities 'A Level Playing Field' became a benchmark for the Sporting Equals Racial Equality Standards for sport (LMU, 2003). In addition, the emerging presence of BEMSport representatives on regional sport committees came at a point of interest convergence where BEMSport was at its most active and the public sector was at its most receptive in terms of requirements to consult stakeholders; due to the spirit of Best Value and the threat of external auditors requiring proof of 'community consultation'. These mutual agendas or 'shared systems of meaning' (Nahapiet & Ghoshal, 1998) are evidence of various sport agencies' value of BEMSport's executive members as its human capital began to be changed into the currencies of bridging capital through its increased networking and extant successes. The Forum offered increased opportunities for bonding across the regional black community as a trusted, community oriented organization and as its presence in the mainstream sport community developed it increased its status and ability to bond with those members also.

The siting of a Lottery Sports Fund (LSF) road show in Yorkshire was an example, like the earlier Active Communities case, of BEMSport's structural connectedness through its raised regional and national profile. The methodology behind the LSF distribution has been shown to be spurious, ad hoc and inequitable, with funding going to a limited number of sports and worthy causes. These issues were further explored by Sia (1996): National Development Agency for the Black Voluntary Sector who brought to the attention of policymakers in sport that the lack of a robust ethnic monitoring system raised serious concerns for the black voluntary sector. As a result of such an intervention into the impact of the national lottery on the black voluntary sector Sia ensured that representation from the black voluntary sector with Lottery Sports Awarding groups at a strategic level would lessen the funding inequalities that came out of previous practices. The mass of bureaucracy to be sifted through for lottery funding was a big drawback for many of the groups that BEMSport was set up to be an advocate for;

this includes barriers like language, supportive lottery officers and consequently a lack of community expertise. The LSF managers were aware of the disparity in funding from the Lottery to the black community and wanted to be more proactive in eliciting feedback on their funding processes from an informed black presence in grass roots sport. The request by the national Sports Council's Lottery Unit to pilot one of their two national road show workshops in Yorkshire is a significant indicator of BEMSport's relational embeddedness in sport networks as these opportunities could only come about through mutual trust and respect. These indicators of social capital are clearly linked and not mutually exclusive. The structural connections do not necessarily lead to the relational embeddedness but they are a necessary condition for good quality relationships to develop.

Micro objectives

On a micro level BEMSport worked with individuals in geographical communities and from the regional black community involved in voluntary community development, with the aim to build their capacity to facilitate sports development initiatives, including advising on LSF. The training and education of these individuals enhanced their human capital and the expertise database for BME contacts whilst widening the range of BEMSport's activities. These community development volunteers or 'community development facilitators' and positive action sports development courses for black sports development workers meant that the internal strengthening or bonding social capital of black professionals and volunteers in sport occurred where previously it was more ad hoc. It is due to these kinds of successes and other externalities from BEMSport's influence with network members such as improved facilities and services, increased participation and strengthened local networks that Sport England advocated the need to be bold in the face of any criticism of organizations like BEMSport. Whiteley and Winyard's (1987) critique of interest groups posits that 'the question of interest group effectiveness is probably the least adequately researched aspect of the study of pressure groups'. The problem here stems from trying to link action with effect. An action by one group of people on an institution or network is very rarely attributed to them due to the plethora of agendas, both personal and political, of actors surrounding the organization and network (see also Blom-Hansen, 1997; Marsh, 1998a). However, BEMSport was established as a vehicle to build and reinforce bonds and empower black officers working with them from local authorities stymied by racial inequalities that meant that their authorities were colour-blind in a multi-cultural environment (Gardiner & Welch, 2001; Hylton, 2003; Swinney & Horne, 2005). This colour-blindness also meant that the networks that these local authority representatives serviced were also hamstrung in relation to racial equality. It could be argued that the benefits of BEMSport's growing social capital could be experienced by these agents in a 'learning network'. For the black sports professionals in BEMSport their feelings of isolation and alienation gave way to those of unity, shared experiences, solidarity and trust, thus enhancing and accumulating intra-bonding social capital. Similarly the bringing together of disparate individuals within this black network simultaneously acted to stimulate bridging social capital across their network. So intra-group bridging and bonding occurred in the development of BEMSport. Cote and Healy (2001) might argue that the inter-group or linking social capital across the regional sports network would be more important in this case, especially as BEMSport also aimed to influence the practices of policymakers and practitioners. The essence of BEMSport's activities ultimately involved transforming actors within the regional sport networks through awareness raising and the strategic manoeuvring of key individuals and organizations able to challenge the racial inequalities in sport policy and practice. This could be described as a dialectical process where each interaction in the network became a reciprocal learning situation for BEMSport and the network's members. Therefore the longer BEMSport stayed constituted and working in the sports network they became more astute and experienced and recognized as being worthy members through the attribution of status, respect and the learned behaviour that Bourdieu described as cultural capital.

BEMSport: A healthy paradox?

On reflection, BEMSport's investment in social relations for themselves, sport networks and the externalities for those experiencing the impact of positive outcomes from these exchanges can be seen as forms of social capital. Lin (2001) considers a process of social exchange with expected returns in the marketplace as his version of social capital. Lin's version is analogous to Putnam's (2007) earlier version of social capital being *social networks and the associated norms of reciprocity and trustworthiness*. But in particular the most persuasive definition for this chapter by Nahapiet and Ghoshal (1998) which sees social capital as *the sum of the actual and potential resources embedded within, available through, and derived from the network of relationships possessed by an individual and social unit* reaffirms that BEMSport has been successful in stimulating social capital and has clearly been a positive influence on actors in sport networks in Yorkshire. However, what we cannot ascertain is the relative outcome of this social capital on BEMSport, actors in sport networks or the externalities that accrue through this process. Hero's (2007) argument that racial inequality is the 'evil twin' of social capital is a little dramatic but forces a further consideration of the relative impacts of social capital for racialized groups and how we effectively consider the material difference emerging from strengthened social networks and institutional environments in sport.

By opening up alternative lines of enquiry that include often under-valued sources of information on racialized experiences BEMSport produce an oppositional account that rejects the claims of progress in public sector sport by emphasizing the salience of social capital in networks of power in sport that few like them have access to. BEMSport produces contradictions as caveats for more complacent policymakers and practitioners and incentives for more forward looking ones. The report of PAT 9 on community self-help outlined how community groups like BEMSport are in fact a paradox. They are necessary *because of* the actions or inactions of public authorities and institutions. Their emergence occurs as a response to the perceived need of a black community that sees disparity in the quality and quantity of sports facilities and services available to it. The unequal distribution of facilities, services and employment opportunities in sport can be explained with recourse to social capital that is useful to explain these disparities in sport. As noted earlier, the emergence of BEMSport in itself sends a message to local authorities and other sports governing agencies that others in their network wish to go beyond gestural resistance to inequality and racism in sport, and that black people in the region are taking action to address these imbalances. The PAT 9 view of organizations like BEMSport as being an unwitting by-product of public policy is relevant here. However, contrary to popular pluralist ideologies BEMSport's inception is not a regular consequence of public dissatisfaction with sport policy and provision otherwise there would be more groups like it.

The impact of a contract culture in the UK is being felt across the country and the resultant motivations to broaden out the consultative network in the local government sector are a direct consequence of that. Where public sector consultation processes differ, lies not in the fact that they have inconsistent individual circumstances that include their locale, demographics, size and history, there is also the notion of quality of provision. For some local authorities such as Birmingham their investment in consultative mechanisms in the past has meant that the black voluntary sector has been able to have a degree of influence on local policy (Solomos & Back, 1995). In Yorkshire BEMSport's experience evidenced that some local authorities actively consult community and interest groups whilst others do not show the same willingness to operate beyond minimum levels (Hylton, 2003). However, where local authority representatives are involved in consultation and therefore stimulating social capital they are more likely to consider and act upon the advice of significant others in influential professional networks. BEMSport constitutes part of this proximate group in Yorkshire which enables it to gain a robust picture of each authority's work on racial equality. The ability to do this is important for an organization like BEMSport that relies upon its local contacts and up-to-date knowledge of practice and policy development across the county.

As an indicator of Best Value in local authorities BEMSport can be seen as very useful evidence of consultation. However, the outcomes of these consultations in terms of results, real power sharing and sensitivity to causes can easily be overlooked. On one level the motivation for consultation may not matter to BEMSport as long as consultation and change are taking place however, this state of affairs is not likely to successfully impact long-term practices unless they are institutionalized. In the case of the local authorities in Yorkshire who are all members of the Yorkshire Sports Board (YSB)[3] that BEMSport has a representative on some will see this relationship as sufficient in terms of racial equality in sport. The adoption of the *Level Playing Field* framework by the YSB (and therefore all of the governing bodies and established voluntary sector) for some authorities was more of a gesture as BEMSport monitoring evidenced that only a limited number of authorities were implementing these Standards in practice. This could mean that the local authorities were active and not publicizing their work or they were choosing to do the minimum towards racial equality in sport for the time being (see Swinney & Horne, 2005). A number of reasons for the dearth of action plans could be suggested although given the historical inertia in this area they are likely, unfortunately for BEMSport, to be

---

[3]Today's equivalents are the Regional Sport Boards.

perennial ones. This highlights the relative nature of social capital as improved social capital for BEMSport does not necessarily translate into analogous benefits for the community groups it supports.

BEMSport's work with the Active Sports Forums[4] found a key sports forum willing to impose upon its members the requirement of having to produce an equity policy before any resources were released. Given this requirement from the funders, the Sports Council, they could offer something new to racial equality in the county by merging the mutual agendas and cognitive dimension for members of their network and BEMSport. The Active Sport Forums need to produce the equivalent of an equality statement that equality professionals would agree are ineffective without a plan of action, and a fuller racial equality policy.[5] Given the profile of the PAT 10 (DCMS, 1999) recommendations on social exclusion and the general profile of inclusion in sport the coming years could be seen as some of the most conducive since the early 1980s for equality work to have an interested political and professional audience. So anomaly, paradox, or both, BEMSport is well placed in the region to influence this transformation if it manages to stay on the same developmental trajectory.

Social commentators like Goldberg (1993, 2002), Solomos and Back (1995), Skellington (1996) and Hero (2007) are critical of the well known disparities between those who have the blend of social capital that keep some on the inside of sport that those outside of the system clearly do not. Thus sport has a role in enhancing social inclusion and consequently social capital even if its role in this task is perhaps not as clear as the Government's. However, a cursory reading of the related sports literature in the UK identifies an institution repeatedly accused of advantaging the social capital of white people as players, spectators

---

[4]Now County Sport Partnerships (CSPs). There were forty-five sports partnerships that cover whole counties or parts of larger ones as in Yorkshire. Each sports partnership in Yorkshire was, made up of the local authorities in those areas, relevant governing bodies and people who have the local knowledge, expertise and experience of sport in their area. Each partnership is responsible for ensuring local delivery of the programme to young people and this includes accessing and utilizing lottery sports fund awards for named projects.

[5]Having seen the initial policy from one Sports Forum BEMSport refused to endorse it on the basis of it not stipulating plans and procedures for monitoring, harassment and also due to the lack of clarity and consistency in the language used. In terms of BEMSport exercising influence over local authorities in parts of the region this is an example of it making matters very difficult for those who have traditionally ignored these issues due to the relatively low figures for black people in their area.

and employees over those from African-Caribbean and Asian backgrounds even in those sports where success amongst these groups is more conspicuous (Jarvie, 1991b; Back, Crabbe & Solomos, 2001; Carrington & McDonald, 2001; Long & Hylton, 2002; Swinney & Horne, 2005).

Appendix: BEMSport milestones

Year 1

Conference to establish the efficacy of a black sports forum. Speakers from the Sports Council HQ, Senior Local Authority staff, and academics. 20 local authority staff, 8 from national governing bodies, 5 Sports Council staff, 4 from voluntary groups and 1 from a Race Equality Council.

Sport England subsidize a partner university to run two sports development courses for black sports development officers (SDOs) in the region. The courses enabled a number of people directly involved in sports development for black and ethnic minorities to receive very valuable education and training which will help them with their future work. A number have progressed into high profile roles.

BEMSport invited to delegate a representative to sit on the executive of the Yorkshire Sports Board. An influential group made up of all of the local authorities and governing bodies in the region.

Annual General Meeting – BEMSport is invited as a stakeholder in discussions on lottery bids in the region.

BEMSport invited to discuss the work of a regional coordinator for BMEs.

Year 2

National Race Advisory Group chooses the region for one of its two lottery road shows (BEMSport link and reputation raised in their discussion as an influencing factor). Aim to consult on the weaknesses of lottery distribution by ethnicity.

The second SDO course.

BEMSport administration/secretariat being put in place for example logo, letterhead, leaflet.

Adjacent County Sports Forum wanting BEMSport representation.

Chair of BEMSport sitting on a national race equality group.

Starting to receive membership applications from local authorities and individual members.

Prospective black National Coaching Foundation (now Sports Coach UK) tutors identified and application forms submitted for a bespoke course.

Lottery Road Show

Delegates included LSF staff, Senior Officers in local authorities, Councillors, range of community groups some representing specific South Asian and African-Caribbean sports organizations.

Overall Workshop Objective – to make recommendations to improve the effectiveness of the service offered by the Sports Council Lottery Unit and Local authority Lottery Officers, in processing applications to the Fund and addressing the problems of equality of access to the LSF.

Commitment from the road shows for ethnic monitoring to be written into the funding award process.

2nd Annual General Meeting – Main concern was the lack of funds held by BEMSport.

Year 3

English Sports Council Development Officer for the National Junior Sports Programme and Equity Service Team reported successful activity with BME groups in the region and plans for similar links nationally.

Year 4

Visit by the Head of Policy @ Sport England to discuss local initiatives and possible ways for BEMSport to access Sport England funding.

BEMSport encouraged by the regional Sport England to lobby local authorities who do not posses an equality action plan.

BEMSport write an adapted version of the CRE race equality standards for local authorities in the region which is adopted by the YSB.

Year 5

£12,000 – Funding for BEMSport *directly* from Sport England nationally for Community Sports Development Facilitators.

A Level Playing Field – Racial equality in Local Authorities seminar. Most Local authorities in the county attended. Subsequent document sent to all local authorities.

BEMSport asked to monitor two local authorities' sport equity work.

Regional Information Seminar for BME communities to raise awareness of funding, products.

Active Sport manager in the region seeking representation from BEMSport.

The regional Sport England advisory group for Black and Ethnic Minorities made up of interested parties in the region to become a *sub-committee* of BEMSport's. The financing of this group will be paid for through BEMSport funding. (After 4 years the more established group in the regional network becomes a subsidiary of BEMSport. The work in this area becomes independent of the regional Sport England.)

References

Back, L., Crabbe, T. & Solomos, J. (2001). *The Changing Face of Football*. Oxford: Berg.

Blom-Hansen, J. (1997). A new institutional perspective on policy networks. *Public Administration, 75* (Winter), 669–693.

Bourdieu, P. (1989). *Distinction*. London: Routledge.

Brownill, S., Razzaque, K., Stirling, T. & Thomas, H. (2000). Patterns of inclusion and exclusion: Ethnic minorities and urban development corporations. In G. Stoker (Ed.), *The New Politics of British Local Governance* (pp. 234–248). London: Macmillan.

Cantle, T. (2002). *Community Cohesion: A Report of the Independent Review Team*. London: Home Office.

Carrington, B. & McDonald, I. (2001). *Race Sport and British Society*. London: Routledge.

Clarke, A. (1994). Leisure and the new managerialism. In J. Clarke, A. Cochrane & E. McLaughlin (Eds.), *Managing Social Policy* (pp. 163–181). London: Sage.

Commission for Racial Equality (CRE) (1995). *Racial Equality Means Quality*. UK: Commission for Racial Equality.

Cote, S. & Healy, T. (2001). *The Well Being of Nations*. Paris: OECD.

Delgado, R. (2000). Storytelling for oppositionists and others: A plea for narrative. In R. Delgado & J. Stefancic (Eds.), *Critical Race Theory: The Cutting Edge* (pp. 60–70). Philadelphia: Temple University Press.

Denham, J. (2001). *Building Cohesive Communities: A Report of the Ministerial Group on Public Order and Community Cohesion*. London: Home Office.

Department of Culture Media and Sport Policy Action Team 10 (DCMS) (1999). *PAT 10 – A Report to the Social Exclusion Unit*. London: Department of Cultural Media and Sport Policy Action Team 10.

Department of Culture Media and Sport (DCMS) (2001). *Building on PAT 10: Progress Report on Social Inclusion*. London: Department of Cultural Media and Sport.

Department of National Heritage (1995). *Sport: Raising the Game*. London: The Stationary Office.

Field, J. (2003). *Social Capital*. London: Routledge.

Fukuyama, F. (2001). Social capital, civil society and development. *Third World Quarterly*, 22(1), 7–20.

Gardiner, S. & Welch, R. (2001). Sport, racism and the limits of 'colour blind' law. In B. Carrington & I. McDonald (Eds.), *'Race', Sport and British Society* (pp. 133–149). London: Routledge.

Goldberg, D. (2002). *The Racial State*. Oxford: Blackwell.

Goldberg, D. (1993). *Racist Culture*. Oxford: Blackwell.

Hain, P. (1976). *Community Politics*. London: Calder.

Halpern, D. (2005). *Social Capital*. Cambridge: Polity Press.

Hemingway, J. & Wood Parr, M. (2000). Leisure research and leisure practice: Three perspectives on constructing the research–practice relation. *Leisure Sciences*, 22, 139–162.

Henderson, K. (1988). The need for critical theory in the study of leisure and minority groups. *Leisure Information Quarterly*, 15(3), 1–3.

Hero, R. (2007). *Racial Diversity and Social Capital: Equality and Community in America*. New York: CUO.

Home Office (2001a). *Strengthening the Black and Minority Ethnic Voluntary Sector Infrastructure*. http://www.homeoffice.gov.uk/acu/strng2.html.

Home Office (2001b). *Strengthening the Black and Minority Ethnic Voluntary Sector Infrastructure*. Foreword by Paul Boateng: http://www.homeoffice.gov.uk/acu/strng1.htm.

Hylton, K. (2003). *Local Government 'Race' and Sports Policy Implementation*, unpublished PhD thesis, Leeds Metropolitan University.

Hylton, K. (forthcoming). *Critical Race Theory in Sport*. London: Routledge.

Hylton (1999). Where Are the Black Leisure Managers? *Leisure Manager*, 17(9), 32–34. K/ILAM

Hylton, K. & Totten, M. (2007). Community sports development. In K. Hylton & P. Bramham (Eds.), *Sports Development: Policy, Process and Practice* (pp. 77–117). London: Routledge.

Jarvie, G. (1991a). There ain't no problem here? *Sport and Leisure*, Nov/Dec, 20–21.

Jarvie, G. (1991b). *Sport, Racism and Ethnicity*. London: Falmer Press.

Johal, S. (2001). Playing their own game: A south asian football experience. In B. Carrington & I. McDonald (Eds.), *Race Sport and British Society* (pp. 153–169). London: Routledge.

John, P. & Cole, A. (1995). Models of local decision making networks in Britain and France. *Policy and Politics*, 23(4), 303–312.

Ladson-Billings, G. (1998). Just what is critical race theory and what's it doing in a nice field like education? *Qualitative Studies in Education*, 11(1), 7–24.

Lin, N. (2001). *Social Capital: A Theory of Social Structure and Action*. New York: CUP.

Ledwith, M. (2005). *Community Development: A Critical Approach*. Bristol: Policy Press.

LMU (2003). *Raising the Standard: An Evaluation of Progress*. Leeds: Coachwise.

Long, J. & Hylton, K. (2002). Shades of White: An Examination of Whiteness in Sport. *Leisure Studies*, 21(2), 87–103.

Long, J., Hylton, K., Dart, J. & Welch, M. (2000). *Part of the Game? An Examination of Racism in Grass Roots Football*. London: Kick It Out.

Lyons, A. (1991). The Racial Equality Plan. *Sport and Leisure*, Nov/Dec, 12.

McLeod, M., Owen, D. & Khamis, C. (2001). *Black and Minority Ethnic Voluntary Organisations: Their Role and Future Development*. York: JRF.

McDonald, I. (1995). *Sport for All – 'RIP' in Policy and Politics in Sport PE and Leisure*. London: LSA.

Marsh, D. (Ed.) (1998a). *Comparing Policy Networks*. Buckingham: Open University Press.

Marsh, D. (1998b). The utility and future of policy network analysis. In D. Marsh (Ed.), *Comparing Policy Networks* (pp. 185–215). Buckingham: Open University Press.

Marsh, D. & Rhodes, R. (1992). Policy communities and issue networks: Beyond typology. In D. Marsh & R. Rhodes (Eds.), *Policy Networks in British Government* (pp. 249–287). Oxford: Clarendon Press.

Nahapiet, J. & Ghoshal, S. (1998). Social capital, intellectual capital, and the organizational advantage. *Academy of Management Review*, 23, 242–266.

Nebeker, K. (1998). Critical race theory: a white graduate student's struggle with this growing area of scholarship. *Qualitative Studies in Education*, 11(1), 25–41.

Neighbourhood Renewal Unit (NRU) (2005). *Community Cohesion*. www.renewal.net. London: NRU.

Office for National Statistics (ONS) (2001). *Social Capital: A Review of the Literature*. London: Social Analysis and Reporting Division (ONS).

Phillips, T. (2005). *Trevor Phillips, CRE Chair, Speaking at 'Building an Integrated Society – Delivering Good Race Relations'*, 12 July, London.

Polsby, N. (1963). *Community Power and Political Theory*. New Have: Yale University.

Putnam, R. (2007). *E Pluribus Unnum:* Diversity and Community in the Twenty-First Century – The 2006 Johan Skytte Prize Lecture. *Scandinavian Political Studies*, 30(2), 137–174.

Putnam, R. (2000). *Bowling Alone*. New York: Simon & Schuster.

Rhodes, R. (1997). *Understanding Governance: Policy Networks, Governance, Reflexivity and Accountability*. Buckingham: OU Press.

Rosenberg, D. (1989). *Accounting for Public Policy*. Manchester: Manchester University Press.

ROTA (2001). *Briefing No. 5: Supporting the Black Voluntary Sector*. http://www.rota.org.uk/briefing/support.html.

Schaap, L. & van Twist, M. (1997). The dynamics of closedness in networks. In W. Kickert, E.-H. Klijn & J. Koppenjan (Eds.), *Managing Complex Networks: Strategies for the Public Sector* (pp. 62–78). London: Sage.

Sia (1996). *Whose Lottery Is It Anyway? The Impact of the National Lottery on the Black Voluntary Sector*. London: Sia.

Silverman, R. (2004). *Community Based Organisations*. Detroit: Wayne State University Press.

Skellington, R. (1996). *'Race' in Britain Today*. London: OU.

Smith, L. (1999). *Decolonizing Methodologies: Research and Indigenous Peoples*. London: University of Otago Press.

Smith, M. (1993). *Pressure, Power and Policy*. Hemel Hempstead: Harvester Wheatsheaf.

Solomos, J. & Back, L. (1995). *Race, Politics and Social Change*. London: Routledge.

Sports Council (1994). *Black and Ethnic Minorities and Sport: Policy Objectives*. London: Sport Council.

Sport England (2002). *Active Communities Experimental Projects*. http://sportengland.org/active_communities/acf/active_communities_projects.htm.

Sport England (2000). *Sports Participation and Ethnicity in England: National Survey 1999/2000*. London: Sport England.

Swinney, A. & Horne, J. (2005). Race Equality and Leisure Policy: Discourses in Scottish Local Authorities. *Leisure Studies*, 24(3), 271–289.

Torkildsen, G. (1999). *Leisure and Recreation Management*. London: E and FN Spon.

Verma, G. & Darby, J. (1994). *Winners and Losers: Ethnic Minorities in Sport and Recreation*. London: Falmer Press.

West Midlands Council for Sport and Recreation (1990). *Equal Opportunity? Sport, Race and Racism*. Birmingham: West Midlands Council for Sport and Recreation.

Wheeler, J. (2000). *Leicester Racial Equality and Sport Project Preparation Report*. Leicester: Leicester City Council.

Whiteley, P. & Winyard, S. (1987). *Pressure for the Poor*. London: Methuen.

Wilson, R. (1999). What Is Social Capital? *Knowledge Management Review*, 6(January–February), 7–8.

Young, K. (1992). Approaches to Policy Development. In P. Braham, A. Rattansi & R. Skellington (Eds.), *Racism and Antiracism* (pp. 252–269). London: Sage.

CHAPTER 13

Stepping into community? The impact of youth sport volunteering on young people's social capital

Steven Bradbury
and Tess Kay

Introduction

Since 1997 the UK has energetically deployed sport in pursuit of diverse social policy agendas including enhancing health, engaging disaffected youth, countering anti-social behaviour and contributing to community well-being. Initially focussing on issues of social inclusion, the policy discourses have progressively shifted to those surrounding active citizenship and social capital. The extent to which the intended social outcomes are definable, realistic and measurable has however been queried, as has the causal role that sport can play in achieving them. In this chapter we address aspects of this debate through a focus on the capacity of youth sport volunteering to develop social capital. In many senses youth sport volunteering 'ticks the boxes' of a number of topical UK policy agendas, providing a form of social participation that potentially engages young people in community-oriented activities, empowers them as resourceful individuals and contributes to the development of citizenship and social capital. These concepts are however much disputed and the debate surrounding the associated policy agendas is intense. Here we analyse the extent to which young people's experiences of volunteering in sport may match or fall short of these policy expectations.

We start by setting the context for our analysis through a review of the debates surrounding social capital itself and its location in UK social policy and sport policy. These issues have been the subject of detailed analyses by previous writers (e.g. see Coalter's (2007) examination of sport, social capital and social regeneration) and by other authors in this volume, and our purpose here is to provide a sufficiently detailed but reasonably concise overview to locate this chapter in relation to these wider debates. Like Cuskelly (this volume), our interest is in the relationship between volunteering activity and social capital, and we therefore also examine key literature related to volunteering in the UK. We pay particular attention to patterns of youth volunteering, and the experiences of young people who engage in it.

We then turn our attention to the specific case of youth sport volunteering. Our main purpose here is to explore whether, and in what way, experiences of volunteering in sport may contribute to the development of social capital among young people. As the editors of this volume stress, there is a need to move beyond 'intuition, suggestion and political opportunism', both in analysing the concept of social capital, and applying it in policy. We aim to contribute to this by providing an empirically based analysis that draws on extensive monitoring and evaluation data for the Step into Sport (SIS) programme, a major national initiative in the UK that trains young people as volunteer sport workers and provides them with placement opportunities through which they gain direct experience of volunteering. SIS began in 2002 and at the time of writing had been running for almost five years, during which time an estimated 60 000 young people had participated in its various stages. It is a high-profile and long-term initiative, jointly funded and managed by a consortium of national sport agencies and government departments, and recently given further impetus by Britain's successful bid for the 2012 London Olympics. The programme provides a series of structured 'Steps' that progressively develop young people's skills and abilities to undertake effective sport volunteering, and provide them with opportunities to actively volunteer in school and community settings. In the later stages the 'Community Volunteers (CV)' element of the programme allows older teenagers (from age 16) to undertake extended sport volunteering placements that actively engage with their communities. Drawing on quantitative and qualitative data from young people participating in this element of the programme, we examine whether being actively engaged in this way impacts on the social connectedness that underpins social capital.

Social capital and UK social policy

The concept of social capital has become increasingly popular in UK policymaking circles in recent years as a result of its perceived capacity to contribute to greater social cohesion and civic renewal (Policy Action Team 10, 1999; Cantle, 2001; Harper, 2001). The conceptualization of social capital as a panacea for economic growth, political engagement and active citizenship has also become a subject of increasing academic debate in economics, political science, sociology, and leisure studies in North America, the UK and France (Bourdieu, 1984, 1999; Coleman, 1990, 1994; Putnam, 1993, 1995, 2000; Fukuyama, 1995; Blackshaw & Long, 2005). This has led to a range of competing and contested definitions of social capital and some confusion as to what constitutes social capital and the way in which its effects become manifest to impact upon social relations and civil society.

The most popularly utilized academic conceptualization of social capital has been Putnam's (1995, 2000) definition of it as *'networks, norms and trust that enable participants to act together more effectively to pursue shared objectives'*. Putnam's central

287

argument is that increased social connectedness encourages greater social solidarity and social cohesion through 'bonding' and 'bridging' individuals into a larger collective whole. Broadly speaking, bonding capital refers to the value assigned to social networks between homogenous groups of people where ties, interaction and familiarity are relatively strong. In contrast, bridging capital refers to social networks between socially heterogeneous groups of people where social ties and bonds may be looser and more diverse. From this perspective, social capital is conceptualized as a collective property based on shared norms, trust, reciprocity and establishment of a range of formal and informal social networks. Whilst other 'social capitalists' have argued that social capital is also premised on rational individual action (Bourdieu, 1984, 1986; Coleman, 1990, 1994), there is a more general agreement with Putnam that social capital underpins a more productive, supporting and trusting society and allows society's mechanisms to operate with greater efficiency to the benefit of the wider population. Conversely, however, an identifiable withdrawal from networks of collective reciprocity and cultural participation can weaken social capital and have direct negative consequences for the productive and cohesive functioning of society.

As has been noted elsewhere in this volume, the work of Putnam and the 'positive' social capital thesis has not been without criticism and contestation, especially in its implication that social capital is a force for individual and collective good. Whilst Putnam also recognizes the potential for a 'dark side' of social capital, a number of authors have further elaborated on some of the processes of exclusion which can inhibit an increased and unproblematic engagement in wider civic society amongst some groups (Portes & Landolt, 1996; Blackshaw & Long, 2005). For example, Putnam's conceptualization of 'bonding' social capital can lead to the exclusion of outsiders across a range of group settings, with particular reference to sustaining patterns of racism, sectarianism, xenophobia, sexism and homophobia and the closed hegemonic structures within which such attitudes and behaviours flourish. Further, social capital of this kind may operate to impose conformity and social division at the expense of tolerance and inclusivity. Putnam's overly nostalgic overview of the immediate postwar period in America as the peak of social connectedness and civic virtue largely downplays some deep-rooted societal fractures and the institutionalized marginalization of racialized minority communities and gender discrimination prevalent in the US at this time. In this sense, social capital can have distinctly exclusionary effects on civic and social participation and can limit access to decision-making hierarchies amongst a range of more marginalized groups.

A key challenge to Putnam's functionalist conceptualization of social capital and its potential for collective good is that it neglects the central issue of the unequal distribution of access to material and symbolic resources which shape power relations in society. Bourdieu (1986) utilizes the theoretical concepts of field, habitus and capital to offer a more complex understanding of the way in which social, cultural and economic capital synthesize the relationship between individual and society. Whilst the work of Bourdieu (like Putnam) is interested in structural determinants and social connections there is also a strong account of individual agency and the implications for the way in which social capital can be acquired through 'profits of membership' and civic associations at an individual level by those with the material and symbolic resources to do so. In this sense, Bourdieu is interested in the acquisition and effects of social capital as a way of explaining inequalities in society. From this Bourdieuian perspective, social capital is:

'on the one hand, a tangible resource made by advantage of family, friendship or other kinds of social networks, and, on the other hand, like all forms of capital, it has a symbolic dimension, which contrives to hide networks of power woven into the fibres of familiarity'.
(Blackshaw & Long, 2005: 251)

Whilst Bourdieu's more complex sociological conceptualization of 'capital' which alludes to the interplay between real and perceived individual agency and structural relations of power in society has found significant favour across a range of academic disciplines, it has had less influence in UK policymaking circles. In the UK, Coleman's rational choice theory and, especially, Putnam's more structural functionalist approach to social capital have found strong favour with New Labour's 'third way' approach to governance which has sought to establish a 'middle ground' between the state and the free market and which depends significantly on the capacity and effective functioning of third sector provision of a range of public services. Central to the appeal of social capital in UK policy circles is its linkage with public policy concerns around social exclusion and civil renewal and the idea that social capital can contribute to increased individual and collective citizenship and strengthen fractured communities through increased social participation and social interaction. The convergence of these theoretical and political approaches to understanding and managing civil society are philosophically informed by civic communitarianism (Giddens, 1991) and the belief that high levels of social capital are necessary for the effective functioning of modern liberal democracies. For some authors, the civic communitarianism/social capital approach ignores the pervasiveness of market forces in society and their consequences for disenfranchised groups (Blackshaw & Long, 2005). For other authors, these approaches prioritize social order over social justice and can lead to a downward levelling of norms and values which are imposed upon marginalized groups (Portes & Landolt, 1996). Nonetheless, it is probably the case, that the influence of Putnam and Coleman's social capital thesis on UK policy is also reflective of a general commitment on the part of the New Labour Government to re-introduce a distinctly social dimension into late-modern capitalism in the UK and marks a concerted effort to engage citizens in the wider, albeit flawed, democratic process, through the medium of active community participation.

Despite significant contestation over the meaning and processes of social capital, a number of UK Government departments have sought to come to a consensus around its measurement and application in a policy context (Babb, 2005). The Office for National Statistics has identified five key indicators of social capital: social participation, civic participation, social networks and social support, reciprocity and trust and views of the local area (Whiting & Harper, 2003: 7). These indicators feature both objective and subjective dimensions, ascertain individual attitudinal and behavioural processes and evaluate levels of engagement with wider community networks. This approach recognizes social capital as a multi-dimensional concept which is located within relational networks of sociability and civil society and follows from the Organisation for Economic Co-operation and Development (OECD) definition of social capital as *'networks together with shared norms, values and understandings that facilitate co-operation within or among groups'* (Cote and Healy, 2001: 41).

Within this conceptualization, social participation is defined in terms of involvement (and frequency of involvement) in organized groups, clubs and associations. The 2001 Home Office Citizenship Survey indicates that around 65 per cent of a broadly representative sample of the population surveyed had been involved socially in groups, clubs or organisations at least once in the previous 12 months and that 52 per cent were involved in social participation of this kind on a more regular monthly basis. High levels of social participation were equated more strongly with key socio-demographic factors such as higher socio-economic status, higher educational achievement, with males and with people from White-British and Black-British ethnic groups. The survey findings also identified some correlation between high levels of social participation and other indicators of social capital such as positive views of the neighbourhood, length of residence in the neighbourhood, feelings of trust and safety, and stronger social networks.

It is in the light of these conceptualizations, we are interested in exploring the potential role of (sport) volunteering to contribute to the development of social capital. In recent years, volunteering has increasingly become a focus for UK Government attention because of its perceived potential to encourage active citizenship and civil renewal (Social Exclusion Unit, 1998; Home Office, 1999; Attwood et al., 2001; Munton & Zurawan, 2003; Kitchen et al., 2005). The driving force behind the linkage of voluntarism with wider policy issues has been the New Labour project which has sought to establish a devolved 'third way' approach to governance and which is philosophically underpinned by notions of civic communitarianism (Giddens, 1991) and the social capital thesis expounded authors such as Putnam (1993, 1995, 2000) and Coleman (1988, 1990, 1994). Within this ideological framework, volunteering is viewed as a key element of social participation with the potential to increase individual and collective citizenship through the medium of active community participation. In this respect, volunteering is construed as a site where social capital can be measured and increased through key policy interventions designed to encourage greater voluntary activity.

The tendency within UK Government policy to view volunteering as having a positive integrative function with wider social benefits of increased citizenship and social solidarity can be problematic. For Rojek (2000), such assertions are reflective of an overtly functionalist approach to linkages and networks in civil society and risk reducing volunteering to a 'rationalist-purposive activity'. Blackshaw and Long have also questioned the assumptions inherent within functionalist conceptualizations of volunteering as a causative force for 'good' social capital and which 'neglect the role of power in social networks and voluntary associations [and] ignore the way social capital within this [functionalist] thesis is divorced from economic capital' (2005: 249). From these more critical perspectives, UK Government policy and its theoretical informants overplay the capacity of volunteering to contribute to increased social cohesion and, conversely, underplay some key dimensions of power, access to economic resources and exclusionary practices within voluntary organizations. In the next section we examine how these structural issues are evident in patterns of engagement in volunteering.

Volunteering in youth policy in the UK

In the UK's 1997 National Survey of Volunteering (Davis-Smith, 1998) volunteering is defined as 'Any activity which involves spending time, unpaid, doing something that aims to benefit (individuals and groups) other than or in addition to, close relatives, or the benefit of the environment', indicating a popular perception of social participation and citizenship in political thought as one based on individual and collective involvement in communities. Volunteering has therefore been seen as a key element of strategies to promote social participation and increase individual and collective citizenship, especially among young people (Social Exclusion Unit, 1998; Home Office, 1999; Attwood et al., 2001; Munton & Zurawan, 2003; Kitchen et al., 2005).

In some respects volunteering appears suitable for this function: there is broad parity in rates of formal and informal volunteering between males and females, and little significant difference in rates of formal and informal volunteering between UK born majority ethnic and minority ethnic communities (Kitchen et al., 2005). However, differences have been evident in relation to socio-economic status and voluntary activity. The National Volunteering Survey showed that people employed in higher management and professional occupations were almost twice as likely as people in routine and semi-routine occupations to be involved in formal volunteering, and differences in rates of formal volunteering were also constant when measured against educational achievement and geographical indices of deprivation. Overall, these 'classed' patterns of voluntary activity suggest that participation in formal volunteering is more characteristic of the volunteering culture of people drawn from more affluent than lower-income neighbourhoods. There was much less of a gap in rates of informal volunteering between people drawn from a range of socio-economic groups. This was largely accounted for by a greater tendency and increasing likelihood of people drawn from less affluent backgrounds to engage in less formalised networks of mutual aid and social support and to recognize this form of social participation within these terms.

The interplay of socio-demographic, interpersonal, perceptual and infrastructural factors can limit opportunities for participation in formal and informal volunteering. The Home Office Citizenship Surveys of 2001, 2003 and 2005 (Munton & Zurawan, 2003; Attwood et al., 2001; Kitchen et al., 2005) identify lower levels of engagement in volunteering amongst groups which experience lower socio-economic status, income and educational attainment. Similarly, reduced patterns of engagement with volunteering are also evident across key indicators of social capital with reference to less neighbourhood satisfaction, trust, safety, length of residence and limited social networks. These findings strongly suggest that a lack of key social, cultural and material resources limits access to and participation in formalized volunteering in the UK.

Research exploring the link between volunteering and social exclusion in the UK (Davis-Smith et al., 2002) has shown the significance of psychological and perceptual barriers to formal volunteering amongst socially excluded groups. These include individuals' lack of confidence, self-esteem and personal value, and their sense that volunteering is perceived as an overly formal and limited activity undertaken primarily by and for mainstream groups in society. In some cases, these perceptions were rooted in local realities and negative experiences of volunteering in formalized settings on the part of marginalized groups. Other discouragements included previous experiences of volunteering as being poorly organized, overly difficult, and lacking enough flexibility and variety to maintain sufficient interest and sustained engagement; a tendency to feel unappreciated and issues around the non-payment of out of pocket expenses were also felt particularly strongly by groups experiencing wider social exclusions. These more infrastructural challenges to the public image of volunteering and practical management of volunteers form a constant theme in UK policy and academic debates around voluntarism and social participation and have informed new initiatives designed to recruit and retain volunteers, especially young people.

Within this broader political context youth volunteering has taken on added resonance as a key element of social participation. In particular, youth volunteering has been seen as a mechanism for addressing a range of youth orientated policy concerns around physical health, education, crime and risk reduction, individual and collective citizenship and community cohesion. Since 1997 the New Labour Government has sought to respond to increasing concerns over youth alienation and disaffection and has implemented a range of policy directives and initiatives designed to encourage greater levels of active citizenship amongst young people, with particular reference to civic engagement and social participation (National Centre for Social Research, 2000; Armstrong, 2002; Catan, 2002; Department for Education and Skills, 2003). Whilst these policy concerns have considered some of the structural determinants of issues of crime, poverty and educational underachievement, they have also been keen to encourage a shift in human agency amongst young people premised on notions of citizens' rights and responsibilities and the maximizing of individual potential. Such notions reflect New Labour's civic communitarianism philosophical informants and a practical 'third way' approach to national governance (Giddens, 1991).

Young people's participation in volunteering has not always matched the policy expectations laid upon it. In the UK there were sharp declines in rates of youth volunteering between 1991 and 2001 and a small, but significant, upturn in rates of youth volunteering from 2003 onwards (Lynn & Davis-Smith, 1992; Davis-Smith, 1998; Attwood et al., 2001; Munton & Zurawan, 2003; Kitchen et al., 2005). The proportion of 16–24 year olds volunteering formally at least once in the previous 12 months fell from 55 per cent in 1991 to 40 per cent in 2001. Volunteer rates among 16–19 year olds subsequently rose from 41 per cent in 2003 to 53 per cent in 2005 although they remained fairly constant amongst 20–24 year olds (43 per cent in 2003, 42 per cent in 2005). Rates of formal youth volunteering are currently broadly comparable to older, middle-aged, cohorts of volunteers, but it is notable that there is a marked drop off in levels of formal volunteering across the transition from youth to early adulthood. On the whole, young people are much more likely to engage in volunteering in relatively informal settings: 78 per cent of 16–19 year olds had done so in 2005, and 75 per cent of 20–24 year olds.

The sharp decline in youth volunteering throughout the 1990s led to a more general shift and re-branding of youth volunteering in the early twenty-first century. A key element was the 1999 launch of the Millennium Volunteers (MV) programme, designed to promote sustained volunteering amongst young people aged 16–24 years old. The MV programme aimed to increase the number and range of youth volunteering opportunities and to provide accreditation and recognition for young people's voluntary efforts, engendering increased personal and professional development and encouraging wider community benefit. MV programmes have been administered through a range of local delivery agencies with a key interest in youth work and social care and have been organized around a series of key principles, including sustained personal commitment, community benefit, voluntary participation, inclusiveness, ownership by young people, variety, partnership, quality and recognition. In some locales, MV programmes have been used a targeted mechanism to re-engage socially excluded and 'at risk' young people and to help engender greater social cohesion and empower communities in economically deprived areas.

In their evaluation of the MV project Davis-Smith et al. (2002) identified a range of personal, professional and community benefits arising from young people's involvement in organized voluntary activity. In this he echoed the work of Gaskin (1998) who identified a range of benefits and motivations among young people. Davis-Smith et al. (2002) found that volunteering contributed to young people's professional development through attainment of a range of 'hard-edged' vocational skills and qualifications which enhanced routes to permanent employment and improved access to further and higher education. Youth volunteering had also contributed to the parallel acquisition of a range of 'soft-edged' skills such as self-confidence, self-esteem, communication and organization skills which enhanced employability, especially amongst socially excluded groups of young people where these forms of personal growth had much wider ramifications and impact. Alongside these instrumental motivations, more altruistic views were in evidence, and the two often worked in tandem to shape young people's voluntary activity. Youth volunteering was seen as a key mechanism through which young people had become active members of local communities and their ongoing commitment to sustainable volunteering was perceived to be a measure of increased citizenship. Youth volunteering was also perceived to have made a significant contribution to the capacity of service providers to maintain and increase the delivery of services to a range of client groups, especially in the social sector. This increased human capacity had clear cost/benefits in terms of economic returns and had also enhanced the quality of life and experiences of, often vulnerable and socially excluded, service user groups. Improvements to the wider social and physical environment of communities were also cited as a benefit of targeted youth volunteering projects. Youth volunteering had also contributed to improvements in inter-generational relations and had helped break down negative stereotypes about young people held by older cohorts and had contributed to increased social capital indicators of improved trust, confidence and reciprocity.

In the opening years of the twenty-first century, youth volunteering in the UK therefore presented a mixed picture. While there was evidence that young people's individual motivation to volunteer was declining, or being compromised by competing demands, it was also apparent that structured programmes of volunteering could be effective vehicles for engaging them. Those who did participate in such initiatives obtained multiple benefits and generated gains for their local communities.

Adopting such approaches in sport, where youth were a primary policy concern and the dependency on a declining volunteer population was impacting community delivery, was timely.

The SIS project

SIS was launched in 2002. The project operates nationally in England offering a framework of structured opportunities for young people to participate in volunteering and leadership training in sport. It aims to establish a clear pathway to progression designed to empower of participants with knowledge and experience to make a positive voluntary contribution to local sporting communities. The project has two key components. Firstly, it offers five programmes for young people aged 14–19 years, providing progressive training and experience in sport leadership and volunteering: Sport Education, Level One Sports Leadership, Top Link, Level Two Community Sports Leadership and Community Volunteering. The programmes are facilitated by PE Teachers in schools within the national school sport partnership framework with the support of the Youth Sports Trust and Sports Leaders UK. Secondly, the project involves the development of capacity building networks involving school sport partnerships, local authorities, county sport partnerships, national governing bodies of sport and Sport England, to help strengthen local sport infrastructure and provide high-quality volunteer placement opportunities for young volunteers.

Since 2002 the Institute of Youth Sport has been responsible for the monitoring and evaluation of the SIS programme. Phase One (2002–2004) of the SIS project was funded by the Department for Culture, Media and Sport (DCMS) and the Home Office 'Active Communities' Unit and Phase Two (2004–2006) of the SIS project by the DCMS alone. SIS is managed and co-ordinated by Sport England, the Youth Sport Trust and Sports Leaders UK (formerly the British Sports Trust), building on the skills and expertise of these organizations' work in this important area. The evaluation has been wide-ranging in its evaluation of the measurable impact of SIS upon active participants and the way in which the various components of the project link together in a co-ordinated and structured way to provide clear pathways of progression for young people as volunteers and sport leaders. The research has utilized quantitative and qualitative methods of investigation, including large-scale surveys of young participants,

County Sports Partnerships, National Governing Bodies, and former CV, and interview-based research with County Sports Partnerships, School Sports Partnerships, Placement Providers, PE Teachers and former Community Volunteers.

In this chapter we are concentrating on the impact that direct experience of sport volunteering, delivered through SIS, has on young people. Our focus is on the CV element of the programme, designed for young people aged 16+, who are first trained in sport leadership, and then undertake placements as volunteers. During the placement element, young people are encouraged to achieve certain levels (amounts) of active volunteering experience, ranging from a target of 50 hours to achieve Bronze level to 100 for Silver and 200 for Gold. Placements may take place in young people's schools, where they may assist in either curricular or extra-curricular activities, and/or in local community sport clubs or other sport facilities. Young people's placements may take place at more than one venue/setting, involve one or more volunteer roles across single or multiple sports, and may entail working with a variety of types of participants. The placements therefore provide a very direct experience of working with others, providing a resource of expertise and increased capacity that is of use to them, and through this has the potential to foster social connectedness. Alongside this, however, it offers a substantial training element that allows young people to enhance their skills and provide evidence on their curriculum vitae that they have done so. We are therefore mindful that engaging in volunteering can have instrumental as well as altruistic motives, and that both may be expected among SIS' young participants.

The account given here draws on data collected between November 2005 and June 2006. Research with the Community Volunteers themselves comprised an initial self-completion 'tracking survey' of 160 volunteers who had first engaged with the CV programme in March and April 2003, and a follow-up set of in-depth interviews with a sample of respondents ($n = 10$). The young people who participated had first taken part in the evaluation in the first year of SIS, when the research team had carried out an initial questionnaire-based survey of young people attending either the CV four-day residential training camp and/or one of the CV one-day training camps held at a range of venues nationally. This first survey resulted in 631 completed questionnaires with home addresses provided by 613 (97 per cent) participants. Sixteen months later, in August 2004, the IYS research team administered a questionnaire-based survey direct to the homes of those 613 pupils who had since been encouraged to complete up to 200 hours of 'Community Volunteering' in local sporting communities as part of their ongoing engagement with Step Five of the SIS project. After a relatively sluggish initial response to our requests for information and following two further questionnaire mail-outs in October 2004 and December 2004, the IYS eventually received a total of 160 completed questionnaires from our target sample group, resulting in an acceptable 26 per cent response rate for postal surveys of this kind. All questionnaires were completed fully by our respondent sample group and many respondents added more qualitative comments which illustrate further some of the key themes to emerge from the more statistical findings featured in this report. Subsequently a set of 10 in-depth interviews was conducted with a sub-group of these respondents to further illuminate these key themes.

Young people's experience of sport volunteering through the SIS project

The survey of Community Volunteers sought wide-ranging information on the young people's socio-demographic and educational background, and their experiences of sport, volunteering, the Community Volunteering programme and the SIS project overall. Here we concentrate on the data relating to the impact of the experience of the volunteer placement on the young people.

The parameters of participation

The results we report here are based on the returns from 160 young people who responded to the tracking survey. This represents a response rate of 26 per cent which while adequate, suggests some caution is appropriate. The response rate was affected by changes in the circumstances of the young people who were aged 17–20 at the time of the survey. Many had left their parental home and entered work or further/higher education and were no longer contactable at their original address. In addition, we assume that as is usual with self-completion surveys, there is a level of selectivity among respondents, with those most interested and satisfied with their experiences of Community Volunteering being most likely to respond. In this respect we acknowledge that we are likely to be dealing with the most favourable accounts of the CV programme. This does not undermine the validity of those accounts for the individuals concerned, but we would be cautious about assuming that they would be more widely replicated.

Community Volunteers is aimed at young people 16+, and all respondents were aged between 17 and 20 years old at the time of the survey. Most respondents were female (65 per cent), White British (92 per cent), and from relatively affluent 'middle income' geographical locales: relatively few (<12 per cent) respondents were from the 20 per cent of wards classed as the most deprived nationally (Neighbourhood Renewal Unit, 2004). There were few respondents from Black and Minority Ethnic (BME) communities ($n = 13$; 8 per cent), and very few with self-reported physical disabilities, learning difficulties or a sensory impairment ($n = 3$, 2 per cent). At the time of the tracking survey many young people had completed their school education and 70 per cent had moved on to continue their education elsewhere (50 per cent to University and 20 per cent to Further Education), while 16 per cent were in full-time employment, 34 per cent were employed part-time and 2 per cent were unemployed.

The profile of the Community Volunteering respondents reflects the overall profile of participants in the SIS programme, which in its opening years tended to be dominated by white, middle class young people with high educational aspirations. Pupils from poorer neighbourhoods, BME communities and pupils with lower educational achievement records were generally under-represented. This pattern reflects the issue often raised by analysts of social capital – that it may be those who already have capital that may be most likely to engage in opportunities for social connectedness, thus obtaining cumulative benefit. It also resonates with Coalter's reminder of the specifically non-inclusive tradition in organized sport (Coalter, 2007).

As might be expected with a voluntary, sport-based programme, most respondents had an established interest in sport and in sport leadership roles. Prior to their involvement in SIS about four-fifths (81 per cent) had taken sport leadership awards, half (52 per cent) had obtained sport-specific coaching awards and a third (34 per cent) general sport coaching qualifications. A high proportion (79 per cent) had also taken school-based academic qualifications in Physical Education, and a quarter of those currently at school/college (25 per cent) intended to pursue a sport-related degree at university. Many young people therefore brought considerable knowledge and established interest to their sport volunteering placements. In addition, the great majority had also had previous experience of volunteering: again, around four-fifths had done so (80 per cent) overall, and most of these (89 per cent) in sport. Much of this volunteering was however relatively low-key, with most reporting it as an 'occasional' rather than 'regular' undertaking.

Volunteering through SIS did not necessarily engender a wholly new experience for all participants: most of the research respondents had been predisposed to volunteering prior to joining the CV programme, and most had had some experience of doing so. In contrast to the more intermittent volunteering that young people had done previously, however, the CV programme offered an opportunity to undertake a substantial, structured and continuous volunteer placement, to undergo the associated training, and, in some cases, to experience diverse roles in varied contexts. Perhaps most crucially from the perspective of social capital, the placement experience required young people to engage with 'others' – young sport participants with whom they had usually had little previous contact, and who in many cases had been wholly unknown to them. As earlier volunteer placements had mainly built on young people's existing networks, the CV placement had the potential to provide a better basis for developing a form of 'bridging' capital than young people may have obtained previously, through the new opportunities for social connectedness it offered.

The survey findings captured young people's diverse experiences during their CV placements, with regards to the scale of their volunteer activity, the contexts within which they operated, the roles they undertook, the sports they were involved in and the client groups with whom they worked. The structure of the CV programme allowed participants to undertake up to 200 hours of volunteering. On average respondents had completed 113 volunteering hours, with 29 per cent completing 200 hours of volunteering (SiS 'Gold Certificate' standard) and around one-third (34 per cent) more than 100 hours of volunteering (Silver Certificate). Of the remainder, 18 per cent had completed more than 50 hours of volunteering (Bronze Certificate) and a similar proportion (19 per cent) fewer than 50 hours of volunteering.

Young people could obtain their volunteer hours by volunteering in more than one capacity and/or at more than one venue, local sport infrastructure permitting. Generally those who had undertaken higher hours of volunteering were most likely to have had the most diverse experiences. Among the research respondents as a whole, a slight majority (52 per cent) had undertaken volunteer placements at more than one venue, most (78 per cent) had volunteered in more than one sport, and most (56 per cent) had also taken on more than one type of volunteer function. School-based volunteering was prominent, and most respondents (71 per cent) had carried out at least some of their volunteering in school-based placements (covering both curricular and extra-curricular school-based sport); however, many had volunteered at sport clubs (53 per cent), sport and leisure facilities (15 per cent) and youth clubs (12 per cent). During their placement the majority (94 per cent) had undertaken sport leadership and/or coaching activities; almost three-quarters (73 per cent) had officiated at games and tournaments; and smaller numbers had undertaken administrative support (20 per cent), sport maintenance (15 per cent), information technology (5 per cent) or more general support (5 per cent) activities. As volunteers they had worked with a range of client groups, including primary school children (82 per cent), secondary school pupils (72 per cent), people with learning difficulties (36 per cent), physical disabilities (21 per cent) or sensory impairments (8 per cent), BME groups (18 per cent), socially excluded groups (15 per cent) young adults (26 per cent), older adults (14 per cent), and elderly groups (6 per cent).

There was some indication that structural factors were impacting on patterns of placement activity. Some aspects of volunteering were differentiated by gender: on average males undertook more volunteer hours than females and all males had taken on leadership/coaching roles; although these were also widespread among females (89 per cent), they were not universal. Types of sport were also differentiated along traditional gender lines with, for example, males featuring highly in football and cricket placements and females in those involving hockey and netball. More female volunteers (41 per cent) than males (27 per cent) had worked with people with learning difficulties, and also with those with physical disabilities (25 per cent females, 13 per cent males) and with sensory impairments (9 per cent females, 7 per cent males). We might tentatively suggest that there are some indications that males were more likely to volunteer within established sport contexts and females were more likely to volunteer outside them, but the small sub-sample sizes mean that such observations should remain purely speculative.

There was also some evidence of differentiation rooted in factors associated with privilege and disadvantage. Practical difficulties in undertaking placements – notably cost and travel – were most likely to be reported by respondents from less affluent areas; correspondingly, these respondents were less likely than those from more affluent neighbourhoods to travel to placements further from their homes. Probably as a consequence of this, respondents from more deprived areas were less likely to undertake their placements in community sport clubs and particularly likely to do so in schools settings. Once again this resonates with the suggestions that those who are most materially and socially well-resourced may be best positioned to take up further opportunities to extend their social connectedness.

We are cautious, however, about couching such observations in overly critical terms. It is unrealistic to expect deep-rooted social structural processes to be over-turned by sport projects, and it is especially unrealistic to expect this of projects that are in their early years and whose impact will inevitably be strongly influenced by their close association with established educational institutions through which patterns of inequality are often sustained. The most striking impact of the CV programme was that it gave a large number of young people opportunities to engage with others in a reciprocal relationship through the medium of sport. We now go on to consider how the young people who accessed these experiences were affected by them.

Being a sport volunteer: The impact on participants

Our analysis of how young people were affected by their volunteer placements focuses on two themes. Firstly, like Gaskin (1998) we recognize that instrumental motives sit alongside altruistic concerns: volunteering can enhance employability and access to educational opportunities. For many young people, participation in the CV programme was undoubtedly attractive because it gave the opportunity for significant skill development in a structured programme that could be formally recorded on curriculum vitaes and application forms. We therefore recognized that one key set of benefits would be those surrounding the personal and skill development (human and sporting capital) that was a pre-requisite for equipping young people to be effective volunteers. Secondly, and more obviously connected to the issue of developing social capital, we focussed on the impact of the volunteer experience on the social connectedness of young people – how much it provided positive, and often new, experiences of working with and for others, with the possibility of engendering a longer-term sensitivity and commitment to 'community'. Both of these themes were strongly represented in the research findings, from both the 'tracking survey' and the subsequent series of in-depth interviews with 10 of the survey respondents.

Developing human and sporting capital: Personal and skill development through sport volunteering

The respondents to the tracking survey reported multiple impacts from their experience of their CV placement(s), with benefits in personal skill development most widely reported. A large majority of respondents reported impacts such as improvements in leadership skills (88 per cent), communication skills (80 per cent) and organizational skills (65 per cent) (Table 13.1). Many also reported increased confidence (85 per cent) as a result of undertaking their CV placement.

There were a number of indications that the greatest benefits were obtained by those who undertook most volunteering, and/or volunteered in diverse contexts. The respondents who were most likely to report personal development

Table 13.1 The impact of the CV placements on respondents ($n = 160$)

Item	Respondents (%)
It has increased my leadership skills	87.5
It has increased my confidence	85
It has improved my communication skills	80
It has improved my organizational skills	65
It made me think more about other roles in sport	60
It made me want to do volunteer work with children/young people	49.4
It has made me think more about different groups	48.8
It has made me want to do paid work in sports	46.3
It has made me want to do volunteering in sports	35.6
It has made me want to do other sports leadership/volunteering awards	35.0
It has made me want to go to university	28.1
I think more about health and fitness than before	25.6
It has made me think more about the community where I live	16.9
It has helped me to better understand other subjects at school/college	16.3
It has made me want to do volunteering in areas other than sports	16.3

improvements were those who had volunteered for more than 100 hours, and/or had done so at more than one venue, and/or undertaken a variety of volunteer activities. Some findings were gendered: males were more likely than females to report improved organizational skills, communication skills and increased confidence, and females were more likely than males to report improved leadership skills.

The findings from the CV survey provided substantial evidence that volunteers obtained considerable benefits from their placement experience, and that many also developed a stronger orientation to active involvement in their community. Following the analysis of the survey data, 10 in-depth interviews were conducted to obtain more detailed explanations about how undertaking placements affected the volunteers in these ways. A sample of survey respondents was selected that provided a mix of male and female volunteers, from white and BME groups, and with varying levels Community Volunteering experience as measured in total hours undertaken.

In line with the survey findings, interviewees gave frequent accounts of personal and skill development. Improvements in sport-specific leadership skills were widely reported:

My coaching skills have definitely improved, for example, breaking up a skill, I couldn't do that when I first started, but as I went on I knew how to break it down to suit that person.

(Female, aged 20)

I definitely improved my teaching and coaching skills in general, like warm-ups and stretching and to pay more attention to that because when it's just you, you don't really bother, but when it's with the children I realised how important it was to warm-up properly. Also, I learnt the key basic skills to teaching PE really.

(Male, aged 20)

I did the course because I want to be a Primary School Teacher. It gave me the skills to be able to handle a sports day and doing the different parts of the organising and coaching. It helped me learn skills and [see] where my strengths and weaknesses lay as a Teacher.

(Female, aged 20)

Many respondents referred to improvements in more generic skills, especially increases in confidence and communication skills:

I got quite a bit of confidence in talking to younger age groups and learning that I could talk to people without getting speechless and things like that really

(Female, aged 20)

My confidence has gone up loads and loads. I used to be really nervous about planning a session and now it just seems like nothing. I don't get nervous at all anymore and I'm not worried about speaking in front of big groups of people, I just get on with it now whereas before I wouldn't even speak in front of 2 people!

(Female, aged 20)

Several also commented on the impact that volunteering had on how they organized themselves:

It improved my organisation skills and I now know that if I am going to be doing something I need to be organised and I need to know beforehand exactly what I am doing and what I am going to be saying.

(Female, aged 20)

In describing these benefits, many examples were given of *how* the experience of delivering sport opportunities through the CV placement had provided the opportunity for this development. Data of this sort are of particular value for the insight they give into the process through which engaging in sport – in this instance, as volunteers – impacts on individuals. In the quotations below, the respondents describe a range of situations which engendered skill development:

It boosted my confidence because I was standing in front of a group of 30 children and they were listening to me and that feels quite good when they know your name, look up to you and have respect for you

(Female, aged 20)

I think I am more organised now, because I learnt that if you haven't organised everything that you are going to do from the start then it's not going to work because the kids know that you are not prepared to do it so they just mess about. If you come prepared the kids are willing to learn. I have learnt that for myself.

(Male, aged 20)

I used to do all the coaching techniques, all the coaching points that were part of the lesson plan, making sure the whole session goes smoothly. Making sure every aspect of the coaching was covered. I looked into coaching manuals and the Internet and that gave me a different aspect on how coaches around the world teach sport. It really did open my eyes, how to teach things effectively and the kids really did follow it. It was brilliant. It really did help me.

(Male, aged 20)

For many interviewees, an important part of this development came from their progression during the placement, from an initial role as a helper/supporter role to one in which they had sole responsibility for aspects of organization of the session.

> We had to do risk assessments as well and the mentor would help me but as time went on and I grew in confidence I would do them myself and check the sports hall and outside areas as well. I would also get all the equipment out and basically get it all organised.
>
> (Male, aged 20)

> Because the Teacher could see that I was getting more confident with the children, she would feel more at ease with me leading things, so she would say 'can you think of things to do with this lot?' or to get me to have more of a role within the classes really. Rather than just demonstrating, I would chat to the children and help them a lot more so it became more of a teaching role rather than assisting role really.
>
> (Female, aged 20)

In several cases volunteers progressed to lead the session themselves:

> I was built-in to the lessons gradually, so at first I would just take a warm up at the beginning of the session and eventually I was taking the whole session and doing my own thing.
>
> (Male, aged 20)

> At first it was just observing and then progressing to giving the children some praise. It then progressed to taking parts of the session and then we eventually took the whole session but with the mentor overseeing it.
>
> (Female, aged 20)

> At first we were just training and then as it went on the teacher would give us the responsibility to take over the whole PE class and teach the children how to do the sports, how to warm-up properly and stretch. We started off as just basic volunteers and then later we got our own group of children that we had to work with.
>
> (Female, aged 19)

> I started off in the corner and for the first couple of weeks I just helped put the mats out and the equipment and I wasn't really sure what to do because everyone else around me seemed so confident. But at the end after a bit of encouragement I was leading the warm-ups and we had a massive games at the end, like an obstacle course thing, which I led on the last session. With everyone's support it just made me grow in confidence throughout the volunteering.
>
> (Female, aged 20)

Overall, young people's accounts of their experiences during the CV programme indicated a high level of personal and skill development. This encompassed both 'hard', more technical–professional, skills, and 'soft' ones relating to personal development and social interaction. The combined impact of the programme's formal training elements coupled with the practical experience gained through the placement had therefore equipped young people with the attributes they required to be effective volunteers – an important prerequisite for building social connectedness. In the next section we now consider whether the experience of actively undertaking sport volunteering did facilitate this.

Developing social capital: Building social connectedness through sport volunteering

One of the issues that was initially addressed through the tracking survey was the question of young people's 'community orientation'. While quantitative data can be limited in the insights it provides into such complex topics, it can be helpful in offering an initial departure point. The survey therefore sought information on whether the experience of taking part in the CV programme, and the volunteering placement especially, had had an impact on participants' attitude to volunteering in future, and to their views on engaging with others. In this way we sought some indication of the impact the programme might have on social connectedness.

The survey data suggested that the CV programme had a positive impact in this respect for several participants. Most respondents (60 per cent) reported that the experience had encouraged them to think about being further involved in sport and more than one-third (36 per cent) that it had made them want to do further volunteering in sport. A similar proportion (35 per cent) wanted to obtain other sport leadership/volunteering awards as a result of their experience of doing CV 'hours'. Those who had volunteered at a local sport club or a sport and leisure facility were more likely to want to engage with sport in these ways than those who had volunteered in school settings.

The CV placement experience also had a broader impact on many respondents' (49 per cent) interest in doing volunteer work with children and young people. There was also evidence that undertaking the placement had widened many participants' perspectives on a range of social issues, including almost one-half (49 per cent) who felt that they now thought more about the various social groups in their community.

Many interviewees expressed strong altruistic views towards volunteering and contributing to their community:

I think respect and confidence are important contributions to life and through volunteering and community work we can all help.

(Female, aged 17)

I think volunteering is of utmost importance in your community and you can learn more about yourself and influence the lives of others.

(Male, aged 17)

Volunteering has helped me to learn and gain new skills. I have been able to use these skills to help others to develop their own abilities.

(Male, aged 18)

Volunteering is a very worthwhile and rewarding activity. I see it as an opportunity to use my knowledge and skills to help others.

(Female, aged 17)

My perception of volunteering is purely to contribute what you can towards society. The reward is the happiness you get from it.

(Female, aged 16)

I feel that volunteering is the ultimate in self-less acts and the person that takes part should be commended. My father once told me 'If you don't need help, help some-one who does'.

(Male, aged 17)

The placement experience made a significant impact on many volunteers' attitudes to working with young people:

I felt a great sense of achievement, especially with younger children as I saw myself as a role model.

(Female, aged 18)

Some friends thought I was silly doing it for free but they didn't real-ise the amount of fun and satisfaction I got out of seeing the children learn new things.

(Female, aged 20)

I have thoroughly enjoyed all of my volunteer work to date and I think my enthusiasm has radiated to the children and my colleagues. As long as the children and myself are enjoying it I will continue doing it.

(Male, aged 18)

Many of the young volunteers had evidently engaged closely with those they were working with and during the interviews they reflected on how they interacted with them and the experiences that their coaching had provided:

I thoroughly enjoyed the fact that I can help children take part in sports they may not have had the chance to do before. I also found it very rewarding to see children doing and improving in the activities that I have taught them.

(Female, aged 19)

You get to know the children and their strengths and weakness and who needs help and who doesn't [you learn that], if someone keeps doing something wrong you don't keep picking on them because they probably can't actually physically do it, so you learn things about individuals, about children.

(Female, aged 20)

To introduce new sports and techniques to the kids was brilliant because you are giving them a positive experience on different sports and hopefully they are still doing them now.

(Male, aged 20)

In several cases the experience of undertaking placements in schools made the CV volunteers more aware of the social dynamics involved, both between themselves and the pupils they were assisting, and in their relationships with school staff:

Because there wasn't so much an age gap between me and them [pupils], and their teachers are much older than them so they could connect more with the younger volunteers. They also really enjoyed themselves and they had some-one that they could ask questions about high school too.

(Female, aged 20)

Our teacher had prepared us to be role models and told us how we should dress and how we should think about the things we are saying when we go in and how we should talk to the headmaster for example. The teachers said that the children looked up to me as a role model.

(Female, aged 19)

Some particularly strong impacts were reported by those who had had the opportunity to work with youngsters with disabilities:

I really enjoyed working with children and that's what I'm doing now as a career. It showed me just how diverse children were and I really enjoyed it, especially working with the disabled children. It was amazing and is something that I would like to get into in my teaching.

(Female, aged 20)

In one class, one child had a mental condition and we had to adapt the session. We did Gymnastics and ... he was really excited and wanted to do it, he had a carer with him who helped him and he really enjoyed it. The carer said it was the first time anyone had involved him, which was a really good feeling. I spoke to his mother and she said how much he had enjoyed it and how much he would like to do it again, so we did some more sessions right up until the end of the summer term.

(Male, aged 20)

One respondent summarized the all-round individual and community benefits she had experienced through her placement:

I really enjoyed volunteering at my placement, as there was such a variety in abilities, attitudes and activities. I was forever kept on my toes and always learning something new. My leadership skills and confidence have grown enormously in all areas and not just in the sporting environment. Step into Sport has given me the chance to grow as an individual whilst doing something good for the community.

(Female, aged 20)

Conclusions

In this paper we set out to examine whether young people's involvement in a structured programme of sport volunteering empowered young people with skills, knowledge, experiences and commitment that appeared likely to contribute to the building of social capital. We did so in the context of the general prominence of social capital as a focus in UK social policy, and the wide-ranging deployment of sport to contribute to this and other social outcomes.

Our first consideration was whether the volunteering programme gave young people the opportunity for the personal and skill development that would allow them to better actively engage with their communities. In this sense we were concerned to consider the extent to which sport volunteering contributed to the development of sporting capital (sport-related technical skills and foundation knowledge) and human capital (transferable social skills and increased sense of self-worth) amongst young people. Not only did both sets of respondents identify this occurring, but they also explained the process through which such benefits had accrued. Several illustrations were given of how particular tasks produced specific benefits: for example, the experience of planning activity sessions leading to improved organizational skills; the experience of leading sports sessions resulting in increased confidence in interacting with people. These accounts of causality explicitly identified how experiences of sport volunteering engendered a positive attitudinal and behavioural impact amongst young people and encouraged a greater tendency towards active citizenship and civic participation through the medium of voluntary sport engagement.

Our second concern was with the extent to which undertaking a volunteer placement facilitated 'social connectedness', both by providing opportunities for young people to engage with others in their communities, and by fostering a greater awareness of the needs of others and the positive experience to be gained from interacting with them. It was certainly the case that volunteer placements engendered increased interaction between young volunteers and a range of 'others' (young children, other pupils, teachers, club workers, etc.) in a largely productive capacity. Quantitative and qualitative responses also indicate that this increased interaction contributed to a greater sense of altruism and citizenship amongst many of the young people and helped maintain and extend sport provision within local school and community sport infrastructures.

The increased social connectedness brought about by volunteer placements was also effective in facilitating 'bonding' and 'bridging' social capital, although these forms of capital formation were rarely singularly manifest or mutually exclusive, but, rather, were dependent on the relational 'habitus' of young volunteers and the contextual framework in which volunteering took place. For example, the majority of volunteer placements took place in geographically local sport venues or in schools where young volunteers were already involved as players or pupils and which provided a relatively familiar (and more sustainable) sporting environment in which to volunteer. However, within these relatively limited social networks, young volunteers were simultaneously likely to be involved in coaching, officiating and more general sport leadership activities with a more diffuse network of younger children, and, in many cases, with disabled groups, under the tutelage of older teachers, coaches or sport development professionals. In this respect, the sites and activities for sport volunteering and the social connections engendered through this process contributed to the maintenance of 'bonding' capital and the emergence of newer forms of 'bridging' capital within particular social milieu. In this sense, our study questions the 'like us/unlike us' dichotomy at the heart of Putnam's conceptual separation of 'bonding' and 'bridging' capital and offers empirical evidence which suggest these forms of capital are intrinsically linked across a range of different contexts and overlapping social networks.

Bourdieu's conceptualization of capital, field and habitus provide a useful theoretical framework for making sense of the way in which our empirical findings relate to the issues of social connectedness outlined above, and, with particular respect to issues of pre-disposition, access and sustainability of youth volunteering. Bourdieu is concerned with the way in which differential access to social, material and symbolic resources shapes wider engagement with civil society and defines social capital as 'the aggregate of the actual or potential resources which are linked to a durable network of more or less institutionalised relationships of mutual acquaintance and recognition' (Bourdieu, 1986: 51). From this perspective, the tendency of SIS to attract large numbers of young people with a prior disposition to and pre-existing active engagement in sport clubs as performers and volunteers, suggests that many were already favourably situated within formal social (sporting) networks or 'fields' through which to expand upon and further their existing social connectedness and social capital, than were other less 'connected' young people. Furthermore, the tendency for greater sustainability of volunteering amongst pre-placed youth volunteers further illustrates the link between the relational (and distributional) 'habitus' of youth sport volunteers and the increased potential for and realization of human, sporting and social capital.

This latter point raises the question of how widely the benefits of social capital can be accessed through the specific form of sport engagement evaluated in this study. Although stakeholders described the capacity of the programmes to attract some disaffected and challenging young people, in its early years participants from low-income households, BME communities and people with disabilities have been underrepresented in SIS. These are groups whom policymakers often perceive as having some of the greatest needs for greater social cohesion and active citizenship. As Coalter has argued, such approaches derive from a community-deficit model and 'an analysis of the supposed inadequacies of socially excluded communities' (2007: 543) and ignore wider social and cultural changes which have informed the apparent reduction in social connectedness and social capital within Britain. Nonetheless, the material, structural and symbolic facets which underpin social and sporting exclusions seemed apparent within our study of youth sport volunteering and are mirrored by wider demographic patterns of participation in formalized volunteering nationally. This may be where the structural characteristics of projects can be seen to affect the response of participants. A schools-based sport leadership and volunteering project which targets young people engaged in the post-compulsory school-age education sector may have limited capacity to attract pupils disaffected from the school itself and has a limited resource pool of potential participants from (increasingly gendered) BME communities, or from disabled groups and young people from economically disadvantaged backgrounds. Further, the role of sport development professionals and PE teachers as 'cultural intermediaries' in shaping the 'feel' of the project and the conscious selection of 'appropriate' young people to engage in volunteer placements might further limit opportunities in sport participation of this kind amongst more disengaged young people. This does not negate the impact that sport volunteering can have, but does point to the greater challenge of stimulating participation among groups who may have most potential to benefit from their involvement.

We have mixed conclusions. On the one hand we are persuaded that the study yielded sufficient evidence to show that for many young people, sport volunteering can 'work' as a mechanism for fostering human and sporting capital and encourage the practical, emotional and intellectual connectedness which underpins the idea of social capital. When it does, the benefits experienced are clearly identifiable and this study suggests they can be causally attributed. In this respect, we argue that sport researchers may be able to be less tentative in some of their claims about whether sport can yield social benefits. Nonetheless, on the other hand, we make no claims as to the permanence of such causality. Rather, we remain acutely aware that the capacity of youth sport volunteering to engender social capital in its various forms is shaped by a range of personal and structural factors, not least of all, the capacity of individuals to possess and utilize the material and symbolic resources to access and negotiate those social networks through which social capital might be best realized. In turn, the benefits of youth sport volunteering to social capital formation will also be informed by the capacity of social (sporting) networks to exhibit a greater egalitarianism and inclusivity in dealing with and valuing the contribution made by young people from a range of socio-economic, racialized and differently abled backgrounds.

References

Armstrong, D. (2002). *Pathways into and out of crime: Risk, resilience and diversity*. Swindon: Economic and Social Research Council.

Attwood, C., Singh, G., Prime, D. & Creasey, R. (2001). *2001 Home Office citizenship survey: People, families and communities*. London: Home Office.

Babb, P. (2005). *Measurement of social capital in the UK*. London: Office for National Statistics.

Blackshaw, T. & Long, J. (2005). What's the big idea? A critical exploration of the concept of social capital and its incorporation into leisure policy discourse. *Leisure Studies, 24*(3), 239–258.

Bourdieu, P. (1984). *Distinction: A Social Critique of the Judgement of Taste*. London: RKP.

Bourdieu, P. (1986). The forms of capital. In J. Richardson (Ed.), *Handbook of Theory for Research in the Sociology of Education* (pp. 241–258). Westport, CN: Greenwood Press.

Bourdieu, P. (1999). *The Weight of the World: Social Suffering in Contemporary Society*. Cambridge: Polity Press.

Cantle, T. (2001). *Community cohesion: A report of the independent review team*. London: Home Office.

Catan, L. (2002). *Youth, citizenship and social change*. Swindon: Economic and Social Research Council.

Coalter, F. (2007). Sports clubs, social capital and social regeneration: 'Ill-defined interventions with hard to follow outcomes'? *Sport in Society, 10*(4), 537–559.

Coleman, J. (1988). Social capital in the creation of human capital. *American Journal of Sociology, 94*, 95–120.

Coleman, J. (1990). *Equality and Achievement in Education*. Boulder: Westview Press.

Coleman, J. (1994). *Foundations of Social Theory*. Cambridge MA: Belknap Press/Harvard University Press.

Cote, S. & Healy, T. (2001). *The Well-Being of Nations. The Role of Human and Social Capital*. Paris: Organsiation for Economic Co-operation and Development.

Davis-Smith, J. (1998). *The National Survey of Volunteering*. London: Institute of Volunteering Research.

Davis-Smith, J., Ellis, A. & Howlett, S. (2002). *UK-Wide Evaluation of the Millennium Volunteers Programme*. London: Institute of Volunteering Research.

Davis-Smith, J., Ellis, A., Howlett, S. & O'Brien, J. (2004). *Volunteering for All? Exploring the Link Between Volunteering and Social Exclusion*. London: Institute of Volunteering Research.

Department for Education and Skills. (2003). *Every Child Matters, Government Green Paper*. London: Cabinet Office, Department for Education and Skills.

Fukuyama, F. (1995). Social capital and civil society. *Foreign Affairs, 74*(5), 89–103.

Gaskin, K. (1998). *What Young People Want from Volunteering*. London: Institute of Volunteering Research.

Giddens, A. (1991). *Modernity and Self Identity: Self and Society in the Late Modern Age*. Cambridge: Polity Press.

Harper, R. (2001). *Social Capital: A Review of the Literature*. London: Social Analysis and Reporting Division, Office for National Statistics.

Home Office. (1999). *Voluntary and Community Sector Activities: Policy Action Team 9*. London: Home Office.

Kitchen, S., Michaelson, J., Wood, N. & John, P. (2005). *2005 Citizenship Survey: Active Communities Topic Report*. London: Department for Communities and Local Government.

Lynn, P. & Davis-Smith, J. (1992). *The 1991 National Survey of Voluntary Activity in the UK*. Berkhamstead: The Volunteer Centre UK.

Munton, T. & Zurawan, A. (2003). *Active Communities: Headline Findings from the 2003 Home Office Citizenship Survey*. London: Home Office.

National Centre for Social Research (2000). *Political Interest and Engagement in Young People*. York: Joseph Rowntree Foundation.

Neighbourhood Renewal Unit (2004). *Indices of Deprivation 2004 for Super Output Areas*. London: Office of the Deputy Prime Minister.

Policy Action Team 10 (1999). *Arts and Sport: A Report to the Social Exclusion Unit*. London: Department of Culture, Media and Sport.

Portes, A. & Landolt, P. (1996). The downside of social capital. *American Prospect*, 26(94), 18–21.

Putnam, R. (1993). The prosperous community: Social capital and public life. *American Prospect*, 4(13), 11–18.

Putnam, R. (1995). Bowling alone: America's declining social capital. *Journal of Democracy*, 6(1), 65–78.

Putnam, R. (2000). *Bowling alone: The collapse and revival of American community*. New York: Simon and Schuster/ Touchstone.

Rojek, C. (2000). *Leisure and culture*. Macmillan: Basingstoke.

Social Exclusion Unit (1998). *Bringing Britain Together: A National Strategy for Neighbourhood Renewal*. London: HM Cabinet Office Social Exclusion Unit.

Whiting, E. & Harper, R. (2003). *Young People and Social Capital*. London: Office for National Statistics.

CHAPTER 14

Soccer and social capital in Australia: Social networks in transition

Daniel Lock, Tracy Taylor and Simon Darcy

This chapter starts with the general premise that sport clubs have the potential to build social capital. Following on from this assumption, we specifically examine the role that soccer played in Australian society in relation to social capital development in the last century. Prior to 2003 the term soccer was officially used to describe football in Australia. We then discuss the present situation, recent governance and strategic positioning changes implemented in the sport of soccer, and the impact these initiatives have had on the sport's social capital and its constituent communities.

In a country where Australian Rules, Rugby Union and Rugby League have traditionally been the dominant football codes and held power bases across other institutions, why are we focussing in this chapter on the sport of soccer? The rationale for this choice is located in the historical and cultural significance that soccer assumed in Australia, with particular reference to migrant communities. Soccer was a particularly popular physical activity in the post-migration life of many Europeans in the twentieth century and it acted as a conduit for the development of personal and social networks. This was especially important for migrants who were struggling to come to terms with a new environment, language and culture. Soccer provided a non-threatening social milieu where community networks could develop and thrive. In particular, ethnically aligned clubs offered a place for the development of reciprocity and trust, by being mutually supportive within a framework of a commonly understood set of social norms. Broadly speaking, many newly arrived migrants were marginalized from mainstream societal institutions of influence and power, such as political and education establishments, in their initial years of settlement. To this end for most of the twentieth century soccer provided a relatively neutral ground on which to develop personal and collective identity.

However, by the new milenium the increasingly negative public image of soccer and growing frustration about the sports' failure to attract a larger supporter base, despite growing participation levels at junior and youth levels, led to concerns that the global commercial potential of the sport would remain unfulfilled. These compounding problems eventually culminated in the federal government's review of the sport in 2003 (Crawford, 2003). The resulting report called for major changes in soccer's governance, to improve the administration and increase mainstream acceptance of the sport in Australia. In this chapter, we outline the position soccer has held in Australian society and discuss how recent changes in the structure and delivery of the game have affected its potential to develop social capital in constituent communities.

Building social capital through sport

In the introductory chapter of this book the editors have provided an overview of social capital as a concept and its broader applications in the sporting arena, and we draw on this work as the basis for framing discussion in this chapter. Furthermore, Hall (1999: 418) has suggested that measurements of social capital are premised on the 'extent to which individuals have regular contact with others, beyond the sphere of the family or the market, and notably the kind of face-to-face relations of relative equality associated with participation in common endeavours, whether *recreational, social,* service-orientated or political' (italics added). The social capital available to those engaged in sporting clubs can also depend on the volume of capital existing in the network (Bordieu, 1983). Specifically it is noted that 'a well-connected individual in a poorly connected society is not as productive as a well-connected person in a well-connected community' (Putnam, 2000: 20).

In essence, the volume of social capital available depends upon the reciprocal benefits and opportunities maintained by the network. Within the sporting world, the sport and size of club may provide the basis for determining the social capital available through engagement. For example, membership of a youth soccer club in a lower socio-economic area, which encourages participation through affordable joining fees and enjoyable participation, may have limited potential to develop social capital due to the socio-demographic composition of the club's members and their parents. Conversely, a youth soccer club, which encourages player talent identification and skill development, may facilitate a far greater volume of social capital due to its links with higher profile coaches, well-connected patrons, business support and regional association affiliations.

Discussions about the scope of sporting clubs to contribute to the development of social capital for participants have circulated in the public arena for the last 20 or so years (Bellah et al., 1985). The contributions that sport can make to social capital, through voluntary associations and in strengthening communities (Dyreson, 2001), and via building self-confidence and widening social contact (Uslaner, 1999) have been noted. While research on sport and social capital are growing, the body of empirical evidence on the relationship between participation in sporting clubs and the development of social capital is still relatively unexplored.

In consequence, wide-ranging 'unproven' claims about the significant role of sport in social capital development have elicited cautionary responses. Daly (2005: 6) posited that sport 'generates social connections that may be more associated with markets and consumers than with democracy' and noted the need for research to investigate how membership of sport clubs and associations may contribute to building social capital. In balance (Jarvie, 2003: 152) argued that it is unrealistic to expect that sport can totally sustain a sense of community, but that it can make a 'valuable contribution' with the sporting club as a central mechanism in this process.

In one of the few empirical studies of social capital and sport, Seippel (2006) found that members of voluntary sport organizations (in Norway) develop social capital which is conducive to generalized trust and political commitment. This finding supports Jarvie's notion that sport clubs can make a valuable contribution to the development of social capital. However, the effect of sporting organizations was weaker than for voluntary organizations in general. Recognizing that we need more evidence about the relationship between sport and social capital Seippel (2006) concluded his article by calling for future studies that focus explicitly on sport and the social and political effects of social capital across different national situations in order to understand the effects of institutional contexts.

The concept of social interaction, the connections available in a social network, and the nature and role that sport has been found to play in developing unity and solidarity among club supporters (MacClancy, 1996), provide us with profitable avenues for investigation. An additional consideration is the size of the social network and its potential to increase social capital (Bordieu, 1983). Furthermore, Bordieu (1983) maintained that social capital development depends on individuals being able to 'effectively mobilize' social benefits available from the network. More specifically, a network rich in social capital will only provide individual benefit for those that are able to access the network.

Therefore, the degree to which social capital is accessible to members of the network is a central element in the ability of any organization to provide positive social benefits to its members. As such, sport clubs can engage with their social environment and provide opportunities to develop social capital and facilitate bonding. Hague and Mercer's (1998) study of a town in Scotland noted that the local football team contributed to the development of a sense of identity and provided a basis for the formation of bonding social capital. Tonts' (2005) case study of the Northern Wheat-belt of Western Australia found that sport was an important avenue for the creation and maintenance of social capital. In this study of rural Australia,

93 per cent of respondents ($n = 285$) indicated that sport was an important way of keeping in touch with friends and neighbours, and 91.2 per cent noted that it was important in promoting a local 'sense of community' (Tonts, 2005). However, Tonts' noted with concern that there has been a steady decline in the state's rural population, and this, together with increased pressures on the volunteer workforce that sustain the clubs, is contributing to an erosion of sporting opportunities.

While sport can provide opportunities to develop positive social capital, conversely, there is evidence that suggests sport can reinforce bad behaviour, isolation and exclusion. For example, sporting clubs have been found to promote masculine aggression, tensions (Kerr, 2005) and crowd violence (Hughson, 2000a). In Tonts' (2005) Western Australian study noted above, it was demonstrated that some of the social networks created by engagement in sport were exclusionary. Exclusion can range from direct prohibition of certain groups, for example not allowing female participation, to a product of a clash of the social norms of the sport and that of the wider community. In the latter instance, sport teams and associated individuals that have violated community expectations of alcohol consumption, recreational drug use and loutish behaviour can create a subculture where social networks may support antisocial behaviour. Tonts (2005) also noted that in the rural context, where sport plays a central social role to group identity of individuals and town identity, the atmosphere created can be intimidating for those people who are excluded. Furthermore, the antisocial behaviour of players may be tolerated because of the perceived importance of their sporting performance to the team and the town's reputation based on sporting success.

Through the case study of soccer in Australia we explore the notion of social capital and its relationship to the development of positive social and cultural networks, as well as investigating if bonding social capital contributes to exclusion or negative impacts.

Soccer in Australian migrant communities

Soccer's prominence in the life and social settlement of many of Australia's migrant communities is extensively documented (Mosely, 1987, 1995; Hughson, 1992, 2000a, 2000b; Adair & Vamplew, 1997; Mosely et al., 1997). In particular, the links between soccer and expressive ethnicity that emanated after World War II have been well established (Hay, 1994; Vamplew,

1994; Mosely, 1995; Hughson, 1996b). Migrant influence first began in the 1880s when mass British migration introduced football to Australia (Mosely, 1995). By the early 1900s, it was the English and Scottish who controlled the game. However, the UK ex-patriots' dominance of soccer only lasted until mid-century. A large influx of players from predominantly non-English speaking countries that arrived in the post-World War II migration boom shifted the sport's player base, this lead to derisory references and soccer was labelled as a 'wogs' game.

Soccer's 'minority' sport status certainly played a part in its relatively easy appropriation by newly arrived migrants. Unfamiliar with the more popular football codes and sports such as cricket, many newly arrived Europeans gravitated to the sport that they were most familiar with – soccer. There was both a cultural and gender dimension in the establishment of many ethnic-specific soccer clubs. For example, Georgakis (1999: 32) noted that soccer was used by the Greek community to keep traditions alive and build the masculine traits they believed that young males needed. 'First of all sport would masculinize the boys so counteracting the influences of the feminized home. Secondly, because sports were conducted in Greek clubs and organizations, they would ensure traditional allegiances to Hellenism and to Greek traditions' (Georgakis, 1999). Acculturation for migrant groups was not straightforward as 'denigration and discrimination was practiced, qualifications and experience among migrants devalued [and] racism was rampant' (Hay, 1994: 44). The soccer pitch provided welcome relief as playing experience was recognized and expertise and skills in soccer were valued, unlike the situation of many migrants in the workplace.

The cultural composition of soccer clubs and players in the 1940s–1950s led to intense rivalries, on and off the field, between the various ethnically aligned soccer clubs (Mosely et al., 1997). Soccer's visible representation of 'ethnic enclaves' existed at a time when migrants were expected to *assimilate* into mainstream Australian society, thus the non-integrative structure of the sport precipitated its ghettoization and led to claims of exclusivity. On one hand, many migrant groups were able to develop successful social links and community networks through soccer. However, paradoxically these same ethnic-specific clubs and competitions that created high levels of bonding social capital also increasingly marginalized some communities from mainstream Australia by 'seeming parochial and offensive to outsiders' (Hay, 2006: 171). The apparent stranglehold that specific ethnic communities had on soccer, combined with long-term financial mismanagement, as Hay (2006) lamented, did not help the image and acceptance of soccer into mainstream Australian society.

Social capital and soccer

Migrant experiences in Australia can be widely varying, Galvin and West (1988: 47) noted, 'the migrant experience in Australia combines absolute opposites: accounts of human effort overcoming seemingly impossible odds contrast stories of exploitation, loneliness and despair'. This comment seems especially pertinent when discussing the potential for social capital development within ethnically based soccer clubs. A lack of competency in the English language obstructed many newly arrived migrants from being able to participate in established Australian social networks. Sport, and especially soccer, provided these migrants with a point of communication. Furthermore, by being able to speak their native tongue and engage in a sport from their homeland, soccer provided a notable avenue for migrants to prosper, develop ties and network with compatriots (Mosely et al., 1997). In this respect engagement in the soccer community was a way to develop social inclusion (Jarvie, 2003).

Soccer clubs were 'frequently the first organisation established by a migrant community' (Mosely, 1995: 20). The environment created by soccer clubs and playing the game gave immigrants a sense of being better at something [soccer] than their native oppressors (Hay, 1994). Soccer clubs were an 'instrument through which all elements of life could be aided ... [the club] enabled people [migrants] to interact, to establish patronage links, support networks and social contacts' (Mosely, 1995: 21). Soccer clubs formed around ethnic groups to assist with them in the settlement process, and soccer represented an activity in which the participants were already acculturated. The clubs provided a common ground for migrants to express an affiliation to their motherland; thus creating a forum for nationalistic values to thrive within Australia (Vamplew, 1994). Nationalism was overtly expressed through soccer, and the majority of clubs in Australia held an obvious ethnic affiliation of some kind (Hay, 1994; Mosely, 1995; Mosely et al., 1997).

With reference to the work of Coleman (1988) and his argument regarding human capital, it seems salient that contacts established through soccer clubs provided many migrants with a social network, which through reciprocal benefits enabled migrants to develop a feeling of worth, employment links and most critically individual benefit. Social networks eventually usurped the soccer club as ethnically based clubs grew in stature (Mosely et al., 1997). Through the growth of migrant clubs, the associated soccer administrators obtained key roles in national body governance, which increased their standing, network reach and club profile. The opportunity to develop cohesive communities perpetuated itself at all levels of soccer from the grass roots community clubs through to the clubs and teams in the national league.

Through involvement in soccer, migrant communities developed significant social capital as it provided a space to develop social ties with compatriots, develop social networks and reap the reciprocal benefits these interactions provided. As claimed in relation to the Croatian community, 'Perhaps the sphere that has come closest to uniting the Croatian-born is sport, and especially soccer, in which many Croatian teams and players have competed with great distinction in the top grades' (Department of Immigration and Multicultural Affairs, 1999: 3).

The place of reciprocity and opportunity are salient factors in understanding how social networks developed within soccer clubs. The actors' 'engagement' with soccer encompassed individuals who were involved in activities relating to the sporting club including participants, supporters, administrators, volunteers, spectators and sponsors. Through soccer, these individuals associated together on a regular basis, to develop trust and engage in community-minded activities. The soccer club provided companionship, camaraderie, contacts and social networks that would have not been available otherwise. From this perspective the development of social capital via soccer was an enabling experience for many migrant communities.

The changing context of soccer

The development of social capital through soccer has to this point been discussed in a positive sense. However, as Putnam (2000) warns there can be negative external effects of networks. Consequences of exclusivity can lead to inequalities and social divisions, such as Jarvie and Burnett (2000) found encapsulated in the secretive, exclusive and elitist nature of many Scottish golf clubs. In the opening chapter of this book, the editors cite the work of Portes and Landolt (2000) and Jarvie (2003) to illustrate the potentially negative effects of social capital. Portes and Landolt (2000) denote exclusion of outsiders as a potentially negative connotation of social capital. The social ties that provide 'privileged access to resources [can] bar others from securing the same assets' (Portes & Landolt, 2000: 533). Notions of exclusivity applicable to individuals outside of the social network are one such consequence. It is therefore plausible that the inextricable ethnic links maintained by soccer clubs served to alienate some sections of the general community.

While no other sport in Australia was more closely linked with immigrants and ethnic communities than soccer, the centrality of soccer in the development of community networks was not inclusive of all ethnic groups. The strong bonds formed with ethnic-based soccer clubs and the homogeneous membership certainly created a perception of not being inclusive towards outsiders (Lock et al., 2007b). 'Names like Croatia, Juventus and Hellas served to antagonise rather than allure' (Mosely, 1995: 24). There are two specific dimensions to the negative effects of social capital in soccer, namely ethnic group exclusivity and the publicly perceived hooligan problems associated with some soccer clubs.

The exclusivity created by ethnically aligned soccer clubs created some negative impacts for individuals outside of the specific culturally based social network. While few soccer clubs were 'exclusively' one culture; by virtue of their name, colours and associated supporters, many clubs were perceived as representative of a particular ethnic grouping. For example, APIA Leichhardt were viewed as an Italian club that represented the Italian community in Australia. Conversely, the Italian club Marconi Stallions possessed weaker links to the Italian population, which helped the club to draw a more diverse audience (Hughson, 1997). Hughson's (1997) extensive research with the Croatian soccer club Sydney United (formerly Sydney Croatia) explicitly detailed the strong relationship between the club's supporters and the Croatian community. Clubs such as Sydney United provided Croatian migrants a fervent forum to express their nationality and a place where young Croatians could be educated in the customs and culture of their parents' homeland (Hughson, 1997).

In consequence, the level of nationalistic expression visible in clubs like Sydney United built up a strong Croatian social network (Hughson, 1996), which was inaccessible for those outside of that specific community. Towards the end of the 1980s, this limiting aspect of soccer club structures contributed to a reduction in crowd numbers. In a report on the soccer environment in Australia, Bradley (1990: 2) asserted that 'ethnic communities are no longer providing the support to their clubs that they once did'. Bradley noted that the diminishing support of ethnically based clubs was linked to decreasing migration of Europeans (Vamplew, 1994).

In essence, the influx of migrants that developed the sport to such an extent post 1940 were no longer arriving in the same numbers and the role of ethnically aligned soccer clubs in the transition phase of the acculturation process diminished. In the 1970s official policies which had resulted in discrimination against all non-British immigration were removed and assimilation and integration policies were being replaced by the concept of multiculturalism (Collins, 1995). During the period 1980–1990 positive social capital within migrant clubs declined and the soccer club no longer provided the once integral role in the acculturation of new migrants into Australian life. By the 1980s, new arrivals were not expected to separate themselves from their cultural origins and the *National Agenda for Multicultural Australia* recognized the right of all Australians, within carefully defined limits, to express and share their individual cultural heritage (McAllister & Moore, 1989). The agenda and other anti-discrimination legislation recognized the importance of removing barriers of race, ethnicity, culture, religion, language, gender or place of birth. However, in a review of progress the National Multicultural Advisory Council (1995) concluded that although significant advances had been made, racism in sport was an issue of concern.

Hooliganism amongst soccer supporters has also been mooted as a consequence of the perceived ethnic exclusivity that surrounded some soccer clubs, although it has been suggested that the extent of the problem was exaggerated by the media (Hughson, 2001). The negative image of soccer created by its association with violent behaviour and crowd disruptions limited the game's audience. Hughson's ethnographic research into soccer hooligans in Australia provides an insight into the subcultures that developed via soccer clubs (Hughson, 1996, 2000a). The soccer hooligan problem in Australia was largely attributed to ethnic grievances (Hughson, 2002). In creating an image that soccer grounds were 'ethnic battlegrounds' the hooligan problem created another roadblock for those outside the soccer network.

The declining strength of social networks of many soccer clubs during the 1980s and early 1990s (Bradley, 1990; Vamplew, 1994), together with growing concerns about the 'dark' side of ethically aligned soccer clubs, provided the basis for major changes to the sport, its strategic direction and its place in Australian society.

Transforming soccer into football

To this point, the narrative on soccer's historical relationship in specific ethnic communities has highlighted how the game served as an avenue to develop social capital for many newly arrived migrant groups and acted as a focal point of community life bringing people together for meaningful social interaction. The role of bonding capital was clearly evident in the ethnic pride created amongst supporter groups. However, competition between soccer teams was generally seen as synonymous with competition between ethnic communities. The resulting strong social bonds in support of particular clubs created rivalries which resulted in hooliganism and violence. Exclusivity and its associated negative consequences were important driving factors behind the changes to soccer's governance structure. The structural change focussed on removing the sports' historical ties with ethnically aligned clubs. The effect of transforming soccer into 'football' on networks of social capital is explored in this section.

In many senses, social policy movements to de-ethnicize soccer contradicted the Australian policy of multiculturalism (Brabazon, 1998; Hughson, 2000b). However, the driving agenda for de-ethnicization was not just related to social concerns for it was also a business decision (Mosely et al., 1997). The business of soccer concerned the development and expansion of the sport's supporter bases outside of a small number of ethnic communities. During the 1990s, this agenda became more evident with the development of 'Australian' soccer clubs. Notable examples included Perth Glory, Northern Spirit, and Adelaide United, all clubs that attracted large supporter bases. However, the degree to which these clubs acted as social facilitators or provided opportunities for social networking was unproven. There has been discussion that such clubs attracted a mainly British following (Brabazon, 1998), although there is no empirical evidence to support such claims.

Several attempts to de-ethnicize the National Soccer League (NSL) in 1977, 1992 and 1997 had proved unsuccessful (Mosely et al., 1997). Finally, in 2003, low attendances, minimal media exposure, negative public images associated with soccer violence and poor international performances convinced the Australian Federal Government to commission a review into soccer. The resulting report into *The structure, governance and management of soccer in Australia* (Crawford, 2003) proposed a radical overhaul of the governance and management of the Soccer Australia. Australian businessperson Frank Lowy was appointed as the Chairman to manage the change.

Lowy then commissioned a further investigation, *The report of the NSL Task-Force into the structure of a new National Soccer League competition* (Kemeny, 2003). This latter report outlined several recommendations for a reformed national league structure. In 2004 the NSL was disbanded amidst waning crowd attendances and an almost total media blackout (Solly, 2004), foreshadowing a 'sea change' for the sport. In the ensuing change, ethnically aligned NSL clubs such as the Marconi Stallions, Sydney United, Wollongong Wolves and Sydney Olympic were relegated to state league competitions such as the NSW Premier League. The only NSL clubs to enter the A-League were culturally pluralist clubs of Perth Glory and Adelaide United.

Prosaically, in August 2005, following an 18-month break from any form of national competition, the A-League was launched and presented an ambitious mandate to transform 'soccer' into 'football'. The changes to the structure of Australia's domestic football league made a concerted effort to quell expressive forms of nationalistic identity. To break the ethnic nexus and the ethnically aligned power bases in the sport, Football Federation Australia (FFA) made a distinct and strategic effort to separate the game from traditional ethnic affiliations. Although a distinct marketing pitch was developed to attract the younger supporters, FFA Chairman, Frank Lowy made it clear that the continued attendance of ethnic communities would be vital to the A-League's success (Cockerill, 2005). The consequences of the change process are now explored. The questions addressed are: Has the removal of ethnically based clubs from top-level football diminished or affected networks of social capital within the communities? If so, has this changed the role of ethnically based soccer clubs as a conduit to assimilate, network and access reciprocity? Finally, has restructuring of football led to new networks of social capital formation?

Have new networks of social capital developed?

In Putnam's example of ten-pin league bowling, engagement with sport provided a form of 'social interaction and even occasionally civic conversations' (Putnam, 2000: 113). Putnam's argument suggested that those elements of interaction are salient factors in participation. Additionally, the size and scope of potential networks are key factors regarding the volume of social capital within a network (Bordieu, 1983). Therefore, we discuss potential social networks, their scope and reciprocal benefits as experienced through engagement in A-League supporter groups. This discussion elaborates on football development schemes implemented in the community since 2003.

In his scathing review of Australian football Bradley (1990) commented that in the NSL, only Marconi met the standards of development required to be a successful club, although he conceded that the club needed to broaden their fan base outside of the Italian community. The broader point to which Bradley alluded was that clubs in Australia needed to grow financially to support a functional and successful national league. *The Report of the NSL Task-Force* drew further attention to this problem outlining the acute issues NSL clubs experienced with insolvency (Kemeny, 2003). It was contended in this report that the general resilience of NSL clubs relied on the 'commitment and passion of club members, rather than successful business models' (Kemeny, 2003: 3). To obtain a license to compete in the A-League, each club had to satisfy criteria defined by the FFA regarding adequate finance. Additionally, the FFA imposed strict salary cap restrictions on all clubs in attempt to curb the excessive spending on players that had crippled some NSL clubs.

The FFA outlined stringent and clearly defined business models that all clubs in the A-League followed as a criterion of entry into the competition. The A-League clubs were structured on a business model and concentrated on engaging city-wide followings, not local communities. Therefore, networks of social capital around these football clubs have shifted since the restructuring of the A-League. In the case of the FFA and the A-League, there is ample evidence of the existence of national social/business networks and city-specific social/business networks of the clubs (Lock et al., 2007a).

The social networks that developed around football clubs still play an important roles in the lives of these communities both at the ground and at the social clubs adjacent to them (Hughson, 1996). For example, in a recent study into Victorian club Springvale White Eagles it was established that despite an agenda of de-ethnicization at state level, the White Eagles maintained their links with Serbian culture in defiance of laws to the contrary. As Hallinan, Hughson and Burke (2007) stated, 'collective Serbian identity is maintained through a social network with soccer in pivotal place'. They concluded (2007: 18), that it is unlikely that football's ethnic roots will ever be severed, despite the presence of the A-League and state and national level de-ethnicization policies.

Independent supporter groups as social networks

In the disbanded NSL, expressive supporter groups classified by ethnicity were commonplace (Hughson, 2002). Furthermore, these groups served as a vehicle to celebrate ethnicity and openly display artefacts of culture (Hughson, 2000a). However, as previously noted negative consequences and deviant behaviour accompanied of some of these highly nationalistic acts of expression (Hughson, 1996).

Since the inception of the A-League into the Australian sporting marketplace, new subcultures of support groups have developed that stand independently from their 'team'. Notable examples include: The Cove (Sydney FC); The Union Rebels (Melbourne Victory); The Marinators (Central Coast Mariners); The Orange Army (Queensland Roar); The Squadron (Newcastle Jets); The Glory Boys/Boys from the Shed (Perth Glory) and The Red Army (Adelaide United). Each group provides expressive, colourful and exuberant support for their team (Lock et al., 2007a). As elaborated on in research into the Melbourne Victory, the Union Rebels, 'organise away game travel, social activities and country supporter links' (Hay, 2006: 100). The social component of club involvement is a common function of supporter groups. The organization of activities as defined by Hay (2006) utilizes Internet-based contact, namely web-based forums. Web-based forums 'allow people to get to know other people and seek out affiliation, companionship and support' (Girgensohn & Lee, 2002: 136). Therefore, in addition to providing a vehicle for fans to organize trips and social activities, fan forums act as a hub for social interaction and the development and continuation of social networks.

The Cove is an example of an A-League subculture (Lock, 2006; Lock, Taylor & Darcy, 2006, 2007a). Organizationally, The Cove is an independent group, which operates outside the governance and control of Sydney FC. The Cove is independently funded by its members. As stated in its charter (a virtual list of rules and guidelines), The Cove's primary aim is to provide unconditional support to the team in the colours of the club (sky and navy blue) (The Cove, 2007a). The actual function of The Cove appears to be fundamentally similar to The Union in Melbourne (Hay, 2006) and centralized through the groups' online discussion forum. In 2007 The Cove's online forum boasted 2411 members (The Cove, 2007c), which is a significant population. The unofficial Sydney FC forum, run by The Cove does not have barriers to entry, although it is strictly moderated based upon the sites, user policies and guidelines (The Cove, 2007b). The in-ground supporter composition of

The Cove is similar, with no explicit barriers to supporter participation within the group.

The apparent inclusiveness of supporter groups such as The Cove provides a point of comparison with the previous exclusive social networks (Portes & Landolt, 2000) that formed around NSL football clubs. By removing expressive ethnicity from football clubs, the FFA hoped to develop inclusive supporter bases. The following quote from a Sydney FC fan and Cove member underlines this philosophy, 'basically, if you can get there and learn a song or two, you're in it' (Huxley, 2006: 3). In an earlier interview, further insight into the inclusive nature of the Cove was provided by one of its leaders: 'We've got Scots, Greeks, Romanians, Anglos, the lot ... It's really exciting to be in on something like this from the start' (Cubby, 2005: 7). This departure from the culture that was perpetuated in ethnically based clubs is significant. It is notable that unofficial supporter groups have embraced the notion of inclusiveness. In their official charter (a virtual mission statement), The Cove articulate (under point five):

The Cove does not tolerate or support racism, sexism or homophobia – Sydney is a multi-racial society. The Cove reflects this and welcomes everyone.

(The Cove, 2007a)

In essence, restrictions on membership are the result of personal choice, not intra-group exclusivity. An individual offended by vociferous support would fall outside of The Cove's Charter, although they are free to converse on the unofficial forum. However, there appears to be a perception amongst some of these groups that attempts to integrate supporters were specifically designed to completely expel ethnicity. In addition to inclusive supporter groups, Hay (2006) pointed out that rogue elements still exist, 'the Northern outskirts of Melbourne represent the ethnic groups whom David Hill (Former Soccer Australia officianado) and others were trying to root out' (Hay, 2006: 100). This assertion suggests that certain ethnic groups have not been ostracized from football support following football's restructure, as they still attended games 'to see good-standard football' (Hay, 2006: 101).

The official mandate of Australia's football governing body has been less about 'rooting out' ethnic groups, but rather it is based on integrating all supporters into larger, more diverse consumer bases. In effect, broader cross sections of the community who want to support football in Australia now have an avenue to do so. The empirical findings from a survey of

Sydney FC's fan base support this notion; the findings noted that the primary motivation for Sydney FC's members to support the club was to support football (Lock et al., 2007a). There is mounting evidence that the A-League has provided the football community, many of whom felt disenfranchized by the previous NSL structure, an opportunity to engage in the new competition (Cockerill, 2005) and that a 'new' market has emerged. Lock et al. (2007b) found that 45 per cent of Sydney FC's members had not previously supported an Australian domestic football club.

Support groups in the A-League have formed on a fundamentally different premise to the NSL. Evidence would suggest that fan groups in the A-League are larger and more inclusive than the former ethnically dominated supporter bases (Hughson, 2000a). The extent to which the increase in size and inclusion of fan groups in the A-League has increased the volume of social capital is unclear for two reasons. Firstly, the volume of social capital that can be derived from a social network is determined by the standing and reciprocal benefits available through membership (Bordieu, 1983). Although the size of fan groups in A-League clubs would suggest that reciprocal benefits would be higher, there is little indication of the networking opportunities. However, using Putnam's (2000: 112–113) example of league bowling in the US, the 'social interaction' and 'civic engagement' accrued through participation in teams, or broad social groups generally is a significant source of social capital. The nature of interaction provides fans with additional benefits through the official membership benefits, which are enhanced through team success, and the visibility of the A-league as a high status 'mainstream' sport with its associated, social, business and celebrity capital. For the dedicated fan, the role of Internet-based forums provides fans with a vehicle to extend their social networks and ties then externally to the support system outside of playing seasons.

Secondly, to limit a discussion of social capital in football to the A-League fan bases is misleading. Since the redevelopment of football governance in Australia, considerable efforts by the FFA to raise the profile of football in the community underpinned a mission to develop the game's profile and network in the antipodes. Two specific initiatives in particular have advanced this mission. Prior to Australia's historic world cup qualification in 2005, the FFA developed the Australian football family, which provided a preferential service for individuals who already engaged in football in some capacity (Football Federation Australia, 2007b). The most significant bonus of membership of the Football Family was pre-release tickets to the Socceroos, international games and newsletters that the general-public could not access. Membership of this social network was beneficial to the FFA and provided members with a source of social capital. Members of the Football Family obtained reciprocal benefits in terms of ticketing and news. The FFA obtained contact information for football enthusiasts across Australia through which they could develop a broader network.

The second initiative acknowledged the importance of actively pursuing community relations. As the FFA stated, 'grassroots football is the "foundation" of the game in this country and provides the base that is necessary to continue to produce talented players, coaches, referees and administrators' (Football Federation Australia, 2007a). In the terms and conditions of the A-League the FFA noted that, 'clubs are also part of this engagement and as part of their participation agreements, are to be actively involved in their community' (Football Federation Australia, 2007a). Engagement, as defined by the FFA, includes school visits, local club visits, appearances at events, charity functions, coaching clinics and sponsor events (Football Federation Australia, 2007a). Such community involvement serves a distinct purpose in the fostering of social capital between A-League clubs and local society. For clubs, compulsory community involvement forces each organization to pursue links with local businesses, football clubs and communities. In doing so, it provides clubs with the opportunity to develop brand awareness and public support within their local community. Conversely, this agreement provides local businesses with an opportunity to affiliate themselves with high-profile athletes for promotional purposes and local clubs have access to A-League players to promote the game in their region. Although in its infancy, the FFA community development programmes appear to provide distinct guidelines dictating A-League clubs to be active in their region, which should (in time) yield significant social benefits for both A-League clubs and the communities in which they operate.

To consider only the new social networks that have developed since the restructure of Australian football would negate the above elements. As with other codes, the professional National Leagues do not necessarily represent the social networks at local community club level or in the state leagues. Therefore, the degree to which social capital in local football communities may have altered following relegation to state competitions and the impact that the changes have had on local community clubs requires further investigation.

Conclusion

There is ample evidence that over at least a 50-year period soccer clubs played a significant role in developing social networks and capital in many migrant communities. Not only did the clubs provided an opportunity for physical activity but, perhaps more significantly, they offered a welcoming place for social interaction and engagement, and formed the basis for both the creation and expression of social capital. The intense sense of pride and ethnic community identity that accompanied the clubs reflected the formation of 'bonding capital'.

However, as the level of interest in football from migrant communities diminished through the 1980s and 1990s, new arrival migrant numbers decreased, and migrant communities acculturated within Australia, the football club served less of a focus for social networks than it once had. This is not to say that the football clubs' function in ethnic communities changed completely but that the clubs' cultural importance was in decline, particularly in second-generation migrant communities.

The changes to football and the development of a new league structure have impacted on networks of reciprocity in migrant communities and the relegation of ethnically orientated clubs to State league competitions across Australia has led to broader and more diverse social networks within A-League football clubs. All indications suggest that social networks continue to exist in relation to football clubs in Australia. However, further research is necessary to delineate with more certainty the extent that social networks in ethnically based football clubs changed post 2004. The impact of sport clubs and associations in particular on the social interactions and engagement are fundamental to building social capital (Daly, 2005). Further empirical work could test this assumption.

In summary, the restructure of football in Australia has changed the nature and function of the game in this country. In addressing a number of issues during the course of this chapter, our position has been that football was historically a significant source of social capital for ethnic groups. However, dropping migration levels and the reduced role that football played in the acculturation process of post-World War II European migrants led to the soccer club assuming a diminished role in ethnic communities. This, coupled with a number of attempts to de-ethnicize the NSL, disenfranchised both ethnic groups and fans of football in Australia that did not identify with the expressive ethnicity of the former league.

Football continues to provide an avenue for social capital development, albeit in a different form. The new business model and the de-ethnicized A-League competition appear to have enforced a noticeable shift into a broader and more diverse supporter base, providing a different spectator base, detached from expressive ethnic groups. The social networks of supporters, new participants and the increased numbers of individuals engaging in football seems to have developed following the changes made to the league structure. New networks appear to be less connected with the negative outcomes that were associated with the previous structure. Specifically, the culturally based exclusivity once associated with football related social networks of ethnic-specific teams has not resurfaced in the new A-League and the sport is now playing an important bridging role between people from diverse ethnic groups.

The extent to which these social networks are still prevalent at the State league, community club level and the reciprocal benefits and social ties available through engagement in A-League clubs is an area for further investigation. The preliminary evidence suggests that the restructure of football in Australia has created greater mainstream acceptance, increased spectatorship of the professional game and broader membership of the A-League clubs replacing the marginalized sport of soccer that was played by *Sheilas, Wogs & Poofters* (Warren et al., 2002) throughout most of the twentieth century.

References

Adair, D. & Vamplew, W. (1997). *Sport in Australian History*. Melbourne: Oxford University Press.

Bellah, R.N., Madsen, R., Sullivan, W.M., Swidler, A. & Tipton, S. (1985). *Habits of the Heart: Individualism and Commitment in American Life*. Berkeley: University of California Press.

Bordieu, P. (1983). Ökonomisches kapital, kulturelles kapital, soziales kapital. In R. Kreckel (Ed.), *Soziale Ungleichheiten (Soziale Welt, Sonderheft 2)* (pp. 183–198). Goettingen: Otto Schartz & Co.

Brabazon, T. (1998). What's the story morning glory? Perth Glory and the imagining of Englishness. *Sporting Traditions, 14*(2), 53–66.

Bradley, G. (1990). *Australian Soccer Federation: Final Report*. Canberra: Australian Soccer Federation.

Cockerill, M. (2005, August 9th). Lowy targets young, welcomes old. *Sydney Morning Herald, 38*.

Coleman, J. (1988). Social capital in the creation of human capital. *The American Journal of Sociology, 94*, 95–120.

Collins, J. (1995). *A Shop Full of Dreams: Ethnic Small Business in Australia*. Sydney: Pluto Press Australia.

Crawford, D. (2003). *Report of the Independent Soccer Review Committee: Into the Structure, Governance and Management of Soccer in Australia*. Canberra: Australian Sports Comission, April, 2003.

Cubby, B. (2005, August 27th). Tribes unite to kick off a league of their own. *Sydney Morning Herald*, 7.

Daly, S. (2005). *Social Capital and the Cultural Sector: Literature Review*. London: Centre for Civil Society, London School of Economics.

Department of Immigration and Multicultural Affairs (1999). *Croatia Born Community Profile*. Canberra: DIMA.

Dyreson, M. (2001). Maybe it's better to bowl alone: Sport, community and democracy in American thought. *Sport in Society*, 4(1), 19–30.

Football Federation Australia. (2007a). *Community Relations*. Retrieved June 22 2007, from http://www.a-league.com.au/default.aspx?s=hal_schooldays.

Football Federation Australia. (2007b). *My Football*. Retrieved June 22 2007, from http://www.myfootball.com.au/.

Galvin, M. & West, P. (1988). *A Changing Australia: Themes and Case Studies*. Sydney: Harcourt Brace Jovanovich.

Georgakis, S. (1999). *Greek Sporting Traditions in Australia: An Historical Study of Ethnicity, Gender and Youth*. Sydney: University of Sydney.

Girgensohn, A. & Lee, A. (2002, 16th–20th November). *Making Web sites be Places for Social Interaction*. Paper presented at the CSCW'02, New Orleans.

Hall, P.A. (1999). Social capital in Britain. *British Journal of Political Science*, 29(03), 417–461.

Hallinan, C.J., Hughson, J. & Burke, M. (2007). Supporting the 'world game' in Australia: A case study of fandom at national and club level. *Soccer & Society*, 8(2), 283–297.

Hague, E. & Mercer, J. (1998). Geographical memory and urban identity in Scotland: Raith Rovers FC and Kirkcaldy. *Geography*, 83, 105–116.

Hay, R. (1994). British Football, wogball or the world game? Towards a social history of Victorian soccer. *Australian Society for Sports History: Studies in Sports History*, 10, 44–79.

Hay, R. (2006). Fan culture in Australian football (Soccer): From ethnic to mainstream?. In M. Nicholson, B. Stewart & R. Hess (Eds.), *Football Fever: Moving the goalposts* (pp. 91–106). Melbourne: Maribyrnong Press.

Hughson, J. (1992). Australian soccer: Ethnic or Aussie? The search for an image. *Current Affairs Bulletin*, 68(10), 12–16.

Hughson, J. (1996). *A Feel for the Game: An Ethnographic Study of Soccer Support and Social Identity* (unpublished Ph.D thesis): UNSW.

Hughson, J. (1997). The Croatian Community. In P. Mosely, R. Cashman, J. O'Hara & H. Weatherburn (Eds.), *Sporting Immigrants* (pp. 50–62). Sydney: Walla Walla Press.

Hughson, J. (2000a). The boys are back in town: Soccer support and the social reproduction of masculinity. *Journal of Sport and Social Issues*, 24(1), 8–23.

Hughson, J. (2000b). A tale of two tribes: Expressive fandom in Australian soccer's A-League. In: G. Finn & R. Giulianotti (Eds.), *Football Culture: Local Contests, Global Visions* (pp. 10–30). London: Frank Cass.

Hughson, J. (2001). 'The Wogs are at it again': The media reportage of Australian soccer 'riots'. *Football Studies*, 4(1), 40–55.

Hughson, J. (2002). Australian soccer's 'ethnic' tribes: a new case for the carnivalesque. In E. Dunning, P. Murphy, I. Waddington, A. E. Astrinakis & (Eds.), *Fighting Fans: Football Hooliganism as a World Phenomenon* (pp. 37–48) Dublin: University College Dublin Press.

Huxley, J. (2006, March 2nd). More than just dribblers – these coves are committed. *Sydney Morning Herald*, 3.

Jarvie, G. (2003). Commuitarianism, sport and social capital: 'Neighbourly insights into Scottish sport'. *Internation Review for the Sociology of Sport*, 38, 139–153.

Jarvie, G. & Burnett, J. (2000). *Sport, Scotland and the Scots*. Edinburgh: Tuckwell Press.

Kemeny, A. (2003). *Report of the NSL Task-Force: Into the Structure of a New National League Soccer Competition*. Sydney: Australian Soccer Association.

Kerr, J.H. (2005). *Rethinking Aggression and Violence in Sport*. London: Routledge.

Lock, D. (2006, 15th–21st August). *The Development of Social Identity in Fans of a New Sports Team: Sydney FC, a Case Study*. Paper presented at the International summer school for young researchers: Sport, Globalisation and Cultural Diversity, Copenhagen, Denmark.

Lock, D., Taylor, T. & Darcy, S. (2006, 6th–9th September). *Sport Fan Identity & The New Kid on the Block*. Paper presented at the European Academy of Sports Management, Nicosia, Cyprus.

Lock, D., Taylor, T. & Darcy, S. (2007a). Fan identity formation in a new football club and a revamped league: The A-League. *Sport Marketing Europe*, 1, 30–35.

Lock, D., Taylor, T. & Darcy, S. (2007b, 18th–19th April). *Restructuring and Repositioning 'Soccer' as 'Football' in Australia*.

Paper presented at the SportBusiness Campus 2007, Birkbeck, The University of London.

MacClancy, J. (1996). *Sport, Identity and Ethnicity*. Oxford: Berg.

McAllister, I. & Moore, R. (1989). *Ethnic prejudice in Australian society: Patterns, intensity and explanations*. Canberra: Office of Multicultural Affairs.

Mosely, P. (1987). *A Social History of Soccer in New South Wales 1880–1957*. Unpublished Ph. D, University of Sydney.

Mosely, P. (1995). *Ethnic Involvement in Australian Soccer: a History 1950–1990*. Belconnen, ACT: National Sports Research Centre.

Mosely, P. (1997). Soccer. In P. Mosely, R. Cashman, J. O'Hara & H. Weatherburn (Eds.), *Sporting Immigrants: Sport and Ethnicity in Australia* (pp. 155–173). Crows Nest N.S.W: Walla Walla Press.

National Multicultural Advisory Council (1995). *The Next Steps: Multicultural Australia, towards and Beyond 2000, a Report of the National Multicultural Advisory Council*. Canberra: Australian Government Publishing Service.

Portes, A. & Landolt, P. (2000). Social capital: Promise and pitfalls of its role in development. *Journal of Latin American Studies, 32,* 529–547.

Putnam, R. (2000). *Bowling Alone: The Collapse and Revival of American Community*. New York: Simon & Schuster.

Seippel, O. (2006). Sport and social capital. *Acta Sociologica, 49*(2), 169–183.

Solly, R. (2004). *Shoot Out: The Passion and the Politics of Soccer's Fight for Survival in Australia*. Milton: John Wiley & Sons Australia, Ltd.

The Cove. (2007a). *Cove Charter*. Retrieved June 20 2007, from http://www.sfcu.com.au/smf/index.php?topic=1738.0.

The Cove. (2007b). *Forum Guide*. Retrieved August 31 2007, from http://www.sfcu.com.au/smf/index.php?topic=62.0.

The Cove. (2007c). *Forum Stats*. Retrieved August 31 2007, from http://www.sfcu.com.au/smf/.

Tonts, M. (2005). Competitive sport and social capital in rural Australia. *Journal of Rural Studies, 21*(2), 137–149.

Uslaner, E.M. (1999). Democracy and social capital. In M. Warren (Ed.), *Democracy and Trust* (pp. 121–150). New York: Cambridge University Press.

Vamplew, W. (1994). Violence in Australian soccer: The ethnic contribution. *ASSH Studies in Sports History, 10,* 1–15.

Warren, J., Harper, A. & Whittington, J. (2002). *Sheilas, Wogs & Poofters: An Incomplete Biography of Johnny Warren and Soccer in Australia*. Sydney: Random House Australia.

CHAPTER **15**

Sport facilities as social capital

Mark Rosentraub and
Akram Ijla

Introduction

For more than 20 years debates regarding the wisdom and equity of using tax dollars to pay for the facilities used by professional teams or for mega-events like the Olympics have focused on the economic returns to the public sector. While there are policy issues and normative dimensions to the distribution of the benefits from the use of tax dollars for sport facilities, it may well be that too little attention has been paid towards understanding social capital issues. Sport is a business generating profits for team owners and international organizations, handsome salaries for a substantial number of athletes, and real estate profits for capable investors. Sport's success as a business, however, is derived from its impact on a region or nation's social systems and therein exists the possibility that sport facilities are integral parts of the social capital of a society.

Sport and its facilities as social capital – if avoided or ignored by economists and other policy scientists – has been an important field of study for many social scientists. For example, social scientists from several disciplines have long-noted the important role of sport as a social and socializing institution (Edwards, 1973; Andrews, 2004). Ancient and modern societies have relied on sport for both entertainment and for celebrations associated with civil and religious holidays (Rosentraub, 1997a). Several ancient civilizations joined religious commemorations to sport events to unify a society. In modern times there are numerous examples of the staging of sport events on notable civic holidays to celebrate a society's achievements and success while underscoring loyalty to governments and countries. More recently, religious days are also seen as important opportunities to attract large crowds and audiences to sporting events (Rosentraub, 1999). The political dimension of sport is readily apparent in the connections made by political leaders of games to nationalistic feelings and this phenomena has also been repeatedly analysed (Wilson, 1994; Rosentraub, 1997a). Sport has also been associated with opportunities to highlight military prowess as when aircraft or other symbols of power are flown over facilities before a match (Lipsyte, 1975; Bale, 1989; Johnson & Sack, 1996; Swindell & Rosentraub, 1998; Eckstein & Delaney, 2002; Foer, 2004; Szymanski & Zimbalist, 2005).

At a less severe or manipulative level, people in virtually any community can point to celebrations when teams win championships and the excitement or 'electricity' that seems to change daily life (Euchner, 1993; Chema, 1996). When all of these social components of sport are analysed or considered, it is clear that the venues in which games are played may be part of the social capital of a society. Sport as social capital can be defined by separating the two concepts or words. The capital component involves the facilities constructed to host the events. The social dimension involves one set of outcomes or benefits from sporting events that increases the interactions between members of a society or between individuals and the social support for a governance system or a society. Therein lies the potential for meeting the definition of social capital as defined by several including Putnam (2000), Portes (1998), and Coleman (1988).

This chapter is designed to consider the role of sport facilities as elements of the social capital of a society. After exploring and defining the term social capital – as used in this chapter – the different ways in which a sport facility is used to advance, change, or interact with a culture and society will be discussed in an effort to form a typology of elements that define the social capital components of sport facilities.

What is social capital?

Before considering if sport facilities can be considered social capital or contribute to the building of social capital, a working definition of the term social capital is needed. This task is undertaken recognizing that other chapters in this volume might offer readers a different perspective.

At first blush, even before considering the works of various social scientists that have long-studied social capital, it might seem that sport facilities by their role in city planning and development have a prima facie case leading to their classification as social capital. The Roman Empire made facilities an intricate part of the design of their cities and indeed if one looks to Rome or any of the cities of Decapolis – the 10 cities on the Eastern rim of the Roman Empire – the integral role of sport facilities in the design of those cities is readily apparent. The Colosseum (or Coliseum) remains a lasting symbol of the design of City of Rome, as do arenas in many places including Pula (Croatia) and Caesarea (Israel). Those facilities were built when those areas were part of the Roman Empire.

The use of sport facilities as part of the design of cities was not limited to the Roman Empire. The Ottoman Empire built its hippodrome for horse racing at the centre of Constantinople. Sport facilities, then, have been an integral part of physical capital of cities for more than two millennia (Rosentraub, 1997a). As physical assets for their society a great deal of social dialogue and interaction occurred at or because of the existence of these facilities. Does the physical importance of sport facilities in the design of cities constitute social capital or are facilities catalyst for the formation of social capital?

Durkheim (1982) noted that an individual's participation in collective or group activities that underscore social – cultural or economic linkages and associations reduces anomie in highly competitive economic societies. These linkages and associations can be seen as responses to social problems, social isolation, and self-destructive tendencies as individuals became bound to important aspects of a culture. Sport can indeed provide these linkages for people when they constructively identify with a team and this relationship reduces feelings of social isolation. If identification with a team reduced an individual's feelings of isolation then sport facilities would be a catalyst helping people deal with the levels of isolation endemic in post-industrial societies. In this manner, sport facilities would be contributing to social capital by minimizing isolation and feelings of anomie.

Lefebvre (1991, 1996) offers important extensions on this logic and line of reasoning by noting that places within a city that encourage dialogue and identification with a group help individuals forge relationships that can enhance identity within large urban environments. The social activity that takes place within public space gives the image of collective activity that helps reduce the stresses of isolation.

Bourdieu's (1986: 198) definition of social capital as 'the aggregate of the actual or potential resources which are linked to possession of a durable network of more institutionalized relationships of mutual recognition' establishes a basis for including sport facilities as part of a society's social capital. These facilities create the potential for associations or linkages, and in that potential lies the identification of arenas and stadia as part of a society's social capital. Putnam (2000) draws attention to the connections among individuals and the norms of reciprocity and trustworthiness to identify what is social capital. In his view a 'society of many virtuous but isolated individuals is not necessarily rich in social capital' (Putnam, 2000: 19). The World Bank has also entered this intellectual fray noting that social capital refers to 'the institutions, relationships, and norms that shape the quality and quantity of society's social interactions … social capital is not just the sum of institutions which underpin a society – it is the glue that holds them together' (World Bank, 1999: 32).

Other perspectives on social capital emphasize the value of building social relationships to resolve collective problems, while some authors have noted that social capital also permits the building of trust through repeated interactions. A recurring theme is that for these associations and situations to occur public spaces need to be developed. Movements in the late nineteenth century stressed the need for public parks as places where people from different economic groups could mix while also providing a respite from the drudgery of industrial work (Olmsted, 1870). Physical space was thus identified as a catalyst for the building of social capital in eras when large public space and parks were the vehicles for recreation. In this regard it has been long recognized that a link exists between a city's amenities and the quality of life of its residents. Efforts to restore and revitalize urban centres have almost without exception been accompanied by a commitment to build public spaces including parks and other venues that attract crowds to centre cities. This has become an especially important policy issue as suburban and decentralized lifestyles have developed in many countries. As Heckscher noted (1977: 2):

McCoffin of San Francisco, Johnson of Cleveland, Lawrence of Pittsburgh, Clark and Dilworth of Philadelphia, La Guardia and more recently Lindsay in New York, have perceived that the vitality of the city was related to park-building and park use and to innovative planning of open space. In the use of open space, the population has found a sense of unity as well as of pleasure in revealing to itself the varieties of age, class, nationality and race of which the great city is composed.

Garvin and Berens (1997) amplified this concept by noting that fiscally successful cities have created new open and public spaces even while they had to address other pressing social service and policy matters. Urban revitalization strategies in the USA, Canada, and the UK have, in many instances, included the building of sport facilities and other civic assets to re-attract crowds to centre cities. These public spaces largely focused on entertainment have replaced the role that retail venues previously offered in terms of attracting crowds to the downtown areas of some central cities (Rosentraub, 1997a).

However, it must also be noted that there is a qualitative difference between the public space created by a park or open land and the 'public space' that exists as a result of the building of a sport facility and the excitement generated by a team's success. Parks and open space generally require no admission fees and thus have lower access costs than the private recreation facilities built for sport and mega-events. While post-victory celebrations and other activities associated with mega-events could have no access fees, the interactions produced or possible at those gatherings are different from those that would take place at a Hyde, Central, or Victoria Park.

However, the real issue is not the form of the space, but whether the interactions that occur create anything that can be described as social capital. Does the behaviour and social interactions at a sport facility or from a team's success constitute the social capital envisioned and valued by social scientists and community leaders? If social capital is created, the issue of access fees may not be as relevant since areas without access fees could still be relied upon to also create social capital.

Lofland (1998) noted that individuals who frequent public space develop, at best, fleeting relationships among people they do not know and with whom they are unlikely to develop lasting or semi-permanent relationships. If these people remain largely unknown to each other, how does social capital form and how is it sustained? The relationships forged in public space probably have a very brief duration and as such, by themselves, are unlikely to be the basis for the formation of social capital in a classical or formal sense. It is also likely that fleeting relationships do not include verbal exchanges on substantive matters or matters unrelated to shared interests beyond a celebration (as in a sporting event) or the enjoyment of a day's outing. This is a result, of course, of the large number of people, who are alone or in small groups. In this regard the social interactions at a sport facility may well be quite similar if not identical to those developed in any form of public space.

Can these loosely coupled interactions constitute social capital formation or do they offer the potential to form social capital that can be called upon at a time of crisis or need? Clearly the sort of interactions that Lofland notes are substantially different than those anticipated when cities built areas such as New York's Central Park or Rockefeller Center, Cleveland's Public Square, and Boston's Common (and Public Gardens). Yet, Webb (1990: 132) in an earlier assessment asked a more fundamental question that can be used to decide if an area constitutes the space with which social capital can be built:

It is a place in which you want to meet your friends and observe strangers? Is it the first choice for community celebrations? Does it offer a sense of place, a feeling of historical continuity, a vision of what urban life should be? Is it maintained with respect or vandalized; does it serve as oasis or for parking? Ask another question: if not, why not? Actors and décor have changed over the centuries, but the need for stage has remained a constant.

Following this view, public parks as well as sport facilities and the celebrations they engender create a stage in which confidence, public spirit, and a sense of optimism regarding the future of a community and city could be created or generated. Beem (1999), Rosentraub (2006a), Putnam (2000), and Webb (1990) each point to the value of different forms of public space for creating images of cities and the perception of the value and future of urban space. Beem's ideas also include specific discussions of the value of these interactions for building a sense of community and in encouraging people to (1) commit themselves to collective goals and (2) support the creation of a sense of identity. As regards the redevelopment and a city's image, Rosentraub (2006a: 220) noted:

... sports facilities have the potential to create important intangible benefits that although more difficult to quantify, are nevertheless important ... When teams are successful, there is a sense of excitement in a community. If a true public benefit was created, then its absence would represent a social loss. In terms of the matrix of intangible benefits, 'social mixing' refers to the role sport teams can assume in attracting people to downtown areas from the suburbs who might otherwise avoid a center city. In regions with high levels of economic class and racial segregation, the attracting of large numbers of people creates opportunities to showcase a city to people who otherwise might not visit a down town areas. This social mixing or the simple attraction of people events in the downtown creates the potential to change the image of a downtown area.

Finally, one needs to also recognize the role played by sport facilities and teams for Americans in the aftermath of the September 11th terrorist attacks. The outpouring of emotion and the celebration of the USA's identity and resiliency were most evident when the Major League Baseball season resumed. Everywhere New York City's two teams played – including cities where fierce rivalries existed with other clubs – there was vibrant support for New York City. For New York City itself the resumption of games created a sense of normalcy that became a rallying point for the recovery and healing that still takes place. In this sense, there would appear to be no debate that sport facilities and the teams that play matches or games at those venues offer the potential for the formation of social capital.

Returning to the issue of image, Gottdiener (2001) is among the urban scholars who have noted the importance of a city's image and its impact on perceptions, and pride. Shared positive images create a potential for collective action and that benefit creates an important form of social capital. Hannigan's work (1998), while focusing on the business aspects of civic images and the creation of entertainment venues for illusions of fantasy, also identifies the possible role of these images for the building of local pride and a sense of identification for individuals. If these potential benefits and attachments can be accessed in building effective policies and programmes to advance a region, then indeed potential social capital becomes vibrant social capital harnessed for public purposes. If sport facilities contribute to or help to redefine a city's image, real social capital is created.

From this discussion, if facilities or public spaces create opportunities for people to congregate, the potential for relationships to be created exists. The relationships can become part of the social capital of a society that reduces feelings of social isolation while enhancing a sense of political and social unity. However, in offering this conclusion, it is recognized that if the definition of social capital is so broad as to include anything that creates the potential for social interaction then it is hard to imagine what is not an asset. There must be more sensitivity to the application of the definition, at least when sport facilities are concerned, and that issue is directly addressed in the next section of the chapter.

Public goods, social capital, and sport facilities

To identify sport facilities as part of the social capital of a society four elements must be considered. *First*, sport facilities must create positive externalities. By themselves, of course, facilities have limited opportunities to accomplish this task, although if a facility was an architectural icon it could indeed create positive externalities from its artistic impacts on people. Without addressing that possibility, what is of concern here is whether or not a team that plays in or events that take place at a facility generate positive externalities. If teams or events can be classified as having some of the characteristics of public goods and produce either tangible in intangible positive externalities, then the facilities in which they play represent social capital for a society as those sport centres permit the externalities to exist.

Second, these externalities must engender the formation of linkages, support, or connections between people and either cities, collective goals, or public life to satisfy the idea that there is a social return or a form of capital that is created. That is, the associations that are created among people must have some measurable tangible or intangible components that create real social capital.

Third, it must also be determined if the building of a capital asset that also produces private benefits and the accumulation of private wealth can simultaneously be, as a result of the existence of positive externalities, a catalyst for social capital.

Fourth, should sport facilities designed for participation also be classified as part of the social capital (or a social capital catalyst)? Again, there is a range of private benefits generated from participation in sport (the benefits of exercise largely accrue to the participant). But does that participation create its own form of social capital through the formation of social linkages with others who engage in sport activities? Is participation in team events different from individual activities such as running or riding a bicycle? This section of this chapter considers these issues before the construct of a typology of social capital from sport and the catalytic role of sport facilities is presented.

Sport facilities, positive externalities, and public goods

Sport facilities involving professional teams are built for the production and delivery of private goods. Fans purchase tickets to attend events and admission is easily restricted to those who pay the required fees. Even when the issue of televised, broadcasted, and web cast sport is considered, games and matches are still private goods as supporters pay fees or accepts other costs in exchange for their ability to watch, hear, or follow a match. In nations that permit advertising to be included in the transmission of games, the fans 'pay' for the benefit of enjoying an athletic event through their consumption of advertising messages. Internet presentations of events involve pay-for-viewing fees and the frequent presentation of advertisements, so these too must be considered private market transactions with viewers receiving a benefit for the payment demanded (even if that payment is merely the advertisements that are inserted). It is also easy to exclude non-payers even though there will also be those able to view games without paying the required fee. Where are the public good elements of sport facilities and how do they generate positive externalities?

Public goods and their positive externalities or benefits – relative to sport facilities – are created by the excitement, good will, and impact on the quality of life of residents resulting from the games held at the facility and enjoyed by people who do not attend matches. When trying to conceptualize these benefits one need to only think about the excitement that exists in many cities when important games/matches are held and the civic celebrations that accompany the winning of a championship. To be sure fan violence and the vandalism that sometimes take places after the winning (or losing) of a championship must also be considered. However, most celebrations of championships generate mainly positive externalities. In addition, the large crowds that gather in public spaces to view matches are another example of the positive externalities that do exist.

Measuring the value of these positive externalities and how much people would be willing to pay to ensure their existence has become a topic for social scientists in recent years. Using contingent valuation survey methods, scholars have begun efforts to quantify the intangible benefits both in terms of their pecuniary value to residents of a city and state and their willingness to pay for these benefits. These studies have included the measurement of how much people might pay in higher taxes to ensure that the intangible benefits from professional sport remained part of a community's social infrastructure. While there is always a likelihood that people will decide not to honestly report their preferences or respond in different ways to hypothetical choices, evidence of a willingness to pay for the intangible benefits from teams has been found. Rosentraub et al. (2008) found residents of Indiana were willing to pay for a substantial portion of a new stadium to ensure the continued presence of a National Football League franchise in the state. Those data sustain the perspective that (1) sport facilities aid in the production of intangible benefits that create positive externalities resulting from a team's presence and (2) residents are willing under the appropriate circumstances to pay taxes to ensure that the potential for intangible benefits is sustained through the team's continued residency. Even transferred to the societies where teams cannot and do not move between cities, the question of intangible benefits may be related to the provision of some level of public money to ensure that a team can remain competitive by retaining skilled players.

Turning for a moment to facilities designed for participation, this is again a situation where there are primarily private benefits. Individuals pay for these facilities through user fees or through their taxes in the situation where a government assumes responsibility for building parks, pitches, and the like. Regardless, there is an exchange here between individuals and either a private vendor or the public sector so there is payment for benefits received. Are there any externalities that are generated? While that it is entirely possible, it is a bit harder to imagine or conceptualize. Certainly participants' families may well enjoy a match or race when their relative competed, but that is not the sort of externality that is shared by non-relatives or people not familiar with the participant. It may be more appropriate to consider facilities that serve participants as private exchanges with the same potential for social capital formation as might exist in an office building where people share similar experiences. Teammates or even those running with others on a track do have a shared experience that can produce opportunities for social capital and relationships to develop. However, in the absence of classical externalities it seems more prudent to focus on the issue of social capital formation in those facilities that create externalities.

Can sport facilities really be considered social capital for a society?

To be sure, the introduction of sport facilities as part of a society's social capital will be a troubling concept for some. Sport facilities, even though they may well produce intangible benefits, are built to facilitate private transactions and the development of successful and profitable businesses. Sport facilities also fit the definition of a classic private good in that goods and services are provided for a fee to customers. It is very easy to exclude non-payers from watching the event and the amount that spectators are willing to pay is established through market transactions.

However, from a public and private goods perspective there is no contradiction in a particular asset producing both public and private benefits. In this regard, then, while the majority of benefits from sport facilities may be private, the externalities generated can be classified as public. In addition, the other opportunities for social bonding also create a form of social capital. While there might be a normative objection, the analysis and discussion clearly illustrate that sport facilities do generate benefits that create social capital.

Before moving to the presentation of a typology that helps to identify and classify the social capital aspects of sport facilities, mention must be made of the potential for negative externalities and a sort of social 'discapital'. Fan violence, while rare in some societies, is more frequent in others. When the violence leads to injury and death – which is all too frequent in some areas – then it is fair to observe that the disunity that is created by sport and promulgated by facilities generates substantial and significant social and individual costs. These costs must be recognized and accorded the warranted tangible and intangible costs. This aspect will not only be noted in the typology, but so too would other costs including increased traffic and noise which would be annoyances and nuisances, but costs never the less which diminish the social capital produced by sport facilities. The destructiveness wrought by fan violence is a far greater concern and must be part of the assessment of the social capital value of sport. Recognition is also made of excessive nationalism that can be created, but that too can be included in the fan violence *dis*capital identified in the typology.

A typology of the social capital aspects of sport facilities

Industrial and economic change brought with it substantial demographic shifts in several countries. Population declines in cities that were once leading economic centres reduced feelings of confidence as well as the sheer number of people in some areas. For example, Cleveland, home to more than 950 000 people at the height of America's post-World War II manufacturing era, had fewer than 475 000 residents by 2000. Cleveland was a city that was once one of the USA's most prosperous, but by 2005 was an annual competitor for the central city with the highest concentration of households classified as 'poor'. Cleveland's fate was shared by several other US cities including St Louis, Pittsburgh, Indianapolis, and Detroit. In discussing their public policy focus on sport to rebuild people's confidence in the future and their city, mayors and public leaders in St Louis, Indianapolis, and Cleveland ruefully acknowledged that the building of sport facilities to create excitement was a chosen tactic to advance social capital. For these leaders, people had begun to accept the notion that the community's best days were behind it, and in that environment they could not forge majorities for social programmes designed to advance the quality of life. New sport facilities were built to improve those images (Rosentraub, 1999).

Were these cities able to capitalize on a potential for social capital from sport into the reality of social capital and enhancements to the quality of life? There are data to sustain that positive conclusion. Austrian and Rosentraub (2002) pointed to the ability of Cleveland and Indianapolis to retard decentralization and enhance job levels in downtown areas through the building of sport facilities. Rosentraub (2006b) quantified the economic returns for the city of Cleveland from the region's financing of the sport facilities despite the fiscal losses for the county. Cleveland's residents and property owners pay a portion of the public sector's investment, but the more populous and wealthy county residents reduce the burden to the point where the city realizes positive net income. Indianapolis's downtown area has been completely rebuilt and it is doubtful the same level of accomplishments could have been achieved without the emphasis on sport (Rosentraub, 2000; Leland & Rosentraub, 2008).

Would redevelopment strategies for a central city have been as successful or acceptable to county residents if it were not wrapped in sport and the social capital it forms? While no empirical work exists to sustain that perspective, sport and its public externalities did create a social bond or social capital that several cities could access to help with a redevelopment strategy. At a time when suburban areas continue to grow at rates that surpass those of central cities in America's Midwest, the sport strategy seems to have been among the most successful at galvanizing a level of social capital to support redevelopment with a spatial redistribution element that might not have been possible with other policy foci. In repeated interviews community leaders have noted that sport seems to galvanize more support for suburban commitments to centre cities then other policy proposals (Chema, 1996; Rosentraub, 1997a). This outcome was again sustained when the suburban counties that surrounding Indianapolis agreed to support a food and beverage tax collected at restaurants in their areas to help pay for a new stadium for the Indianapolis Colts to be built in downtown Indianapolis.

Could a city restore its image and reposition itself through the building of venues for participation in sport by its residents? While that is certainly a distinct possibility, and there can be little disagreement with the notion that the presence of venues and space for participatory sport is an integral component of the quality of life of any city, one is pressed to find an example of an economic recovery and image overhaul linked solely to participatory sport. Because something has not been tried, does or has not been analysed does not mean it will not work and could not outpace spectator sport for economic development and image enhancement. It must simply be noted that there is not yet sufficient evidence to sustain the image enhancing and economic development effects of participatory sport. There is, however, more evidence of the impact of and intangible benefits produced by sport venues where spectator events occur. Hence, it is safer to suggest that there are externalities and development benefits that can accrue in close proximity to a facility that changes the location of economic activity. Given the spatial decentralization of economic activity in metropolitan regions, concentrating some of this activity in central cities especially when there is a substantial local component to tax revenues is as important (and in some instances more so) than an increment to regional economic activity (Rosentraub, 1997b).

What then becomes a typology of social capital from sport facilities?

One begins with group identity or identification that counters the isolation inherent in a post-industrial society replete with opportunities for individualistic activities and work and leisure isolation. The popular labels of 'Red Sox Nation', the Yankees as part of an 'Evil Empire', the international identity of the 'Red Devils' of Manchester United, and the samba beat of FC Barcelona are just some of the examples that one could discuss. In the USA and the UK authors have identified numerous teams that hold particular symbolism for their communities. The fact that Walter O'Malley is still held in extreme contempt for the movement of the Brooklyn Dodgers to Los Angeles 50 years after the heinous act and after several championships by their replacement team, the New York Mets, attests to the existence of identification from sport teams that reduces social isolation and instills a sense of civic pride (Kahn, 1998). Art Modell still cannot safely return to Cleveland having moved his National Football League franchise, the Browns, to Baltimore even now that a new Cleveland Browns warms the hearts of the fans in the 'Dawg Pound'. The damage inflicted on the social identity of people was so severe that Art Modell is ranked with Walter O'Malley as one of the great villains of American sport. In turn, Baltimore never forgave Indianapolis for stealing the Colts, even though the renamed Browns they took from Cleveland brought the city a Super Bowl title (Rosentraub, 1999).

The first part of the typology, 'Group Identity Benefits', is divided into three parts. In the first cell are the private benefits that accrue to individuals or groups from their attendance at events or at locations where sport events are shown. This identifies the exchange or private benefits that are created. The second part within the 'Group Benefits' comes from the positive externalities generated for identity and social cohesion because of a team's presence and the facility's existence. The third part of the 'Group Identity' component is the social linkages built among fans from opposing teams that in some facilities sit in segregated areas. This proximity of supporters creates the possibility for social capital formation (see Figure 15.1).

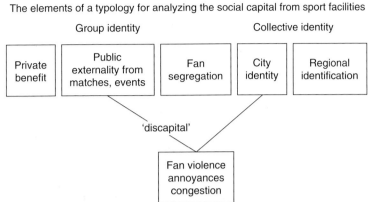

The elements of a typology for analyzing the social capital from sport facilities

Figure 15.1
A sport facility – social capital typology

Underneath all of these benefits – from those classified as private to those that are clearly positive externalities – runs the possibility of '*dis*capital' from fan violence. That violence can exist as part of the private exchange, but when it occurs the negative image for a city or region – as well as for the team, facility, and sport – clearly generates a negative externality. Those costs, as well as any others identified as annoyances or nuisances including traffic, etc., must also be enumerated and accounted for in any measurement of the social capital.

The second element of the social capital typology is the identity that teams generate for a region in the core city. When one speaks of identification with many US central cities, that identity is often inexorably bound to a team. The Greater Cleveland metropolitan area contains more than 100 cities and that pattern is similar in many parts of the country. Yet a team's name is usually connected to the central city and that benefit for Chicago (the Bulls, Bears, White Sox, and Cubs), Cleveland (Browns, Cavaliers, Indians), and St Louis (Cardinals) is not lost on mayors and public leaders (Rosentraub, 1997a). At a time when there is substantial movement of people to suburban and exurban areas, the value of this level of identification is not lost on community leaders. Detroit's leadership wanted to bring the National Football League Lions back to the downtown area from the suburbs following the policy direction of other cities (e.g. Cleveland). In addition to individual identity there is a regional identity component created and for cities struggling to attract residents and businesses, that regional identity is as important as the individual identity created to reduce individual isolation. In a sense central cities are fearful of a collective economic isolation and the identity bestowed by events that take place in a downtown facility creates a form of social capital whose value is not doubted by elected leaders.

The last form of social capital created is the potential from regional identification among residents of decentralized and fragmented areas for regional responses to numerous public policy issues. Building consensus to frame regional responses to public policy issues is a concern for both fast-growth and slow-growth areas. Finding threads of commonality to bind divergent populations is a daunting task and the identity forged by professional sport is an asset that is repeatedly used for economic development plans, regional transportation and environmental strategies, and for the redevelopment of central cities. This may well be the exact form of social capital envisioned when public space and parks were discussed as aspects for the building of urban centres in the industrial age.

Conclusions

Sport facilities should be considered part of a society's social capital for the group identification benefits that can be created. This is concluded even though the potential for fan violence and 'discapital' is recognized as a clear liability of sport facilities and more prevalent in some societies than in others. If this social capital exists, the question that then emerges is how can governments, organizations, or individuals use it for positive outcomes?

Probably the best examples of the positive use of the social capital from sport facilities emerge when regions, characterized by fragmented units of local government, seek collaboration to achieve area-wide goals or objectives. In the USA where local governments have more direct responsibility for financing and delivering a broader range of social services, regional identities are necessary to secure passage of tax base sharing programmes. Under these programmes there is an important level of transfer of wealth from higher income areas to lower ones. In the absence of a commitment or interest in a regional identity such programmes are very difficult to implement. Simply put, wealthier suburban areas if they follow their narrow and short-term best interests would vote not to participate in any regional redistribution programme. The existence of a regional identity, forged by a sport team's identity and success, creates an environment in which leaders can speak of the region's needs and the shared value in insuring that there are needed public services for all citizens in an area. There are even instances where the financing arrangements for a sport facility were tied to the fiscal benefits that accrued to a centre city. These sort of voluntary transfers of wealth where suburban areas pay a larger share of the costs and allow centre cities to enjoy a larger share of the fiscal benefits are difficult to imagine with other policy initiatives. When these arrangements are developed it is difficult not to conclude that sport played a large role in building a level of social capital.

Note should also be made of the urban regeneration benefits of placing sport facilities in downtown areas. As Nelson (2001) observed, where sport facilities are located does have an impact on their contribution to economic development. His research, and the work of others, sustains the point that location in the downtown areas of centre cities increased the value of regional investments in sport facilities. This is not to suggest that regional development levels necessary increase. However, the placement of facilities in downtown areas does maximize their effect on spending patterns and that in turn has a more robust impact on the finances of centre cities. The impact on suburban cities was found to be far less, and others have sustained this perspective (Austrian & Rosentraub, 2002). Similarly, the location of some Olympic facilities distant from a city's centre has meant that after the games are a memory the facility's use is often far less.

To be sure the benefits noted above do not come without important costs. Sport facilities are not notable for the equality of access and thus there are inherent equity problems. With the prices for tickets continuing to escalate one cannot argue that the opportunity for social capital formation does not come with substantial equity issues, especially when public resources are used to pay for part or all of the cost of a sport facility. Simply put, sport is no longer the mass entertainment vehicle it was when it comes to attendance at matches of premier leagues. Sport in this regard has become the purview of the middle and upper classes even if financing schemes serve to increase the wealth of centre cities.

Contrast that point, however, with the intangible benefits Rosentraub et al. (2008) found for a National Football League team in Indiana, and those benefits were reported by higher and lower income households. If that research is validated and sustained in other studies, then it is possible that the positive externalities generated by sport create far less inequities than many have feared.

Building sport facilities is not a matter of creating a 'Field of Dreams' relative to the creation of social capital. It is, instead, a strategic decision or investment. Like other strategic investments it must be carefully managed with its benefits channelled into positive returns while care is taken to minimize the chances of severe *dis*capital events. This is neither an easy set of tasks nor responsibilities for governments that would prefer to simply have a facility built. To the contrary, formation and utilization of the social capital from sport facilities require oversight and management strategies and without those a government would be well advised to look for other mechanisms to develop social capital. However, sport facilities offer a potential for social capital formation unlike many others if community leaders properly use the asset.

References

Andrews, D. (2004). Sports in the late capitalist movement. In T. Slack (Ed.), *The Commercialization of Sport* (pp. 3–28). London: Routledge.

Austrian, Z. & Rosentraub, M. (2002). Cities, sports, and economic change: A retrospective assessment. *Journal of Urban Affairs*, 24(5), 549–565.

Bale, J. (1989). *Sports Geography*. London: E & F.N. Spon.

Beem, C. (1999). *The Necessity of Politics: Reclaiming American Public Life*. Chicago, IL: University of Chicago Press.

Bourdieu, P. (1986). The forms of capital. In J. Richards (Ed.), *Handbook of Theory and Research for the Sociology of Education* (pp. 241–258). New York: Greenwood Press.

Chema, T. (1996). When professional sports justify the subsidy: A reply to Roberta A. Baade. *Journal of Urban Affairs*, 18(1), 19–22.

Coleman, J. (1988). Social capital in the creation of human capital. *American Journal of Sociology*, 94(supplement), 95–120.

Durkheim, E. (1982). *Rules of Sociological Method*. New York: The Free Press.

Eckstein, R. & Delaney, K. (2002). New sports stadiums, community self-esteem, and community collective conscience. *Journal of Sport and Social Issues*, 26(3), 235–247.

Edwards, H. (1973). *Sociology of Sport*. Homewood, IL: The Dorsey Press.

Euchner, C. (1993). *Playing the Field: Why Sports Teams Move and Cities Fight to Keep Them*. Baltimore, MD: Johns Hopkins University Press.

Foer, F. (2004). *How Soccer Explains the World*. New York: Harper Collins.

Garvin, A. & Berens, G. (1997). *Urban Parks and Open Space*. Washington, DC: The Urban Land Institute.

Gottdiener, M. (2001). *The Theming of America: American Dreams, Media Fantasies, and Themed Environments*. Colorado: Westview Press.

Hannigan, J. (1998). *Fantasy City: Pleasure and Profit in the Postmodern Metropolis*. New York: Routledge.

Heckscher, A. (1977). *Open Spaces: The Life of American Cities*. New York: Harper and Row.

Johnson, A. & Sack, A. (1996). Assessing the value of sports facilities: The importance of noneconomic factors. *Economic Development Quarterly*, 10(4), 369–381.

Kahn, R. (1998). *The Boys of Summer*. New York: Harper and Row.

Lefebvre, H. (1991). *The Production of Space*. Oxford: Basil Blackwell.

Lefebvre, H. (1996). *Writings on Cities* (E. Kofman & E. Lebas, trans. and Eds.). Oxford: Basil Blackwell.

Leland, S. & Rosentraub, M. (2008). Consolidated and fragmented governments and regional cooperation: Surprising lessons from Charlotte, Cleveland, Indianapolis, and Kansas City. In D. Armonk (Ed.), *Who Will Govern Metropolitan Regions in the 21st Century*. New York: M.E. Sharpe, Inc., forthcoming.

Lipsyte, R. (1975). *Sportsworld: An American Dreamland*. New York: Quadrangle Books.

Lofland, L. (1998). *The Public Realm: Exploring the City's Quintessential Social Territory*. New York: Aldine De Gruyter.

Nelson, A. (2001). Prosperity or blight? A question of Major League stadia locations. *Economic Development Quarterly*, 15(3 August), 255–271.

Olmsted, F. (1870). *Yosemite and the Mariposa Grove: A Preliminary Report*, Yosemite, California: Yosemite Assn., 1995. A collection of Olmsted's early reports on his landscape work. *Frederick Law Olmsted Papers*, located in the Manuscript Division, Library of Congress, Washington, DC.

Portes, A. (1998). Social capital: Its origins and applications in modern sociology. *Annual Review of Sociology*, 24, 1–24.

Putnam, R. (2000). *Bowling Alone: The Collapse and Revival of American Community*. New York: Simon and Schuster.

Rosentraub, M. (1997a). *Major League Losers: The Real Cost of Sports and Who's Paying for It*. New York: Basic Books.

Rosentraub, M. (1997b). Stadiums and urban space. In R. Noll & A. Zambalist (Eds.), *Sports, Jobs, and Taxes: The Economic Impact of Sports Teams and Stadiums* (pp. 178–207). Washington, DC: Brookings Institution.

Rosentraub, M. (1999). *Major League Losers: The Real Cost of Sports and Who's Paying for It* (2nd edition). New York: Basic Books.

Rosentraub, M. (2000). City–county consolidation and the rebuilding of image: The fiscal lessons from Indianapolis's UniGov Program. *State and Local Government Review*, 32(3), 180–191.

Rosentraub, M. (2006a). The local context of a sports strategy for economic development. *Economic Development Quarterly*, *20*(3), 278–289.

Rosentraub, M. (2006b). Sports facilities and urban redevelopment: Private and public benefits and a prescription for a healthier future. *International Journal of Sports and Finance*, *1*(4), 213–227.

Rosentraub, M., Swindell, D. & Tsvetkova, S. (2008). *Justifying Public Investments in Sports: Measuring the Intangibles*, unpublished paper, Cleveland, OH: Cleveland State University.

Swindell, D. & Rosentraub, M. (1998). Who benefits from the presence of professional sports teams? The implication for public funding of stadiums and arenas. *Public Administration Review*, *58*(1), 11–20.

Szymanski, S. & Zimbalist, A. (2005). *National Pastime: Why Americans Play Baseball and the Rest of the World Plays Soccer*. Washington, DC: The Brookings Institution.

Webb, M. (1990). *A Historical Evolution: The City Square*. London: Thames and Hudson Limited.

Wilson, J. (1994). *Playing by the Rules: Sport, Society, and the State*. Detroit, MI: Wayne State University Press.

World Bank (1999). What is social capital? *PovertNet Newsletter* 4 (April 30). Retrieved September 6, 2007. Available at http://www.worldbank.org/poverty/scapital/calendar.htm.

Subject and Author Index